Tales
for
Little
Rebels

Tales for Little Rebels

A Collection of
Radical Children's Literature

Edited by JULIA L. MICKENBERG
and PHILIP NEL
Foreword by JACK ZIPES

NEW YORK UNIVERSITY PRESS

New York and London

NEW YORK UNIVERSITY PRESS
New York and London
www.nyupress.org

Image credits, text sources, and further copyright
information can be found on pp. 287–289.

Library of Congress Cataloging-in-Publication Data
Tales for little rebels : a collection of radical children's literature /
edited by Julia Mickenberg and Philip Nel ; foreword by Jack Zipes.
p.   cm.
Includes bibliographical references and index.
ISBN-13: 978-0-8147-5720-8 (cl : alk. paper)
ISBN-10: 0-8147-5720-0 (cl : alk. paper)
1. Children and politics—Literary collections. 2. Children's
literature, American. 3. American literature—20th century.
4. Children's literature, American—Political aspects. 5. Children's
literature, American—Social aspects. 6. Politics and literature
—United States—History—20th century. 7. Radicalism in
literature.   I. Mickenberg, Julia L. II. Nel, Philip, 1969–
PS509.C519T36 2008
810.8′09282—DC22   2008020926

New York University Press books are printed on acid-free paper,
and their binding materials are chosen for strength and durability.
We strive to use environmentally responsible suppliers and
materials to the greatest extent possible in publishing our books.

Manufactured in the United States of America

c 10 9 8 7 6 5 4 3 2 1
p 10 9 8 7 6 5 4 3 2 1

Contents

Foreword

The Twists and Turns of Radical Children's Literature

JACK ZIPES

"Radical" is a word that has often been misunderstood and been confused with extremism of some kind. The word "radical," however, stems from the Latin *radicalis*, which means "having roots" or "being rooted." Radical qualities form the essence of a person or a thing. A radical person is someone who endeavors to understand the world by going to the root of a phenomenon, issue, or problem. A radical literature, especially a radical children's literature, wants to explore the essence of phenomena, experiences, actions, and social relations and seeks to enable young people to grasp the basic conditions in which they live.

Julia Mickenberg and Philip Nel's book, *Tales for Little Rebels*, is a radical work in a very genuine sense. Not only do the authors recover neglected and "essential" works of children's literature, but they also challenge us to rethink the essence of children's literature and the way this literature has been transformed. As Mickenberg and Nel frankly state, their purpose is not to reclaim "great" literature for children that has been obfuscated; rather, they want to excavate the roots of children's literature and to rewrite its history by shedding light on what has been dismissed and repressed. It is not by chance that their book is the first anthology of radical children's literature in the United States that brings back to print unusual works of social and historical importance. We tend to repress the crucial issues that children need to know to adjust to a rapidly changing world. We tend to repress what is at the heart of the conflicts that determine our lives. We have tried to "nourish" children by feeding them literature that we think is appropriate for them. Or, put another way, we have manipulated them through oral forms of communication and prescriptions in print to think or not to think about the world around them. Mickenberg and Nel's anthology is bound to be both enlightening and disturbing because it touches on the traumatic.

It brings forth uncomfortable moments in American cultural history and challenges us to reconsider what we mean when we think and speak about children's literature.

The political nature of children's literature is at the core of their anthology. But it would be wrong to think that they view children's literature only through a political lens. All literature is political or ideological to a certain extent. Yet, it is impossible to separate aesthetics from politics, just as it is impossible to separate entertainment or education from politics. From the very beginning, when books were first explicitly printed for children in the sixteenth century, politics played a "radical" role in primers, the Bible, and alphabet books. To become literate did not mean simply to develop the ability to read; literacy entailed (and still does) a learning process that produced responsible citizens who functioned in a hierarchical society according to its rules. To become literate involved learning to read the world according to letters and words that were to govern one's beliefs and views and that were regulated according to specific guidelines and norms established by the church and state. Children's literature always carried with it a social code that was part of the civilizing process. For instance, one of the earliest alphabet books, *The Childes Guide* (1667), included such phrases as "In Adam's fall / We sinned all"; "This Book attend, / Thy life to mend"; "The idle Fool / Is whipt at School." Every alphabet book from the sixteenth century to the present was and is ideological. Children's literature was never pure and objective, never just for instruction or just for amusement. Each book depended on artful and technological modes of production, communication, and distribution to convey messages and impart values and rules that might help a child adjust to a changing world and find a place within it. This place was often an *assigned* place, a place filled with signs that the child was taught to recognize. No matter whether it was a nursery rhyme, fairy tale, Bible story, myth, anecdote, or legend, the signs provided information that contributed to a child's understanding of the way the world works.

Yet, understanding is a complex process. In the past, if children were born white and male into an educated and well-to-do family, these children generally found their family's views on life and society represented and reinforced in a children's literature intended to facilitate their understanding of the way the world operated. Understanding meant self-understanding and reconfirmation of privileges. The mainstream of children's literature was their stream. If children were born of a different color, not to mention female, and if they were from the lower classes, children's literature rarely, until the late nineteenth century, depicted and explained the world from their perspective. They were generally deprived of skills that enabled them to succeed in a world not of their making. If they wanted to succeed, they would have to adapt and prove their merits. Children's literature was neglected by the majority of children, if, in fact, they read, or were taught to read, and children often felt that the teaching of reading was an imposition on their time, just as school was. Their concerns were not the concerns of upper-class literature, and they preferred popular literature. Even well into the middle of the twentieth century, the stories, images, plots, and views of "approved" children's literature were predominantly those of people from educated and wealthy white classes. There might have been radical elements in some books that undermined the hegemonic social code of the civilizing process, but for the most part young people were not exposed to radical political ideas in the literature produced specifically for children that was flourishing by the nineteenth century. The beginnings of a radical literature for children can be seen in the pioneer essays and stories of Lydia Maria Child and in her journal *Juvenile Miscellany* (founded in 1826), the abolitionist literature published in the magazine *The Slave's Friend* (1836–1839), and works by Harriet Beecher Stowe, Louisa May Alcott, and other authors who published in the *St. Nicholas Magazine* (founded in 1873). Yet, the majority of American children were not encouraged to read or "compelled" to go to school until the latter part of the nineteenth century. If there were radical or different views represented in children's literature, they were few and far between and were generally conveyed to "enlighten" privileged young readers.

With the great rise of literacy and compulsory schooling, with the end of slavery, with the beginning of the suffrage movement, with the introduction of the ideas of Darwin, Marx, and Freud, all toward the end of the nineteenth century, writers and illustrators began addressing problems in history, science, sociology, and politics in children's literature in a much more explicit manner than they had ever done before. Mark Twain is a good example in books such as *Tom Sawyer* (1876) and *Huckleberry Finn* (1884). But he was only the tip of the iceberg at the end of the nineteenth century. The rise of strong political and social oppositional groups led to the formation of socialist, communist, anarchist, feminist, and civil rights organizations at the beginning of the twentieth century, and they produced diverse works for children that countered, contradicted, and opposed the mainstream products. It is impossible, I would contend, to understand L. Frank Baum's fourteen Oz novels (1900–1920), initiated at the beginning of the twentieth century, without grasping how he was influenced by the suffrage and union movements, the political machinations of governments, and wars. But was Baum a radical writer? Did he consider himself a radical? What makes for a radical writer or illustrator? What were the conditions that brought forth radical writers at the end of the nineteenth century, not only in America but also and especially in England? These are some of the important questions that are raised in Mickenberg and Nel's anthology.

As we know, there were all types of radical writers and illustrators who represented a wide array of political positions throughout the twentieth century. As Mickenberg and Nel point out in their numerous informative biographies, some were members of communist and socialist parties, some were nonaligned, and some were simply dissidents. Their focus is mainly on American radical writers and illustrators who took clear stands in their books. What is strikingly similar about all the works included in this anthology is that the writers and illustrators sought to clarify on behalf of children what it meant to grow up in America in a particular sociopolitical context. They addressed the roots of social problems. It did not matter whether these writers and illustrators produced nonfiction, realistic fiction, or fantasy. There was always a didactic purpose behind their works that apparently drove them to write, draw, and compose. As Mickenberg and Nel point out, sometimes the didacticism was heavy handed and ruined their purpose, while at other times the authors were remarkably creative and innovative and were able to convey their messages in startling ways. Many of the writers and artists, who were nonaligned with a particular party, or who did not want to push a specific ideology, became so involved in grasping the roots of lived experiences and of social developments that they unconsciously produced "radical" books. In fact, any writer or illustrator who takes children seriously, who reflects critically and honestly on the way children are treated in the United States (and elsewhere), must, I contend, produce radical works.

What is interesting about the development of children's literature in the latter part of the twentieth century and beginning of the twenty-first century is its general "radical" tendency. That is, almost all the *best* writers and illustrators, such as Maurice Sendak, Judy Blume, Jane Yolen, Robert Cormier, Chris Van Allsburg, Virginia Hamilton, Russell Hoban, Walter Dean Myers, Francesca Lia Block, Laurence Yep, Milton Meltzer, Julius Lester, and hundreds of others, no matter what their ideological bent may be, were and are sadly compelled to produce works with "radical" qualities if they want to be honest with children. I say "sadly" because the conditions under which children live today are deplorable. If we just think of the themes of books for children from five to seventeen, they concern child abuse, pedophilia, rape, anorexia, dysfunctional families, divorce, alcoholism, drug addiction, racism, corruption, abortion, perversion, dystopias, injustice, bullying, and so on. Most of the writers and illustrators who address young people endeavor to grasp the roots of social and political problems. One could generalize and argue that the social and political tendencies in American society drive writers to become radical. Politics plays a role in determining the scope and purpose of their works. Whether or not the writers and illustrators take a conscious ideological position in their writing, they must explore what causes social problems if they are going to be true to their craft and readership.

There is, however, a clear dividing line among writers and illustrators for children today. There are still many who write and illustrate for commercial reasons and self-aggrandizement and who produce banal and empty literature. They are still the majority and form the mainstream that "dumbs down" content for children. They write to maintain the culture industry as it is. But, to write and illustrate for children today, in my opinion, demands a conscious radical approach to social and political conditions. Fortunately, during the past forty years numerous writers and illustrators, along with publishers, educators, and critics of children's literature, have responded to the "plight" of children, their families, and the education system by producing works that contain radical critiques, enabling children to think for themselves. The question, we must ask, is whether this strong radical tendency in children's literature and scholarship has a chance to have an impact on children, given certain continuities in the mainstream of children's literature. These continuities are fostered by the corporate tidal wave of consumerism and the production of books, toys, and other articles that promote violence, sexism, and racism. Not only does the culture industry frame the way in which life is mediated through cultural products, but it also contributes to an instrumentalization of the imagination. In this regard, Mickenberg and Nel's anthology is a strong antidote to the dominant tendency of consumerism in our times. Not only do the works in their anthology reveal how vibrant and experimental the writers and illustrators were and still are, but by offering this wide selection of mostly out-of-print works, they uncover the historical roots of radical children's literature in America and keep the "radical" tendency alive at a time when American culture must take stock of itself. Radical children's literature will not guarantee a better future for American children, but it will certainly challenge them to think critically and creatively about their choices, and this can only have a positive impact on the future of American society.

Acknowledgments

For his foreword, thanks to Jack Zipes.

For general research assistance, including (but not limited to) helping us find authors, illustrators, or their heirs, we thank Steve Allen, Peter Bearman (Columbia University), Pam Boiros (Modern Age Books), David Bonner, Anna Burgard, Ron Carden (South Plains College), Tara C. Craig (Butler Library, Columbia University), Sara Duke (Library of Congress), Maria Felizardo (Scholastic), Victor Garlin (Sonoma State University), Rich Gibson, Eric Gordon (The Workmen's Circle), Dee Grimsrud (Wisconsin Historical Society), Andrew Hemingway (University College London), Julie Herrada (Special Collection Library, University of Michigan), Karen Hoyle (Children's Literature Research Collections, University of Minnesota), Michele Janette and Mary Siegle (Kansas State University), Leonard Lehman (Elie Siegmeister Society), Robbie Lieberman (Southern Illinois University), Kathleen Manwaring (Syracuse University), Denise M. Marshall (Fairleigh Dickinson University), Jane Martin (New York Artists Equity Association), Michelle Martin (Clemson University), Tony Marzani, Charlie McGovern (College of William and Mary), Paul Mishler (Indiana University, South Bend), Joann Miyamoto, Blair Mosner, Sharon O'Neil (Brown, Jacobson law firm), Sandrine Pechels de Saint Sardos and Shannon Speck (Classic Media), Dean M. Rogers (Vassar College Library), Mara Sapon-Shevin (Syracuse University), Laura Schwartz (University of Texas Art Library), Phillip Serrato (San Diego State University), Sarah Shumway (Dutton Children's Books), Avi Soifer, Ken Steacy, Michelle Pagni Stewart (Mt. San Jacinto College), Superior Court Records of New Jersey, Jan Susina (Illinois State University), Truusje Vrooland-Lob, Daniel Vuillermin (La Trobe University, Melbourne, Australia), Alan Wald and Rebecca Zurier (University of Michigan, Ann Arbor), and Diane Waterhouse Barbarisi (Eric Carle Museum).

For translations, thanks to Jerold Frakes (SUNY Buffalo) and Dolora Chapelle Wojciehowski (University of Texas).

For his guest introduction, thanks to Jerold Frakes.

For allowing us to reproduce their work (or work they control), we thank Lara Anderson (Curtis Brown Ltd.), Jose Aruego, Tom Barry, Caryn Burtt and Dominique Giammarino (Random House), Herb Cheyette and Jill Jones (Dr. Seuss Enterprises), Amanda Cooper (UNITE Here!), Stewart I. Edelstein (Estate of Ruth Krauss), Kamili Feelings, Shari Segel Goldberg, Anthony Gould, Gene Gropper, Betty Howe (Institute for Intercultural Studies), Ronald Hussey (Houghton Mifflin), Kathleen Johnson, Pete Kelly, Alfred Stephen Kreymborg, Dee Michel, Greg Pason (Socialist Party U.S.A.), Marian Reiner (for Eve Merriam's estate), Mimi Ross (Henry Holt and Company), Elie Rubinstein (The Workmen's Circle Arbiter Ring), Shari Segel, Marc Simont, Betty Smith (International Publishers), Christine Smith (Harcourt, Inc.), Craig Tenney (Harold Ober Associates), Nanda Ward, Sandra Weiner, and Doug Wixson. For various reasons, some of the works for which we gained permissions were not included in the collection.

For the many authors, illustrators, and heirs who not only allowed us to reproduce their work but also took the time to talk with us or answer our queries, thanks to Barbara S. Brauer, John Broderick, Pat Carbine, Jacqueline Chwast, Jeanne Desy, Roy Doty, Tom Feelings, Erwin Fleissner, Joan Goldfrank, Lewis Goldfrank, Gene Gropper, Friso Henstra, Lawrence Koering, Gil Leaf, Julius Lester, Ann L. Margetson, Dr. Julia A. Miller, Joe Molnar, Charlotte Pomerantz, Debra Preusch, Robin Ward Savage, Galvin Swift, Leslie Udry, Victoria Williams, and Beth Wood.

For scans of images, thanks to Roger Adams and Cindy Von Elling (Morse Department of Special Collections, Kansas State University), Karen Bauer (Children's Literature Research Collections, University of Minnesota), Charles Cohen (The Whole Seuss), Uri Kolodny (University of Texas Libraries Digitization Services), Kathleen Manwaring and Nicolette A. Schneider (Special Collections, Syracuse University Library), and Rita Smith (Special Collections, University of Florida at Gainesville). And very special thanks to Donna Davey, Michael Nash, and Leo Rodriguez (Tamiment Library, New York University).

Phil thanks Tim Beal and Kurt Koenigsberger for inviting him to speak on this project at Case Western

Reserve University's Humanities Week in April 2006, and Julia and Phil thank Syracuse University for their invitation to speak about the book in February 2008.

At New York University Press, thanks to Aiden Amos, Despina Papazoglou Gimbel, Ciara McLaughlin, Emily Park, Eric Zinner, Emily Wright, and Richard Hendel.

For helping to underwrite the project, thanks to Kansas State University for a Big 12 Faculty Fellowship and a University Small Research Grant, and to KSU English Department Head Linda Brigham for funding a part-time research assistant.

Phil would also like to thank each of those Research Assistants: Melissa Glaser, Carla Schuster, and Cliff Starkey.

For underwriting NYU Press's production costs, we are *very* grateful for a University of Texas Cooperative Society Subvention grant, and to Frances Granatino of Downhomebooks (Malvern, PA).

For general support, we thank Sidney Lock (Adams House, Austin, Texas), Valerie Millholland (Duke UP), and David Barker (Continuum).

We also wish to thank the anonymous readers for New York University Press, who influenced the book in important ways. Special thanks to Stephen Johnson for helping to reconceive the cover.

And most importantly, for donating a family member to the cause, we give special thanks to Karin Westman, and to Dan, Lena, and Edie Birkholz.

Introduction

In 1912, an unhatched revolutionary chick cries, "Strike down the wall!" and liberates itself from the "egg state," a metaphor for the work each individual must do to overthrow capitalism. In 1940, ostriches pull their heads out of the sand and unite to fight fascism. In 1972, Baby X grows up gender free and happy about it.

These snippets of stories from *Nature Talks on Economics*, *Oscar the Ostrich*, and *X: A Fabulous Child's Story* may be unfamiliar to you. *Tales for Little Rebels* brings together these little-known stories and others in a collection of forty-four children's texts that exemplify the ideals of radical politics as they evolved over the twentieth century. The pieces gathered here reflect the concerns of their times, as seen in the examples above: chickens protest capitalism in the 1910s, ostriches fight fascism in the 1940s, and a genderless baby challenges the construct of gender in the 1970s. All of these tales address or attempt to create a liberated, informed, questioning, activist child.

The very idea of "radical children's literature" may be surprising, because we do not commonly think of the connections between children's literature and politics. But children's literature has always been ideological. Consider an ABC from the 1680s: "A. In Adam's Fall / We Sinned all." And, next to a picture of a Bible, "B. Thy Life to Mend / This Book Attend." *The New England Primer* teaches more than just literacy.

From the Puritans to the present day, the didactic tendency of books for younger children suggests that adults have no problem prescribing a moral framework for the young. Yet there is the tendency to fear that "political propaganda" will taint a young child's "innocence." Children's literature is necessarily involved in both morality (making distinctions between right and wrong) and politics (which are about the power to effect change). Teaching children to obey a higher authority may be understood as a moral lesson, but it can also be understood as a political lesson.

Rather than teach children to seek redemption through prayer, twentieth-century leftists of various stripes used literature to encourage them to question the authority of those in power. Radicals taught children to take collective action to effect change, to trust their own instincts, to explore alternative social arrangements, and to use history to understand how and why today's world has developed as it has.

For those who would argue that politics have no place in children's literature, we maintain that there is no way to keep politics out. Stories that uphold the status quo (arguably the majority of works published for children) may not seem political, but they represent efforts to teach children that the current social, political, economic, and environmental orders are as they should be. McGuffey readers (widely used in nineteenth-century American schools) and Sunday school literature were extremely popular up through the early twentieth century and tended to advance a conservative agenda. More subtly, stories that showed African Americans in subservient roles—if in any role at all—were the norm until the 1960s. Modern works uphold norms that glorify individualism and promote free enterprise; emphasize girls' and women's physical appearance and marriage as an ultimate goal; normalize car culture; or generally teach children to obey authority, to trust adults, and to avoid confronting the problems we face as a society. Notwithstanding the regressive tendencies of some books, children's literature is very often marked by utopian feelings of possibility: children represent the chance for creating a better world.

Perhaps it is not surprising that conservatives condemn the domination of children's literature by liberals. In recent years, right wingers have made efforts to counter "insidious left-wing propaganda" with such books as Katherine DeBrecht's *Help! Mom! There Are Liberals under My Bed!* (2005) and its sequel *Help! Mom! Hollywood Is in My Hamper!* (2006).[1] Bill O'Reilly's *Kids Are Americans Too* (2007) and Lynne Cheney's *America: A Patriotic Primer* (2002) and *Our Fifty States: A Family Adventure across America* (2006) have had considerable success, as has Jerry B. Jenkins and Tim LaHaye's *Left Behind: The Kids* (forty titles between 1998 and 2004). There is also *faux* radical children's literature, such as the infamous *Black Panther Coloring Book* (1968) created by the FBI's Counter-Intelligence Program (COINTELPRO) in order to discredit the Black Panthers—a radical, black nationalist organization.

Ironically, while right wingers have perceived a liberal conspiracy in children's literature, people on the left have tended to overlook the long tradition of truly radical children's literature: witness educator Herb Kohl's 1995 "plea for radical children's literature," which, he says, is almost impossible to find.[2] Yet, in recovering a radical tradition in children's literature, we discovered far more work than we had room to include. We've collected texts that offer a taste of the U.S. Left's "social imagination" (to borrow Kohl's term) as it evolved over the course of the twentieth century.

Prominent trends evolved over time across a spectrum of the Left. There was never a unified voice of the Left, just as there was never a unified vision of the child. Much of what we found is compelling and still relevant today: the playful but incisive lessons about pesticides' effects upon ecosystems in Charlotte Pomerantz and Jose Aruego's *The Day They Parachuted Cats on Borneo: A Drama of Ecology* are as important now as they were when the book was published in 1971. Going even further back, Ruth Brindze's *Johnny Get Your Money's Worth (and Jane Too)!* (1938) offers a much-needed corrective to the overwhelming tide of contemporary advertising directed at children. Carl Sandburg's mockery of war in his *Rootabaga Pigeons* (1923) and Ruth Benedict and Gene Weltfish's calls for human brotherhood in *In Henry's Backyard* (1948) should encourage a new generation of children to reject war as a solution to conflicts based on race or religion. Parents looking for a "practical princess" whom their daughters might emulate can find one in Jay Williams's 1969 story of that title. Look inside this book, and you'll find a great deal more that feels unexpectedly contemporary.

Participants in a variety of radical and progressive movements have created literature for children as part of organized and informal efforts to educate young people. In the United States, this tradition stretches back at least to the abolitionists, who published journals such as *The Slave's Friend* (1836–1839) and wrote stories for other children's magazines. In the twentieth century, participants in most radical movements wrote and published stories for children: Socialists and lyrical leftists at the turn of the century; labor unionists, Communists, and antifascists in the 1930s and 1940s; pacifists and civil rights activists in the 1950s and 1960s; feminists and environmentalists in the 1970s and 1980s; and gay liberationists in the 1990s. Within a tradition of leftist politics in the United States, children

have been at the center of radicals' deepest aspirations, and traces of those aspirations can be found in literature they wrote for young people.

The children's literature field represents a relatively free space for unconventional ideas. Juvenile publishing began to develop as its own division of the book field only in the 1920s. Led by educated, progressive women who had worked in libraries, as social workers, and in education, juvenile publishing tended to exclude material seen as inappropriate for children: violence, sex, and, at least in the baldest sense, politics. Still, the field absorbed something of librarians' commitment to intellectual freedom. This fact, and a lack of critical attention—combined with significant interest in preparing children for the "real world"—sometimes translated into a surprising openness. Children's literature became one of the main avenues open to radical writers during the McCarthy era, in part because no one thought it important to monitor a field largely controlled by women, whose authority on matters concerning children was considered unshakable. Langston Hughes, one of the few children's authors called before the House Committee on Un-American Activities, was not actually targeted for his children's books. In fact, he wrote children's books to escape the blacklist—books like *The First Book of Negroes* (1950), *The First Book of Rhythms* (1954), and *The First Book of Africa* (1960). Many reds in political trouble found work writing for major series published in the postwar period, including the First Books, the Real Books, the Landmark Books, and even the Little Golden Books.[3]

Some of the most famous twentieth-century American authors of children's books leaned left. Syd Hoff, best known today for books like *Danny and the Dinosaur* (1958) and his *New Yorker* cartoons, published his first children's book as A. Redfield, the pseudonym he used when writing for the communist *Daily Worker* and *New Masses*. His editor at *New Masses*, Crockett Johnson, is best remembered for *Harold and the Purple Crayon* (1955). And when Wanda Gag wrote *Millions of Cats* (1928), her reputation rested in part on the artwork she too had created for *New Masses*.[4] Radical politics influenced Caldecott-winning author-illustrator Lynd Ward; Eve Merriam and Lilian Moore, both winners of the National Council of Teachers of English award for excellence in poetry for children; and William Steig, creator of *Shrek* (1990) and *Sylvester and the Magic Pebble* (1969). Their books are not transparently political, but they do encourage children to use their imaginations, to question received authority, and to trust their sense of what feels right and true. And in a world where books get challenged for "encouraging children to disobey authority," promoting independent thinking is political.[5]

In *Tales for Little Rebels*, we present works that have a more self-evident political dimension—although a few works' politics are quite subtle. Most of the authors and illustrators would have identified themselves as left of center, but they were not necessarily part of a radical political party or movement. We have consciously pushed boundaries with what we have included: by not overemphasizing political affiliation, by including some pieces in which the political content is not immediately self-evident, and by including pieces that, while they may represent radical *intent*, are frankly dogmatic in their execution.

Some of the pieces reprinted here were published originally in movement periodicals, such as the *New Pioneer*, the communist magazine for children; *Freedom*, the radical black newspaper; or *Ms.* magazine, which had a "Stories for Free Children" column. Most selections, however, were published by major book publishers, but have gone out of print. Bringing forgotten, out-of-print texts back to life reminds us of the fickleness of both the market and the canon: we find great richness in these works, and in their broader project. Thus this book represents an act of recovery. If familiar radical children's stories such as Dr. Seuss's *The Lorax* (1971) or Jon Scieszka and Lane Smith's *The Stinky Cheese Man and Other Fairly Stupid Tales* (1992) seem strangely absent, our larger message is that the longer legacy of radical children's literature is hidden. If that legacy is not always one that current progressives would embrace, it is one that they—and their children—could learn from.

We concentrated on the twentieth century so that we could offer historical breadth but include works that still felt timely. We incorporated works published in the United States (or, in a few instances, works translated for American audiences) mainly for the sake of coherence, but it should be noted that comparable traditions can be found elsewhere. For instance, in Britain, Fabian Socialists like E. Nesbit and H. G. Wells wrote stories for children, and nonsense writing and fairy tales by people such as Edward Lear, George MacDonald, and Oscar Wilde had radical dimensions.[6] Likewise, in Weimar Germany radicals rewrote traditional fairy tales with new messages.[7]

The balance of ethnic and racial groups represented leans strongly towards African Americans. For many years, African Americans represented the nation's largest minority, and, furthermore, were the minority group most outspoken on civil rights and most prominent in American letters. As a result, there were simply more African-American texts available to us. We also sought texts for younger readers that had a political dimension more overt than simply an effort to represent minority experiences. We do include texts representing Mexican Americans, Puerto Rican Americans, and Native Americans, but these texts are by white authors. Our recommended reading list, at the back of this volume, offers a starting point for readers seeking more.

While we emphasize that major literary figures are part of the tradition we aim to recover, we also want to share the work of lesser-known authors. Some of the authors and illustrators are familiar figures from American arts and letters in general or children's literature specifically: Lucille Clifton, Syd Hoff, Langston Hughes, Walt Kelly, Norma Klein, Munro Leaf, Julius Lester, Eve Merriam, Charlotte Pomerantz, Carl Sandburg, Dr. Seuss, Jay Williams, and Lynd Ward. Others are relatively unknown today, but we hope their work will find admirers among contemporary readers. To give only a few examples, Alfred Kreymborg was a major modernist poet and anthologist, William Gropper a well-known painter and radical political cartoonist, Alex Novikoff a world-renowned scientist, Caroline Nelson a popular lecturer and birth control agitator, and Ruth Brindze an important consumer advocate.

The book's general introduction, section introductions, and introductions to each selection give readers tools for making sense of the pieces, offering biographical and historical backgrounds and, in some cases, interpretive frameworks. When possible, introductions to each story provide a biographical sketch of the author and illustrator, and describe how their lives intersected with the work's political concerns. In those cases where we could uncover little information about a piece's creators, we focused on situating the story in historical, social, political, and/or literary context. Generally speaking, however, the eight section introductions work towards providing that broad sense of context.

"R Is for Rebel," the first section, highlights literature for the youngest children. The subsequent sections represent broad themes in left-leaning children's literature, and cross boundaries between fiction and nonfiction, offering picture books, poetry, comics, drama, and song.

Our inclusion of a section on science—"Subversive Science and Dramas of Ecology"—demonstrates that an interest in science and technology animated many of the twentieth century's radical movements. Teaching children about science can give them skills in critical thinking and make them question racist logic. It can expose the unjust distribution of resources and promote an ecological consciousness. But there was also a more practical incentive to write about science: postwar defense concerns and the space race created a ready market for juvenile science books in the United States. Thus, this genre became an important outlet for teachers who had been dismissed for political reasons and who reinvented themselves as juvenile authors.[8]

"Work, Workers, and Money" reflects the economic concerns that have inspired Marxist-influenced leftist movements, particularly socialism and communism. We have also included a story reflecting second-wave feminism's concern with opening up professions for women and obtaining equal pay for equal work. "Organize" could have included many stories in this book, given the fact that collectivity and solidarity have been guiding principles of most leftist movements.

"Imagine" contains stories such as Lydia Gibson's *The Teacup Whale* (1934), which, though not obviously radical, point to the potentially subversive power of imagination. When writers encourage children to speculate about what *might* be, they also invite them to question what *is*. Although fairy tales appear throughout this book, the "Imagine" section discusses how radicals have adapted the fairy tale form to advance subversive messages.[9]

"History and Heroes" highlights stories that look to the past to help children imagine a better future. Radicals recovered the stories of groups omitted from historical narratives, debunked myths used to uphold the existing social order, and used history as a lens to critically examine the present. The tales in "A Person's a Person" treat difference—such as race, ethnicity, class, gender, or political affiliation—as a positive quality and challenge discrimination based on such difference. This section underscores the fight to grant full rights to each member of humankind as a central goal of most leftist movements in the twentieth century.

"Peace," *Little Rebels*' final section, emphasizes an-other major objective—one that, sadly, seems all the more relevant today. These stories advocate resolving conflict through peaceful means and, in some cases, suggest how to prevent the prejudices that can inspire war.

Tales for Little Rebels deliberately focuses on picture books and illustrated books geared at preteen readers. We have not ventured towards young adult literature because YA is so explicitly political that an anthology of radical young adult literature would comprise several more volumes. That said, a few texts are more appropriate for older children; these were included because of their historical significance, or because we did not find a text for younger children that addressed the same concerns. There are also several selections—such as Art Young's *Socialist Primer*—that fall into the tradition of using the children's book form as political commentary for adults. We've included as many illustrations as we can because they are so integral to the way children's literature is conveyed.

All the stories are products of their times, and we found some material that, in hindsight, was not liberatory. In seeking a body of children's literature written with the goal of creating progressive social change, we made the conscious choice to be honest about what we found. Our goal was not to whitewash history but to unearth it and make sense of it. Some selections in the very first section highlight the darker side of the Left's social imagination. Nicholas Klein's *Socialist Primer* traffics in the stereotype of the fat capitalist, and it is hardly progressive to attach moral values to a particular body type (or profession). Even more troubling, both "Pioneer Mother Goose" and "ABC for Martin" recall the communist Left's rather blind worship of the Soviet Union. One hopes that readers today would take a very different lesson from selections such as these, a lesson about the dangers of mindlessly following a doctrine or dogma. They are included here because of their historical relevance and, taken together with the rest of the selections, their representation of a range of concerns taken up by twentieth-century leftist movements. They also serve as important reminders that truly progressive politics involve critical thinking, not blind devotion to a cause or an ideology.

Now is an opportune moment for this collection of radical children's literature, both because many social, economic, and environmental efforts associated with the Left have been rolled back and because the long legacy of radical children's literature—a "usable past" for contemporary progressives—has been largely forgotten.[10]

Today, children's literature continues to be a vehicle for expressing visions of a more just world, as our working list of recommended books begins to suggest. We wish to place such new work within a much longer tradition of radical children's literature, but we also want to complicate that tradition. In this book, through largely forgotten children's literature, we show the ideals the Left has fought for—but we also ask readers to think critically about how the stories invite children to wage those battles. In other words, in documenting a tradition of "radical children's literature," we want to call all of those terms—"radical," "children," and "literature"—into question.

What sort of literature is appropriate for children? What responsibility do adults have to children to keep them informed about critical issues of the day, such as global warming, terrorism, political corruption, and corporate greed? At what point must an ideal of "protection" end and one of preparation necessarily begin?

As you read the pieces collected here, we invite you to think about how they address issues that have animated radical thinkers of the past—as well as concerns still very much with us today. The next generation will face many challenges. Progressive tales, old and new, can help them address such problems, and inspire them to create a better future for everyone.

NOTES

1. Stephanie Simon, "Publisher Aims to Teach Kids Right from Left," *Los Angeles Times*, 1 June 2007: <http://www.latimes.com/news/nationworld/nation/la-na-kidbooks1jun01,0,7059853.story?coll=la-home-nation>.

2. Herbert Kohl, "A Plea for Radical Children's Literature," *Should We Burn Babar? Essays on Children's Literature and the Power of Stories* (New York: New Press, 1995), 60.

3. For further discussion see Julia Mickenberg, *Learning from the Left: Children's Literature, the Cold War, and Radical Politics in the United States* (New York: Oxford UP, 2006).

4. On Wanda Gag's politics, see Richard W. Cox, "Wanda Gag: The Bite of the Picture Book," *Minnesota History* 44 (Fall 1975): 239–54.

5. Larra Clark, "Harry Potter Series Tops List of Most Challenged Books Four Years in a Row," *American Library Association*, 13 Jan. 2003: <http://www.ala.org/ala/pressreleasesbucket/pressreleases2003/harrypotterseries.htm>. 20 Jan. 2007.

6. On the political dimensions of nonsense writing, see Kevin Shortsleeve, *The Politics of Nonsense: Civil Unrest, Otherness, and National Mythology in Nonsense Literature*, University of Oxford, dissertation, 2007.

7. See Jack Zipes, *Fairy Tales and Fables from Weimar Days* (Hanover, NH: UP of New England, 1989).

8. For further discussion, see Mickenberg, *Learning from the Left*.

9. For a fuller discussion of this practice, see the classic work by Jack Zipes, *Fairy Tales and the Art of Subversion: The Classical Genre for Children and the Process of Civilization* (New York: Methuen, 1988).

10. There has also been considerable scholarly interest of late in the subject of children's literature's radical possibilities. In addition to *Learning from the Left*, see, for instance, Michelle Martin, *Brown Gold: Milestones of African-American Children's Picture Books, 1845–2002* (New York: Routledge, 2004); Katharine Capshaw Smith, *Children's Literature of the Harlem Renaissance* (Bloomington: Indiana UP, 2004); and Kimberley Reynolds, *Radical Children's Literature: Future Visions and Aesthetic Transformations in Juvenile Fiction* (New York: Palgrave Macmillan, 2007).

part 1

R Is for Rebel

JULIA MICKENBERG & PHILIP NEL

Beside the letter "A," a picture shows a man and a woman holding hands and a serpent twisted around an apple tree. To the right, we read, "In *Adam's* Fall / We Sinned all." Following through B, C, D, and nearly to the end, we find "Y" beside a split picture; the left side shows people eating and drinking at a table while the right side shows a skeleton. Beside this image, we read, "While youth do chear / Death may be near." This picture alphabet, originally printed in London in *A Guide for the Childe and Youth* (1667) and then adapted for the *New England Primer* (1690), reminds us that even literature for the youngest children is ideological.

Throughout the *New England Primer*, Puritan children were taught basic moral lessons in the course of gaining literacy. A section on "Words of Five Syllables" includes "A-bo-mi-na-ble," "Be-ne-dic-ti-on," "E-du-ca-ti-on," and "For-ni-ca-ti-on." "A Lesson for Children" includes "Pray to God / Love God / Fear God / Serve God / Take not God's Name in vain / Do not Swear / Do not Steal / Cheat not in your play / Play not with bad boys."[1]

Alphabet books, primers, and nursery rhymes represent some of the earliest forms of children's literature, and the forms traditionally read or spoken to the youngest children. This section of *Tales for Little Rebels* includes excerpts from two radical alphabet books, along with portions of two socialist primers and an anticapitalist revision of Mother Goose. In rewriting genres for the youngest children, authors of these selections challenged oppressive social hierarchies, economic injustices, and biases in education. As this book's only section organized according to genre instead of theme, "R Is for Rebel" provides vivid examples of the ways in which values and ideology—in this case, radical values and ideology—can be boiled down to their most elemental forms. Likewise, it illustrates ways in which groups opposed to the dominant power structures have recast these simple forms to teach children the language of rebellion. In adapting these stories, radicals and progressives deploy a genre against itself, inviting children to subvert—instead of submit to—dominant power structures.

As Lissa Paul notes, "the links between literacy, power, and a Christian education are very deep."[2] Paul notes that the name "primer" originally referred only to prayer books, but because children learned to read from these books, the term came to mean "any elementary book used to teach children to read."[3] The doctrinal character of most early primers and alphabets grows from the fact that the earliest organized effort to promote universal literacy came from the church: in the late eighteenth century, the Sunday School movement arose to "train up the lower classes in habits of industry and piety."[4] In the United States, by the end of the nineteenth century, free, state-supported elementary education was available in every state. Although separation of church and state in theory might have minimized doctrinal power over school texts, the readers that young children used in schools—most famously, the McGuffey Readers—taught lessons that affirmed religious values and, like most religious texts, inculcated respect for authority.

But the push for public schooling came not only from powerful business and religious leaders hoping to create a docile workforce and well-mannered citizens. Groups calling for greater democracy and members of the labor movement were also instrumental in the movement to provide universal, free public education.[5] However, they quickly recognized that children in public schools would not learn to think critically about capitalism or the state.

Hence the move to create alternative institutions—and literature—for adults as well as children. As part of the Socialist Sunday School movement, Francis Wayland's Appeal to Reason—probably the leading socialist press of the early twentieth century—published Nicholas Klein's Socialist Primer (1908). The book offered practical language lessons while seeking to raise class consciousness. Its "Language Lessons" seem unideological when they tell us, "Names like tree, horse, chair, pair, are common nouns." However, the accompanying illustration shows "Socialism will win" on the chalkboard. Further emphasizing the political lessons, the primer's earliest images include a "HOG—See the fat Hog!" and "MAN—Why does the man beg?" Tying these illustrations to pictures of ax, cat, rat, and hat, the book provides an explanation with revolutionary connotations: "The Ax will cut down the Tree. The Cat will go for the Rat. Man will not beg."

The next selection, Art Young's Socialist Primer, was published in 1930 by the Socialist Party of Chicago. This book may have been intended more as adult humor than as a primer for children, but its form marks it as children's literature. Like Dan Piraro's The Three Little Pigs Buy the White House (2004)—a satire of George W. Bush, Dick Cheney, and Donald Rumsfeld—Young's "primer" plays with the children's book form. Recognizing the power and immediacy of simple lessons for

very young children, Young adapts the plodding didacticism of the elementary primer to playfully criticize capitalism. As in Klein's Socialist Primer, many of Young's lessons take the form of questions and answers: "Is this a spider? It is. What is its other name? The capitalist system." The apparently adult content in Young's primer points to the fact that radical "children's literature" was often created not only for children but also for semiliterate, working-class adults.

Satire mixed with dogmatism likewise characterizes Ned Donn's "Pioneer Mother Goose," published in the communist New Pioneer in 1934. Mother Goose rhymes are products of folklore rather than formal educational institutions. As Lucy Rollin points out, nursery rhymes "communicate the most elementary of concerns of the culture to its children—concerns about nature, food, sex, and language. They also express, in their bodily rhythms and symbols, the most elementary concerns of the child."[6] The rhymes often come from children themselves and, like folklore, have many variations. Even in printed form, nursery rhymes' simple, memorable, and familiar form has meant that they are endlessly rewritten—sometimes, as this selection shows, to radical ends.[7]

As an oral-based genre often carried or created by children themselves, many nursery rhymes revel in absurdity, raucousness, and nonsense. In Donn's "Pioneer Mother Goose," "Pease porridge hot" serves as a lesson on the injustice of the rich getting the "hot" and the poor getting the "cold," and offers the revolutionary promise that one day "bosses will search the garbage pot, for anything—nine days old!" Donn's rhymes are striking because they manage to mix humor and wordplay with a message that is frankly dogmatic and sectarian. Indeed, cries of "Down with capitalism! Long live the Soviet!" demand a fair amount of explanation—so much so that parents may want to avoid sharing Donn's rhymes with very young children. The same should probably be said of "ABC for Martin."

Although the earliest alphabets reinforced religious principles, the form has long invited playfulness. Indeed, the invention of the picture alphabet—with its didactic and religious purposes—derives from the idea that children will learn more easily if they are enjoying themselves. In the mid-eighteenth century, the printer John Newbery built the first children's publishing empire out of this pleasure principle. His Peter Piper's Practical Principles of Plain and Perfect Pronunciation (1813) contains what Gillian Avery calls "a series of lunatic tongue twisters," starting with

> Andrew Airpump asked his aunt her ailment;
> Did Andrew Airpump ask his aunt her ailment?
> If Andrew Airpump asked his aunt her ailment,
> Where was the ailment of Andrew Airpump's aunt?[8]

As George Bodmer has observed, "As one of the most rigid forms of children's literature, the alphabet book is ripe for innovation and exploration. The alphabet book looks like a teaching tool for children, but its entertainment value has always lain in the stretching of its borders."[9] Bodmer's focus is on the second half of the twentieth century, but the example above points to a longer trend of playing with the alphabet book's didactic form.

"ABC for Martin" consciously plays with conventions of the alphabet book in its attempts to create little rebels. Many contemporary (older) readers will probably find themselves laughing at its earnest lessons: "A stands for Armaments—war-mongers' pride; B is for Bolshie, the thorn in their side. C stands for Capitalists, fighting for gold; D for destruction, they've practiced of old." But if there is humor in this alphabet it partly comes from the recognition that the earnest lessons were so profoundly misplaced. As with the "Pioneer Mother Goose," the simple form and language belie the fact that this ABC—mixed up as it is with communist dogma and adulation of the Soviet Union—is probably not so appropriate for the very young. At any rate, it demands a fair amount of explanation. The intent may have been liberatory, but the message winds up mixing violent sentiments with praise for a dictator—not lessons progressives want to teach their children.

On the other hand, contemporary parents may be very pleased to share Lucille Clifton's The Black BC's (1970) with their children. The selection from that book offers an Afrocentric challenge to Eurocentric education, reflecting the consciousness that grew out of the Black Power movement, and teaching beginning readers about African and African-American history—again, through the alphabet book form. The first entry, "A is for Africa," explains that Africa "covers as much land as the United States, Western Europe, China, and India put together." With "the greatest variety of wild animals, at least 16 different major languages, and about 225 million people," Africa, Clifton's book implies, demands our attention. "B is for Books" offers a brief lesson about such African-American authors as Phillis Wheatley, James Baldwin, and Gwendolyn Brooks. "C is for Cowboys" tells of black cowboys, and "D is for [Frederick] Douglass / giant of men / who freed himself / and mastered the pen."

The pieces in this section distill revolutionary ideas into their simplest forms, and show that an accessible medium may be a powerful vehicle for radical messages. Whether very young children can or should absorb all of these messages will probably depend on the message. An ABC praising Soviet Russia uses the genre uncritically, to proselytize for Communism; in contrast, an ABC conveying black history uses the genre to bring forth important figures who have been neglected. If the former is important primarily for its place in the history of radical children's literature, the latter remains significant for contemporary children. So, although most of the works in this section were written for the very young, we urge parental guidance in the reading of them.

NOTES

1. The New England Primer (1690; 1777 edition), reprinted in Norton Anthology of Children's Literature: Traditions in English, ed. Jack Zipes, Lissa Paul, Lynne Vallone, Peter Hunt, and Gillian Avery (New York: Norton, 2005), 93.

2. Lissa Paul, "Primers and Readers," in Norton Anthology, 77.

3. Ibid., 78.

4. Hannah More, qtd. in ibid.

5. Thomas Jefferson made these links between liberal democracy and education; they are also articulated in the writings of John Locke, Mary Wollstonecraft, and other Enlightenment thinkers; the twentieth-century thinker who best articulated this connection is John Dewey. See his Democracy and Education (1916). On labor's agitation for public education, see George G. Dawson, "Doctoral Studies on the Relationship between the Labor Movement and Public Education," Journal of Educational Sociology 34:6: 260–69.

6. Lucy Rollin, Cradle and All: A Cultural and Psychoanalytic Reading of Nursery Rhymes (Jackson: UP of Mississippi), 16.

7. See Rollin, 131–44; also see Ronald Reichertz, "The Generative Power of Nursery Rhymes," Children's Literature Association Quarterly 19:3 (Fall 1994): 100–104.

8. Gillian Avery, "Alphabets," in Norton Anthology, 5.

9. George R. Bodmer, "The Post-Modern Alphabet: Extending the Limits of the Contemporary Alphabet Book, from Seuss to Gorey," Children's Literature Association Quarterly 14:3 (Fall 1989): 115.

1

Excerpt from *The Socialist Primer: A Book of First Lessons for the Little Ones in Words of One Syllable* (1908)

Written by Nicholas Klein (dates unknown), Illustrated by Ryan Walker (1870–1932)

EDITORS' INTRODUCTION

In March of 1910, the *New York Times* featured two articles on the *Socialist Primer*, calling it "one of the most remarkable books ever issued, and probably one of the most dangerous."[1] Published in 1908 by The Appeal to Reason, a socialist press and newspaper in Girard, Kansas, the *Socialist Primer* bore the subtitle "A Book of First Lessons for the Little Ones in Words of One Syllable." It was one of the first texts to be written specifically for use in the Socialist Sunday Schools (SSS) that were opening throughout the United States in the early twentieth century.[2]

Socialist Party activists founded approximately one hundred English-speaking Sunday schools between 1900 and 1920, in locales ranging from New York City to Kenosha, Wisconsin, and Portland, Oregon. The goal of these schools, like the anarchist "Modern schools" and the radical ethnic schools in existence at this time, was to counter and supplement the education that working-class children received in the public schools. In the SSS, children learned lessons about "striking and scabbing," "working and shirking," war and peace, and other themes illustrating the problems inherent in industrial capitalism and the benefits found in socialism.[3] Texts like the *Socialist Primer* were taken as evidence that Socialist Sunday Schools were "subverting the minds of the young."[4]

Widely advertised in the socialist press and probably used in most of the SSS, the *Socialist Primer* mixes lessons in grammar and language with socialist philosophy, boiled down to its simplest form with the aid of images from the prominent socialist cartoonist Ryan Walker. Walker's illustrations utilize many typical conventions of the socialist press, perhaps most notably stereotypical images of the fat, cigar-smoking capitalist (aka "the Fat Man"), and the bedraggled, laboring

child. The book's thirty-two lessons become increasingly complex (more words to a page), starting by introducing characters, settings, and issues (Shirk, Work, World, etc.) and developing these over the course of the lessons. The book sticks to the promised monosyllabic verbiage until the final lesson, which advises the teacher or potential teacher to "give each pupil a little bow made of red ribbon" and to explain the objects of the school: "to develop the body, to develop the mind, to develop the morals, [and to] show the connection of one to the others." In contrast to what the *New York Times* pegged as the primer's "malice-breeding, hate-stirring ideals," for a slogan, Klein advised,

I LOVE EVERYBODY
I HATE NOBODY
I WANT EVERYBODY TO BE HAPPY.[5]

The "ten rules of life," included here along with six lessons and a theory review, became the basis for a socialist "ten commandments" that were recited in several SSS.

Nicholas Klein was a prominent Socialist, lawyer, and politician in Ohio who ran for the U.S. House of Representatives on the Socialist Party ticket in 1906. After the 1920s Klein remained active in Ohio politics but repudiated his earlier radicalism. In fact, the public library in Klein's home town of Cincinnati apparently had to keep its copy of the *Socialist Primer* in a locked vault to prevent Klein from destroying it in an effort to hide his embarrassing past.[6]

Parents reading these selections with children will probably want to consider some of the problematic assumptions built into the text: Are fat people bad and thin people good? Are fat people rich and thin people poor? Are there any "lessons" here that are valuable and still relevant today?

NOTES

1. "Primer Teaches Children Socialist Doctrines," *New York Times*, 27 Mar. 1910, SM14. ProQuest Historical Newspapers, The New York Times (1851–2003).

2. Kenneth Teitelbaum, *Schooling for "Good Rebels": Socialist Education for Children in the United States, 1900–1920* (Philadelphia: Temple UP, 1993), 150.

3. Teitelbaum, 37, 215–16 n.1, 40–41, 140, 138.

4. "Pastor Denounces Socialist Primer," *New York Times*, 21 Mar. 1910, 2. ProQuest Historical Newspapers, The New York Times (1851–2003).

5. Nicholas Klein, *The Socialist Primer* (Girard, KS: Appeal to Reason, 1908), 44–45.

6. The Political Graveyard, <http://politicalgraveyard.com/geo/OH/ofc/usrep1900s.html>; Teitelbaum, 240, n.20.

LESSON IV

HOUSE
This is a House.

SHED
Is this a shed?

SHIRK
O, see the Shirk!

WORK
Who does the Work?

WORLD
Who has the World?

WAGE
Who gets the Wage?

LESSON V
All men will Work.
We want no Shirk.

HERE IS A MAN who begs. Why does he not go to work? He would, but he can not get a job. Can he not go to work in a shop? No; for a Fat Man owns the shop. Can he go to work in a mine? No; for a Fat Man owns the Mine. Can he go to work on the Land? No; for a Fat Man owns the Land. IT IS A GREAT SCHEME! When the Thin Man can get work, he must work for the Fat Man. The Thin Man is poor. Is the Fat Man poor? The Thin Man makes the Fat Man rich. Would you like to be the Thin Man?

WHO WORKS FOR THE FAT MAN?
WHO IS A SLAVE?

LESSON VII

HERE is a shop.

Who owns the shop? Who works in the shop? Where should the child be? Do you like the school? The child is in the shop to make the Fat Man rich. Is it good for the child? See the Shirk, who lives on the work made by the poor child.

See the Box that men will fill when they vote right. Then we all will own the shop. Then we all will own the mine. Then we will all own the land. Will you vote right when you are big? Then the Fat Man will go to work. We will all be free.

I LOVE TO BE FREE.
I HATE TO BE A SLAVE.

LESSON XVII

Child	Wheels	Love
Works	Big	Hate
Shop	Near	Wrong

O, see the shop! The child is in the shop. See, the big wheels! They are near the child. The child works hard. The child should be in the school, and not in the shop. You don't want to go to the shop to work all day? You like play; and you like a good time as well as you like the school. Can the child in the shop play? It must work. Why must such a small child work? Are there no men who want to work? A child works cheap. The Big, Fat Man owns the shop. This is a crime. The child is a slave. Men are out of work. Men beg. The child dies. The time will come when there will be no child in the shop. Men will not be out of work. They will not need to beg.

"CHILD SLAVE" will be no words in use, for we will have no slave. All will be free. That will be nice for all. Joy and love will take the place of hate and wrong.

THE CHILD NEEDS PLAY. ALL MEN WILL WORK

LESSON X

See	You	What
The	May	You
Earth	Own	Use

Here is the World. The World is round like a Big Ball. Is it big? Yes it is big. Do you want to see the world? Who owns the Earth? Is it good for the Rich to own the earth? It Is very bad for the poor. We are not rich. We do not own the earth. If the rich own the earth, the poor must pay to live on the earth. Is this fair? Why not? Should any man own the earth? No; all the men should own the earth. The earth was made for all. We can not live if we have no earth, so you see it was made for all, and not for the few. By the earth we mean the shops, the land, the mills, the mines, the cars, the street, the store, and all the things in which we all must work so that we may live. If the few own these things the many will be poor.

THE WORLD IS FOR ALL MEN. WE WILL HAVE NO SLAVE HERE.

LESSON XXX

See the oil well! The oil comes from the ground. Did any man make oil? No, it was found here in this world. No man made the oil wells. Then why do we let the Big, Fat Man own the oil wells? The Big, Fat Man did not make the oil. It is here for all men. The oil wells will be held by all men when the man who works wakes up and votes right. I wish the Thin Man would wake up, don't you? We all use oil in some form; we all need oil. The Fat Man did not make it. Who should own the oil wells? All the folks, of course. And not the Big, Fat Man. Now the Fat Man owns them, and he sets the price on oil. He also sets the wage of the men who work by the oil wells.

He can give or not give us oil. We have night and day. We must have oil just as we must have coal. Would you like it if the Big, Fat Man would own the air and make us all pay for the use of it? Is not the case of the coal and oil just as bad? We need air, coal and oil, and a whole lot of things. These things should be held by the States for all the folks.

THOSE THINGS USED BY ALL THE FOLKS, THE STATES, THAT IS TO SAY ALL MEN, WILL OWN. THEN WE WILL HAVE NO BIG, FAT MEN TO ROB US. WE WILL ALL DO OUR SHARE OF THE WORLD'S WORK, AND WE WILL ALL HAVE JOY.

THE TEN RULES OF LIFE

1. Love your school fellows, who will be your fellow-workmen in life.
2. Love learning, which is the food of the mind: Be as grateful to your teacher as to your parents.
3. Make every day holy by good and useful deeds and kindly actions.
4. Do not hate or speak ill of anyone: Do not be revengeful, but stand up for your rights and resist oppression.
5. Honor good men and women: Be courteous to all: Bow down to none.
6. Do not be cowardly: Be a friend to the weak and love justice.
7. Remember that all the good things of the earth are produced by labor: Whoever enjoys them without working for them is taking what belongs to labor.
8. Observe and think in order to discover the truth: Do not believe that which is contrary to reason, and never deceive yourself for others.
9. Do not think that he who loves his own country must hate and despise other nations or wish for war, which is a remnant of barbarism.
10. Look forward to the day when all men will be free citizens of one fatherland and live together as brothers in peace and righteousness.

THEORY REVIEW

The ax will cut down the tree.
The cat will go for the rat.
Man will not beg.

The box will be full.
The slave will be free.

Men need love and joy.
The child is in the shop.
All men will work.
We want no shirk.
Who works for the fat man?
Who is a slave?
He is a slave who dare not be,
In the right with two or three.
I love to be free.

I hate to be a slave.
I love all. I hate none.
I want all to have joy.

I want to be free.
I want all to be free
The world is for all men.

We will have no slave here.
Let us be free.

No whip.
No wage slave.

THEORY REVIEW

The babes of the ape do not starve.
All men must have nice homes.
All men must have good food.
All men must own
What all men must have to live.
The land, tools and cars
Are for all men.
That which gave us life
Gave us the right to be free.
The child needs play.
All men will work.
The world was made for all men.
Not for the few.

That which you use yourself
You will own yourself.
The rule of gold is good.
But it will not work in this state of things.
Change the state of things
Not the rule.
Do not find fault with the man.
Change his mode of life
And you will have a real rule of gold.

2

Excerpt from *The Socialist Primer* (1930)

Art Young (1866–1943)

EDITORS' INTRODUCTION

Art Young was a Socialist, but he started out as a Republican. He grew up in Monroe, Wisconsin, where his father ran a farm and a general store—"a gathering place for politicians, . . . other leading citizens, and . . . farmers."[1] Instead of weighing and packaging groceries, Young preferred to observe and sketch customers.[2]

Freelancing to underwrite his education, the 17-year-old Young studied at Chicago's Academy of Design (today, the Art Institute of Chicago). Next, working as an artist for Chicago newspapers, he covered the trial of the eight anarchists accused of throwing a bomb during the May 1886 Haymarket Square labor rally. Although Young at that time did not question the guilty verdict, sympathy emerges in his sketches of the imprisoned men, whose wrongful convictions became a rallying point for labor (Illinois executed four, one killed himself in prison, and Illinois governor John Altgeld pardoned the remaining three in 1893).

As his political awareness burgeoned, Young drew for Joseph Pulitzer's *World* in New York, studied art in Paris, and worked on the *Chicago Inter-Ocean* with cartoonist Thomas Nast. After Altgeld's death in 1902, Young read the former governor's pamphlet on why he pardoned the surviving Haymarket men and realized that Altgeld was right. By 1910, Young decided that he "belonged with the Socialists" and would devote his pen "—in so far as circumstances would permit—to attacking the System which engendered so much woe."[3]

Subsidizing his efforts by working for the commercial press, Young cofounded the *Masses* in 1911 and ran as the Socialist candidate for the New York State Assembly in 1912 (he lost). The following year, a Young cartoon accused the Associated Press of deliberately clouding the truth of a West Virginia miners' strike. The AP sued him and *Masses* editor Max Eastman for libel, but, unable to support its case, quietly dropped the charges a year later. Young's next cartoon to land him in court, "Having Their Fling" (*Masses*, September 1917), shows an editor, capitalist, politician, and minister dancing to the sounds of a devil's orchestra, with weapons for instruments. The U.S. attorney general charged this cartoon and three others of violating the Espionage Act. Despite strong public sentiment for the war, the first (April 1918) and second (October 1918) trials ended in hung juries, allowing Young and his *Masses* codefendants to walk free. During the trials, Young ran as a Socialist candidate for the New York State Senate and wrote a pamphlet in support of Scott Nearing, Socialist candidate for the U.S. Congress. (Young and Nearing lost their races.)

In 1930, Young transformed the Nearing pamphlet into *The Socialist Primer*. Though these pages deliver "adult" political messages, Young may have imagined children as a potential audience: he believed that changing the world begins with educating young people. As he put it, "human nature is 'manufactured,'" and if "one generation of young men and women were taught that the human race is one family, . . . a better kind of human nature would develop out of this teaching."[4]

Though these pages from the *Socialist Primer* express their convictions bluntly, Art Young himself harbored doubts and contradictions. He was a Whitmanesque radical with a tendency to get caught up in the enthusiasms of people from different political persuasions. As he said, "I am with every ism, creed, thesis, or scientific experiment that gives a reasonable hope of improving, however little, the happiness and character of human beings in the mass."[5]

NOTES

1. Art Young, *Art Young: His Life and Times*, ed. John Nicholas Beffel (New York: Sheridan House, 1939), 39.

2. Art Young, *On My Way: Being the Book of Art Young in Text and Picture* (New York: Horace Liveright, 1928), 27; Young, *Art Young*, 40.

3. Young, *Art Young*, 262, 269.

4. Young, *On My Way*, 167.

5. Ibid., 269.

The Socialist
Primer

BY Art Young

Public

SEE THE COW

20

10 CENTS
Published by the
SOCIALIST PARTY OF AMERICA
2653 WASHINGTON BOULEVARD
CHICAGO, ILL.

PRICE: FIVE CENTS

HAVE MOTHER AND FATHER A WORRIED LOOK? THEY HAVE. WILL THE WORRIED LOOK COME OFF? NO. NOT UNTIL THEY GET SENSE ENOUGH TO VOTE IN SOCIALISM. WHAT IS SOCIALISM? IT IS—BUSINESS, OPERATED FOR PUBLIC BENEFIT INSTEAD OF PRIVATE PROFIT.

SEE THE PROFITEER? DOES HE MAKE ALL THE PROFIT HE CAN OUT OF THE THINGS THAT LABOR PRODUCES FOR HIM? HE DOES! WHETHER HE IS THE PRESIDENT OF A WOOLEN TRUST OR A COAL MINE—DOESN'T MATTER —HE IS IN BUSINESS FOR BIG PROFITS—FOR HIMSELF AND A FEW STOCKHOLDERS. IS HE TO BLAME FOR BEING A PROFITEER? NO. NOT SO LONG AS THE PUBLIC TOLERATES THE PRIVATE OWNERSHIP OF A PUBLIC NECESSITY.

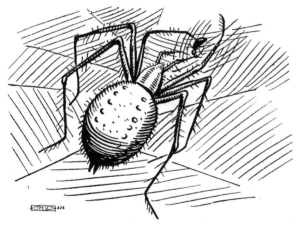

IS THIS A SPIDER? IT IS. WHAT IS ITS OTHER NAME? THE CAPITALIST SYSTEM. HAS HE GOT AN ANT IN HIS WEB? HE HAS. WHAT IS THE ANT'S OTHER NAME? WORKINGMAN. DOES THE SPIDER LIKE TO HAVE THE ANTS ORGANIZE? NO, HE PREFERS TO DEAL WITH THEM "INDIVIDUALLY."

SEE THE OIL WELL ON THE LEFT OF THE PICTURE AND THE RIVER ON THE RIGHT. WHO OWNS THE OIL WELL? A PRIVATE COMPANY OF SPECULATORS. WHO OWNS THE RIVER? THE PUBLIC. IS NOT OIL USED BY THE PUBLIC JUST AS WATER IS? OF COURSE. THEN WHY DOESN'T THE PUBLIC OWN THE OIL WELL? THAT'S WHAT SOCIALISTS WANT TO KNOW.

SEE THE BOSS AND THE WORKER. WHAT ARE THEY DOING —DIVIDING UP? THEY ARE. IS IT A FAIR DIVIDE? NEVER MIND, THE BOSS DECIDES THAT.

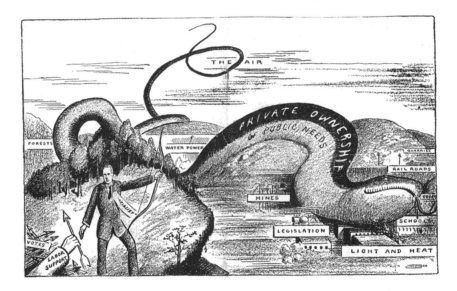

WILL THERE EVER BE ENOUGH ARROWS TO KILL THE MONSTER? SOME DAY. IN THE MEANTIME, EVERY ARROW HELPS.

Selections from "Pioneer Mother Goose" (1934)

Written by Ned Donn (dates unknown), Illustrated by Bill Gropper (William Gropper, 1897–1977)

EDITORS' INTRODUCTION

Fairy tales and nursery rhymes have often been adapted to advance a particular social message. Indeed, some of the original versions have political origins. Published in the December 1934 issue of the communist children's magazine New Pioneer, Ned Donn's "Pioneer Mother Goose"—a group of eight poems, three of which are reproduced here—uses nursery verses in support of working people in general and communist revolution in particular.

The original version of the first poem comments on homelessness, but its precise sympathies are not clear: "Hark, Hark, / The dogs do bark, / The beggars are coming to town; / Some in rags, / And some in jags, / And one in a velvet gown." The "velvet gown" could suggest that the beggars are deluded, inviting a laugh at their expense; on the other hand, such clothes may also be seen as defying class status, and "rags" worn by other beggars may solicit our concern. In contrast, Donn's version clearly aligns itself with strikers, in a year during which a million and a half workers went on strike.[1] In the spring and summer of 1934, longshoremen on the west coast struck and were joined by teamsters and maritime workers, shutting down the ports. Police killed two strikers, San Francisco workers called a general strike, and finally the longshoremen settled with management. During the summer, teamsters in Minneapolis struck for a full month, police killed two, and the teamsters ultimately won their demands. In the fall, textile workers in the South and in New England struck.[2] As in the other strikes, there were confrontations between strikers and police—"The Nightstick flies, the Mass defies," as Donn writes in his verse.

Donn's variation on "Pease porridge hot" cites widespread hunger as a cause for revolution. As Donn's poem suggests, surviving on "Mulligan stew" (made of odds and ends of vegetables and meat) or "smelly soup in a pot" breeds resentment against those who can afford a more nourishing meal. During the Great Depression, hunger and malnutrition led many to take action. In June 1933, unemployed Ford workers and their families held a "Ford Hunger March," in which they demanded a minimum wage, no discrimination against black workers, and an end to the "speed-up"[3] —a practice in which management forced assembly-line labor to work, without added compensation, at a sometimes dangerously fast pace. In 1938, the Fair Labor Standards Act addressed many of these problems, establishing the 40-hour work week and the minimum wage. But at the time these poems were published, such reforms lay an uncertain four years in the future.

The revolutionary update of "This little pig went to market" reflects the Communist Party's aggressive stance in the early 1930s. The month before Donn's verses were published, the Daily Worker's Milton Howard cited the "shooting of workers on picket lines, the police terrorism against the unemployed, the growing movement toward the outlawing of strikes" as reasons for "the smashing of the Wall Street dictatorship and the setting up of a government of workers' and farmers' councils, a Soviet America."[4] Donn's conclusion —"Down with Capitalism! / Long live the Soviet!"— endorses precisely this message.

We could discover nothing about the verses' author, Ned Donn. To learn about William Gropper, see the introduction for The Little Tailor (pages 76–77).

NOTES

1. Howard Zinn, A People's History of the United States, 1942–Present (New York: HarperCollins, 1995), 386.

2. Zinn, 387–88.

3. "ALL OUT: Ford Hunger March," Dearborn, Michigan, 5 June 1933 (flyer), Radical Responses to the Great Depression, University of Michigan Special Collections Library: <http://www.lib.umich.edu/spec-coll/radicaldepression/work_page_601.html>.

4. Milton Howard, "Revolution Alone Can Solve Problem of Ending Crisis: Terrorism and Starvation of New Deal Show That American Working Class Must Prepare for Seizure of Power," Daily Worker, 7 Nov. 1934, 3.

Hark, hark! The Bosses bark,
The Strikers are fighting to win.
The Nightstick flies, the Mass defies,
And frightens the Scab with their din!

Pease porridge hot,
Mulligan stew cold,
Smelly soup in a pot,
Nine days old.

Rich get the 'hot,'
Poor get the 'cold,'
Others get it in a pot,
Nine days old.

Some eat stinking hash,
Others stale gruel—
Help the worker smash
This capitalistic rule.

Workers will get the 'hot,'
There won't be any 'cold,'
Bosses will search the garbage pot,
For anything—nine days old!

This bloated Pig masters Wall Street,
This little Pig owns your home;
This war-crazed Pig had your brother killed,
And this greedy Pig shouts "More!"
This Pig in Congress shouts "War, War!"
All the day long.

These Pigs we'll send to market—
And will they squeal? You bet!
Down with Capitalism!
Long live the Soviet!

4

"A B C for Martin," from
Martin's Annual (1935)
M. Boland (dates unknown)

EDITORS' INTRODUCTION

"A B C for Martin" comes from Martin's Annual, a collection published simultaneously in the United States and Britain by the communist presses International Publishers and Martin Lawrence and edited by Joan Beauchamp.

As a picture alphabet, this selection might seem geared toward very young children. However, it probably demands the most explanation of any text in Little Rebels. To contemporary readers, the sectarian, revolutionary, and occasionally violent rhetoric would surely make this ABC seem quite inappropriate as children's reading. However, the selection is of historical interest, and it is worth including as a somewhat chilling artifact of left-wing illusions and the pedagogy of revolution. That said, the piece may also strike contemporary adult readers as absurdly funny, precisely because the stridency turns out to have been so misplaced.

Several elements of the text and illustration merit discussion. Most troubling, the references, in text and pictures, to "Bolshie" (short for Bolshevik), Kremlin, Stalin, Lenin, and the Soviet Union point to Communists' deference to the USSR and Soviet policy. In hindsight, "T is for Trials" is ironic because the crackdowns that would culminate in the infamous Moscow show trials (1936–1939) were already beginning when this piece was published. In these trials, leaders of the 1917 Russian revolution who opposed Stalin's policies were forced to confess to trumped-up charges or face execution. Along with preventable famine and forced collectivization in the same decade, these trials were some of the first signs that revolutionary rhetoric would justify an ongoing pattern of violent repression. In mentioning "trials" Boland more than likely had in mind the sedition trials in the United Kingdom, such as a 1925–1926 trial of prominent Communists, and the Meerut Conspiracy Trial in India in which thirty-one trade unionists and suspected Communists were tried between 1929 and 1933.[1]

The more general references to "the Holocaust we'll fight to the end," "the Nemesis long overdue," the "Revolution we're going to win," and "You who will know how to fight" attest to the ultraleftism of what was known as the "third period" (1928–1934), during which Communists believed that a final and decisive revolutionary upheaval was just around the corner. Although worldwide depression seemed to give some credence to the idea of capitalism's imminent demise, the depression actually wound up showing capitalism's staying power.

This selection forces the "radical" parent to think carefully about whether children should be taught that systemic transformation requires violent revolution. (The word "holocaust" here means "complete destruction"; during and after World War II, "Holocaust" came to refer to the Nazi murder of six million Jews, Gypsies, and others.)

A few other details merit attention. The stereotypical image of the fat capitalist "warmonger" reiterates an image seen in other selections—Mr. His (pages 123–27) and Klein's Socialist Primer (pages 10–13). As we've noted elsewhere, today overweight people are more likely to be poor than rich. However, the "S stands for Stomachs that wages can't fill" points to the literal and metaphoric hunger of the working class at this time, and the perception that workers were going hungry while capitalists were getting fat from their labor. In "F is for Fascists," the three figures depicted are probably Hitler, Mussolini, and Hirohito. "I is for India" refers to the Indian movement for independence from Britain, which had been underway since 1857 but accelerated with mass struggles in the early 1930s (and culminated in Indian independence in 1947). The W for "World and Workers" refers to the slogan from Karl Marx's The Communist Manifesto: "Workers of the world unite: You have nothing to lose but your chains." The uniformed children depicted next to "Z is the Zeal" are probably meant to be Young Pioneers, a communist version of the Boy Scouts and Girl Scouts.

Nothing is known about M. Boland, but he or she was probably British, as were most contributors to Martin's Annual. Joan Beauchamp, the editor of Martin's Annual, was a member of the Communist Party in Britain and the author or editor of several other books, including Poems of Revolt (1924), British Imperialism in India (1935), and Women Who Work (1937).

Although the book's title suggests that Martin's Annual was a yearly periodical, there do not seem to have been additional volumes.[2] It may be that the revolutionary content of *Martin's Annual* did not sit well with the new rhetoric of the Popular Front, declared at the Seventh World Congress of the Comintern in 1935. During the Popular Front, Communists muted demands for revolution as they emphasized the more pressing need to defeat fascism, and called for cooperation with all democratic forces.

NOTES

1. Thanks to Steve Allen for these references.

2. There are no references to *Martin's Annual* in the most reliable source for information about children's periodicals. See R. Gordon Kelly, *Children's Periodicals in the United States* (Westport, CT: Greenwood, 1984).

A stands for Armaments—
   war-mongers pride;

B is for Bolshie,
   the thorn in their
   side.

C stands for Capitalists,
   fighting for gold;

D for destruction
   they've practiced of
   old.

E stands for Empire,
   built upon blood;

F is for Fascists,
   a murderous brood.

G stands for Glory,
   they try to defend;

H is the Holocaust
   we'll fight to end.

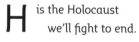
I stands for India,
   never yet quelled;

J is for Jail,
   where good rebels
   are held.

 K stands for Kremlin, where our Stalin lives;

S stands for Stomachs that wages can't fill;

L is the Lead he so ably gives.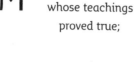

 T is for Trials that won't break our will.

 M is for Marx, whose teachings proved true;

 U stands for Union of "Soviet's fame";

N is the Nemesis long overdue.

V was the Victory when our Lenin came.

 O stands for Ownership, which we demand;

 W stands for World and for Workers;

 P is for Poverty, stalking the land.

X crosses out the misleaders and shirkers.

Q is the Quandary those rulers are in;

Y is for You who will know how to fight;

 R Revolution, we're going to win.

Z is the Zeal that will add to your might.

5

Excerpt from *The Black BC's* (1970)

Written by Lucille Clifton
(b. 1936), Illustrated by
Don Miller (1923–1993)

EDITORS' INTRODUCTION

Born Thelma Lucille Sayles, Clifton grew up in a working-class community in Depew, ten miles east of Buffalo, New York. Her father worked in a steel mill, and her mother worked in a laundry. Neither finished elementary school, but her father told stories, and her mother wrote poetry. As a girl, Clifton also wrote poetry but never considered it a career: "The only poets I ever saw or heard of were the portraits that hung on the wall of my elementary school—old dead white men from New England with beards. Of course it didn't seem a possibility to me."[1]

She kept writing and began meeting other poets. Clifton graduated from high school at sixteen and won a scholarship to Howard University, where she met poet and playwright Amiri Baraka (then LeRoi Jones). Unwilling to study anything unrelated to poetry, Clifton left Howard for Fredonia State Teachers College (now SUNY Fredonia), where she joined a small group of black writers, including novelist Ishmael Reed and University of Buffalo professor Fred Clifton—whom she would marry in 1958.[2] Reed showed her poems to Langston Hughes, who included some in *The Poetry of the Negro, 1746–1970*, an anthology he and Arna Bontemps edited. In 1969, the *New York Times* named Clifton's first volume of poetry, the ironically titled *Good Times* (1969), one of the ten best books of the year. Then thirty-three years old with six children under ten, Clifton felt "too busy to take it terribly seriously. I was happy and proud, of course, but had plenty of other things to think about."[3]

Hearing her children referring to Africa as "the dark continent" inspired Clifton to write *The Black BC's*, an Afrocentric challenge to Eurocentric education.[4] (One update for the book's "A is for Africa": though Africa did have 225 million people in 1970, by 2005 its population had risen to 840 million.) Teaching beginning readers about African and African-American history, *The Black BC's* offers an early exploration of Clifton's

core themes. *Good News about the Earth: New Poems* (1972) and *Quilting: Poems, 1987–1990* (1991) include poems dedicated to black heroes, both famous and unknown. The courage and dignity of everyday people emerges in her eight *Everett Anderson* children's books (1970–2001) and in *Generations: A Memoir* (1976), which tells the story of her much-admired great-great-grandmother Caroline—a brave, strong matriarch abducted from the Dahomey people of West Africa and sold into slavery.

A National Book Award winner (1999) and Maryland's poet laureate from 1979 to 1985, Clifton has written a dozen collections of poetry and over twenty books for children. Today a distinguished professor of the humanities at St. Mary's College in Maryland, Clifton continues to write because, she says, "writing is a way of continuing to hope."[5]

The book's illustrator, Don Miller, turned to children's book illustration after seeing the *Dick and Jane* books that his son was reading in school: "The families illustrated in these books were middle class suburbanite blue-eyed blondes," he said. "My son and other black children could not see themselves in these books."[6]

Born in Jamaica, Miller and his parents emigrated to the United States when he was an infant. They lived in Montclair, New Jersey, where his father worked as a school custodian. As a child, he drew pictures of his heroes: Paul Robeson, Joe Louis, and Frederick Douglass. Serving in the U.S. Army during World War II, Miller illustrated his base's newspaper, edited by novelist Dashiell Hammett.

After the war, he earned a degree from Cooper Union. There, he met his wife, Judy Miller, who became the director of African-American Studies at Seton Hall University. He became a freelance artist, creating paintings (the Smithsonian holds some of his work), drawing advertisements, and illustrating children's books.

During the 1960s, Miller heard Dr. Martin Luther King, Jr., speak in Montclair, and participated in the 1963 March on Washington, at which King gave his famous "I Have a Dream" speech—a scene that Miller depicts in *The Black BC's*, accompanying "K is for King." Supporting civil rights nationally and in his community, Miller was an active member of both the Montclair NAACP and the Fair Housing Commission.

In 1983, after a fulfilling year teaching art in Nigeria, Miller abandoned his commercial work, deciding he would "no longer do another thing that didn't absolutely fascinate me."[7] The next year, he proposed and then received a commission to paint a mural in the lobby of the Martin Luther King Memorial Library in Washington, D.C. Unveiled on January 20, 1986—the first observance of Martin Luther King Day—the 56-by-7-foot mural focuses on King but includes other people connected with the struggle for civil rights, such as Rosa Parks; Medgar Evers; Andrew Young; Jesse Jackson; Andrew Goodman, James Chaney, and Michael Schwerner (voting-rights workers murdered in Philadelphia, Mississippi); and Addie Mae Collins, Denise McNair, Carole Robertson, and Cynthia Wesley (the four girls killed in the Ku Klux Klan's bombing of Birmingham's Sixteenth Avenue Baptist Church). Miller considered the mural "the ultimate expression for my goals as an artist."[8]

As Clifton writes in *The Black BC's*, "H is for Heroes / who follow a dream / however impossible / it may seem."

NOTES

1. Vineta Colby, ed., *World Authors, 1985–1990* (New York: Wilson, 1995), 156.

2. Ibid., 156.

3. Ibid., 157.

4. Harriet Jackson Scarupa, "Lucille Clifton: Making the World 'Poem-Up,'" *Ms.*, Oct. 1976, 123.

5. "(Thelma) Lucille Clifton," *Contemporary Authors Online* (Thompson Gale, 2005).

6. Anne Commire, ed., *Something about the Author*, vol. 15 (Detroit: Gale, 1979), 196.

7. Miller, qtd. in Desson Howe, "The Muralist's March with King: Artist Don Miller, Civil Rights Chronicler," *Washington Post*, 20 Jan. 1986, C6.

8. Ibid.

For the children

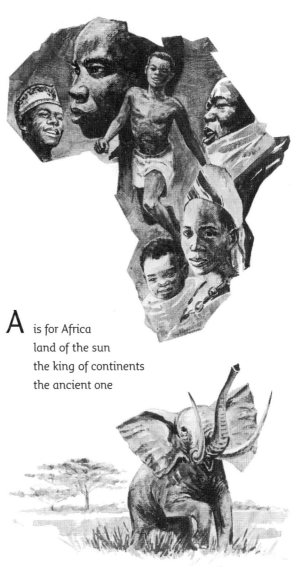

A is for Africa
land of the sun
the king of continents
the ancient one

Many different countries are located on the continent of Africa. It is the second biggest of the world's seven continents; only Asia is bigger. It covers as much land as the United States, Western Europe, China, and India put together. Africa is the land of the biggest desert in the world (the Sahara), the longest river in the world (the Nile), the greatest variety of wild animals, at least 16 different major languages, and about 225 million people.

B is for Books
where readers find
treasures for the heart
and mind

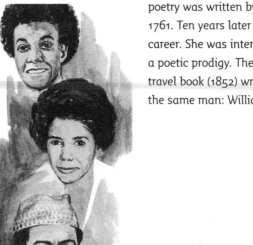

The first poem by a black American dates back to 1746. It was written by a Massachusetts slave girl named Lucy Terry. The first published example of black American poetry was written by Jupiter Hammon and printed in 1761. Ten years later Phillis Wheatley began her literary career. She was internationally known, and hailed as a poetic prodigy. The first novel (1853), play (1858), and travel book (1852) written by a black American were by the same man: William Wells Brown.

There are many other famous black literary names. Among the best-known contemporary ones are:

James Baldwin	Lonne Elder III
Gwendolyn Brooks	Lorraine Hansberry
Eldridge Cleaver	LeRoi Jones
	Ted Shine

C is for Cowboys
kings of the West
some of the black men
were some of the best

There were thousands of black "forty-niners" during the California Gold Rush.

The only known male survivor the Alamo was a black man named Joe.

A black cowboy named Bill Pickett invented the rodeo art of bulldogging.

Isaiah Dorman was an interpreter for General George Custer; they both died at Little Big Horn.

Other famous black cowboys who were scouts and traders were Jim Beckwourth and Nat Love.

D is for Douglass
   giant of men
   who freed himself
   and mastered the pen

Frederick Douglass was born a slave in Maryland in 1817. In 1838 he escaped from bondage and became an abolitionist, lecturing around the world on the evils of slavery. Instead of living quietly and safely, he wrote and lectured about this life as a slave so that everyone would know what slavery was really like. He published a newspaper called the *North Star* and helped recruit black troops during the Civil War. Later in his life he served as U.S. Marshal for the District of Columbia.

E is for Explorers
   brave pioneers
   whose courage made history
   through the years

The first man to ever stand at the North Pole was a black man, Matthew Henson. He explored the Arctic with Admiral Robert E. Peary and reached the North Pole before the rest of the party on that historic occasion.

The first building in the area that is now Chicago was the home of a black man named Jean Baptiste Pointe Du Sable. He became an Indian trader who traveled the Mississippi River region before establishing the trading post and settlement that became Chicago.

Thirty black men were with Balboa in 1513 when the Pacific Ocean was discovered.

York, a black scout, helped to guide the Lewis and Clark Expedition.

There was at least one black man with Columbus when he reached the shores of America.

F is for Freedom
   whatever folk say
   whoever can give it
   can take it away

Many years ago Frederick Douglass, describing a fight he had with a slave-breaker (a man whose job was to break the spirit of "troublesome" slaves), said: "When a slave cannot be flogged, he is more than half free." Douglass recognized the responsibility that men have to free themselves. Black men and women have always tried to free themselves in this country, from Harriet Tubman to today's marchers. In the earlier days of our country most strides toward freedom were solitary endeavors, but in the early 1960's Freedom Rides and Freedom Marches involved many people of different races marching and riding together and freeing themselves.

Part 2

Subversive Science and Dramas of Ecology

JULIA MICKENBERG & PHILIP NEL

Science might seem like an odd subject for radical children's literature: what is science if not "objective," and, therefore, apolitical?[1] However, the tendency to see scientific knowledge as fact makes less visible the reality that this arena is "intensively value laden," according to one historian of science.[2] As cultural critic Raymond Williams put it, "the notion of 'science' has often foreclosed analysis of its own assumptions."[3]

Educators have long found moral and ethical reasons for teaching children scientific subjects. The Nature Study movement, which emerged in the United States in the late nineteenth and early twentieth centuries, developed in concert with romantic ideas about childhood. Followers of this movement believed that studying nature could help preserve children's natural wildness and protect them from the taint of civilization. Nature study was particularly encouraged for girls, who, through better appreciation of nature, could develop feminine traits of sympathy, cooperation, and gentleness.[4]

Early-twentieth-century progressive educators encouraged experimentation and learning through experience. They believed that children were natural scientists—curious, constantly asking questions, interested in novelty and in the natural world. Although all aspects of scientific study were hailed for their value in developing young people's powers of observation and reason, progressive educators believed that biology education would have particular benefits for children. For instance, learning the biological facts of adaptation and the interrelatedness of all living beings could help make the student a "'master of life' rather than a passive victim of his surroundings."[5]

Socialists shared many of progressive educators' assumptions about science as a tool for developing critical consciousness, but their goals in developing this consciousness were more explicitly political. The *Little Socialist Magazine for Boys and Girls* (1909–1912) contained a regular column on scientific themes such as "The Sun and the Stars" and "Gravitation and Inertia." These columns mixed science with commentary suggesting that power came with knowledge. As one column noted, "Ignorant people are the best wage slaves, for they know nothing about the rights of human beings, and their hope lies in the fantasy of a happiness hereafter."[6]

Evolutionary ideas had an enormous impact on Socialists' interest in and discussion of science. Like progressive educators, who tended to embrace the idea that "ontogeny recapitulates phylogeny" (or that the development of the individual mirrors the development of the species), early-twentieth-century Socialists believed that studying evolution would aid in the literal evolution of the child's mind, and, consequently, advance civilization as a whole. Socialists also emphasized that an understanding of evolution would help children grasp the importance of agency in social as well as physical transformation. As one socialist educator noted, "Changes in civilization are the things we wish to impress upon the minds of our students, and the fact that necessity has forced man to think of change and, finally, through action, to bring the change about."[7]

In the early twentieth century, much of the science-oriented children's literature published by Socialists emphasized evolution and suggested continuities between the natural world and human society. The selection included here from Caroline Nelson's *Nature Talks on Economics* (1907), on "Evolution and Revolution," reflects both the conventions of Nature Study and the left-wing socialist understanding that humans must act deliberately in order to effect change (rather than waiting for change to evolve naturally). Likewise, Mary Marcy, editor of the *International Socialist Review*, published *Stories of the Cave People* (1917) and *Rhymes of the Early Jungle Folk* (1922) with the intent of both emphasizing the constancy of change and challenging supernatural or religious explanations.[8]

The Scopes trial of 1925, in which a high school teacher was tried for teaching evolution, highlighted evolution's fundamental challenge to a traditional, religious outlook. *Science and History for Girls and Boys* (1932)—by the ex-communicated communist "bishop" William Montgomery Brown—uses science to debunk Christian theology in particular and religion in general. In addition to emphasizing evolution, his book also highlights several other themes that would inform much radical-authored scientific children's literature in decades to come. Brown emphasized the need to combat superstition with science and rationality; he pointed to the misuse of science under capitalism (in which science for profit replaces science for the public good); and he proposed that true scientific advancement depends upon the free exchange of ideas. Finally, he argued, "It is quite silly to regard the features of different races as marks of inferiority or superiority."[9]

Communists believed that Marxism itself had enormous implications for science, particularly because its philosophy of "dialectical materialism" offered a method for rational inquiry applicable to the sciences and to society. The communist magazine for children, the *New Pioneer* (1931–1939), published a regular column on "Science and Nature for Johnny Rebel," which covered various scientific subjects and their political implications. "The Powder of Empire" (April 1932) explained how gunpowder works, as well as the ways in which gunpowder has supported projects of class domination, from the colonization of the Indians in North America to the German, French, and Belgian control of Africa. Another column, "Can Girls Be Scientists?" (April 1936), suggested that gender inequity in the sciences was a product of capitalism, as men trained "in the spirit of individualism and economy rivalry" prevented women from entering scientific fields.[10]

By the late 1930s, many scientists had been politicized by the Depression, which dramatized the need for a more efficient and equitable distribution of resources. For some, the Soviet Union appeared to offer a model for harnessing science and technology to serve human good. Forced collectivization, purges, show trials—and constricted freedom for scientists, as well as other intellectuals and creative people—eventually muted this enthusiasm for the "New Russia," but the initial excitement did trickle down to children's literature produced in the United States. Although usually only implicitly, American children's books about the technologies of production (see "Work, Workers, and Money," pages 59–94) communicated the technocratic utopianism that marked Americans' enthusiasm for Soviet science. This admiration gained more explicit expression in the enthusiastic reception given to *New Russia's Primer* (1931), a school text written by the Soviet engineer M. Il'in and translated by the American educator George Counts.[11]

American scientists—and science educators—were also radicalized by the specter of fascism. Under the Nazis, science was put in the service of evil: Nazis used concentration camp prisoners as guinea pigs for scientific experiments and rationalized their power by "scientifically" demonstrating the Aryan race's superiority.

Thus both communism *and* fascism helped politicize scientists. In the late 1930s and 1940s, many science teachers connected both the means and the ends of science to a political and social agenda, emphasizing that scientists must "be free to question the orthodox and to consider with open mind the heretical" and must be motivated by a commitment to the common good.[12]

Alex Novikoff's *Climbing Our Family Tree* (1945), from which we include the selection "The Races of Mankind," was part of a series of children's books published by the communist International Publishers (under the imprint of Young World Books). It speaks to many of the concerns we have been discussing. The longer text incorporates a discussion of evolution; it calls for the rational use of scientific knowledge for the common good; and, particularly in the selection included here, it challenges the racial logic that had driven the Nazi project. Although Novikoff only wrote one other children's book, other books in International's Young World series launched the careers of well-known juvenile science writers, including Irving Adler, Sarah Riedman, and Millicent Selsam.

The dropping of atomic bombs on Hiroshima and Nagasaki in 1945 also sparked a movement among scientists to prevent future use of atomic weapons. The critique of science voiced by scientists in the highest echelons filtered into educational discourse as well, although instructors too outspoken in their politics were likely to find their teaching careers in jeopardy. But quite a few science teachers—working at all levels —discovered that, by writing juvenile literature, they could make a good living and reach more children. Cold War–inspired demands for beefed-up science education contributed to the market for scientific children's literature. In fact, several of the most prominent science writers for children in the 1950s and 1960s —including Adler, Riedman, Selsam, Hy Ruchlis, and Rose Wyler—had been forced to leave teaching jobs for political reasons but were able to launch successful careers as authors for children. Sputnik suddenly made teaching evolution seem not quite so radical (Were we going to keep up with the Russians, or were we going to keep steering clear of controversy so as not to offend conservative Christians?).

The New Left and counterculture of the 1960s and 1970s shared earlier radicals' frustrations that science under capitalism failed to serve the common good. The environmental movement, which grew out of the counterculture, pointed to the costs of industrialism and consumption, citing in particular pollution, deforestation, and the consequences of pesticides. The final two selections in this section—*The Day They Parachuted*

Cats on Borneo (1971), by Charlotte Pomerantz, and *Red Ribbons for Emma* (1981), by Deb Preusch, Tom Barry, and Beth Wood—both speak to the environmental critique that emerged with force in the 1970s. Bill Peet's *The Wump World* (1970) and Dr. Seuss's *The Lorax* (1971) were also early examples of children's books imbued with this ecological consciousness. More recently, Molly Bang's *Common Ground: The Water, Earth, and Air We Share* (1997) and *Nobody Particular: One Woman's Fight to Save the Bays* (2000) have tackled conservation and pollution.

Today, concerns about global warming, toxic waste, and other forms of environmental degradation make scientific, technological, and ecological education more important than ever. The children's film *Happy Feet* (2006), about a penguin interested in combating pollution and overfishing, has been attacked by conservatives for its "global-warming agenda," although the film is actually silent on that issue. The very mention of penguins has come to represent the specter of climate change—which several new books for children do address. Jean-Luc Fromental and Joëlle Jolivet's *365 Penguins* (2006), a charmingly funny story of a family coping with the daily arrival of penguins, appears to be a book about numbers, until the end when Uncle Victor arrives to claim responsibility and explain just why has been mailing these penguins. He says, "The ice caps are melting," shrinking the penguins' territory on the South Pole; so, he has "decided to introduce them to the North Pole," evading restrictions on exporting endangered species by sending one penguin a day to his brother's family.

Science can be subversive to the extent that it offers children tools to question, criticize, understand, and transform society. Continuing debates about teaching Darwinism in schools and the "intelligent design" movement suggest that old victories for science teaching in the schools are precarious at best. Conservative attacks on several recent texts with scientific themes may be direct products of concerns about a "global-warming agenda," but the attacks may also suggest growing recognition that encouraging children to critically evaluate all information they encounter—the essence of the scientific method—is a radical practice.

NOTES

1. Much of the material in this introduction is drawn from Julia Mickenberg, "The Tools of Science: Dialectics and

Children's Literature," in *Learning from the Left: Children's Literature, the Cold War, and Radical Politics in the United States* (New York: Oxford UP, 2006), 175–230.

2. Philip J. Pauly, "The Development of High School Biology: New York City, 1900–1925," *ISIS* 82 (1991): 662.

3. Raymond Williams, *Marxism and Literature* (New York: Oxford UP, 1977), 64.

4. Pamela M. Henson, "Through Books to Nature: Anna Botsford Comstock and the Nature Study Movement," *Natural Eloquence: Women Reinscribe Science*, ed. Barbara T. Gates and Ann B. Shteir (Madison: U of Wisconsin P, 1997), 116–43.

5. Pauly, 675.

6. W. Gundlach, "Law of Gravitation," *Little Socialist Magazine for Boys and Girls* 3:2 (Mar. 1910): 4, 14.

7. William F. Kruse, "How to Teach History in the Primary Grades," *Young Socialists Magazine* 13:11 (Jan. 1920): 7.

8. Discussed in Paul Mishler, *Raising Reds: The Young Pioneers, Radical Summer Camps, and Communist Political Culture in the United States* (New York: Columbia UP, 1999), 113.

9. William Montgomery Brown, *Science and History for Girls and Boys* (Galion, OH: Bradford-Brown Educational Co., 1932), 72.

10. Bert Grant, "The Powder of Empire," *New Pioneer*, Apr. 1932, 15; ibid., "Can Girls Be Scientists?" *New Pioneer*, Oct. 1936, 18–19.

11. For a useful discussion of the Soviet "production book," see Evgeny Steiner, *Stories for Little Comrades: Revolutionary Artists and the Making of Early Soviet Children's Books*, trans. Jane Ann Miller (Seattle: U of Washington P, 1999), 111–67. On American interest in Soviet development, see David Engerman, *Modernization from the Other Shore: American Intellectuals and the Romance of Russian Development* (Cambridge, MA: Harvard UP, 2003).

12. Benjamin Gruenberg, "The Scientific Temperament and Social Values," *Science Education* 22:3 (1938): 128–33. Also see Peter J. Kuznick, *Beyond the Laboratory: Scientists as Political Activists in the 1930s* (Chicago: University of Chicago Press, 1987).

6

Excerpt from *Nature Talks on Economics* (1912)

Caroline Nelson (1868–1952)

EDITORS' INTRODUCTION

Inside the back cover of Enrico Ferri's *Socialism and Modern Science* (1917) is an advertisement by the socialist publisher Charles H. Kerr for Caroline Nelson's *Nature Talks on Economics*. It reads, in part,

> Many Socialist parents are letting their children grow up in ignorance of Socialism and its principles. There are Socialist fathers who let no opportunity pass to talk Socialism to their friends and shopmates and yet leave their sons and daughters to the mercies of capitalistic teachers and capitalistic books. The result is that they grow up with their minds filled with perversions and abominations of capitalism. For a long time there has been a need for a short exposition of Socialism suitable for children. We have that book now.[1]

Nature Talks on Economics, from which "Evolution and Revolution" is taken, is one of several texts designed for use in English-speaking Socialist Sunday Schools, about a hundred of which were founded in the United States between 1900 and 1920.[2] This book, according to its publisher's advertisement, shows the child that "the forces of nature work co-operatively. From that viewpoint it is easy for him to understand the necessity of the Co-operative Commonwealth."[3]

Caroline Nelson was a Danish-born Socialist and west coast organizer of the Industrial Workers of the World (IWW). A regular contributor to socialist and radical journals, Nelson wrote pieces that discussed the role of women in the socialist movement and in the larger society.[4] In the 1910s Nelson became active in the movement to secure safe and reliable birth control for women. Although the Socialist Party refused to take up the issue of birth control organizationally, many of the leading figures in the movement, including Margaret Sanger, came to the issue through socialist activism, and Nelson made clear connections between the two movements. "It does not take a philosopher to see that having many children renders working class parents almost helpless in the hands of their masters," she wrote in 1913. "When they go on strike the children's cry for bread drives them back. . . . The children, in turn, have no chance to become thinking men and women."[5] Nelson first met Margaret Sanger in 1912, and she contributed to Sanger's magazines, the *Woman Rebel* and the *Birth Control Review*, the latter designed to bring broader support to the birth control movement. After Sanger's husband was arrested for distributing her pamphlet, *Family Limitation*, Nelson, along with fellow radicals Emma Goldman, Elizabeth Gurley Flynn, and Rose Pastor Stokes, traveled throughout the United States, speaking at IWW and socialist locals and to women's groups. In 1915 Nelson helped found the San Francisco Birth Control League, and she arranged many of Margaret Sanger's west coast speaking engagements. Nelson, who also published several pamphlets on unionism, was married to an iron worker and union activist, Carl Rave.

The selection reprinted here reflects the radical socialist viewpoint (as opposed to that of right-wing Socialists), which held that the social rupture brought on by revolution could find rationale in the natural laws of biological evolution.[6] The story, told in the form of a conversation between two children and their father, draws upon conventions of the Nature Study movement. Popular at the turn of the century, it held that children could learn life lessons from nature. Here, a chick's hatching is meant to offer a lesson on the need for workers to break the shell of capitalism.

NOTES

1. Enrico Ferri, *Socialism and Modern Science (Darwin, Spencer, Marx)* (Chicago: Charles H. Kerr, 1917 [Italian ed., 1894]), inside back cover.

2. Teitelbaum, Kenneth. *Schooling for "Good Rebels": Socialist Education for Children in the United States, 1900–1920* (Philadelphia: Temple UP, 1993), 37.

3. Ibid.

4. Information on Nelson comes from the following sources: Mari Jo Buhle, *Women and American Socialism, 1870–1920* (Urbana: U of Illinois P, 1981), 276–78; Meredith Tax, *The Rising of the Women: Feminist Solidarity and Class Conflict, 1880–1917* (Urbana: U of Illinois P, 2001 [1980]), 157; Alan Ruff, *We Called Each Other Comrade: Charles H. Kerr and Company, Radical Publishers* (Urbana: U of Illinois P, 1997), 257; Esther Katz, ed., *The Selected Papers of Margaret Sanger. Vol. 1, The Woman Rebel, 1900–1928* (Urbana: U of Illinois P, 2003), 136–40, 191–92.

5. Caroline Nelson, "Neo-Malthusianism," *International Socialist Review* 14:4 (Oct. 1913): 230.

6. Paul Mishler, *Raising Reds: The Young Pioneers, Radical Summer Camps, and Communist Political Culture in the United States* (New York: Columbia UP, 1999), 112.

EVOLUTION AND REVOLUTION

Early one Sunday morning a carpenter with his two children, Johnny and Anna, went to the woods to saw down a tree. The little folks chatted away, asking all sorts of questions.

"Papa, do the flowers sleep?" asked Anna.

"I think they do," said the father. "They fold their petals and droop their heads in the night."

"Why don't they wake up when we go by?" went on the little chatter-box.

"They don't wake up," said the father, "because they have no eyes or ears to see and hear with. If they had they would pull themselves up by the roots and run about."

"They would be funny plants," said Johnny with a laugh.

"They would no longer be plants, they would be animals," said the father. "All animals have grown out of the plant life. They didn't like being tied to the soil."

Just then they were passing a bush that grew by the roadside. Somewhere in the bush there was a great fluttering and screaming of birds. They all stopped and peered into the bush. They saw a bird's nest around which the father and mother birds were circling in distress. In the nest were two tiny baby birds. They were red-skinned, without any feathers. Their heads seemed to be too big for them to carry. In the nest was also a tiny egg, and, as they looked, it cracked and out of it came another baby bird. Johnny and Anna both screamed, they were so excited. And the birds screamed because a little one had dropped out of their nest. The father picked it up from a twig, where it was hanging by one leg, and replaced it in the nest.

"How did the birds grow inside the eggs?" asked both the children.

"The egg," said the father, "is a storehouse of food with a center of life. We don't know what life is. We only know that it is always active, and always changing. First, the yolk of the egg is divided into little sacks, so small that we couldn't see them with our naked eye. The different organs are built out of this prepared material, very much as our cities are built out of lumber, bricks and many other materials. It may be that there are fairy carpenters, plumbers, bricklayers and many other workers at work building the bird. But whatever it is that does this work, it means to give out energy. And energy can only be restored by food. When the food in the egg is gone the builders in the egg must find food in some other way. But these builders had no bosses. They built the bird in co-operation. They became the bird. What one part of the bird needed the whole needed. The governing seat was the head, in the brain. Every part of the organism called for action. There was a revolt against living any longer in an egg state. It meant death and starvation. 'Strike down the wall!' was the cry. And the bird did something he had never done before; he moved his head and struck blow after blow."

"Then he came out," said Johnny with glee.

"Yes, he came out," said the father, "because he didn't remain quiet, and say—'It is no use. I have always been in an egg and therefore always shall be here until I die.' All life has come up from a mere speck, and labored mightily until it so changed that it had to find a new way of living. This laboring mightily is evolution. The cry—'Strike down the wall!'—is the cry of revolution. Life in its onward march has struck down a thousand walls. The workers are the world's mighty builders. They have labored night and day. They have built railroads, steamships, telegraphs, telephones, factories, machinery, and delved in the bowels of the earth for coal to run the whole business, until today we have a mighty organized world. But the working-class is in a shell of Capitalism. What they have built a few idle rich claim as their private property. Every day the workers have less and less food. The army of people who can find no work grows larger and larger; all around the world is heard the cry of revolution for us workers. Strike down the wall of capitalism! is our cry. We must have food or die. And we shall not die while we produce food in plenty."

"What is Capitalism, papa?" asked Johnny.

"Capitalism," said the father, "is a condition in which there goes on a regular system of stealing from the workers what they make. When the workers make a hundred dollars' worth of goods they only get twenty dollars in wages. The bosses get the eighty dollars for doing nothing. But here we are. This is the tree," said the father. "We shall see how many birthdays it has had, after I get it sawed down, and see how it built itself up."

7

Excerpts from *Science and History for Girls and Boys* (1932)

William Montgomery Brown
(1855–1937)

EDITORS' INTRODUCTION

Known as the "Bolshevik Bishop," William Montgomery Brown had been a well-respected and outspoken Episcopal bishop in Arkansas before gradually embracing communism between 1911 and 1920. Brown was born into poverty in Ohio. His father died when he was young, and his mother had him "farmed out" to other guardians starting at age seven. Forced to work from a young age, Brown was determined to get an education. He entered school at the fourth grade and made it up to the eighth grade. Although raised a Methodist, Brown learned of a wealthy Episcopalian philanthropist, Mary Scranton Bradford, who helped him gain an education through the Episcopal church. He later married his benefactor's adopted daughter and devoted his time to writing: his first book, *The Church for Americans* (1895), went through nineteen printings. The book helped Brown earn a position as bishop coadjutor of Arkansas.[1]

Prior to his conversion to communism, Brown was perhaps most known for his vocal defense of racial segregation, which he articulated in his 1907 book, *The Crucial Race Question*. Here, he argued that race prejudice is "a deep-rooted, God-implanted instinct" and that "the Anglo-American citizen is prevented by a law of nature from allowing the Afro-American to be associated with him in the government of these United States."[2] Brown also became infamous for his outspoken defense of southern lynching.[3]

Thanks to his reading of Darwin, English rationalists, Christian Socialists, and other thinkers of his day, Brown's views became increasingly radical. He left his post in Arkansas in 1911. In *Communism and Christianism: Banish Gods from Skies and Capitalists from Earth* (1920), Brown went beyond the Christian socialism that was popular in his day to reject core Christian ideas, proclaiming, "Darwin is my Moses and Marx my Christ!"[4] This book led to Brown's deposition for heresy in 1925, after which he "styl[ed] himself the chaplain to the Communist Party and dressed in a black cassock with a large gold cross hanging from his neck,"[5] spending his remaining years as an outspoken supporter of the communist cause. As part of this conversion, Brown moved away from his embrace of racial doctrines, supporting the American Negro Labor Congress in 1925.[6] In 1930 he published a pamphlet entitled "The American Race Problem," renouncing his earlier views on race.[7]

Reflecting his new faith in Soviet-style communism, Brown dedicated *Science and History* to "the girls and boys of the rising generation of Bolsheviks in the Soviet Union," who, he predicted, "are destined to have an hitherto unequalled influence for good" because of their scientific training and "their freedom from superstition."[8] The chapter from which this selection is taken sums up many of the book's themes and arguments about natural and human evolution, Brown's rejection of Christian doctrine, and the power of science to debunk superstition and improve life.

Brown printed at least twenty thousand copies of the book, but it is doubtful that more than a fraction of that number sold, and many of the volumes that did not sit for decades in an Ohio attic were given away.[9] Still, the book was influential in leftist circles. Radical Marge Frantz entitled the short memoir she published in *Red Diapers* "Science and History for Girls and Boys Infiltrates Alabama,"[10] and scientist Richard Levins, whose grandfather read Brown's book to him as a child, connects that reading to his continuing interest in discovering the links between science and society. According to Levins, "the linking of science and history in the book did not seem at all strange to us. For me it was all part of an exciting finding-out about the way the world worked."[11]

NOTES

1. Ron Carden, "The Bolshevik Bishop: William Montgomery Brown's Path to Heresy, 1906–1920," *Anglican and Episcopal History* 82:2 (2003): 197.

2. William Montgomery Brown, *The Crucial Race Question* (Little Rock, 1907), 118, 125. Qtd. in James W. Vander Zanden, "The Ideology of White Supremacy," *Journal of the History of Ideas* 20:3 (June–Sept. 1959): 388–89.

3. Vincent Vinikas, "Specters in the Past: The Saint Charles, Arkansas, Lynching of 1904 and the Limits of Historical Inquiry," *Journal of Southern History* 65:3 (Aug. 1999): 559.

4. Carden, 200.

5. Carden, 227.

6. Mark Soloman, *The Cry Was Unity: Communists and African Americans, 1917–1936* (Jackson: UP of Mississippi, 1998), 53.

7. William Montgomery Brown, *Heresy: Bishop Brown's Quarterly Lectures. No. 1: The American Race Problem* (Galion, OH: Bradford-Brown Educational Co., Jan. 1930). Thanks to Ron Carden for providing us with this source.

8. William Montgomery Brown, "Dedication," *Science and History for Girls and Boys* (Galion, OH: Bradford-Brown Educational Co., 1932), 4. The English rationalist Joseph Mc-Cabe ghostwrote *Science and History for Girls and Boys* as well as Brown's other book for children, *Teachings of Marx for Girls and Boys* (1935), both of which Brown published through his Bradford-Brown Educational Company. Brown paid McCabe well but never credited him. See Carden, 227.

9. List of books and printings as of May 1937 in Brown's *The Fascist and Communist Dictatorships* (Galion, OH: Bradford-Brown Educational Co., 1937). Email message from Ron Carden to Julia Mickenberg, 26 June 2006. Also see Ronald M. Carden, *William Montgomery Brown (1855–1937): The Southern Episcopal Church Bishop Who Became a Communist* (Lewison, NY: Edwin Mellen, 2007).

10. Marge Franz, "Science and History for Girls and Boys Infiltrates Alabama," *Red Diapers: Growing Up in the Communist Left*, ed. Judy Kaplan and Linn Shapiro (Urbana: U of Illinois P, 1998), 45–53.

11. Richard Levins, "A Science of Our Own: Marxism and Nature," *Monthly Review* 38 (July–Aug. 1986): 3.

RT. REV. WILLIAM MONTGOMERY BROWN, D. D.
Episcopus in partibus Bolshevikium et Infidelium

I. WHAT SCIENCE IS GOING TO DO

The great value of science is, as I told you, that it finds out the truth for us by the study and interpretation of nature, so that we are not going to waste any more time serving imaginary gods who never revealed a truth to the world or did a thing for it, so that we can produce all sorts of good things more abundantly and rapidly and cheaply than ever. Let me remind you again how the workers lived until about a century ago or even less. It is science that has made life far brighter for the great majority of them.

We often feel, when we see so much suffering and poverty, so much anxiety about jobs, so much cruelty and selfishness, that it is difficult to believe that the world is any better at all. But there is no doubt that for the great majority of the workers it is far better. You remember how I told you that a century ago they worked fourteen, fifteen and sixteen hours a day, Saturdays as well as other days, and got far less money than now. They had no trains or street cars or automobiles to go to work in or get out of the town on Sundays. The streets were not paved or lit by lamps and were very filthy. People suffered from disease three or four times as much as they do now, and had almost no shows to go to, no parks nor baths nor schools nor libraries.

Of course, in America, where the population was still small and most people were farmers, it was not so bad, outside the big towns. But at the beginning of the last century (1800 A.D.) there were only about four million people in the United States, and we must think more about the hundred million in Europe. Even the regularly employed workers of Europe get little enough to-day, but they get three or four times as much as formerly, work only half as many hours in the week, go to work in street cars, trains and automobiles, get education free, have public libraries and more variety of food and shows, and have twice the chance of living to be fifty or sixty.

If you ask questions, you will find that science has had by far the greatest share in this improvement. The children of Europe, and a great many in America, a hundred years ago never had sugar or candy or preserves. Now science has shown how to make sugar from beetroots, and everybody has plenty of sugar. No girls or women ever had soft silk stockings, and now science makes a very good imitation silk. And think of all these things: cold storage so that food can be brought from thousands of miles away and kept fresh; wholesome canned foods; central heating systems in winter; ships and trains, the movies and bright streets, the mail service and wireless; daily papers and public libraries; hundreds of things you can buy for five and ten cents, and mechanical toys for boys. I could fill a chapter with things we have which the world never had before, and we owe them all to science. . . .

So science is going to help in producing more wealth also: which does not mean money but all the good things that money can buy. In any country like America and Great Britain to-day we can produce four or five times as much wealth (houses, food and clothing) with the same amount of work as a hundred years ago. We have every reason to think that in another hundred years we shall produce four or five times as much as we do now.

II. HOW THE WEALTH IS SHARED

But what is the good of all this, you will say, if most of this wealth (the good things we grow and make) is to go to rich people or be wasted in wars? So, as I said, we want something else besides science. We want to stop this waste and to see that the wealth is properly shared.

Some people blame science for not putting an end to poverty and war, but that is not fair. We not only never asked science to attend to these matters but, if men of science tried to do that most people would tell them to mind their own business. Those who lived before us, and most people to-day, made the terrible blunder of leaving these things to politicians, and it was as bad as leaving it to churches to preach justice. The politicians, who know no more about science than they do about making dresses or cooking dinners, have made a terrible mess of the world and spoiled much of the good that science did.

Now you see the great mistake do you not? We asked science to help us to produce wealth, but we never asked it to help us to share or, as we say, distribute it. What we need is the help of science all round in planning to produce the physical and cultural necessities of the world and to place them within the reach of all. We want to control all the industries that produce what we want or what we can enjoy, and then (this is the big point) to control the sharing of what they produce. Then the men who have the most ability and experience will get together and make a real scientific plan of the sharing of wealth, so that there shall be no waste and no one without a proper share. . . .

You see again what a mockery there is in the Christian idea of brotherhood. Everybody knows that as long as we keep what we call the industrial system of to-day, in which men and women are employed by capitalists or corporations and are paid wages, there will always be: (1) a very great deal of unemployment or insufficient employment, with terrible poverty as a result; (2) there will always be no care for the weaker and sick workers, who are of no use to the capitalists and nearly every man will be always anxious lest he lose his job, and (3) there will be every few years a horrible depression like the one through which we are now passing.

But the capitalists, whether they are Christians or not, are determined to keep this system, in spite of all the suffering of millions of people. They know quite well that it means that hundreds of thousands can draw a rich share of what the workers produce, though these hundreds of thousands of share-holders and landowners never do a stroke of work. And the capitalists have the full support of all the churches in this. They talk about the brotherhood of men and they support a system in which half the good things produced in a country go to a few who took no part at all in producing them.

It is a mockery to talk of brotherhood when the wealth that is produced is so unjustly shared. And it is a still worse mockery to talk of brotherhood as long as there are armies and navies and wars. Of course, most people to-day, even the churches, say that they want to make an end of war. But what are they doing to prevent it? Talk against war will not end it. Promises on paper not to go to war will not end it. Japan signed that promise three times in the last twenty years, and then made war on China, because it was weak, and took a great deal of its territory. And America and all the other countries did nothing but talk. Naturally, if capitalist China becomes strong enough, it will make war on Japan to get its territory back.

That is how the world has always gone, and so it will go until the workers unite in each country and with the workers in all other countries. All war is for territory or for some advantage in trade. What we want is to see that all land which is held by one nation but really belongs to another shall be given back, the people in that land must be allowed to say which country they wish to belong to, and trade must be arranged by friendly agreements. The kind of greed that leads to a war in which millions suffer or are killed is the most terrible crime in the world.

III. THE REAL REASON FOR JUSTICE

Some people will say to you that it is all very well to want to make an end of war and poverty, but that unless we believe in God and the churches we shall all be very selfish and not even want to do these things. Now that is silly, although you read it in all sorts of books and papers. . . .

What we can see clearly now is that the real reason why we should be just and truthful and kind to each other has nothing at all to do with gods and spirits or heavens and hells. The real reason is that we shall all be much better off in this life if we behave decently to each other, and very much better off if we behave generously to each other.

You know how it is at school or in your neighborhood. There may be a hundred children, and there is a good deal of quarrelling and unkindness and lying. The world has been taught on wrong lines so long by the churches that this can not be helped. But you know what you do. You pick out two or three to be your special friends or pals, and the three or four of you will not be cruel or unkind or untruthful to each other. Why? Certainly not because you believe in heaven and hell, but just because you are very much happier.

You know how you are upset if you find that one of your friends has been unkind in some way. So you know how much happier your little group is (not in heaven, but on earth) when you are all good to one another and help and trust each other.

Well, that shows that to be kind and truthful and honorable is just a rule of life without any reference to gods and heavens. Suppose you attended a school where no child was ever spiteful or cruel or told lies or stole things. What a better time it would be for all! Suppose, when you grow up, you could live in a town where there is no cheating or lying, where all are really friendly and helpful to each other. Suppose all the men and women in the country were like that.

I am afraid we shall have to wait a long time for this! But it shows, does it not, that the reason for behaving well is in this real world not in another and imaginary world. We really do not need any ancient wise men like Buddha or Jesus or Confucius to tell us how much better off we shall all be if we behave to others as we would like them to do to us. That is clear enough. As to the churches, they have made things worse by saying that we must behave well to each other in order to win heaven after death. Not a bit. It is to make a heaven, or help to make it, on earth.

It will be much easier to follow these simple rules of life when wealth is equally shared and there are no more wars. It will be easier to stamp out criminals and grafters of all sorts. No one will need to steal because of his poverty, and each city will take care of the sick and aged and helpless. It is not at all impossible that in another twenty years science will be able to turn a lazy man into one who is ready to work by a few doses of medicine. At all events under communism everybody who can will work, either with his hands or his brain, either producing wealth or serving others as doctors and teachers and entertainers do. Then, when men see that the good things are properly shared, there will be no occasion for greed and envy and bitterness and crime. We are all still full of faults and after what I have told you about history you will not be surprised. But when we have got full justice in our social life and peace and friendliness in all our relations with other nations, we shall gradually get to a real brotherhood of men all over the world.

In spite of all the suffering and ugliness that you see about you, this is really a very great age into which you children have been born. The next fifty years are probably going to be the greatest in history. It is most likely that in them there will be a beginning at least of a quite just and scientific national life and the abandonment of all armies and navies. But these things have to be fought for. There are so many who get a fat living out of the world as it is that they will try to keep on fooling the workers and preventing any change. So everyone who sees the truth, whether child or grown-up, must try to get others to see it and so work for the brotherhood of man, for the making of a heaven in this world.

There is going to be a very wonderful life on this earth for all men, women and children. And science tells us that it is going to last for millions of years, perhaps more than a hundred million years. So we must all help to get that wonderful life started as soon as possible, and then science will make the world richer and richer and everybody will get his or her share. We are not going to waste time any longer on imaginary gods and heavens and hells. We are going to work for the time when no human being shall have a taste of hell in this world, and every man, woman and child of every race and nation shall have its share of a material heaven.

8

"The Races of Mankind," from
Climbing Our Family Tree (1945)
Written by Alex Novikoff
(1913–1987), Illustrated by
John English (1913–?)

EDITORS' INTRODUCTION

Two decades after the infamous Scopes trial (1925), which pitted defenders of creationism against proponents of Darwin's theories, teaching evolution was still illegal in several states (including Tennessee, home of Scopes), and it was a taboo subject in school textbooks. Evolution and communism became closely associated in the minds of Christian conservatives, highlighting the potentially radical implications of evolutionary theory. Hence International Publishers' Young World Books, which published Climbing Our Family Tree as one of its first titles, was cited by the House Committee on Un-American Activities not only for its books with "pro-Communist themes" but also for producing and distributing "books on evolution."[1] Like communism, evolution challenged biblical explanations and suggested that the forces of "science" would produce changes—possibly radical changes—in living things and in society. Young World's editor, Betty Bacon, said that Novikoff's great contribution in Climbing was showing "things in motion." Bacon believed showing children that they "live in an extremely dynamic world where there is a lot of change going on" encourages more change, which threatens the status quo.[2]

The selection included here, "The Races of Mankind," has a message similar to Ruth Benedict and Gene Weltfish's In Henry's Backyard (pages 267–73), which was adapted from a pamphlet likewise called "The Races of Mankind." The message in Novikoff's explanation of racial differentiation was that human beings may look different, but they are all descended from a common ancestor. Moreover, "No race is better or worse, or smarter or more generous than any other race." This discussion comes toward the end of a much longer discussion of evolution.

Novikoff, a biologist and a distinguished researcher, "was a Marxist in the broadest sense of the term," according to his biographer. "His rigorous standards for discovering scientific truth were consistent with the Marxist attempt at an 'objective' analysis of society."[3] Novikoff was born in the Ukraine but emigrated to the United States with his family when he was six months old. Growing up poor in the Brownsville section of Brooklyn, Novikoff excelled in his studies but found some of his academic choices limited by quotas against Jewish students. This perceived discrimination also contributed to his growing radical consciousness.[4] Novikoff became active in the Teachers' Union and the Communist Party in the 1930s, when he was an instructor at Brooklyn College, a center of communist organizing efforts. In addition to his official duties at Brooklyn College, he taught Introductory Biology and The Origin and Evolution of Life at the Jefferson School of Social Science, a Marxist institute. Novikoff's political activism and involvement with left-wing organizations put him under government surveillance for nearly three decades and also jeopardized his career: in a highly publicized case, Novikoff was dismissed from the University of Vermont for refusing to answer questions about his past political involvement.

The open discussion of evolution made Climbing Our Family Tree very unusual for children's literature of this time, and the book received accolades from critics, one of whom said it would be hard to "praise such a book as this account of evolution for the ten or twelve year old too highly, particularly since there has been nothing of its kind before."[5] The book was named as a New York Public Library book of the year and was a Children's Book Club selection of the New York Times.[6] Novikoff followed Climbing with another Young World Book, From Head to Foot: Our Bodies and How They Work (1947), which was equally well received. Although several publishers approached Novikoff about writing additional books, his career demanded that he put his energies into scientific research and academic publishing.[7] After his dismissal from the University of Vermont, Novikoff obtained a position at the Albert Einstein School of Medicine, where his scientific contributions earned him international recognition. In 1983, the trustees of the University of Vermont, which had called for his dismissal three decades earlier, awarded Novikoff an honorary degree.

Little is known about John English. Along with Climbing Our Family Tree, he also illustrated two children's books by Jeffrey Victor: The Train Book (Will Roberts, 1946) and Everything on Wheels (Roberts, 1948).

NOTES

1. Testimony of Walter S. Steele, Chairman of the National Security Committee of the American Coalition of Patriotic, Civic, and Fraternal Societies and Managing Editor of National Republic magazine. 80th Congress, 21 July 1947, 107.

2. Betty Bacon, interview with Julia Mickenberg, 14 Nov. 1998.

3. David R. Holmes, Stalking the Academic Communist: Intellectual Freedom and the Firing of Alex Novikoff (Hanover, NH: UP of New England, 1989), 91.

4. Holmes, 15.

5. Bentley Glass, The Quarterly Review of Biology 22 (Sept. 1947): 227, qtd. in Holmes, 92.

6. John K. Hutchens, "People Who Read and Write," New York Times Book Review, 19 May 1946, 17.

7. Holmes, 92.

Since the days when man climbed down out of the trees, he has spread out all over the earth, in hot countries and cold, in mountains, jungle swamps and fertile valleys. Remember what Darwin figured happened to the birds of the Galapagos when they were isolated on one or another of the islands? They began to develop all sorts of small differences, although they remained generally the same. That is just what happened to men when they became isolated from each other.

Most scientists believe that *Homo sapiens'* birthplace was in Central Asia. From there he spread out to Africa and Europe, to America and to Australia and the South Seas. Wherever men went they lived in ways that suited the climate and geography of the particular place where they settled. For a long time they continued to look pretty much alike. Then there developed differences —in their skin color, in the shape of their heads and in other minor physical features. In Africa, the isolated group developed darker skins; in Asia, yellow skins and slanting eyes; in Europe, fair or "white" skins.

Scientists used the word "races" in speaking of such groups which belong to the same species but which differ from each other in certain inherited features.

The feature most used to distinguish the races of mankind is the color of the skin. All three races—black, white and yellow—are very much the same in other physical features. In each race there are some people who are tall and some who are short; some are long-headed, some round-headed. In each race there are some people who belong to blood group A, some to group B, some to AB and some to O.

But all races are members of the *same species.* Proof of this is that people of different races can mate with each other and produce perfectly normal children.

You may have heard it said that there is a definite connection between the color of a man's skin and his ability to learn or work or think. This is just as unscientific as the notion of the *Beagle's* captain that he could judge Darwin's character by the shape of his nose. The fact that some men built cities while others lived in huts, had nothing to do with the color of their

skins. Wherever and whenever any group of any color had the chance, they did their part in forwarding the march of human progress. History does not belong exclusively to any one race; it is shared by all. No race is better or worse, or smarter or more generous than any other race. You can make an important invention or write a great book or become a hero whatever the color of your skin or the shape of your head may be.

Many birds that lived in the Galapagos were once just like those on the mainland. After a while there developed differences among them so that there were several distinct races. Then after years of evolution, isolated from the mainland, they developed into different species. Is that what is happening to the races of mankind? Is *Homo sapiens* turning into different species, black, yellow and white?

To answer that question, we have to ask another. The Galapagos birds evolved separately because they were isolated from the mainland. Are men isolated from each other today?

Perhaps way back in the early days men in various parts of the world might have grown into different species if they had stayed isolated. But they didn't. Men have always roamed over the earth, first on foot, then on horseback and in sailboats. People from one place settled down in another and mixed with the people who were already there. The English people, for instance, though they live on an island, have among their ancestors the ancient Britons who first came to live there, the Romans from Italy, the Saxons from Germany, the Danes from Scandinavia, and the Normans from France. And they all arrived in the days before railroad trains and steamships made traveling really easy.

Today airplanes and radio have brought men closer together than ever. The remotest valley in Tibet and the farthest island in the South Pacific are no longer isolated. Men can no longer grow and change apart from each other. Some scientists believe that the time will come eventually when there will be what has been called a "fusion of the races in a single greatly variable population."

9

The Day They Parachuted Cats on Borneo: A Drama of Ecology (1971)

Written by Charlotte Pomerantz (b. 1930), Scenery by Jose Aruego (b. 1932)

EDITORS' INTRODUCTION

In 1969, a *New York Times* story inspired Charlotte Pomerantz to write a book. The article, written by the Associated Press, reported on the World Health Organization's use of DDT in Borneo.[1] Although the insecticide killed malaria-carrying mosquitoes, this apparently small change in the ecosystem produced many unintended consequences, which Pomerantz portrays in her book, *The Day They Parachuted Cats on Borneo*. The book was named an Outstanding Picture Book of the Year by the *New York Times* and, in 1977–1978, was one of ten U.S. books chosen for the International Year of the Child.

Born in Brooklyn, Pomerantz grew up in New Rochelle, in a politically active family. She was six when the Spanish Civil War broke out, and her parents supported the Popular Front government. Some of her earliest memories are "the songs of the Lincoln Brigade [American volunteer soldiers in Spain] and the songs of the International Brigade."[2] At sixteen, Pomerantz spent a year in Europe, where her father was deputy chief counsel at the Nuremburg Trials. When he resigned in protest against the U.S. failure to prosecute German industrialists Krupps and Farben, the Pomerantzes returned home.[3] After graduating from Sarah Lawrence College in 1953, Charlotte worked at a variety of jobs, including one for the left-wing publisher Marzani and Munsell. That firm published her first book, an edited collection titled *A Quarter-Century of Un-Americana, 1938–1963: A Tragicomical Memorabilia of HUAC, House Un-American Activities Committee* (1963). In 1966, she married one of the book's publishers, Carl Marzani. He had served nearly three years in prison (1949–1951) for failing to disclose his former Communist Party affiliation while working for the U.S. State Department and Office of Strategic Services during the Second World War.

Pomerantz published her first story for children in 1965 and has since published over thirty more books for children, including *The Piggy in the Puddle* (1974), illustrated by James Marshall, and *Magnaboom* (1997), illustrated by Anita Lobel. Two children's plays have had professional productions, and public schools have staged both *The Day They Parachuted Cats on Borneo* and her *Princess and the Admiral* (1974). A sense of humor characterizes Pomerantz's work for children as well as her approach to politics.

Jose Aruego was born and raised in Manila. At school, he sat next to and became good friends with Benigno Aquino, later the leader of those who opposed Ferdinand Marcos.[4] Aruego's father, a prominent attorney and law professor at the University of Manila, helped shape the constitution of the Republic of the Philippines in 1946. After receiving his B.A., Aruego earned a law degree from the University of Philippines and began practicing law. He lost the one case he tried and left the profession after only three months.

Realizing that his heart was not in the law, Aruego remembered his childhood, when he enjoyed drawing and collecting comic books—so much so that, as an adult, he still thought in terms of comic panels.[5] Aruego's parents supported his decision to pursue art, encouraging him to go to Paris. He chose New York, which he considered the comic book capital of the world.[6]

In 1957, he enrolled in New York City's Parsons School of Design, where he studied with Leo Lionni, then *Fortune* magazine's art director and later the creator of children's classics *Swimmy* (1963) and *Frederick* (1967).[7] After graduating from Parsons in 1959, he worked for advertising agencies and began to sell his cartoons to the *New Yorker*, the *Saturday Evening Post*, and *Look*. With the encouragement of his wife, artist Adriane Dewey, Aruego quit his job to pursue freelance illustration full-time.

Although he has written a few of his own books, Aruego is best known for illustrating the works of others, notably Robert Kraus's *Whose Mouse Are You?* (1970) and *Leo the Late Bloomer* (1971). He and Dewey divorced in 1973, but they have continued to collaborate, co-illustrating over forty-five books together, including more than a dozen by Kraus, and Charlotte Pomerantz's *One Duck, Another Duck* (1984).

The recipient of many awards, Aruego is particularly pleased to have been chosen as an Outstanding Filipino Abroad in the Arts, an honor given by the Philippine government. Some fifty years after changing professions, Aruego still enjoys his job: "Each project teaches me something new and makes me a better artist."[8]

NOTES

1. Associated Press, "DDT Exemplifies Peril in Technological Gains," *New York Times*, 13 Nov. 1969, 20.

2. Charlotte Pomerantz, telephone interview with Philip Nel, 25 July 2006.

3. Ibid.

4. Allen Raymond, "From Law Books to Kids' Books," *Teaching Pre-K–8*, Aug.–Sept. 1987, 48.

5. Ida J. Appel and Marion P. Turkish, "Profile: The Magic World of Jose Aruego," *Language Arts* 54:5 (May 1977): 587.

6. Dorothy Cordova, "Jose Aruego (1932–) Cartoonist, Artist," *Distinguished Asian Americans: A Biographical Dictionary*, ed. Hyung-chan Kim et al. (Westport, CT: Greenwood, 1999), 23.

7. Appel and Turkish, 587.

8. "Jose (Espiritu) Aruego (1932–)," *Contemporary Authors Online* (Gale, 2002).

This is a true story about what happens to our environment when our solutions to one problem have unexpected consequences. The huts on the island of Borneo were sprayed with DDT to get rid of the malaria-infecting mosquitoes. DDT killed the mosquitoes but it also brought on a series of other troubles for the farmers. You will soon find out how parachuting pussycats came to the farmers' rescue.

Cast in order of appearance and disappearance

I	The Island of Borneo	VII	Lizards	XIII	Parapussycats
II	Malaria	VIII	More Lizards	XIV	More Parapussycats
III	DDT	IX	Cats	XV	Still more Parapussycats
IV	Mosquitoes	X	The Rivers	XVI	The Roof Beams
V	Cockroaches	XI	Rats	XVII	The Farmer
VI	Caterpillars	XII	Helicopters	XVIII	The Ecologist

I

I am the island of Borneo,
Where the farmer—poor farmer—bends low, bends low.
I have honey bears, rhinos, and tiger cats,

Great falcons, flamingoes, and foxy-faced bats.
I have gold and quicksilver, rubber and rice,
Cane sugar and spice—but not everything nice:
A land of harsh ridges and savage monsoon,
Of jungles as dark as the dark of the moon.
Land of thundering rains and earthquakes and heat,
Where the farmer's life is more bitter than sweet.
Land of mosquitoes, which carry with ease
The dreaded malaria, scourge and disease.

II

I am malaria, dreaded disease.
I cause men to ache and to shake and to freeze.
Three hundred million a year do I seize.
One million I kill with remarkable ease.
But I'm not the big killer I used to be
In the good old days before—ugh!—DDT;
'Cause that stuff kills mosquitoes—one, two, three . . .

*And the death of them
is the death of me.*

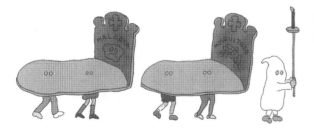

III

My name is dicholoro-diphenyl-trichlorethane
Which you've got to admit is a heck of a name.
But, perhaps, some of you have heard tell of me
By my well-known initials, which are DDT.
An organo-chlorine insecticide,
I come in a powder or liquefied.
I'm death to mosquitoes outside or inside.
I was brought here by copter to Borneo,

Where the farmer—now hopeful—bends low, bends
  low.
My job is to kill that cruel killer of man:
A worthy wise ecological plan.

*If you don't know
what ecology means,
you'll soon find out.*

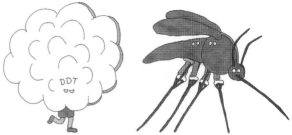

IV

We are the mosquitoes who roam day and night,
Bringing death to the farmer with one small bite.
We like the farmer's hut—it buzzes with life.
There's the farmer, of course, his kids and his wife.
The caterpillars chew on the roof beams there,
While the geckoes, or lizards, roam everywhere.
There are lots of cockroaches, and always some cats
Who pounce on the lizards and scare away rats.
All of us are busy—busy looking for food.
Sometimes we eat each other, which may seem rather
  crude.
But imagine yourself in that hut, and I bet
You would rather eat someone than find yourself et.

Now suddenly—zap!—there is no place to hide,
For they sprayed all the huts with insecticide.
That's the end of our tale.

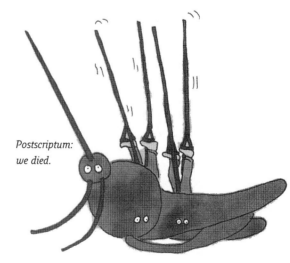

*Postscriptum:
we died.*

Nosh-nosh, nibble-nibble, munch-munch-munch,
For breakfast, supper, high tea and lunch.
Our life is as pleasant as green tea and roses,
Except when the lizards (gulp) poke in their noses.
Then nosh-nosh, nibble-nibble, munch-munch-munch,
The lizards ate half our cousins for lunch.
Those four-legged reptiles ruin our meals . . .

*You'd have to be eaten
to know how it feels.*

VII

We are the lizards, or geckoes, by name.
To the farmer we're useful, we're charming, we're tame.
Over the floors, walls and roof beams we roam,
Of every tropical home sweet home.
For us, cockroaches are scrumptious to eat.
Almost as tasty as caterpillar meat.

*It all seemed to good
to be true—and it was.*

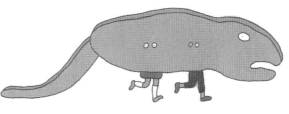

V

We are the cockroaches, homeloving pests.
In most people's huts we are unwelcome guests.
When we all got sprayed with that DDT stuff,
The mosquitoes got killed—not us. We're too tough.
We just swallowed hard and kept right on a-crawling,
Despite the rude comments and vicious name-calling.

People are so anti-roach.

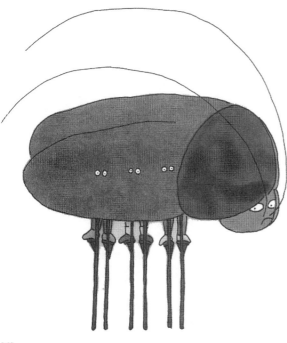

VI

We're the hungry caterpillars of Borneo,
Where the farmer—also hungry—bends low, bends low.
We live on the roof beams, eating and hatching.
We make all our meals out of roof beams and
    thatching.

VIII

Then the copters sprayed, and we lost our appetite.
Now we laze away the days, we snooze the balmy
    night.
For every roach we eat, though they do taste yummy,
Adds DDT to our little lizard tummy,
And makes our tiny nervous system sluggish and slow.
We geckoes—leaping lizards!—got no get-up-and-go.
It's true we're not dying of DDT,
But a slooow gecko ain't nooo gecko,
As the caterpillars can plainly see.
We watch them eating roof beams like there's no
    tomorrow,
While we lizards hold our tummies in pain and
    sorrow.

At night the caterpillars and the roaches walk right up to us and say, Buenas Noches.

IX

We're the cats on the island of Borneo
Where the farmer—who loves us—bends low, bends low.
Eating all those lizards, or geckoes, by name,
Is turning out to be (sigh) a dying shame,
'Cause those lizards are poisoned from tail to head,
And killing those lizards is killing us dead.
We poor cats got a massive overdose.
What's left to say
(Sob)
Except *adios.*

Be careful of the lizard you eat. The life you take may be your own.

X

We're the rivers, the rivers of Borneo.
We watch little man come and go, come and go.
We watched him kill mosquitoes with pesticide.
Saw the roaches poisoned, though not one cockroach died
Till . . .
The hungry lizards ate them, one by one by one.
Oh what a feast they had—it seemed like good clean fun.
But every roach they ate, though they did taste yummy,
Added DDT to their little lizard tummy.
Then the lizards were filled with deadly pesticide.
They felt pretty punchy, though not one lizard died
Till . . .
The hungry cats devoured them, one by one by one.
Oh what a feast they had—it seemed like good clean fun.
But every liz they ate, though they did taste yummy,
Killed the cats by poisoning their DD Toxic tummy.
Now this poor old island is steeped in poison air.
Our waters, too, are poisoned. Little man, take care!

Whoever thought that little man could affect us mighty rivers? But the rain has washed the DDT into our waters, and our tenants, the friendly fish, are feeling pretty rocky.

XI

We're the rats on the island of Borneo,
We never had it so good—heigh—dee—ho.
When the cats who had swallowed the geckoes lay dying,
We crawled in by thousands from forests outlying.
When the farmers saw us, they raised an anguished cry:
"Rats bring plague! Fly in help, or we shall surely die.
Help us, men of science, help us kill the rats;
For the DDT you sprayed has killed off all our cats!"
"Borneo for rent," we sang. "Inquire, please, within.
When the cats die off from DDT, we rats—move—in."

XII

We're the copters who've just flown in thousands of
    cats
And chuted them down on the armies of rats,
On the plague-threatened island of Borneo,
A bright green jewel in the blue sea below.

Once we came with DDT; now we come with cats.
Once we sprayed mosquitoes; now we'll fix the rats.
Looks like no one really thought the whole thing
    through . . .
Soon all the cats and rats will have a deadly
    rendezvous.

*It was, all told,
a rather unusual
assignment.*

And then the helicopters came . . .

XIII

We're the parapussycats they parachuted down
On every cat-killed, rat-filled little village and town
On the dead-cat, dread-rat island of Borneo,
Where the farmer—strictly catless—bends low, low,
    low.

*It's better than
hanging around
fish markets.*

*But let the roof beams
tell their own story.*

XIV

When we parapussycats were dropped to the ground,
What a feast we had—there were rats all around.
Everywhere you looked there were rats and rats and rats
Pursued by our elite corps of parapussycats.
We chased the rats for days, till most of them had fled,
And those who didn't run fast enough were—biff bam!
   —dead.

*Mission accomplished.
All parapussycats have returned to quarters.*

XV

The good farmers gave us a ticker-tape parade.
They heaped us with ivory, gold and silk brocade.
They said they would grant us our most fantastic wish—
So we asked them for five hundred kettles of fish.
We were wined, we were dined, we slept in king-size
   beds,
Till we heard a strange creaking just over our heads . . .

KA-RASH!

XVI

We're the roof beams of thatched huts in Borneo,
Where the farmer—enduring—bends low, bends low.
If a man, now and then, did some roof patching,
Replaced chewed-up beams and half-eaten thatching,
We could keep out the wind, the rain, and the sun,
And shelter a man when his labors were done.
Despite caterpillars, we roof beams stayed strong,
And the lizards, by eating them, helped us along.
For the lizard, you see, was the number-one killer
Of the beam-eating (nosh-nosh) cater- (nosh-nosh)
   pillar.

Now we mourn the little lizards—may they rest in
   peace—
While the greedy caterpillars (burp) get more and more
   obese.

To be frank, we roofs are in a state of collapse.

XVII

Good day, I'm a farmer in Borneo,
Where the coconut palm and the mango grow.
Here are honey bears, rhinos, and tiger cats.
Great falcons, flamingoes, and foxy-faced bats.
Here are gold and quicksilver, rubber and rice,

Cane sugar and spice—but not everything nice:
When they sprayed my hut with insecticide,
My rat-catching cat soon sickened and died.
When the rats crawled in, I was filled with fear:
The plague can kill more than malaria here.
When my roof beams caved in, I moved next door,
Until their roof beams collapsed to the floor.
But please do not think I wish to offend,
For DDT is the farmer's good friend.
Still, perhaps you'll allow a poor man to say,
He hopes men of science will soon find a way
To kill the mosquitoes till all, all are dead—
But save the roof beams which are over my head,
As well as my most useful rat-catching cat.
How grateful I'd be if you'd only do that!
Then, men of science, I would not complain.
But now I must look to my roof—I smell rain!

XVIII

I am an ecologist. Ecology is the study of living things in relation to the world around them—everything around them—air, water, rocks, soil, plants, and animals, including man.

If a tree is cut down, I try to find out what will happen to the birds in the nests, the squirrels in the branches, the insects at the roots. I know that the roots of the tree hold the earth, that the earth holds the rainwater, and that the rainwater keeps the soil moist, so that plants can grow. I am concerned if too many trees are cut down, for then the rain will run off the surface of the soil, making the rivers rise, overflow their banks and flood the land. This is the kind of thing an ecologist thinks about.

Borneo is a huge island in Southeast Asia—the third largest in the world and bigger than all of Texas. It straddles the equator, which is why the climate is hot and steamy. Someone has said that there are two seasons in Borneo—a wet season and a less wet season.

The people are mainly Malays and Dyaks. The Malays, who live near the coast, are rice farmers and fishermen. Some work on rubber plantations or in the oil fields, for Borneo is rich in oil. Inland are high mountain ranges, where most of the Dyaks live. Until recently, they were headhunters—the wild men of Borneo—and they still hunt with blowguns and poisoned darts. The women grow rice, yams, and sugarcane in tiny forest clearings.

Most of Borneo is part of the Republic of Indonesia. Some of it belongs to Malaysia, and a tiny part is a British-protected state run by a sultan. It is an island of dense tropical forests, where vines grow as high as a thousand feet, where orangutans swing through the trees, and where the giant long-nosed proboscis monkey can grow as tall as a man. There is also a great variety of insects, including the anopheles mosquito. This mosquito carries malaria and is the reason I was sent to Borneo.

Mosquitoes breed in wet places, and there are many swamps and rain holes in Borneo. In the old days, we used to fight mosquitoes by draining swamps, when possible, and by spraying a thin film of oil on stagnant waters during the breeding season. Those who could afford to, put screens on doors, windows, and openings to keep the mosquitoes out. All this helped to keep malaria down, but millions of people still got sick.

Then, during World War II, a scientist discovered that a certain chemical compound, called dichloro-diphenyl-trichloroethane—DDT for short—was a marvelous insect killer. The discoverer, Dr. Paul Mueller of Switzerland, received the Nobel Prize for his discovery.

In Borneo, we sprayed the walls and insides of the huts with DDT. You know what happened: we killed the mosquitoes—and ended up with no cats. We had not realized how much DDT can accumulate in the fatty tissues of animals. Even a tiny amount of DDT in food or drinking water, with repeated meals, builds up and up until the quantity is large enough to poison a large animal, such as a cat.

As you know, with the cats dead, the rats took over and brought the threat of plague. So cats were flown in to stop the rats. Then, just when matters seemed under control—the roofs fell down. This is but a small example of the complex and subtle connections and balances which exist among all living things.

Because of the poisonous effects of DDT, it has been banned or restricted in the United States, the Soviet Union, and other industrial countries. In December, 1969, at a world conference of the Food and Agricultural Organization (a body of the United Nations), an attempt was made to ban the use of DDT all over the world. But the majority of scientists, representing the nonindustrial countries, refused to go along with the ban. They knew DDT was dangerous to health, but they needed it to control malaria and other diseases, and to protect food crops from insect destruction. The alternatives to DDT are expensive, and the nonindustrial countries, which contain about eighty per cent of the world's population, cannot afford them, for they are very poor.

In El Salvador, for example, the cost of DDT to control malaria is ten cents a person. Other insecticides would cost at least three times that much. Where is the money to come from?

The wealthy nations pointed out that the danger of pesticides is everyone's responsibility, for when you pollute the atmosphere, and the waters which flow to the oceans, everyone suffers. Ecologically, the nations of the earth are one.

The poor nations replied that the wealthy nations are not faced with malaria epidemics, wholesale destruction of their food supply, and mass starvation. They can afford to worry about the future of the environment. The poor nations can only think of day-to-day survival. Seventy-five per cent of the people in the world go to bed hungry, and the great majority of them are in the poor, nonindustrial countries.

Ecologists from underdeveloped countries, faced with starvation and disease, can only choose the lesser evil —DDT. But the real answer to their problem is to find new solutions. Work is going forward on drugs for the prevention of malaria. Unfortunately, these new drugs have some bad side effects. Others are not effective for all kinds of malaria. And all drugs are very expensive.

A more fruitful road is for scientists to seek an insecticide that kills mosquitoes and nothing else. Scientists have discovered that under crowded conditions, some mosquitoes release a toxic chemical that kills young mosquitoes. If they can isolate and synthesize that chemical, it would be a great step forward in malaria control.

Another possibility, which shows considerable promise, is to breed a variety of mosquito which leaves seventy-five per cent of the female eggs unfertilized. Released among other mosquitoes, this new strain transmits its infertility to all the offspring. Thus each generation would breed fewer and fewer mosquitoes.

canals of Amsterdam and Venice. The Danube is no longer blue. One can no longer swim in the Rhine in Germany, or in the Seine in Paris, or in our own Hudson River. Whole stretches of beaches in Italy, South America, England, and the United States have been polluted with oil slicks from the sea.

This is bad enough, but if the oil spills continue, worse will follow: a thin film of oil will spread over all the oceans. This will cut down the sunlight which very tiny plants, called diatoms, need both to reproduce and to live. These tiny plants, billions and billions of them, are the source of food for all the fishes of the sea. Further, these tiny plants use sunlight to combine with water to form carbon dioxide (used as food by them) and oxygen which is released into the air. Eighty per cent of all the oxygen in the world comes from these tiny plants. If sunlight is cut down and the amount of oxygen is reduced, the whole animal kingdom, including man, will suffer.

We've been talking about DDT and the farmers of Borneo, but ecological problems are extremely varied and serious, and they cover the whole world. For example, the fumes of automobile exhausts have greatly increased the number of people who get lung diseases. Atomic radiation has increased the incidence of certain types of cancer. The hot water from power plants, when poured into lakes and rivers, kills the fishes.

There is pollution by lumber mills in Lake Baikal in the Soviet Union. There is too much sewage in the

We need to know these things, so that we can do something to keep the air and water clean for all the people, as well as for all the animals and plants in the world. The ecologist should not protect the farmer against malaria with one hand and bring the roof down on his head with the other. But the answer is not for the ecologist to do nothing, but to be wiser about what he does. This is the moral of Borneo.

10

Red Ribbons for Emma (1981)

Written by New Mexico People & Energy Collective: Deb Preusch (b. 1953), Tom Barry (b. 1950), and Beth Wood (b. 1947)

EDITORS' INTRODUCTION

Activism inspired this book. In Albuquerque, New Mexico, Deb Preusch was organizing the first undocumented workers' strike when she met reporter Tom Barry, founder of the alternative newspaper *Rio Grande Weekly*. In 1979, galvanized by the plight of these workers and by power companies' impact on native communities, Barry, his colleague Beth Wood, and Preusch founded what would become the International Resource Center (I.R.C.), then called the New Mexico People & Energy Collective. After creating a successful slide show on uranium development in the Navajo Nation, they decided to write a children's book about Emma Yazzie, whom Tom had met when he was working as a journalist.[1]

Yazzie's struggle against corporate pollution is a true story with roots in the 1940s. After the Second World War, Navajos began working in the area's new uranium mines, which then lacked regulations to protect the environment and the workers' health and safety.[2] (Poisoned by radiation, over 450 miners would die from cancer by 1990.)[3] When Navajo Nation leaders agreed in the mid-1960s to coal mining and a coal-fired power plant, they believed that these businesses would bring prosperity. To those who lived nearby, they brought noise and pollution but little money and (ironically) no electric power. For failing to protect them from the pollution, Yazzie and four other Navajos filed suit against the Department of the Interior and the Department of Health, Education, and Welfare in 1973.[4] When that failed, Yazzie joined the Chemehuevi Tribe's suit against the Federal Power Commission. In 1975, the case went to the Supreme Court, which kicked it back down to Appeals Court, extending the long history of government inaction on this issue.[5]

Yazzie and her allies were still seeking their rights when the New Mexico People & Energy Collective came

to tell her story. Barry did most of the writing, Preusch took the photographs, and all three discussed and revised the book's content.[6] *Red Ribbons* won several awards, and teachers encouraged their students to send letters to Emma Yazzie. She "loved" receiving them, Preusch recalls. "It was like she was famous."[7]

The Navajos' struggle for justice stalled, however. Radioactive pollution in the water caused birth defects in animals and people. In 1990, the U.S. government passed legislation to compensate the families of miners killed by the yellow ore, but this mandate lacked funding until 1992 and ran out of money in 1993.[8] For decades, Yazzie, her daughter, and others who lived near the Four Corners Power Plant had no power and no utilities. Emma Yazzie died in 2000, at the age of eighty-nine. In December 2005, Yazzie's daughter and granddaughter—living on the same land—finally received electric power. As of this writing, they still lack running water.[9]

Today, the Southwest Research and Information Center is most closely involved with the struggles depicted in *Red Ribbons for Emma*, but the book's creators continue to work for justice. The author of one play on domestic violence and another on Central America, Beth Wood is a professional researcher and writer who teaches research and fact checking at the University of California San Diego Extension. The coauthors of many books and reports on Central America and U.S. foreign policy, Preusch and Barry still work for the organization they founded. Preusch is executive director; Barry directs policy and the I.R.C.'s *Right Web* (http://rightweb.irc-online.org/), tracking "the work of those, in and outside of government, who have been instrumental in shaping or supporting U.S. policies in the global war on terror."[10]

NOTES

1. Deb Preusch, telephone interview with Philip Nel, 8 Nov. 2005.

2. Bruce E. Johansen, *Indigenous Peoples and Environmental Issues: An Encyclopedia* (Westport, CT: Greenwood, 2003), 393.

3. Ibid., 395.

4. *Emma Yazzie et al. v. Roger C. B. Morton, and Elliot L. Richardson*, No. Civ. 71-601-PHX, 59 F.R.D. 377, U.S. District Court, Phoenix, Arizona, 1973.

5. *Chemehuevi Tribe of Indians et al. v. Federal Power Commission et al.*, No. 73-1380, 420 U.S. 395, U.S. Supreme Court.

6. Preusch, interview.

7. Ibid.

8. Johansen, 399.

9. Associated Press, "Navajo Residents Near Power Plant to Get Electricity," *Daily Times*, 25 Nov. 2005; Valarie Lee, "Bright Christmas," *Red Lake Net News*, 5 Dec. 2005: <http://www.rlnn.com/ArtDec05/BrightChristmas.html>. 18 July 2006.

10. "About Right Web," *Right Web*: <http://rightweb.irc-online.org/about.php>. 19 July 2006.

Sometimes it seems there are no more heroes. Every place, even the moon, has been discovered by explorers. All the fun and brave and exciting things to do, like flying alone across the ocean in an airplane or inventing the light bulb, have already been done. Sometimes it seems we were all born too late to be heroes.

But that's not true.
We still have plenty of chances
to become heroes.

We just need to think
about becoming
a different kind
of hero.

Emma Yazzie is a hero
who is living right now
in the Navajo Nation of New Mexico.
She is a hero in our modern age—
the time we all live in.

Emma is brave and strong and courageous. And she is not alone. Many of her people work and struggle with her. They are brave, strong, and courageous heroes, too. They are the rural Navajo people. They call themselves "grassroots" people because, like the hardy grass on their reservation, they have to be tough to survive. Grassroots means that like the grass, they have their roots in the land.

Emma and the other rural Navajos look different from heroes we usually read about who are mostly men, mostly white men. Emma is a poor Indian woman and a grandmother. She is friendly and fun to be with.

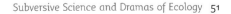

Emma lives on the Navajo Reservation in New Mexico. Reservations are places where the army and the government put Indians after they pushed these people off their lands.

When the Navajos need things they don't make —like canned goods and soap—they go to a trading post near the reservation. A trading post is the same as a store, except occasionally people can also trade things for what they need. For instance, if Emma doesn't have any money, she trades jewelry or wool to get her food and supplies.

Emma lives in a hogan that is near two shady elm trees. A hogan is a round, one-room house that Navajos make from stone and mud. Emma wakes up at dawn every morning because her front door faces east toward the rising sun. Navajos like to start their days with a good feeling by greeting the morning sun. At sunrise, Emma leads her hungry sheep out of the corral.

Many Navajo women and children take care of sheep and goats. The animals are important to Navajo Indians because they eat the meat of the animals and they make clothing and rugs from the wool.

When night comes, Emma puts on her apron and goes to the job she does for money. She cleans the offices and mops the floors of the mining company

nearby. She works until the middle of the night. Emma is glad to have the job because she needs the money. But she says it's not fair that the white people have all the good-paying jobs at the mine and the power plant, while the Navajos have hard and low-paying work.

When her cleaning work is finally done, Emma goes back to her hogan to sleep. The power plant lights up the night sky, but Emma walks home to a dark house without electricity.

Jeanne Joe Boone is Emma's daughter. She helps Emma cook and herd sheep. Jeanne Joe has never been to a big city like Los Angeles. She has never even visited Albuquerque which is only three hours away from her home. She lives near Emma in a two-room house with no lights, no heat, and no running water. Although neither woman has any electric power, they both live near the power plant that feeds electricity to Los Angeles, Albuquerque, Phoenix, and other big cities.

All around Emma's hogan and the home of Jeanne Joe are many different kinds of energy development. Coal trucks rumble along the road in back of the hogan. The power plant makes electricity from the coal and also dirties the blue sky with chemicals and soot. Gas pipelines cross the land, carrying gas to help run the power plant. Emma and Jeanne Joe live in the middle of all this energy development, but they don't have any of this energy to light their homes or to keep them warm at night. They certainly know what an energy crisis is and that those power lines take electricity to the cities so that people living there have lights to read by, refrigerators to keep drinks cold, and fans to keep their houses cool in the summer. Yet with so much energy

coming from their Indian land, they are too poor to have any of it themselves.

Emma thinks that living near the power lines is dangerous for people and animals. The wires crackle loudly because of the electricity charging through them. When you walk under the power lines, they tower over you and your body shakes from all the electric energy in the air. The wires kill all the pretty birds, Emma says sadly. When the birds land on the wires, they get fried because the lines are so hot. To protect the land and the birds, Emma doesn't want any more power lines crossing Indian land.

All of her life, Emma has herded sheep. She walks long distances over sandy land to find grass that is high enough for her sheep to graze on. The sheep and Emma usually pass by the ruins of the hogan where she was born and where her mother lived. Emma says it is the place where she opened her eyes for the first time.

Emma, now an old woman, remembers how beautiful the land was when she was a young girl.

Out of this land a magnificent shadowy rock, Shiprock, juts up high into the sky. When she was a child, Emma would herd sheep with her mother and explore the land. She thought that Shiprock was the tallest thing in the world. Nothing could be higher or bigger than that mighty rock.

The Navajo name for Shiprock is *Tse Bi Dahi*, which means The Rock With Wings.

Emma recalls a time when she could see for miles and miles because the sky was so bright and blue and clear. But the sky isn't so clear now, or the land so beautiful. Near Emma's hogan is the largest coal mine in the United States. It feeds a huge electric power company.

When the companies came 15 years ago, they changed the life of Emma and her neighbors and caused many of her neighbors to move away. The grassroots Navajos opposed the coal and power companies, but the tribal leaders living hundreds of miles away in the cities gave the companies permission to build on Indian land. These leaders said the companies would bring wealth to the Navajo Nation.

Back then, Emma and her neighbors didn't know they would be surrounded by huge holes in the ground, a big smoking power plant, and all kinds of giant machines. They have never seen any of the wealth they were promised, but they hear about Navajo leaders in the cities who drive big cars and buy expensive clothes.

Emma is furious!

Every day when Emma herds her sheep, she sees the huge coal shovels. They are 32 stories high and cost $12 million each. Emma hates how the hungry coal shovels tear up her land, the land of her mother and grandmother.

This land belongs to the Indian people, Emma says, not the companies of white men. *I'm* not going to let all this Navajo land be chewed up by the coal shovels, she says.

The power plant is even bigger than the coal shovels. To Emma, the smokestacks of the power plant are the tallest things in the world, even taller than Shiprock. Emma says the power plant and the coal shovels are like monsters. They make awful, groaning sounds, even in the middle of the night. But Emma is not afraid of them.

The power plant is called the Four Corners Power Plant because it is near the spot where four states —New Mexico, Arizona, Utah, and Colorado—touch corners. Emma has her own name for the power plant. She calls it *X id,* a Navajo word that means smoke.

When she was a young girl, Emma used to be able to see the mountains that surround Navajo land. But now the pollution from the power plant makes it hard to see far away. Emma calls the pollution a disease. The power plant is the worst disease Navajos have ever known, Emma says. The smoke and the ashes are killing us all.

The pollution shoots out of the monstrous stacks next to Emma's hogan. The pollution is so bad that when the astronauts went into space, they could see the smoke from the power plant. Imagine how dirty and grimy the air is where Emma lives!

In the big cities, it is hard to tell where the pollution comes from because it is everywhere. It is easy to tell

where the dirt in the air comes from on the Navajo Reservation because there aren't many cars or factories.

Navajos believe they live between four sacred mountains. Each mountain has a special meaning and a special color—blue, yellow, black, and white. Into this land of color and beauty, the Navajos came from the underground, a place they call the underworld.

Navajos believe that they will keep healthy and strong if they respect nature and treat the land in a good way.

Emma loves the land in the Navajo way. When the land hurts, she hurts. Sometimes she cries when she sees how the land is being destroyed. She says that all the pretty flowers have died because of the smoke. But Emma is determined and brave.

One reason why Emma Yazzie is so brave is because there are other grassroots people all over the Navajo Reservation who are fighting against the destruction of the land by the energy companies. These Indians say that all of the Navajo people should have more to say about what to do with their own land. It gives Emma strength to know that other people love the land the way she does.

Emma went to court to try to stop the power plant and the mine. She and her lawyers told the judge that the companies were polluting all the Navajo land and water. Emma lost her court case, and the power plant and the mine stayed on Navajo land.

Emma has a funny story about how 15 years ago she and Jeanne Joe tried to stop the company from building the power plant. In the middle of the night, when no one could see them, they would hook up their horse to their wooden wagon and drive over to the place where the company was building. The company men had marked the spot with ribbons tied on wooden stakes called survey posts. Emma smiles now when she remembers the way they would yank up those markers. Then they would go home to burn the wood in their stoves. It was a good way to keep themselves warm during the cold winter nights. The two Navajo sheep herders also slowed down the work of the company. But the company managed to build the power plant anyway.

Emma is strong, too. When she goes out herding sheep, it is difficult to keep up with her. She carries her walking staff and takes long strides across the land. Miles and miles she walks in the early morning.

Some days, though, Emma rides her horse, Judy. It is hard for Emma to get up on Judy's back so she stands on a boulder near her house and jumps into the saddle.

It is hard now for Emma to find enough grass for her sheep because so much of the land has been torn up by the mine. When she goes walking or riding with her sheep, she has to cross the roads built for the huge coal trucks. Even their wheels are taller than Emma. But Emma is not afraid of them. She makes the trucks stop for her. At first they didn't, but she threw stones and bottles at them, and cursed them in Navajo. Now the drivers of the giant trucks wait for her to cross the road with her sheep.

One day Emma found a tiny black and white spotted puppy, all cold and shivering by the side of the road.

She took the little dog home with her and helped it get well. She called the puppy Roadrunner because she found the dog along the road. Emma needed a sheep dog so she put Roadrunner in the corral with the sheep and the goats. Roadrunner never got bigger, but now every morning he goes out herding sheep, always barking to keep them together in one group. He runs around and around the sheep.

Each sheep and goat has been branded with a big "E" for Emma. Roadrunner is always watching to make certain the baby lambs don't wander off from the herd and get lost. It is fun to watch such a tiny dog bossing around all the big sheep and goats. That little dog is mean like me, jokes Emma.

Emma is not really mean, but with the companies she acts real mean. The mine would like her to move because she is in their way. She is always causing them trouble.

Indian people have a different way of thinking about the land than the companies do. Emma says the companies only want to make money. They want to take the coal out of the ground, and when the coal is gone they leave the land full of holes. Their big shovels nose their way into the ground to take the minerals out and they tear up the grass roots. Once the grass is gone, the land just blows away in the wind. Then they go to another place to find more coal.

Indian people believe that if you treat the land badly, the land will die. Then the animals will die and soon the people will die, too. The energy companies can find someplace else to go, but the Navajos have no place to go when their land dies.

In the winter, it is so hard for the sheep to find grass that they get hungry and skinny. One winter day Emma tried to get her animals into the land the company had fenced off. This was land her sheep had grazed on before the mine was built. While Emma was trying to open the lock to the fence, a few sheep slipped under the fence and began to eat the greener, tastier grass. Just then, a company guard drove up and told Emma to get her sheep off company land. It makes Emma angry to see that the companies have the things she needs but can't have.

One gray winter day after it snowed, Emma was shivering inside her hogan. It gets cold on the Navajo Reservation. The winter winds blow strong over the open land and Emma gets very cold. She can't turn on a switch for a furnace. She needs coal and wood to put in her potbelly stove.

Emma decided that it didn't make any sense for her to be cold when there was so much coal around. Coal that came from Navajo land. She found an empty bag and walked down to the power plant to the place where the coal is stored. A little bit of coal could fit into her stove and keep her nice and warm. The men at the company told Emma it was not her coal and she couldn't have any.

What do you mean? Emma said. The coal came from Navajo land so you should give me a big pile to keep me warm when it snows, she told them. She thought the men were being unfair and she wanted to show them how cold and angry she was. She picked up a stone and threw it hard at the company men. It was a good thing for them that they were wearing their hard hats.

The summers are dry and hot where Emma and Jeanne Joe live. The bright white sun pours down on their homes. All Jeanne Joe and Emma can do is sit under the two shady trees to be a little cooler in the hot afternoon. If someone visited them and brought them cold, clean water to drink, they would be very happy. Their water is stored in an old metal barrel. The water is warm and rusty. It is not the best thing to drink after a hard, hot morning of sheep herding on the dusty land.

The sheep and goats also have trouble getting water. Before the power plant came, the animals used to drink at a watering hole. Now that spot is a cooling pond—a lake the company made to cool down the machinery when it gets too hot. When the sheep and goats are thirsty, they drink out of this lake. It is a big lake and it is full of white, soapy chemicals. In the summer, Emma says the water is hot and brown like coffee.

Emma and Jeanne Joe have good times, too. The Navajos have many dances, when people dress up. The women wear brightly colored long skirts and velveteen blouses. The men put on their best cowboy hats and bolo ties. Everyone—women, men, and children—wears the beautiful handmade turquoise-and-silver jewelry for which the Navajos are famous.

Many Navajos, young and old, get together to dance and sing. Some come in pickup trucks and others ride their horses over the bumpy roads of the reservation to the dance.

Emma loves to dance and be happy with her people. They sing Navajo songs and dance around in a big circle to the beat of a wooden drum. It is lots of fun because the children dance with the adults and the old people like Emma can be part of the dance. That way, everyone has a good time. There is food at the dance which is cooked over open fires or in ovens made from dried mud.

Navajo legends say the Enemy Way Dance helps a sick person get over disease. Other dances and songs have other meanings. The Song of the Earth Spirit says:

> The strength of the earth
> is my strength
> The thoughts of the earth
> are my thoughts

Another song tells how much the Navajos love their land with its big sky, high mountains, wonderful colors and rainbows.

Inside her hogan, Emma has red ribbons hanging on her wall. They are not the fancy kind people win at state fairs, and nobody gave them to her. She took them! She took them off the wooden stakes the company stuck into the land. Emma knows very well that the stakes are survey markers to show where the company plans to build more power lines and more mines. Every time she or Jeanne Joe see a stake with a ribbon, they pull it out!

One morning, after they had come back from herding sheep, Emma and Jeanne Joe saw a line of trucks coming up the dirt road to Emma's hogan. They were company trucks, and both women knew that trouble was coming.

After herding sheep, Emma and Jeanne Joe are very thirsty and hungry. They were cooking breakfast. They were heating up Navajo fry bread and green chile over the potbelly stove and listening to a Navajo radio program on their transistor radio. Emma took the food off the stove and went outside to greet the men. At first, the men wearing hard hats tried to treat Emma the way most adults treat children. They began talking to her as if she wasn't as smart as they were and they could tell her what to do whenever they wanted.

The company men had come to tell Emma to stop pulling up the survey markers—the ones with the red ribbons. They told her: we need to build a new power line to carry electricity from the plant. You are

slowing our work down. We put the stakes on the land to tell us where to put the power line, which will be on company land.

It is not company land, it is Navajo land, Emma said back to the company men. It is the land where my mother and my grandmother herded sheep. It is not your land. I never gave it to you. The company boss tried to scare Emma. If you don't stop pulling up the stakes, he said, we'll call the police.

Emma is a small woman, but she looked at the boss with mean and angry eyes. I don't care what you do, she said bravely. I don't want this land to be destroyed anymore. I don't care if you hang me up and kill me. I'm ready to die for my land.

And Emma will keep up her fight against the power plant and the mine until the day she dies. The grassroots people like Emma are finding that they can outsmart the monster. When they all get together, they are bigger and more powerful than it is.

When I die, Emma says, I want to be lying right here on the land I love and where I was born.

One night after she fell asleep, Emma dreamed she had died.

She dreamed she had wings and was flying over her land. She looked down from the sky and she could see the giant shape of Shiprock. She could also see her nearby land. She was amazed to see hundreds and hundreds of red ribbons tied on stakes all over the area where she grazes her sheep.

The ribbons surprised Emma. They were the fancy ribbons people get for winning prizes at the state fair. Why, she wondered in her dream, were these ribbons on her land?

When she woke up the next morning, she remembered the dream and thought a lot about it. Were the ribbons rewards for her love and protection of Navajo land?

Then she looked around her hogan and saw the long red ribbons she and Jeanne Joe had taken from the survey stakes. Maybe they were not so fancy, but she liked them just as much. These were grassroots ribbons! The very thought of that made Emma laugh again and she knew that she would never leave her land!

You will probably agree
that Emma is a hero.
She is a different kind of hero—
a hero for the time we live in.

You too can be a hero
if you want to fight against pollution
and against the big companies
that don't care about people.

You too can be like Emma
and protect and love the land.

Hooray and red ribbons for Emma!

Part 3

Work, Workers, and Money

JULIA MICKENBERG & PHILIP NEL

When we imagine an ideal childhood, we may think of a realm apart from economics. Protected from toil, the "innocent child" would exist outside the arena of commerce. Scholars studying the history of childhood argue that modern American childhood as we know it—that is, the child of this imaginative ideal—was made possible by the abolition of child labor, which removed children from the workforce and allowed them to be educated in schools, nurtured, and protected.[1] The proliferation of objects designed to meet children's needs has, perhaps ironically, helped foster the American child's sacralization, but advertising directed toward children remains controversial, and many adults are uncomfortable with the notion of children as consumers.[2] Both premature toil and consumer culture threaten children's presumed innocence. For many people, economics ranks with politics and sex as potential childhood hazards.

Even so, work and workers—and, to a lesser degree, economic principles in general—hold a significant place in twentieth-century American children's literature. We can partly chalk this up to the influence of progressives and radicals, who wished to teach children the value of work, to celebrate the contributions of workers, and to give children a basic understanding of economics. The principles of progressive education, which built upon ideas popularized by John Dewey (such as education through experience and the school as a laboratory for society), gave rise to a vogue in what author-educator Lucy Sprague Mitchell called "Here and Now" stories. These stories emphasized the everyday world of urban children—in contrast to a more deeply rooted pastoral tradition in children's literature. In addition to highlighting the sounds, sights, and smells of city life, they tended to glorify the processes of industrial production. The "Here and Now" philosophy inspired a vogue in books about derricks, locomotives, steam shovels, and engines, with titles such as *Diggers and Builders* (1931), *How the Derrick Works* (1930), and *A Steam Shovel for Me!* (1933). Virginia Lee Burton's *Mike Mulligan and His Steam Shovel* (1939) is perhaps the most enduring title in this genre—with the TV show *Bob the Builder* (1999–) as a contemporary counterpart. These stories, and other "production books," highlight the processes by which commonly used objects are created.[3]

Although stories about industrial labor and production may sound merely informational, they often had a political dimension. Describing production brought attention to labor that was otherwise hidden from view; more significantly, it emphasized the importance of industrial workers, in contrast to stories that glorified those in power. The politics of production books could be expressed in subtle ways, as in *The Lollipop Factory and Lots of Others* (1946), written by Mary Elting and illustrated by Jeanne Bendick. That book showed women of different races working on a production line, and it discussed the need for unions to protect workers against speedups. For older children, Lavinia Davis's *Adventures in Steel* (1938) and *The Company Owns the Tools* (1942) by Henry Vicar (aka Henry Felsen) made these political contexts more explicit. Books for younger children about workers tended to be quite subtle in their politics. For example, Leone Adelson and Benjamin Gruenberg's *Your Breakfast and the People Who Made It* (1959) simply portrayed the "parade" of breakfast workers needed to bring children their eggs and milk and orange juice. Published by a communist publisher, *The Story of Your Coat* (included here) reminds children that the goods we use every day are products of labor by people from all over the world—people who are often exploited and unable to afford the very goods they produce.

Many of the pieces in *Tales for Little Rebels* might have been included in this section on Work, Workers, and Money, including some of the earliest dated pieces in the collection. Note, for instance, the representation of workers (as opposed to the shirkers) in Nicholas Klein's *Socialist Primer* (pages 10–13), or in "Happy Valley" (pages 98–101). However, many of the relevant selections date from the 1930s, a period of radical labor agitation. "Pickets and Slippery Slicks" (see pages 106–9) shows the children of black and white mill workers who ultimately organize for better pay and working conditions. "Revolt of the Beavers" (pages 110–16), a play performed by the Federal Theater Project, shows exploited beaver workers revolting because, like the chickens in "Battle in the Barnyard" (pages 101–5), they were never able to benefit from their labor. Mr. His (pages 123–27) uses humor in its depiction of disenfranchised workers —and also predicts their eventual uprising against an unjust boss who owns everything in the town. "Mary Stays after School," published by the Amalgamated Clothing Workers of America (pages 116–22), teaches the children of workers to take pride in the work their

parents do and to appreciate the efforts of worker-activists to achieve a decent standard of living.

The first selection reprinted in this section, Langston Hughes's 1937 poem about a sharecropper, reminds us that industrial workers were not the only ones facing exploitation. Especially in the 1930s, leftists brought attention to the plight of the tenant farmer or sharecropper. Like the factory worker, the sharecropper did not own the products of his or her labor, and, during the years of the Depression, the tenant farmer became an icon of national suffering. Although they are certainly not as radical as Hughes's poem, several critically acclaimed stories published around this time highlighted the plight of farm workers and their children. For instance, Doris Gates's *Blue Willow* (1940) and Lois Lenski's *Strawberry Girl* (1945), winner of the 1946 Newbery Medal, showed children of migrant farm workers exhibiting heroic determination in the face of difficult circumstances.

The selection following Hughes's poem comes from Ruth Brindze's *Johnny Get Your Money's Worth—And Jane Too!* Part of a larger consumers' movement that sought to create savvy consumer citizens who could resist manipulation by advertisers, *Johnny* recognizes children's growing role in the consumer economy—and urges them to spend their money wisely. The examples in *Johnny* might seem somewhat outdated to today's readers, but the lessons remain as relevant as ever.

William Gropper's *The Little Tailor* builds on themes relating to money, work, and workers in another way, by playing with the theme of what Jewish immigrants called *di goldeneh medina*, a Yiddish term for "the golden land." With the prosperity of the 1950s, it was easy to forget the struggles and sacrifices that an earlier generation had made in their quest for what became known as the "American dream." This simple story echoes numerous immigrant narratives, especially the typical Jewish immigrant narrative, with its depictions of sweatshop labor and the hustle and bustle of New York's Lower East Side. Even so, Gropper's tale offered children a picture of working-class immigrant life that was unusual for the 1950s, when, aside from Sydney Taylor's *All-of-a-Kind Family* stories (first published in 1951), Jewish characters and scenarios were at best on the margins of mainstream American children's literature. In the 1980s, Marilyn Sachs's *Call Me Ruth* (1983) would revisit the theme of immigrant sweatshop labor in more explicitly political terms, recalling the 1911 textile workers strike known as the "Uprising of the Twenty Thousand."

American folklore—which gained in popularity in the 1930s, 1940s, and 1950s as part of a widespread interest in discovering and describing American culture —brought attention to worker-heroes, who outperformed machines or outwitted bosses. For instance, as part of their work with the Federal Writers Project's industrial folklore division, Jack Conroy and Arna Bontemps collected narratives that highlighted manual laborers' ingenuity and strength. They published several of these stories as children's books, among them *The Fast Sooner Hound* (1942) and *Slappy Hooper, the Wonderful Sign Painter* (1946). Irwin Shapiro's *Yankee Thunder: The Legendary Life of Davy Crockett* (1944) and *John Henry and His Double-Jointed Steam Drill* (1945) fit this category as well, as does Elie Siegmeister's songbook for children, *Work and Sing: A Collection of the Songs That Built America* (1944). Julius Lester's story of "High John the Conqueror" (pages 192–99), published for older children in the late 1960s, goes to a more radical extreme, portraying an enslaved worker who is strong and capable but more interested in sabotaging the boss (his master) than in being productive.

By the mid-twentieth century, more and more writers—especially radical ones—were publishing stories depicting African-American life and history. Inevitably, given the extent to which work has been a defining feature in the lives of African Americans, many of these books, including *North Star Shining* (see pages 175–82), showed the important contributions of African-American workers: as involuntary laborers under slavery and as industrial workers, farm workers, doctors, scientists, singers, and athletes. Decades later, Sandra Weiner's *small hands, big hands* (pages 133–36) made visible the labor and the struggles of Chicano farm workers, young and old, galvanized by unbearable working conditions to join forces in the Farm Workers' Union. Bringing an international perspective to work, Edith Segal's poem (pages 283–86), "The Work of the World," depicts a wide variety of labor done around the globe. In doing so, Segal values all kinds of work, be it blue-collar or white-collar, paid or unpaid.

Although most of the texts in *Rebels* focus on manual labor, a wave of white-collar union-organization drives in the 1930s and 1940s helped bring attention to the shared concerns of industrial, agricultural, and professional workers. Several children's stories published in the 1940s portray industrial and professional workers embarking on a shared enterprise. A good example is Helen Walker Puner's *Daddies, What They Do All Day* (1946), showing daddies who are salesmen, doctors, musicians, mail carriers, street sweepers, truck drivers, miners, pilots, and window washers. Of course, this book assumed that children knew perfectly well what *mommies* did all day: stayed home and took care of them. However, by 1961, mothers (and women in general) would also be given their due as workers, with Eve Merriam's *Mommies at Work* (now back in print), which showed mommies who are dancers, doctors, writers, astronomers, television directors, and circus performers. Norma Klein's *Girls Can Be Anything* (included here) followed on the trend that Merriam helped initiate, now more consciously reiterating that girls (whether or not they would become mommies) could aspire to any profession they pleased.

As the story *Elizabeth* (pages 249–53) reminds us, children themselves often take on responsibility for work around the house—such as child care, food preparation, and cleaning. And they sometimes work outside the home, in conditions that can be less than ideal. We hope that some of the stories collected in this section and in this book will make children aware of the dignity of work, will give them tools to be savvy consumers, and will inspire them to imagine new possibilities for their own futures. Adult readers will gain a sense of the variety of ways in which writers and illustrators have understood work, workers, and money as subjects of concern to children.

NOTES

1. In *Pricing the Priceless Child: The Changing Social Value of Children* (New York: Basic Books, 1985), sociologist Viviana Zelizer argued that American children became "priceless" or sacralized at precisely the same moment when the abolition of child labor rendered children economically useless.

2. On children and consumption, see, for example, Daniel Thomas Cook, *The Commodification of Childhood: The Children's Clothing Industry and the Rise of the Child Consumer* (Durham, NC: Duke UP, 2004); Gary Cross, *Kids' Stuff: Toys and the Changing World of American Childhood* (Cambridge, MA: Harvard UP, 1997); Lisa Jacobson, *Raising Consumers: Children and the American Mass Market in the Early Twentieth Century* (New York:

Columbia UP, 2004); Stephen Kline, *Out of the Garden: Toys, TV, and Children's Culture in the Age of Marketing* (New York: Verso, 1993); and Ellen Seiter, *Sold Separately: Children and Parents in Consumer Culture* (New Brunswick, NJ: Rutgers UP, 1995).

3. We're borrowing the term from Evgeny Steiner, who discusses the production book specifically in relation to Soviet constructivism and its necessarily political project of building a communist society. See Evgeny Steiner, *Stories for Little Comrades: Revolutionary Children's Artists and the Making of Early Soviet Children's Books*, trans. Jane Ann Miller (Seattle: U of Washington P, 1999).

11

"Sharecroppers" (1937)
Written by Langston Hughes (1902–1967), Illustrated by Fred Ellis (1885–1965)

EDITORS' INTRODUCTION

One of the most influential African-American writers of his generation, Langston Hughes is best known for his poems, plays, and short stories, but he wrote over a dozen children's books. Children's poems were his first works to appear in a national publication—*The Brownies' Book*, the monthly children's magazine founded by W. E. B. Du Bois. Hughes was just eighteen years old at the time.

Born in Joplin, Missouri, Hughes grew up in several states. He spent most of his first thirteen years with his grandmother in Lawrence, Kansas; after her death, he lived with his mother in Topeka, Lincoln (Illinois), and Cleveland. To supplement the household's meager finances, Hughes at age twelve began delivering newspapers, including—for a short time—the popular socialist weekly, *Appeal to Reason*.[1] After high school, he spent an unhappy year at Columbia University but quickly became a leading figure of the Harlem Renaissance. Following his acclaimed debut volume of poetry, *The Weary Blues* (1926), Hughes attended and in 1931 graduated from Pennsylvania's Lincoln University, where his classmates included future Supreme Court justice Thurgood Marshall.

Racial and social injustice radicalized Hughes. In 1931, an all-white jury convicted the "Scottsboro Boys" —nine young African Americans (whose ages ranged from thirteen to twenty)—of raping two white women on an Alabama train, even though all were innocent of the crime. When the NAACP was slow to act, the American Communist Party's International Labor Defense hired a lawyer and organized public support for a retrial. The party's antiracist platform attracted Hughes, and the facts of the case prompted him to act. He wrote poems and the one-act play "Scottsboro Limited," visited the "boys" in prison, and raised money for their defense by organizing auctions of manuscripts and other items from authors and artists—including W. C.

Handy, Ezra Pound, George Bernard Shaw, Claude McKay, and Anita Loos.[2]

During the 1930s, Hughes was especially active on the Left, spending a year in the Soviet Union, filing reports from Madrid on the Spanish Civil War, and writing revolutionary poetry. "Sharecroppers," one of several works for children from this period, appeared in the communist children's magazine *New Pioneer* in February 1937. Echoing the sentiments of groups like the Southern Tenant Farmers Union, Hughes's poem dramatizes how sharecropping enslaved the sharecropper. Owning no property and paid only after his crops were harvested, the tenant farmer and his family (children worked, too) lived in thrall to their landlord, the "boss man," who "had sole responsibility for keeping accounts and selling the crops."[3] At the end of the year, many sharecroppers learned that they were still in debt and would need to work for another year in order to pay off that debt—even if they believed that their landlords had cheated them.[4]

If the intended audience for this poem seems more "adult" than "child," it's worth remembering that a number of Hughes's poems were published for more than one audience. In any case, as Katharine Capshaw Smith points out, Hughes "rejected any image of childhood as recessed from social realities."[5]

(For more on Langston Hughes, see pages 204–5.)

Born in Chicago, Fred Ellis left school after eighth grade, working first as an office boy for Frank Lloyd Wright, next in an engraving shop, and then in an ice cream factory. During a strike at the Chicago packing houses where he worked, Ellis used the time off to attend art school.[6] In 1919, Ellis was a sign painter for the General Outdoor Advertising Company, when he fell six stories from a scaffold, breaking thirty-two bones. During two years in the hospital, he drew cartoons for the *New Majority*, the Chicago Federation of Labor's newspaper. Ellis, whom Joseph North described as "a quiet, handsome man" with a "refreshing twist of phrase and observation," learned from Robert Minor how to "strip [his] cartoons of everything extraneous" in order to "get at the essence."[7] On the recommendation of Minor, Ellis became a cartoonist for the *Daily Worker* in 1923; he joined the Communist Party the following year.[8] From 1930 to 1936, Ellis lived and worked in Berlin and Moscow, contributing cartoons to newspapers there. Upon his return to the United States, he resumed cartooning for the *Daily Worker* and created illustrations for the *New Pioneer*, where this picture appeared.[9]

NOTES

1. Arnold Rampersad, *The Life of Langston Hughes*. Vol. 1, 1902–1941, 2d ed. (New York: Oxford UP, 2002), 17.

2. Ibid., 283–84.

3. Greta de Jong, "'With the Aid of God and the F.S.A.': The Louisiana Farmers' Union and the African American Freedom Struggle in the New Era," *Journal of Social History* 34:1 (2000): 106.

4. Ibid.

5. Katharine Capshaw Smith, *Children's Literature of the Harlem Renaissance* (Bloomington: Indiana UP, 2004), 240.

6. Alfred Durus, "Fred Ellis: Artist of the Proletariat," *International Literature* 11 (1935).

7. Joseph North, *Robert Minor: Artist and Crusader* (New York: International Publishers, 1956), 157.

8. Durus.

9. "Fred Ellis, 1885–1965," *Life of the People: Realist Prints and Drawings from the Ben and Beatrice Goldstein Collection, 1912–1948*, ed. Harry Katz (Washington, DC: Library of Congress, 1999), 94.

Just a herd of Negroes
Driven to the field,
Plowing, planting, hoeing,
To make the cotton yield.

When the cotton's picked
And the work is done,
Boss man takes the money
And we get none.

Leaves us hungry, ragged
As we were before,
Year by year goes by
And we are nothing more

Than a herd of Negroes
Driven to the field—
Plowing life away
To make the cotton yield.

12

Excerpt from *Johnny Get Your Money's Worth (and Jane Too!)* (1938)

Written by Ruth Brindze (1903–1984), Illustrated by Emery I. Gondor (1896–1978)

EDITORS' INTRODUCTION

Ruth Brindze was an important figure in the consumers' movement of the 1930s, "perhaps the only decade in American history," according to historian Lawrence Glickman, "when commentators could speak of 'consumer society' as a potentially radical force."[1] During the Depression decade, thousands of Americans joined consumer organizations or cooperatives, or participated in "boycotts, educational campaigns, 'don't buy where you can't work' movements, and cost-of-living strikes."[2] The literature of the consumer movement abounded, with pamphlets, articles, and dozens of books, many inspired by Stuart Chase's controversial *Your Money's Worth: A Study in the Waste of the Consumer's Dollar* (1927) and F. J. Schlink and Arthur Kallet's best-selling *100,000,000 Guinea Pigs: Dangers in Everyday Foods, Drugs, and Cosmetics* (1932), a book that popularized the idea of a human "guinea pig." Brindze acknowledged a debt to these books when she published *How to Spend Money: Everybody's Practical Guide to Buying* (1935), a work that "combined radical political critique with practical advice."[3] Historian Kathy Newman calls Brindze "the archetype of the grassroots consumer activist."[4] She was the chair of the Consumer Council of Westchester County, New York, and she began writing a consumer column for the *Nation* in 1935. In 1937 she published *Not to Be Broadcast*, which criticized powerful radio advertisers who prevented stations from representing viewpoints hostile to corporate power.

Johnny Get Your Money's Worth was Brindze's first book for children, but it launched her illustrious career as a juvenile author. The strongest link between her children's books and her consumer activism, *Johnny* was the most political of her dozen-plus works for children. James Henle, then the president of Vanguard Press, encouraged Brindze to write the book. As she recalled, "We were discussing a manuscript on consumer buying I had recently completed when I remarked that someone should write a book telling children how to avoid the tricks of the market place. Jim suggested I tackle the job."[5] Vanguard, which published all of Brindze's early books, had become somewhat notorious as a publisher of what Charles McGovern refers to as "Guinea Pig books" that criticized aspects of American business culture.[6] In the 1940s, the House Committee on Un-American Activities (HUAC) called Vanguard a "communist enterprise" and targeted it in a campaign against books that "undermined advertising by destroying consumer confidence."[7]

Johnny opens by urging children to recognize their own power as consumers: "Every year a fortune is spent by and for the children of America," Brindze says in a chapter called "Why Business Men Work to Please You."[8] Other chapters address advertising, "tests for school supplies," food labeling, beauty products, and consumer organizations. This selection comes from the chapter "Candy—How to Choose It."

Reviewers had high praise for the book: Helen Woodward, writing in the Nation, said it "should be called household equipment" and suggested that while Johnny had been written for children, "there is plenty in it for grown-ups."[9] Anne T. Eaton, writing for the New York Times Book Review, maintained, "Young people and many adults as well will profit by having the sound principle that 'you never get something for nothing' brought home to them." She also praised Brindze for her "sincere belief that boys and girls are intelligent enough . . . to learn to buy wisely and thoughtfully, and thus not only profit themselves, but help to promote honest selling and reliable advertising."[10]

Emerich I. Gondor was born in Budapest, Hungary, where he graduated from the Federal Academy of Art. While he was a young art teacher, his observations of children who had suffered during World War I inspired him to learn more about children's psychological difficulties and to seek ways to help children through art. Moving to Vienna in 1920, he studied with leading researchers on progressive art education for children, and he began working with emotionally disturbed children at the Viennese University clinic. At this time he also exhibited his oil paintings, worked as an illustrator for children's books and newspapers, and became art director at Europe's largest publishing house.

Gondor immigrated to the United States in 1935, becoming a citizen in 1941. During the war, he worked in counterespionage. After the war, Gondor became the head of the art and play therapy groups at the Retarded Children's Clinic and the Psychiatric Child Guidance Clinic at New York Medical College, and he also taught art to juvenile delinquents. He earned his diploma in clinical psychology in 1959 and became director of the art program at the Institute for Mental Retardation at New York Medical College in 1968.[11]

NOTES

1. Lawrence B. Glickman, "The Strike at the Temple of Consumption: Consumer Activism and Twentieth-Century American Political Culture," Journal of American History 88:1 (June 2001): 102.

2. Ibid., 103.

3. Kathy M. Newman, Radio Active: Advertising and Consumer Activism, 1935–1947 (Berkeley: U of California P, 2004), 63–64.

4. Ibid., 64.

5. "Ruth Brindze" (autobiographical sketch), More Junior Authors, ed. Muriel Fuller (New York: Wilson, 1963), 30.

6. Charles McGoven, Sold American: Consumption and Citizenship, 1890–1945 (Chapel Hill: U of North Carolina P, 2006), 246.

7. John Tebbel, A History of Book Publishing in the United States. Vol. 4, The Great Change, 1940–1980 (New York: Bowker, 1981), 89. 1944 HUAC report cited in FBI file of Helen Colodny Goldfrank (Helen Kay).

8. Ruth Brindze, Johnny Get Your Money's Worth (and Jane Too!) (New York: Vanguard, 1938).

9. Helen Woodward, "Young Shoppers," Nation, 31 Dec. 1938, 17.

10. Anne T. Eaton, review of Johnny Get Your Money's Worth (and Jane Too!), New York Times Book Review, 8 Jan. 1939, 10.

11. Information on Gondor from Guide to the Papers of Emery and Bertalan Gondor, Leo Baech Institute, Center for Jewish History, New York. http://www.cjh.org/nhprc/Emery Gondor.html.

USING A WRAPPER AS MONEY

You can't expect the candy manufacturers to tell you not to eat too much candy. After all, they want to sell just as much candy as they possibly can. To encourage you to eat more candy (as if this were necessary!), the manufacturers may say that if you send a certain number of wrappers from their candy by a certain date they will give you a prize.

To get the necessary number of wrappers, you may have to eat far more candy than your regular share, and far more than is really good for you. Sometimes the manufacturers demand so many wrappers that no one could possibly eat that much candy and not get sick. The Curtiss Candy Company, for example, once offered to give a free bicycle to anyone who sent in seven hundred wrappers from its 5¢ bars of candy within a five-month period. It seems like an easy way to get a bicycle for nothing until you begin to do some arithmetic.

To get seven hundred coupons during the prize period you would have to buy about five bars of candy a day. No one could be expected to eat five bars of candy day after day and month after month without getting sick. What the Curtiss people expected was that each boy or girl trying for the prize would spend all his candy money for Curtiss candy and urge all his friends and relations to do the same, so that he could have the wrappers.

It was a good idea for the company. It sold 200 times more candy than usual because it had offered the free bicycles.

Most manufacturers do not offer such expensive prizes, and they do not demand that you send them so many wrappers. They make it easier for you. Giving away prizes is just a method of increasing sales. The manufacturers know that if they offer a prize, you, and thousands of other boys and girls, will buy more of the candy they make. A prize is a first-rate advertisement for them.

Frequently, no customer collects quite enough coupons to get the prize. But even when the prize is actually given it may still be cheaper for the company than spending money to advertise in newspapers or over the radio. To advertise a single time in a newspaper or magazine or over a nationwide hookup may cost hundreds or thousands of dollars. The cost of the prizes may be very much less, and some companies think that these prizes are just as good as advertisements.

When you are collecting coupons or wrappers, you form a habit of buying a certain kind of candy. And long after the prize contest is over, you may continue to buy the same kind of bar. You have developed a taste for it. This is good business for the manufacturer. It helps him to sell more of his candy.

You'd have to eat a lot of candy for that
"bike"!

13

The Story of Your Coat (1946)

Written by Clara Hollos
(dates unknown), Illustrated by
Herbert Kruckman (1904-1998)

EDITORS' INTRODUCTION

Clara Hollos wrote *The Story of Your Coat* in a class at New York City's Jefferson School of Social Science, a Marxist institute founded in 1943 by blacklisted teachers associated with the U.S. Communist Party.[1] In its peak years (1946–1948), the school enrolled five thousand students per term; persecution by the federal government led to its closing in 1956.[2] The institute's offerings included Dashiell Hammett's "Mystery Story Writing Course" in 1948 and the "juvenile writing" course that Hollos took.[3]

That class's teacher, Elizabeth Morrow "Betty" Bacon, was the editor and founder of Young World Books, International Publishers' children's series, launched in the fall of 1945. She advocated books that address "social questions" concerning "the larger ideas of democracy and freedom, of exploitation and discrimination."[4] Though not bestsellers, the books did gain access to a mainstream market.[5] For example, *The Story of Your Coat* won positive reviews in such decidedly non-Marxist publications as *Library Journal*, *Booklist*, and the *New York Herald Tribune*.[6]

Sympathetic to unions and workers, *The Story of Your Coat* makes no explicit reference to Marx or communism. But its title alludes to the first chapter of *Capital* (volume 1), where Marx uses a coat to show how a manmade object becomes a commodity, abstracted from the human labor that created it. Restoring the role of the people who made the coat, Marx traces its value as commodity back to the tailor, weaver, and others who created that value.[7] Hollos's *Story of Your Coat* undertakes a similar task, removing the jargon and adding a more detailed account of the many different types of labor involved.

Clara Hollos wrote one other book, *The Story of Your Bread*, a Young World Book published in 1948. The surname "Hollos" is Hungarian. Nothing further is known about her.

The book's illustrator, Herb Kruckman, taught at the Jefferson School and created cartoons and artwork for *New Masses*, the *Daily Worker*, and the *New Pioneer*. His first book, *Hol' Up Yo' Head* (1936), featured a black Jesus who, as Kruckman later explained, is an activist, a humanitarian, and "practically a Communist."[8] As with many artists of his generation, the Great Depression moved Kruckman towards the left. As he said, "I felt very pained by the scenes of suffering all around me in New York, the bread lines and mass unemployment."[9]

Kruckman was no stranger to suffering. When he was three and his mother was pregnant with his brother, an industrial accident killed his father. At school, antisemitic classmates beat Kruckman because he was Jewish. Kruckman's stepfather was abusive to both boys—an experience that, Kruckman said, "hurt the roots of my feelings."[10] These early experiences instilled in him a deep sympathy for any who suffered. As he wrote late in life, "As a society we are plagued by inhumanity, war, murder and child abuse . . . the artist seeks to become an affirming voice in the midst of this."[11]

This compassion emerges in his paintings and in his work for children, such as *Joey Meets His People* (1940), which describes a boy's imaginary encounter with his Jewish ancestors, and Edith Segal's *Be My Friend* (1952), for which he provided the pictures. Kruckman illustrated seven and wrote three children's books. He also worked directly with children, giving chalk talks in New York City and at the leftist Camp Kinderland, where his son Russell went in the summers. Kruckman was art director of Camp Lakeland, Kinderland's affiliate for grownups.[12] Kruckman worked on many books with Jewish themes and produced work for the Jewish People's Fraternal Order, a branch of the communist-affiliated International Workers Order. Though his identification with Judaism was more cultural than religious, Kruckman felt that Jewish heritage helped "to stimulate a feeling of humanity."[13] Certainly, such a feeling motivates much of Kruckman's work.

NOTES

1. Janet Sillen, "'Story of Your Coat' Xmas Treat for Kids," *Daily Worker*, 7 Dec. 1946, 11; Ellen W. Schrecker, *No Ivory Tower: McCarthyism and the Universities* (New York: Oxford UP, 1986), 50; Alvah Bessie, "School for Democracy," *New Masses*, 27 Jan. 1942, 12.

2. "Selsam Gives Story of Jefferson School," *New York Times*, 14 Apr. 1954, 19; Marv Gettleman, "Jefferson School of Social Science," *Encyclopedia of the American Left*, eds. Mari Jo Buhle, Paul Buhle, and Dan Georgakas, 2d ed. (New York: Oxford UP, 1998), 399.

3. Gettleman, 399.

4. Elizabeth M. Bacon, "Books That Mold the Young Mind," *Daily Worker*, 5 Jan. 1947, sec. 2, 10.

5. Julia Mickenberg, *Learning from the Left: Children's Literature, the Cold War, and Radical Politics in the United States* (New York: Oxford UP, 2006), 145.

6. *Library Journal*, 15 Dec. 1946, 1809; *Booklist*, 1 Feb. 1947, 174; *New York Herald Tribune Weekly Book Review*, 29 Dec. 1946, 9.

7. Karl Marx, *Capital*, volume 1, in *The Marx-Engels Reader*, 2d ed., ed. Robert C. Tucker (New York: Norton, 1978), 308–17. Pages 183–84 and 187 of Peter Stallybrass's "Marx's Coat" (*Border Fetishisms: Material Objects in Unstable Places*, ed. Patricia Spyer [New York: Routledge, 1998]) were enormously helpful in helping us to articulate these concepts succinctly.

8. Isobel Crombie, "Warm Humanity: The Work and Life of Herbert Kruckman," *Warm Humanity: The Work and Life of Herbert Kruckman*, by Isobel Crombie with Swami Shankarananda (Mt. Eliza, Melbourne, Australia: Shiva Books, 1999), 14.

9. Ibid., 12.

10. Ibid., 10.

11. Ibid.

12. Swami Shankarananda [Russell Kruckman], "Pop Remembered," *Warm Humanity: The Work and Life of Herbert Kruckman*, 6.

13. Crombie, 17.

This is the story of your coat.

Do you think your coat is just an ordinary coat? Wait until you hear its story.

Your coat is made of wool. The wool comes from sheep.

Let's see what happens to it before it becomes a coat.

You and I must take a long trip to find out. And we start at the other side of the world.

THE SHEEP RANCH

Here we are in Australia. Just look at this huge meadow covered with grass. And sheep, sheep everywhere. We are on a sheep ranch belonging to Mr. Tick.

Thousands of sheep graze under the bright sun. The best sheep with the finest wool come from Australia. Just touch their backs. How rich and soft their coats feel!

It's all wool.

THE BATH

The sheep are getting a bath. This is something special, for they are washed only twice a year. The sheep act as if they were taking a bath just for fun. Not at all, sheep! You are getting a shampoo before a haircut, just as people do in a barber shop. When the sheep have been washed, the shepherd sees that they keep clean until the big day arrives.

THE SALE

The big day is here! This is the day when the wool is sold. The gentleman over here is Mr. Tack. He is a buyer who has come all the way from the United States to buy wool from Mr. Tick in Australia.

The sheep are lined up, and Mr. Tack takes his choice. Of course, he picks only the ones with the thickest, fluffiest coats. They give the best wool.

THE SHEARING

This place looks like a barber shop. But here the barber is called the shearer, and his scissors are called shears. The sheep shearer uses automatic shears which work like an electric razor.

Do you think it's easy to shear sheep? Not at all. Shorty, the shearer, has been working on this ranch ever since he was a little boy. No wonder he can do such a good job of shearing off a sheep's coat all in one piece.

After it is sheared, the sheep's coat is called the fleece.

Each fleece is rolled into a bundle.

See how funny the sheep are without their woolly coats.

They look all naked.

Well, we are sorry to leave the sheep, but we have other things to do.

SORTING AND SHIPPING

These men are sorting the bundles of fleece in a place called a sorting station. They separate the fleece into three piles—the "very-best," the "next-best," and the "not-so-good."

The packer puts fifty small bundles of fleece into a large bag. Each bag is put onto the scales to see how much it weighs. Then it gets a number—Number 1 for the "very-best," Number 2 for the "next-best," Number 3 for the "not-so-good."

Now all the bags are ready for shipping. They are loaded onto big trucks which line up in front of the sorting station.

Mr. Tack, the buyer, has finished his business in Australia.

Before he goes, he pays Mr. Tick, the rancher, for the fleece.

Everybody says good-by to Mr. Tack. He can even hear the sheep baa-ing far away. By-byeeeee!

The trucks are ready to go to the harbor.

THE HARBOR

What an exciting place this is! We are in Sidney, the largest harbor in Australia. Big ships are coming in from far-off countries. Other big ships are sailing out of the harbor to all parts of the world.

Just look at that crowd of people—Australians, Chinese, Americans, and many others. Everybody is busy. Workers are unloading boxes, barrels, and bags from large trucks. These workers are called longshoremen. Many hands are busy with our bags of fleece. The place is buzzing. Rush, rush, rush!

Everybody is rushing except Mr. Tack. He is taking it easy now, because the shipping company will look after everything.

The boxes and barrels and bags that are loaded onto the ship are called the cargo.

THE WAREHOUSE

We arrive in Lawrence, Massachusetts, near Boston. This big building is a warehouse. Its walls are made of steel and other fireproof materials, for millions of dollars worth of goods are stored here. Some storage rooms are as large as a railroad station. Here the boxes and barrels and bags are kept until their owners need them.

Mr. Toe is the owner of the bags of fleece. He is a textile manufacturer, and he owns a factory where woolen cloth is made. Now Mr. Toe pays Mr. Tack for buying the wool.

Good-by. Mr. Tack. We won't see you again.

Good-by, Australia, land of sheep and sunshine and wide meadows. We are sailing home to the United States.

It's good to be back on land after four weeks on the Pacific Ocean. This is the harbor of San Francisco, California. It's raining cats and dogs. but Mr. Tack is not worried, because the fleece is packed in waterproof bags.

Now the cargo is unloaded. Our bags of fleece are put on trucks to be taken to the railroad station.

The boxes and barrels and bags that are put on the train are called freight.

Mr. Tack is a busy businessman, so he takes an airplane.

THE TEXTILE MILL

This is Mr. Toe's factory. It is a big place that takes up a whole block of buildings. It is called a textile mill, and the workers who run the machines here are called textile workers.

The bags of fleece have arrived from the warehouse, and the workers are ready to start. They have to work very hard to make nice woolen cloth out of that coarse, greasy fleece.

CLEANING AND COMBING

Here are some workers in the textile mill sorting the wool—Number 1, the "very-best"; Number 2, the "next-best"; Number 3, the "not-so-good." Mr. Toe is required by our government to keep the different kinds separate. If cloth is made from Number 3, the "not-so-good," he has to sell it cheaper than cloth made from Number I, the "very-best," or Number 2, the "next-best." The "very-best" has to have a label that says "100 per cent pure wool."

Now comes the cleaning. The workers put the fleece in a machine where it is washed just like dirty laundry. They scour it with soap and chemicals until it is white and fluffy. It is dried by an electric fan.

Then a big machine with wire teeth combs the fleece. It takes the tangles out and makes the fleece smooth just as you smooth your hair with a comb.

But let's go on and see some very interesting work.

SPINNING

Yarn is wool thread out of which woolen cloth is made. How is yarn made?

Take a piece of wool from your mother's knitting bag. Pick it apart until it is soft and fluffy. Now hold it in one hand. Keep twisting it round and round in the same direction with your other hand.

See, it's getting to look more and more like thread! The longer you twist it, the stronger the yarn will be.

The spinning machine works the same way. The machine has a part like a hand that holds the wool. This is the bobbin. It is stuck on the end of a rod called the spindle. A motor makes the spindle, with the bobbin, spin around faster and faster, twisting the wool tighter and tighter.

But this wonderful machine cannot make yarn by itself. It needs a worker to run it. Here is Spike, the spinner, who runs the spinning machine. Spike knows a great deal about the machine. He is going to night school to study textile engineering. What a good engineer he will be, because he already knows so much about spinning!

After the yarn has been twisted round and round until it is strong enough, it is wound onto large rolls.

Now it is ready to be woven.

THE LOOM

A loom is a weaving machine that makes cloth. It has little machine fingers, called heddles, that pick up first one thread and then another. These threads are the warp.

Have you ever watched the way your mother's needle goes in and out when she darns stockings? That's the way the shuttle goes. In and out between the warp threads, across and back, it carries a thread called the weft.

Here William, the weaver, puts the yarn on the heddles, the little machine fingers, to make the warp. Then he gets the shuttle ready to carry the weft. This takes a long time, but William knows his job well. All set? William starts the loom going. But his work is not over. He goes on to do the same thing to the next loom —and the next—and the next. He has to look after several looms at once.

William's father was also a weaver, and William himself has worked in a textile mill for many years.

A hundred years ago, little children used to work in textile mills from sunrise until after dark in the evening. They had no time to play, no time to go to school. And all they got for their long, hard work was a few cents. Their parents worked in the mills too. They were all very poor, very tired, and often hungry.

Finally, these grown-ups and children of long ago became so tired and hungry that they could stand it no longer. They decided to stick by each other to try and make life better for them all. They formed a group which they called a union and agreed not to work until all of them got more money. Of course, the looms could not run without workers. So at last the mill owners gave in.

After this fight, the workers did not have to work from sunrise until after dark. They had more time to talk with their children. They earned more money, too, so their children could leave the mills and go to school.

Ever since that time, their union has kept on making life better for the textile workers. William's father was a member of the union when he worked in the mill and today William is, too.

Now the first loom has finished weaving the yarn to cloth. Other workers, called examiners, go over every inch of cloth very carefully. They take out lumpy knots in the yarn and mend little holes. At last the cloth is perfect.

THE DYEING ROOM

The wool fabric is ready to be colored. We call this dyeing.

Many years ago, before machines were invented,

only rich people could have beautifully colored cloth for their coats.

The colors, or dyes, were made out of vegetable roots, the bark of trees, berries, seeds, and even insects. Some colors were more expensive than others. A doctor, a lawyer, a merchant, a farmer all wore clothes of a different color. You could tell at once what a person did for a living just by looking at the color of his coat. Purple dye was made out of tiny shellfish. It was so hard and expensive to make that only the kings and princes had purple coats.

And oh, how mysterious the dye-makers *were* about the way they made their colors! Imagine a father on his death-bed saying to his son, "Dear son, I leave to you the big secret of how to make canary-yellow dye!"

Nowadays dyes are made in chemical laboratories by scientists. And you don't have to be a prince to have a purple coat!

Here is Clarence, the colorist, in his laboratory. He knows more about colors and dyes than any of those old-timers. And what he knows is no secret either. Clarence understands chemistry very well. He knows how to make purple dye not from rare shellfish but from ordinary coal tar.

Dick, the dyer, is a very important man, too. He puts the wool fabric in the dyeing vat, which is just like an enormous pot. He has to know exactly how many hours the fabric must boil in the vat of dye. Some dyes take a long time to color certain fabrics; others take only a

short time. If Dick didn't know which—what a mess of spoiled cloth there would be!

Now we are in the drying and pressing room. First, the wet fabric is dried by hot air. Then Pete, the presser, draws the fabric between big, hot rollers until it is flat and smooth.

The finished fabric is measured by the yard. Then it is rolled into huge rolls called bolts. Each bolt gets a label with a number—Number 1 for the "very-best," Number 2 for the "next-best," and Number 3 for the "not-so-good."

It's time to say good-by to Spike and William, Clarence and Dick and Pete. We are now ready to take a trip to the biggest city in the world.

THE CLOTHING FACTORY

We are in New York City. In this building there is a factory where children's coats are made. It belongs to Mr. Bing who has just bought hundreds of bolts of woolen fabric from Mr. Toe's textile mill. The factory is in full swing, for many people want to buy children's coats. There are workers of many different nationalities —Jewish, Italian, Irish and others—all busy.

Let's go in and see what everybody is doing.

MAKING THE PATTERN

Up we go in a big elevator to the third floor. First we shall visit Doris, the designer. She knows all about children's coats—how they are put together and which styles look nicest. Doris studied designing in art school before she came to work for Mr. Bing.

Here is the new fabric. Doris likes it. It is Number 1, the "very-best." She looks at it for a long time. Flash! She has an idea. She draws a picture. What a handsome coat!

She calls in Pat, the pattern-maker. He makes a life-size drawing of the coat on pieces of paper which are as long as a person. He figures out how big size 8 has to be, and size 9, and size 10. Then he cuts out all the parts of the drawing and pins them together. Now he has a paper coat that looks just like Doris' picture. This is the pattern from which the cloth coats will be made.

Doris and Pat are pleased. They call in Mr. Bing, and he okays the design.

Mr. Bing wants to make money by selling these coats. That's his business. He figures out how much it will cost to make them—so much money for fabric, so much for buttons and thread. Now comes the question of how much he must pay the workers for making the coats.

And of course, the workers want to earn enough money to buy nice coats for their children like the ones they make. They want enough money to live in nice houses, eat good food, and go to the movies once in a while. They don't want to work so hard and fast that they are too tired to speak to their children in the evening.

Remember how the workers in the textile mill helped themselves by joining a union and working together to make life better for them all? The workers in Mr. Bing's factory belong to a union, too. They hold a meeting and choose Olga, one of the best workers in the sewing room, to speak for them all and tell Mr. Bing how many coats they can make in a day and how much money they think they should get for making them. Mr. Bing and Olga argue back and forth for a long time. At last they agree. The workers will make so many coats in one day, and each worker will get a certain amount of money for a day's work.

Now that's done, and we can follow Olga down to the workrooms on the second floor.

Our first stop is the cutting room where the fabric is cut into pieces.

The man who knows most about this job is Carl, the cutter. He is here, there, everywhere. He spreads the bolts of fabric on long tables. He puts the paper patterns on top of the fabric and outlines them with white chalk. The wool fabric is now ready to be cut —not with scissors, but with electric cutting machines, that look like big knives. They can cut through many layers of fabric all at once. You have to know your job when you handle those big knives. See how carefully Carl does it. It looks easy, but do you really think it is?

Every cutter cuts a different piece of the coat. Hyman cuts the backs, Joe the fronts. Tony cuts the collars, Sammy the pockets. Ivan cuts the right sleeves, and Jim the left ones.

Carl takes the pieces to the sewing room.

THE SEWING ROOM

When we say "sewing room," we mean a huge hall with rows and rows of electric sewing machines. The sewing-machine workers are called operators.

The worker who knows the most about this job is Olga, the operator. We met her before, remember? She can make the pieces of cloth whizz under the needle of the sewing machine so fast that you think it must be magic.

Each operator sews a different part of the coat. Katie sews the backs and fronts together. Myrtle sews in the sleeves. Sarah sews on the collar, and Sonia the pockets. Betty sews up the hem. Mary puts in the lining. Stitch, stitch, stitch—the coat is done.

If one person had to make this coat by hand— s-t-i-t-c-h, s-t-i-t-c-h, s-t-i-t-c-h—it would take days.

If Olga had to make a whole coat by herself, it would still take from morning till night.

But when all the workers work together on electric sewing machines, a coat is done in a very short time.

FINISHING

Now the coats are ready for finishing. Fanny, the finisher, takes care of that. Zip, zip, the coats go under the buttonhole machine. Zing, zang, the buttons are put on—you guessed it, also by machine.

Now the coats are ready. A checker looks at each one to make sure nothing is wrong. Onto the racks they go. Hundreds of coats every day. Little coats and big coats. Girls' coats and boys' coats. Red coats and blue coats. And every coat has a label—Number 1 for the "very-best," Number 2 for the "next-best," and Number 3 for the "not-so-good."

Mr. Bing's order clerk is on the telephone. She has an order. Please send two hundred children's coats to Mr. Bang, who has a department store.

Yes, sir. Thank you. The order will be delivered on time. Good-by, Carl. Good-by, Olga.

THE DEPARTMENT STORE

Here is the Bang department store. A big sale is going on.

What a crowd! Everybody wants to buy children's coats.

Look out. Don't push! Here we are. Which coat do you want? The yellow one? Fine, let's try it on. It fits perfectly. How much does it cost? We buy it.

It is marked Number 1, the "very best."

The coat is made of wool.
The wool came from sheep.
It came from Australia to the United States, from Sidney to San Francisco. From San Francisco to Lawrence. From Lawrence to New York.
It traveled by truck, by ship, by train.
It was cargo. It was freight.

It was on a ranch.
It was in a warehouse.
It was in a textile mill.
It was in a clothing factory.
It was in a department store.
It was fleece.
It was yarn.
It was fabric.

It was sheared.
It was weighed.
It was packed.
It was cleaned.
It was spun.

It was woven.
It was dyed.
It was pressed.
It was measured.
It was designed.
It was cut.
It was sewed.

It was made by
Shorty the shearer
Spike the Spinner
William the weaver
Clarence the colorist
Dick the dyer
Pete the presser
Doris the designer
Pat the pattern-maker
Carl the cutter
Olga the operator
Fanny the finisher
and many others.

It belonged to
Mr. Tick who sold it to
Mr. Tack who sold it to
Mr. Toe who sold it to
Mr. Bing who sold it to
Mr. Bang who sold it to
                                    you.
And now you wear it.

Your coat was not made by one worker alone. It was not made by one machine alone. It was not made in one place alone. It was made by many workers at different machines in different places—all working together.

This is the story of your coat.
Do you still think it is just an ordinary coat?

14

The Little Tailor (1955)

William Gropper (1897–1977)

EDITORS' INTRODUCTION

Dedicated to his mother and father, *The Little Tailor* is the sole children's book authored by Gropper and is his most autobiographical work. The eldest of six children born to poor Jewish Rumanian immigrants, William Gropper grew up on New York City's Lower East Side. His mother, the family's breadwinner, was a seamstress for a sweatshop, often bringing her work home.[1] At age twelve, he left school to support his family, taking a job as a dishwasher in a Bowery restaurant.

In his scarce spare time, he drew, using the sidewalk as his canvas. When a friend from the nearby Ferrer School (named for the anarchist educator) spotted these chalk drawings, he invited Gropper to attend a class taught by Robert Henri and George Bellows, proponents of what would come to be known as the Ashcan School. He learned art from their class and politics from the school's evening lectures by such figures as anarchists Emma Goldman and Alexander Berkman.[2]

As a teenager working at a clothing store ten hours a day, six days a week, Gropper began adding his own caricatures to the postcard advertisements he was addressing. Frank A. Parsons, director of the New York School of Fine and Applied Arts, received one such card and offered him a scholarship. Unable to afford the loss of income, Gropper accepted a half-scholarship and continued working part-time.[3]

In 1918, when Gropper was a staff cartoonist for the *New York Herald Tribune*, his editor sent him and a reporter to cover the Industrial Workers of the World. They arrived, read a leaflet, joined the IWW, and left the *Tribune*.[4] Gropper began contributing to radical publications such as *The Dial*, the *New Pioneer*, the *Labor Defender*, and *New Masses*. Staff cartoonist for the Yiddish communist daily *Morning Freiheit* (Freedom), Gropper did not otherwise charge the radical press for his contributions, taking money from the commercial press to support himself and his family: wife Sophie and two sons, Gene and Lee.

With novelists Theodor Dreiser and Sinclair Lewis, Gropper traveled to the USSR in 1927 to celebrate the tenth anniversary of the revolution. Upon his return, Gropper published one of the earliest American graphic novels, *Alley-Oop* (1930), and gained recognition as a painter, receiving commissions for murals, mounting his first one-man show, and winning a Guggenheim fellowship.

His cartoons made front-page news when his caricature of Emperor Hirohito (published in *Vanity Fair*, 1935) caused an international incident. The Japanese government demanded that the State Department suppress the cartoon (it declined but did offer an informal apology). During the Second World War, Gropper created posters in support of the Allied war effort. Also in the 1940s, the FBI began watching him, compiling a file that ultimately grew to over three hundred pages.

In 1953, when Senator Joseph McCarthy called him to testify, Gropper appeared before the Senate Permanent Committee on Investigations but declined to answer questions, citing his Fifth Amendment rights. Privately, Gropper maintained that he was never a Communist but *was* sympathetic to the cause. "I was not a member of the Communist Party. I did do work for them," he later said.[5] "I am accused of being a red," he told another interviewer. "I don't belong to any political party. If a Negro is attacked, then I am a Negro. Any minority—that's me."[6]

Blacklisted from other venues, Gropper wrote and was able to publish *The Little Tailor*, which draws on his childhood experiences. Though Gropper's political cartoons are sharply (even angrily) satirical, this book does not clearly commit to a partisan point of view. It longs to embrace the American dream, and yet acknowledges that it is a dream. Perhaps that's what the *New York Times'* Ellen Lewis Buell was getting at when she wrote, "If the theme is familiar, Mr. Gropper's handling of the tale is original. His story has something of the quality of a fable, but is also realistic."[7]

Noting that (after being called before McCarthy) some of his friends crossed the street when they saw him, Gropper kept the company of his family and his paintings.[8] Looking back, Gropper observed that, early on, he realized, "in the end my life is no more than a 2 inch column [obituary]. I didn't want to do anything that I would be ashamed of. I couldn't always say what I wanted and the closest to freedom of expression I can get is with my painting."[9]

NOTES

1. Harry Salpeter, "William Gropper: Proletarian," *Esquire*, Sept. 1937, 156.

2. Bruce Hooton, "Tape Recorded Interview with William Gropper," 12 June 1965, Archives of American Art, Smithsonian Institution.

3. Salpeter, 159.

4. Ibid.

5. "Great Neck Profile: William Gropper," *Great Neck Record* [Great Neck, NY], 27 Nov. 1975, 12.

6. John L. Hess, "William Gropper, Artist, 79, Dies; Well-Known Left-Wing Cartoonist," *New York Times*, 8 Jan. 1977, 22.

7. Ellen Lewis Buell, "New Found Land," *New York Times Book Review*, 24 July 1955, 18.

8. Hess, 22.

9. Doris Dann, "Art" [unknown publication], 31 Oct.–3 Nov. 1963, 13. William Gropper Papers, Roll 3502, Archives of American Art, Smithsonian Institution.

Many many years ago, in a sleepy little town called Nochi, which was hidden far away in the darkest end of Europe, there lived a little tailor who made the most beautiful clothes in the world.

People from all corners of the province came to this little tailor for their clothes.

Out of material, he would cut clothes that could make quite ordinary people look really noble. He could dress meek men with the dignity of their profession so that they commanded respect.

The skill of the little tailor was amazing—the way he selected the fabric, designed the style, cut the pattern to measurement, pinned the material into form, basted the fabric to a lining, made pads for sloping shoulders, sewed the sleeves, the collar, cuffs, pockets, and when the garment was finished, the man or woman was dressed with high authority.

Although the little tailor was poor, he was blessed with many children, mainly daughters. Some people like the Rothschilds, inherit wealth, but that is not everything.

He could dress all sorts of women with such charm and beauty that they looked lovely and young.

A man holding a very high official position looked no different from any other person to the little tailor.

When people were undressed, you could not tell the difference between the butcher and the soldier, the poet and the merchant, the fiddler and the lawyer, the baker and the teacher.

They were just sizes—tall, short, stout and thin.

Could a Rothschild sew a patch on his pants? If it were not for the little tailors who make the clothes, the high and mighty Rothschilds would be walking around without pants.

On Sundays, holidays, and at weddings and birthdays, the town seemed to wake up. People would put on their best clothes and parade up and down the boulevard.

The little tailor would recognize one of his coats or suits. When he shook hands with the wearer, he was really greeting the sleeve that he had made. He felt that the parade on the boulevard was mostly a fashion show of his art.

Wherever people went, his clothes were admired. Everybody would ask, "Who made this beautiful costume?" And the proud wearer would always answer, "The little tailor of Nochi."

His clothes traveled all over the country, from village to village, from town to town, from city to city and on to distant lands—flying like birds seeking to settle in a place of sunshine and freedom.

In France, the little tailor became known as "*le petit tailleur.*"

In Italy he was called, "*il sarto piccolino.*"

In Spain they called him "*el sastre pequeno.*"

And in Germany he was known as "*der kleiner schneidermeister.*"

But back home, he was just the little tailor who knew nothing of his fame. He was busy hour after hour, sitting with his legs crossed on his table in his tiny shop.

One day the little tailor received a glowing letter from a friend who had moved to America. The letter urged him to pack up his belongings and come with his family to the wonderful new country where his friends had settled and were happy. Where the buildings were so tall that they reached up into the sky.

Where the sun shined brightest in a land of plenty. Where fruit grew in baskets, apples in barrels, potatoes in sacks, and there were plates full of bread, already buttered.

Where every man was a king in his own castle.
All the streets were paved with gold.
It was a land of the free,
    a land of promise,
        a land of equal opportunity.

The little tailor and his family were assured a home, and his friends would send steamship tickets for them to come to America.

There was great jubilation. The little tailor and his family were leaving for America, the new land of hope, equality, liberty! The town's musicians played folk music and the town's people danced. They rejoiced at the good fortune of the little tailor.

The next morning the little tailor and his family started on their journey.

As they traveled from village to village, the little tailor was surprised to find that the people everywhere seemed to know him.

They had seen the beautiful clothes that he had made for the travelers who had passed through the same places before.

Now the little tailor and his family were on the same road to happiness.

When the little tailor and his family reached the port where they were to board the steamship, they sold their horse and wagon and joined a great many people from different countries who had gathered on the boat.

The passengers were carpenters, bricklayers, merchants, waiters, shoemakers, dancers, butchers, singers, farmers, bakers, students, hatmakers, inventors, tailors—tall men, thin men, short men, stout men, women, children, all together in one big boat, going to help build a free world in a new country.

The newly arrived settlers were welcomed by relatives and friends at New York's Battery Park which was once called Castle Garden.

The little tailor and his family were overjoyed to see all their old friends.

They were taken to a small flat on New York's crowded East side.

It was all strange to the little tailor. People seemed to be living on top of each other. During the hot summer nights, many slept on fire-escapes and on the roofs to keep cool.

No sooner had the little tailor and his family been settled, than he was taken by a friend to a shop where many tailors were making men's clothes. He was seated at a machine and was told to make only sleeves. The machines were lined up like little horses, racing to make hundreds of sleeves without arms or coats to fit them.

Then the piles of sleeves were counted and carried to another group of tailors who sewed the sleeves to jackets.

A line of women then finished the garments by sewing on buttons and making button-holes.

The clothes were pressed and then delivered to stores where they were sold as ready-to-wear clothes.

After months of hard work, the little tailor had made all the sleeves that were needed. The shops then closed for the season. All the tailors were idle and would have to wait until they were called back to work again for the next season's styles.

The little tailor walked the streets, trying to find work. There is nothing that can make a worker so sad as idleness. He tried to recognize one of the thousands of sleeves he had made, so he might feel the same pride in his work that he had in the old country, but the coats and their sleeves were all strangers to him.

The little tailor went to his friend who had written the glowing letters. He asked him, "Where is this dreamland of plenty and opportunity, this land of promise you wrote me about?" His friend assured him, "It is here, all around you. All people with ability and desire to work can have their dreams come true. If you will take a walk around the neighborhood with me, I will show you what I mean."

He took the little tailor over to a pushcart peddler and asked, "What are your ambitions?" The pushcart peddler told them, "First, I plan to open a little store. Then, when business gets better, I hope to get a bigger store in a better section of the city. In time, when I am rich enough, I will open a large department store."

Next the little tailor's friend called a newsboy who was selling papers. He asked the newsboy, "What are you going to be when you grow up?" "When I grow up," said the newsboy, "I'm going to be a reporter and write stories for newspapers. The editor has promised me a job as copy boy when I get out of public school. Maybe some day I'll have my own newspaper."

"See that singing waiter, he writes his own music. Someday he may become America's leading composer. . . . And that little man who wants to improve our city may someday be elected mayor. . . . Ask any of these people, they all have ambitions.

"Liberty-loving people from all sections of the world, people with high hopes of the future, have come here to fulfill their dreams. This is a country where everyone is free to say what he thinks, free to agree or disagree, free to create and build, where there are free elections, equal opportunity and fair play for every race, creed or color. These are the qualities that will make us a great nation."

The little tailor went home, thinking about all he had seen and heard. On the first floor of the building where he lived he was greeted by a neighbor with two free tickets for a concert her little boy was going to perform uptown.

She asked the little tailor if he would make her a new dress and a new suit for the boy.

When he reached his flat, the happy little tailor had news for his wife. He told her that they were invited to a violin concert and that he was going to sew a new dress for her, that he also had an order to make a dress for the woman on the first floor and a suit for her boy —and that he had discovered America!

He was going to create new designs for clothes starting right here in this small room. Some day he would have a fine salon of his own on Fifth Avenue. His would be the garments of people with a future—the people of America.

Clothes for boys, girls, men and women, sailors, nurses, cowboys, fire-chiefs, opera singers, ballet dancers—they would be so beautiful that people from all walks of life, and from every section of the city, would all find their way to the little tailor.

15

Girls Can Be Anything (1973)

Written by Norma Klein (1938–1989), Illustrated by Roy Doty (b. 1922)

EDITORS' INTRODUCTION

After her second daughter was born, Norma Klein decided to write for children. She was already a successful writer for adults, having published sixty short stories and a novel. Her first work for a younger audience, *Mom, the Wolfman, and Me* (1972) began the career for which she is best known—that of a young adult novelist. She published over thirty novels for adolescents, addressing such subjects as divorce, sexuality, racism, and sexism.

Girls Can Be Anything (1973), Klein's second book for children and first picture book, is "a merry assault on sexism," as *Publishers Weekly*'s reviewer noted.[1] Klein described herself as "an ardent feminist" who regarded "equal rights for women as the most important issue of the modern world."[2] She dedicated the book to her older daughter "Jenny (who when she grows up, would like to be a painter, join the circus, and work at Baskin-Robbins, making ice cream cones)." If this dedication reflects the flexibility of childhood ambition, it also reflects a sense of possibility inspired by the feminist movement, which was gaining ground when Klein wrote the book. The year before the book's publication, the Equal Rights Amendment passed the U.S. Senate and the House of Representatives for the first time. That same year, the E.R.A. was ratified in twenty-two of the thirty-eight states required to amend the Constitution. And, as *Girls Can Be Anything* notes, two prominent world leaders were women: Golda Meir, prime minister of Israel (from 1969 to 1974), and Indira Gandhi, prime minister of India (1966–1977, 1980–1984).

As a child growing up in New York, Klein knew "bright, thoughtful, idealistic" people.[3] As she writes in an autobiographical sketch, "My parents were non-religious Jews, politically left-wing, intellectual."[4] As a child, Klein attended private progressive schools; as a college student, she majored in Russian, receiving her B.A. from Barnard in 1960 and an M.A. in Slavic Languages from Columbia in 1963. She had intended to pursue a Ph.D., but after marrying scientist Erwin Fleissner, she decided to write full-time.

When her daughters were born—Jenny in 1967, Katie in 1970—she became disappointed in the quality of the children's books available to them. As she said a few years after she started writing for children, "I especially want to write for girls . . . who are active intellectually, who are strong, interesting people."[5] She was equally insistent that the books not be didactic. Klein said she felt that these messages should be delivered "nondidactically, humorously in books that are fun to read."[6] In so doing, she encouraged girls and young women to be independent, and to realize that they can be anything.

Her daughters have apparently taken this message to heart. Now grown up, Katie has been an artist, has run her own natural foods baking company, and now teaches yoga. Her other daughter—Jennifer, to whom the book is dedicated—is associate professor of English at the University of Indiana at Bloomington.[7]

Born in Columbus, Ohio, Roy Doty had an independent streak that began in grade school. As he said, "From fifth grade on I had only one desire, and that was to draw cartoons. I fought off the attempts of every art teacher to switch me to the finer kinds of art, and I continue my merry and most happy way, doing what I started out to do in the fifth grade, draw cartoons."[8]

During the Second World War, Doty got his big break as a cartoonist. When a strip he was cowriting for his army camp's newspaper got picked up by other armed forces papers, someone in the Pentagon saw it, liked it, and sent Doty to Paris to set up the French bureaus of *Yank* and *Stars and Stripes*. While working on those, Doty began contributing to other publications, including the *London Daily Mail*; *Elle*, which was then a new magazine for teenage girls; and *Overseas Woman*, a magazine for American women (nurses, WACs, Red Cross workers, civilians) in the European theater of operations. He got the jobs for both *Overseas Woman* and *Elle* because, as he recalls, he was one of the few cartoonists there who could draw women without resorting to the typical caricature of the day—what he describes as "big feet, big noses, have big boobs or what-have-you."[9]

Returning to the States with an impressive portfolio, Doty embarked upon a career as a freelance cartoonist. He has illustrated over 170 books, the most famous of which is probably Judy Blume's *Tales of a Fourth Grade Nothing* (1972). His illustrations regularly appeared in

Newsweek, *Business Week*, and the *New York Times*. For over fifty years, he has drawn "Wordless Workshop," which runs in the magazine *Family Handyman*.

Though not known as a political artist, Doty has used his art to make a difference. As he said, when he and his colleagues came back from the war, "we wanted things to change."[10] With Ben Shahn, Doty worked on the art for Progressive Henry Wallace's 1948 presidential campaign. Doty also worked on Democrat Adlai Stevenson's 1952 and 1956 presidential campaigns. For three years (1968–1971), Doty wrote the nationally syndicated strip for the irreverent television show, *Rowan & Martin's Laugh-In*. His books *Where Are You Going with That Tree?* (1976), *Where Are You Going with That Coal?* (1977), and *Where Are You Going with That Oil?* (1976) all teach the reader how each item is used, but they also advocate conscientious use of our natural resources. The *Oil* book suggests ways to conserve energy—a subject of particular interest to Doty, who for many years lived in a solar-powered house.

Most of his works express ideas with a sense of humor. As *Booklist*'s reviewer said of *Girls Can Be Anything*, "the cartoon-like illustrations . . . make the point with a smile."[11] This description also aptly describes Doty's outlook. Asked if he still enjoys the freelance illustrating that he has been doing for over sixty years, Doty replies, "Oh, what could be nicer? I sit and draw funny pictures and people send me money."[12]

NOTES

1. Jean Mercier, review of *Girls Can Be Anything*, *Publishers Weekly*, 21 May 1973, 50.

2. "Norma Klein," *Fifth Book of Junior Authors and Illustrators*, ed. Sally Holmes Holtze (New York: Wilson, 1983), 180.

3. Sally Holmes Holtze, "Klein, Norma," *Children's Books and Their Creators*, ed. Anita Silvey (Boston: Houghton Mifflin, 1995), 375.

4. "Norma Klein," *Fifth Book of Junior Authors and Illustrators* (1983), ed. Holtze, 179.

5. "Klein, Norma 1938–," *Something about the Author*, vol. 7, ed. Anne Commire (Detroit: Gale, 1975), 153.

6. Ibid., 153.

7. Irwin Fleissner, telephone interview with Philip Nel, 27 Mar. 2006.

8. "Doty, Roy 1922–," *Something about the Author*, vol. 28, ed. Anne Commire (Detroit: Gale, 1982), 100.

9. Roy Doty, telephone interview with Philip Nel, 4 Feb. 2006.

10. Ibid.

11. Review of *Girls Can Be Anything*, *Booklist*, 1 May 1973, 856.

12. Doty, telephone interview, 4 Feb. 2006.

"Now we will play Hospital," said Adam Sobel. "I will be the doctor and you will be the nurse."

Adam Sobel was Marina's best friend in her kindergarten class. They went home on the bus together and at school, in the yard, they sat and pretended to fish. They were the only ones in the class who could do the lion puzzle and get all the pieces of the mane together. Usually Marina liked the games Adam thought up, but this time she said, "I want to be the doctor too."

"You can't be doctor if *I'm* doctor," Adam said.

"Why not?" said Marina.

"There can't be two doctors," Adam said.

"So, *you* be the nurse and *I'll* be the doctor," Marina said.

"That's not the way it goes," Adam said. He was already putting on the white doctor costume that was in the costume box. "Girls are always nurses and boys are always doctors."

"Why is that?" said Marina.

"That's just the way it is," Adam said. "Could I have the stethoscope, please, Nurse?"

That night Marina told her father at dinner, "I don't like Adam Sobel at all."

"Oh?" Father said. "I thought he used to be your favorite."

"He used to be," Marina said, "but you know what he said today?"

"What?" asked Father.

"He said girls can't be doctors. They have to just be nurses."

"Well, that's just plain silly!" her father said. "Of *course* they can be doctors."

"They can?" asked Marina.

"Certainly they can," Father replied. "Why, your Aunt Rosa is a doctor. You know that."

"But is she a real one?" Marina said.

"She sure is, as real as they come," Father said.

"Does she work in a hospital and wear a white uniform?" Marina wanted to know.

"She does," Father said. "In fact, she works in the very hospital where you were born. You know what she does there?"

"What?" said Marina.

"She's a surgeon," Father said. "That's hard work, you know."

The next day at school, Marina said to Adam, "I have an aunt who's a doctor. She's a surgeon."

"Is she a real doctor?" Adam wanted to know.

"Of *course* she's real," Marina said. "She comes to our house for dinner. She even has a white uniform. . . . Lots of women are doctors. I might be one. I might be one that takes care of animals."

"That kind is called a veterinarian," Adam said. He knew a lot of long words.

"I could have my own hospital and dogs and cats would come to see me and I would make them better," Marina said. "That's the kind of doctor *I* want to be."

"I don't even want to *be* a doctor," Adam said.

"What do you want to be?" asked Marina.

"I think I want to be a pilot," Adam said.

"You mean, you'd have your own airplane and fly it from place to place?"

"Yes," Adam said. "Why don't we play airplane right now?"

"Okay," said Marina. "How do we do it?"

"Well," said Adam, "this is the plane and I sit in front driving."

"What do *I* do?" said Marina.

"You're the stewardess," Adam said. "You walk around in back and give people drinks."

So Marina poured some water in paper cups left over from juice and crackers time and walked around and gave them to all the imaginary passengers. She always asked them first if they wanted tea, coffee, or juice.

Finally, she went over to where Adam was and asked "What are you doing?"

"I'm still driving the plane," Adam said. "Oh oh —here we come. . . . It might be a crash landing. . . . Better look out."

"You know what?" Marina said.

"What?" said Adam, who was keeping his eyes on the place where the plane had to land.

"I think *I* want to be a pilot," Marina said. "*You* can't be a pilot," Adam said.

"If I want to, I can," Marina said.

"Girls can't be pilots," Adam said. "They have to be stewardesses."

"But that's dull," said Marina. And she went off and began to drive her own pretended plane.

That night in bed Marina said to her mother, "Adam Sobel is so *bad.*"

"Is he?" her mother said. "What did he do?"

"He said girls can't drive planes," Marina said. "He said they have to be stewardesses."

"That's not true," Mother said.

"Then, how come he said it?" Marina asked.

"Maybe he didn't know," Mother answered. "There was a picture of a woman in the newspaper just the other day, and she's been flying her own plane for fifteen years."

"Does she fly with people in it?" Marina asked.

"Of course!" said Mother.

"Does she fly it all by herself?" Marina said.

"Well, she has a co-pilot," Mother said. "Pilots always have co-pilots to help them."

"Mommy?"

"Yes, darling."

"If I was a pilot, would you and Daddy fly with me in my plane?"

"We certainly would."

"Would I be a good pilot, do you think?" Marina asked.

"I think you would," Mother said.

The next day at school Marina told Adam, "Today you can be my co-pilot. I'm going to be a pilot like that lady in the paper who has her own plane."

"What lady is that?" Adam said.

"Oh, I guess you didn't see her picture," Marina said. "Her plane has people in it and everything. Even her mother and father fly in it with her."

"Who is the stewardess in that plane?" Adam said.

"It's a self-service plane," Marina said. "In the back there's a little machine and you get your drinks by putting in a nickel."

"That sounds like a good idea," Adam said. He let Marina be pilot and he was co-pilot and read the map and told her where to go. There was almost a crash landing, but Marina landed in a grassy field and everyone got out safely.

That afternoon Mrs. Darling read them a story about a king and queen. They wore long red robes and had yellow crowns on their heads.

On the way home in the bus Marina said, "How about being a king? Or a queen?"

Adam thought about that for a minute. "No."

"You could have a red robe," Marina said. "You could have a crown."

Adam shook his head. "That wouldn't be comfortable. Anyway, kings and queens don't *do* anything anymore. It would be dull."

"Maybe that's true," Marina said.

"What I'd *like* to be," Adam said, "is president. That's *better* than being a king."

"President of what?" Marina wanted to know. "Just president."

"You mean *The* President?" Marina said. "That's right," Adam said.

"What would you do if you were president?" Marina asked.

"Oh," answered Adam, "I would sit in a big room with a rug on the floor and a big desk and I would sign papers and everyone would have to do whatever I said,"

"Maybe tomorrow we can play President," Marina said.

"Okay," Adam said.

"Only, the thing is," Marina said, "what would I be while you were president?"

"You could be my wife."

"What would I do if I were your wife?" asked Marina.

"Well, you could cook dinner and get the newspaper ready when I got home," Adam said. "Sometimes you could ride in a car with me and we could wave at people and they would throw confetti at us."

"That sounds like fun," Marina said, "only, Adam?"

"Listen," Adam said. "One thing I *know*. There's *never* been a woman president."

That night after supper Marina said to her mother and father, "I don't know what we're going to *do* with Adam Sobel. He says such silly things."

"What did he say today that was so silly?" her father said.

"He said there never was a woman president," Marina said.

There was a pause.

"Isn't he a silly boy!" Marina said. "I call him a dum-dum."

"Well, it's true, there's never been a woman President of the United States," Mother said.

"Have there been women presidents of other places?" said Marina.

"Other countries have had important women leaders," Father said. "Mrs. Gandhi in India. Mrs. Meir in Israel."

The next morning Marina said to Adam, "Adam, you know, *you* can be a pilot or a doctor. You know what I'm going to be?"

GOLDA MEIR INDIRA GANDHI

"What?" Adam said.

"I'm going to be the first woman President! . . . You can be my husband."

"What would I do?" Adam said.

"You would fly our plane and fly me from place to place so I could give speeches," Marina said.

"It seems like according to you girls can be anything they want," Adam said. "Well, that's just the way it is now," Marina said.

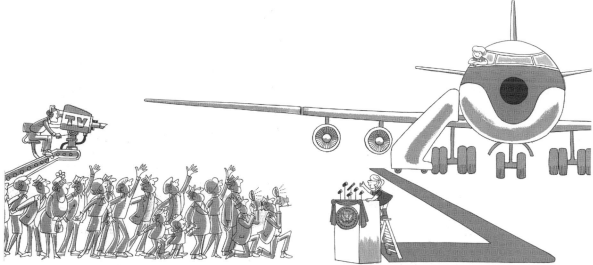

TV

"Will you fly me to where I can give my talk?"

"Okay, but after you give your talk, you have to fly me back so I can give *my* talk," Adam said.

"Okay," Marina said.

So Adam flew the plane to where Marina had to give her talk, and she gave it.

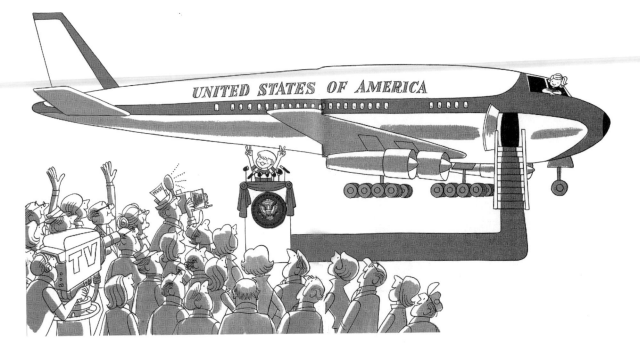

Then Marina flew Adam to where he had to give his talk, and he gave it.

Then there was a big Presidential dinner with potato chips, Coca-Cola, lollipops, Marshmallows, Juicy Fruit gum, and Tootsie Rolls for dessert.

Both Presidents thought it was delicious.

part 4

Organize

JULIA MICKENBERG & PHILIP NEL

The final verse of Florence Reese's 1930s pro-union anthem advises, "Don't scab for the bosses, / Don't listen to their lies. / Us poor folks haven't got a chance / Unless we organize." This song, with its rousing chorus of "Which side are you on?", appears in Elie Siegmeister's *Work and Sing: A Collection of the Songs That Built America* (1944), an illustrated book intended for children. As this song and *Little Rebels'* fourth section show, collective action is an important theme of the Left. Whether fighting for better working conditions, equal rights for women, or civil rights for homosexuals and people of color, those on the Left have understood that there is power in numbers. Likewise, they have recognized both the symbolic value of children in organizing campaigns, and—as these stories reflect—the importance of teaching children about unions.

In 1903, the socialist Mother Jones organized a "Children's Crusade" in which thousands of striking child mill workers joined her in a march from Philadelphia to Oyster Bay, Long Island, where President Roosevelt summered. The march highlighted the terrible working conditions in the mills that employed children. If organizing children was a dramatic way to remind people of the excesses of capitalism, an even simpler but no less powerful way was to teach children this message through literature, so that it might seem natural to them by the time they became adults.

An allegory for unions in general and socialism in particular, "Happy Valley" appeared as the opening story in *The Child's Socialist Reader* (1907), published one year after the Labour Party's first major victory in Britain. In 1906, Labour won twenty-nine seats in Parliament, leading to the passage that year of the Trade Disputes Act, which legalized picketing and granted other rights to unions. Echoing the increased support for workers' rights, "Happy Valley" chronicles the invasion of the giant Monopoly and his servants Capital and Competition. They dupe the formerly happy residents into becoming slaves of Capital—until Fairplay and his followers take action. Working together, they kill Monopoly, and Competition flees; Capital marries Fairplay, and the two "worked for the people and were happy ever after."

During the 1920s, labor gained strength in Britain while losing strength in the United States. By 1922, the Labour Party became the official opposition party in the House of Commons, having gained 144 seats. Although the first Labour government (1924) lasted only nine months, the party continued to make gains, holding 287 seats after the 1929 elections. In the United States, after a surge of strikes in the 1910s and early 1920s, the steel and coal industries all but crushed unions—though the causes for union members' grievances remained intact.[1]

The Socialist Party and radical organizing in general also suffered great setbacks in the 1920s. The party was riven by internal factions around the issues of support for World War I and the newly established Communist Party. It is significant that one of the last successful efforts of a united socialist coalition in the 1920s centered around children. This second "Children's Crusade," modeled on Mother Jones's effort two decades earlier, was organized by Kate Richards O'Hare, coeditor of the *National Rip-Saw*. In 1922, O'Hare convened the children of Socialists who were jailed as political militants or conscientious objectors during World War I for a march on Washington, with the idea of using public sympathy to unite the children with their fathers. The efforts were largely successful, with many prisoners released during or shortly after the March on Washington. But the relative dearth of radical organizing in the 1920s is reflected in our collection.

It's no coincidence that most of the stories in this section come from the 1930s. During that decade, unions grew rapidly and won legal rights in the United States. Between 1932 and 1939, union membership increased from under three million to nearly nine million.[2] Section 7(a) of the National Recovery Act (June 1933) granted employees "the right to organize and bargain collectively through representatives of their own choosing" and stated that employers did not have the right to obstruct efforts to unionize.[3]

In 1933, the Amalgamated Clothing Workers Union's membership had declined to 60,000 from nearly 180,000 in 1920. Seizing the opportunity provided by the NRA's Section 7(a), Amalgamated undertook successful organizing campaigns, nearly doubling its membership by the end of that year.[4] Published later in the decade, Amalgamated's "Mary Stays after School —or What This Union's About" (1939) shows both the hardships that strikers' families faced and the optimism that the union would prevail. When Mary, teased for being poor, laments her family's economic woes, the fairy Bright Future appears to explain that Mary's parents are courageous, fighting for a better life for their family and other working families.

Published the year the Supreme Court declared the National Recovery Act unconstitutional, Myra Page's "Pickets and Slippery Slicks" (1935) depicts workers uniting across racial lines, creating opportunities for the children of white and black workers to become friends. Though many unions had excluded black workers, a few went against that trend—notably the United Mine Workers, the driving force behind the creation of the Congress of Industrial Organizations (CIO), also in 1935. Beyond the support it garnered for industrial (and white-collar) unions, the CIO also stood out in welcoming radicals into its leadership. Though its leader, John L. Lewis, was no revolutionary, he recognized the enthusiasm and commitment that Communists, Socialists, and other radicals would bring to the organization—a move that made business leaders view the CIO as subversive.[5]

In this collection, several stories' aims are more subversive than those of major unions in the 1930s. Helen Kay's "Battle in the Barnyard" (1932), Oscar Saul and Lou Lantz's *The Revolt of the Beavers* (1936), and A. Redfield's *Mr. His* (1939) present organizing as a means not just for securing better working conditions but for overthrowing capitalist rulers. In "Battle in the Barnyard," chickens kill the selfish rooster (who has been in charge) and drive out the barnyard aristocracy, creating a community in which each member gets a fair share of the food. Similarly, the title character of *Mr. His* flees Histown when its citizens unite to reclaim the resources for the people. In *Revolt of the Beavers*, two children aid the beavers in returning their exiled leader and liberating Beaverland from its corrupt Chief and his gang, securing ample food and clothes for all.

The year after *Revolt of the Beavers* was published, the Supreme Court upheld the Wagner Act (passed initially in 1935), ushering in a new era for labor. Before the act, companies—often aided by the police—literally battled workers on strike, often killing strikers. The Wagner Act established the right of workers to organize and created a mechanism for addressing labor disputes: the National Labor Relations Board. Though labor disputes still resulted in some violent confrontations outside of factories, the struggle began moving off the streets and into committee rooms and courtrooms.[6]

During World War II, unions pledged not to strike —and, although there were strikes (especially in 1943 and 1944), there were far fewer, as union leaders worked to keep the lid on discontent during the war.

Published just before the U.S. entry into the war, Jerome Schwartz's *Oscar the Ostrich* (1940) stresses the need for unity against fascist tyrants, represented by a tyrannical ostrich who hoards all the sand dunes. Henry Felsen's *The Company Owns the Tools* (1942, written under the name Henry Vicar), a novel for older readers, reflects labor's wartime truce with capital. Although the novel does depict battles between workers and management, its solution is not to overthrow the bosses. Instead, the novel asks each group to recognize its responsibilities and to work together.

At the end of the war, the labor movement's numbers were at record highs: its 14.5 million members comprised more than 35 percent of the civilian labor force.[7] Reflecting unions' new power, progressive children's fiction of the 1940s tends not to emphasize the struggle of labor versus capital, but rather presents the need for unions as a given. In the midst of teaching children how ice cream and lollipops are made, Mary Elting Folsom's *The Lollipop Factory* (1946) briefly mentions why unions are important: they can oppose speedups. Likewise, Clara Hollos's *The Story of Your Coat* (1948) focuses on the many different jobs involved in the production of a coat but also notes (in passing) how unions have improved working conditions in the garment industry.

Unions suffered a setback with the Taft-Hartley Act (1947), which severely amended the Wagner Act. It prohibited union contributions to political campaigns, required leaders to sign statements affirming that they were not Communists, and instituted several means through which the government could intervene to avert strikes. But unions continued to thrive in the 1950s and 1960s. Perhaps reflecting this strength, Leo Lionni's *Swimmy* (1963) tells of one little black fish (the title character) who organizes other little red fish to swim in the shape of a big fish—the black fish serves as the eye. Though Lionni says the book's "central moment" is Swimmy's artistic vision,[8] the united little fishes' ability to swim safely amidst dangerous large fishes certainly emphasizes the notion that a union can empower the apparently powerless.

In the 1960s, Cesar Chávez's attempts to secure higher wages for California grape pickers captured national attention. Echoing this interest in farm workers' rights, Sandra Weiner's *small hands, big hands: Seven Profiles of Chicano Migrant Workers and Their Families* (1970) highlights the need for union representation.

Frustrated that her parents and seven siblings receive a total of seven dollars for twelve hours' work, Doria Ramirez speaks up, asking the growers for more money. Then, she works to organize a union, hoping, as she says, that "the dream of a union will come true. It's just like Martin Luther King when he said, 'I have a dream too.'"

Recent decades have brought many children's books that show what can be accomplished when people work together. Angela Johnson and Eric Velasquez's *A Sweet Smell of Roses* (2005) follows children joining a civil rights march in the early 1960s. If that book uses realism to demonstrate the power of unity, many other works deliver this message more fancifully. Martin Waddell and Helen Oxenbury's *Farmer Duck* (1991) shows farm animals uniting to expel a lazy farmer, alleviating the great burden carried by the overworked duck (who did all the chores while the farmer relaxed). After the farmer's departure, the animals share the labor of running the farm. In Doreen Cronin and Betsy Lewin's *Click, Clack, Moo: Cows That Type* (2000), cows and hens strike until Farmer Brown gives them electric blankets. They succeed, as do the title characters of Toby Speed and Barry Root's *Brave Potatoes* (2000). Rising up against Chef Hackemup, the brave potatoes toss him into the soup and triumphantly lead the vegetables out of the kitchen, and to freedom. Though these stories are more comic than their twentieth-century predecessors, they nonetheless underscore the lesson that —to paraphrase Florence Reese—those without power haven't got a chance unless they organize.

NOTES

1. Robert H. Zieger, *American Workers, American Unions*, 2d ed. (Baltimore, MD: Johns Hopkins UP, 1994), 9.

2. Zieger, 26.

3. *National Industrial Recovery Act*, 16 June 1933. *Historical Documents*: <http://www.historicaldocuments.com/National-IndustrialRecoveryAct.htm>. 13 Jan. 2007.

4. Zieger, 31.

5. Zieger, 52.

6. Zieger, 40.

7. Zieger, 100.

8. Leo Lionni, *Between Worlds: The Autobiography of Leo Lionni* (New York: Knopf, 1997), 232.

16

"Happy Valley," from
The Child's Socialist Reader (1907)

Illustrated by Walter Crane
(1845–1915)

EDITORS' INTRODUCTION

Born in Liverpool, Walter Crane was the son of Thomas Crane, a portrait painter. In his father's studio, Crane displayed a talent for drawing, creating portraits of his own when he was but six years old. A few months before his father's death in 1859, Crane gained an apprenticeship to wood engraver William James Linton, who was so impressed with Crane's work that he took him on without the usual fee.[1]

Linton was Crane's mentor in more ways than one: he prepared him for a career in book illustration, but he also guided the teenaged Crane's sympathies towards socialism. Before Crane became "the artist of socialism,"[2] however, he became famous for his children's books. Following three years with Linton, he went to work for printer Edmund Evans, where his bold use of color, detailed style, and carefully integrated design earned Crane the reputation as "the father of the illustrated children's book."[3] As illustrator or author-illustrator, Crane created over eighty books for children, including *The Absurd Alphabet* and adaptations of nursery rhymes and fairy tales such as *One, Two, Buckle My Shoe*, *Jack and the Beanstalk*, *The Frog Prince*, and *Puss in Boots*. After he became a father (he had married in 1871), Crane also created picture books for his three children—Lionel, Lancelot, and Beatrice.

He illustrated *The Child's Socialist Reader* (1907), in which "Happy Valley" appears, after he had become a Socialist. Key to this political affiliation was Crane's friendship with William Morris, Socialist and founder of the Arts and Crafts Movement. In the 1880s, Crane joined this movement, which, as he saw it, sought to restore "design and craftsmanship" to even "the humblest object and material," as a protest against the ugliness wrought by industrialization.[4] His own work as an engraver and Arts and Crafts' emphasis on the work of craftsmen made Crane a natural convert to socialism. Speaking of his leanings in that direction, Crane later said, "I imagine that as people can be roughly divided into Socialists and Individualists, so they can be subdivided into conscious Socialists and unconscious Socialists. I believe I really belonged to the latter long before I knew I belonged to the former."[5] In 1883, he joined the Socialist Democratic Federation and began giving speeches and creating artwork for the cause, his winged "Freedom" (1885) and "Triumph of Labour" (1891) being two of his most famous. He aligned himself with the Fabians, whose best-known members were George Bernard Shaw, Hubert Bland, E. Nesbit, and H. G. Wells. Crane shared the Fabians' belief that education, rather than revolution, was the best way to defeat capitalism and adopt socialism. However, when in 1900 the Fabians failed to oppose British participation in the Boer War, Crane parted ways with the group.

As demonstrated by his illustrations for socialist publications and for children's books like *The Child's Socialist Reader* and Frederick James Gould's *Pages for Young Socialists* (1913), Crane remained committed to socialism until the end of his life. In its obituary for Crane, the London *Times* wrote, "More even than [William] Morris, he was the artist of the Socialist movement."[6]

The author of *The Child's Socialist Reader* is not known.

NOTES

1. Isobel Spencer, *Walter Crane* (New York: Macmillan, 1975), 15.

2. Ibid., 8.

3. Susan E. Meyer, *A Treasury of the Great Children's Illustrators* (New York: Abrams, 1997 [1983]), 82.

4. Crane, qtd. in Spencer, 101.

5. Crane, qtd. in Spencer, 141.

6. "Death of Mr. Walter Crane," [London] *Times*, 16 Mar. 1915, 12.

Once upon a time—when the world was still beautiful, and, instead of ugly factory chimneys belching forth hideous smoke, fair gardens and orchards made the air sweet and fragrant, and the sun shone golden on the corn; when good fairies flew from home to home in the broad daylight, and were not afraid, and men and women welcomed them, and were glad the live-long day—far away, in the heart of the country, there lay a pretty valley.

Poppies nodded amongst the corn, and grew rosy when a bold ear stooped and tickled them. The children never wanted to steal apples, for they could always pick them for the asking. No notice-boards, saying "Trespassers will be prosecuted," were to be seen, so there were no naughty little elves to run round and whisper into children's ears how nice it would be to trespass. But then there were no fences to climb over, although there were plenty of trees to climb up, and I daresay the children tore their clothes sometimes, and gave their mothers plenty of trouble in this way. Still, on the whole, children and grown people, too, were very happy, and the good fairies grew fat and lazy through having no work to do.

One day the people were startled to hear a curious, rumbling sound, and the whole earth seemed to shake. If they had ever heard of such a thing they would have thought it was an earthquake—but they never had.

The noise grew louder and louder, until a crowd of people, with scared faces and eyes and mouths wide open with fright, came running into Happy Valley. When they had recovered themselves they were able to tell what they had seen.

A terrible monster—a giant, they said—was coming, and with him two horrible dwarfs, who seemed to be his servants, as they were carrying his baggage, consisting of two enormous sacks, upon their shoulders.

Sure enough, they had no sooner finished their story than the rumbling grew louder, and the people saw a hideous giant, with the two misshapen dwarfs on either side.

When the giant saw the prosperous little valley his eyes began to sparkle, until the country-side was lit up, as though with lightning; but seeing the men and women running from him in fear, he stopped short in his descent, and sent one of his servants on in front to speak to them.

GIANT MONOPOLY
ENTERING THE HAPPY VALLEY

Seeing that the giant appeared inclined to be friendly, the people gathered round the dwarf to hear what he had to say.

"My good people," said he, "I come from my master, Monopoly, who, seeing that you are unnecessarily frightened of him, bids me tell you to be of good cheer. For, though he could easily crush you with one stamp of his foot, he has no such unkind intention; but, indeed, only wishes to be your very good friend and to render you all the service in his power."

At this the people began to pluck up courage, and although a few still had some misgivings (for the dwarf was so terribly ugly) yet most of them began to feel ashamed of their fears.

"My name," continued the dwarf, "is Capital, and I and my fellow-servant, Competition, have worked many years for our master, who is the best of all possible masters, and treats us exceedingly well. Seeing your poor little valley, with its miserable orchards, and knowing how hard you have to work to make your corn grow and how few nice things you get in return for your work—my master (with his usual kindness of heart) has taken pity on you, and will show you how, by working for him, you can have a great deal more comfort. Indeed, if you are industrious, you may become rich as he—look!

With that the dwarf opened the sack he was carrying, and poured out its contents—a number of glittering gold pieces, which came tumbling out before the astonished gaze of the people.

Now a curious thing happened—at the sound of the tinkling gold all the good fairies spread their wings and flew right away.

It was not long before the dazzled people were persuaded to accompany the dwarf to his master; and, following the servant's instructions, knelt at the feet of the giant to receive his blessing and words of advice. First he flattered them by telling them how sensible they were to come to him as they had done; and the people were just beginning to think that they were very wise indeed, when he began to call them fools.

"See here!" he said, "have you not been spending all the best years of your life in growing a little corn and fruit for yourselves, when under your cornfields there lies a gold-mine, which would make you and your children rich for ever?"

At this the people looked at each other in astonishment, and some were for running to dig at once to see if it were true. But the giant roared with laughter. "Do you think, with your foolish little spades, that you can unearth the gold which lies deep hidden in the earth?" he said. "No, no! my friends." Then, seeing their disappointment, he added: "But I will tell you what I will do. I will give you spades with which to dig all the gold you want, but I shall expect you to give me a share in return."

At this the people were delighted, and cried out how good and generous kind Giant Monopoly was, and they set to work to build him a great palace to live in, for none of their homes were large enough for him.

If you could have seen Happy Valley a year after the giant came you would have been surprised at the change which had come over it—surprised, and sorry, too, I think. For instead of the laughing cornfields and orchards, great ugly pits yawned everywhere; even the sparkling rivulets were turned to dirty, muddy streams, as the people threw the earth into them and washed their gold in them. Oh, yes! there was gold, plenty of it. The giant's spades (each of which took 100 men to dig with) tore up a whole cornfield with one spadeful, and there it lay—a great glittering mass.

But now, see how cunning old Monopoly was!

He took a great sack and held it out before the people. "When this sack is full," he said, "the rest of the gold shall be yours, and I will only take this for my share."

"Very reasonable," said everyone; "of course there will be plenty left for us." So they shovelled up the gold with a will, and poured it into the sack.

But (poor, silly things!) they could not see the hole in the other end of the sack, and that as fast as they filled it the gold ran out, and was gathered up by Monopoly and carried off to his palace.

Soon, however, the people grew very weary of trying to fill a sack that was never full. They began to want food, but no one had any time to get it, and their orchards and cornfields had all been dug up. The giant, seeing that they were likely to die from hunger, and that he might have to turn to and dig up his own gold, called his servant Competition, and bade him throw a handful of gold amongst them. This the people scrambled for, and some were knocked over and killed in the tussle, and some who got a few lumps gave it away to their fellows in exchange for the food they were so sorely needing.

So this went on for years, and the people grew more and more afraid of the giant, and many hated him because they had seen the hole in the sack, but they dared say nothing about it.

One day a young man, called Fairplay, instead of going to work in the gold-mines, sat down to think. Now, everyone knows that if you want to do more work than you can manage in a day, it is no use to sit down and think about it, or you will not do any at all. And this is what happened to Fairplay. The more he thought, the more disinclined he was to work, and the end of it was that, instead of going to work at the goldmines he went wandering away and away, until at last he lost sight of Happy Valley altogether, and found himself in the heart of the country.

"What beautiful fields and woods," thought he; "why should I not stay here, and live on berries and mushrooms?" So he set to work, and built himself a little home of wood, and here for a short time he lived very happily.

But he had not been long in his little hut when he began to feel very, very sorry for his fellowmen toiling so miserably without enough to eat.

"How can I free them," thought he, "from that terrible tyrant, Monopoly? We must kill him; but I, alone, cannot do it. I must get others to join me."

So back he went to the Valley, but when his fellows

saw him they all began to jeer. "Here is a lazy fellow, who won't work," said they; and they threw stones at him. "Better stone Monopoly," cried Fairplay, "for not only will he not work, but he grabs all the gold for which you work so hard for himself."

But they hooted and stoned him all the more for that; only some went home and thought over what he had said.

These few sought out Fairplay afterwards, and asked him what he meant.

"Have you seen the hole in the sack?" said he. And they nodded silently.

Then he told them his plan, of how they must free themselves from the giant and his servants, and they agreed to help him.

Lo! one night, when the giant was asleep, a long procession wound round the valley. First came Fairplay, with his followers; after them the women and children; and after them quite an army of fairies, each with a glittering sword in his hand. They knocked at the door of the palace, and killed the terrible giant, and his servant, Competition, ran away and was seen no more in Happy Valley.

"But what about Capital?" you ask.

Well, I am coming to that. When they tried to find him they could not see the ugly old dwarf anywhere, but, instead, found a beautiful princess, whose long, golden hair reached to the floor.

"The giant wanted to marry me," she told them; "and when I would have nothing to do with him he turned me into an ugly dwarf, and made me work for him. Dear people, you have made me free! To show you my gratitude I will work for you all my life."

So Princess Capital married Fairplay, and they worked for the people, and were happy ever after.

17

"Battle in the Barnyard," from *Battle in the Barnyard: Stories and Pictures for Workers' Children* (1932)

Written by Helen Kay (Helen Colodny Goldfrank, 1912–2002), Illustrated by Juanita Preval (1905–?)

EDITORS' INTRODUCTION

In the mid-1930s, when *New Masses* writer Jean Simon surveyed the "small but sturdy collection" of works for children "which are making an honest attempt to tell children just what is happening around them," the book she singled out for having the widest appeal was Helen Kay's *Battle in the Barnyard*. "It ought to be an excellent supplementary text in Class Struggle, expressing the struggle between exploiter and exploited in terms of ants, chickens, and pelicans," she wrote. Simon felt the excellent illustrations and the picture-book form could make the book appealing to younger children. Still, she conceded, "children of picture-book age would probably fail to make the desired and necessary association between the barnyard and its human counterpart."[1] Whether or not children would have picked up on the class warfare that is central to the tale's moral, the animal drama makes the book's title story more than dreary dogma. It also gives present-day readers a rather striking look into how the revolutionary fervor of the early 1930s translated into literature for children.

Beyond positive reviews in the left-wing press, *Battle in the Barnyard* (intended for use with the communist children's organization, the Young Pioneers) did not attract a great deal of attention. Ironically, when Helen Kay did earn notoriety as a red author, it was for the apolitical *Apple Pie for Lewis* (1951), her first story to win critical acclaim. That story also has the dubious distinction of being the only book for young children to be banned from U.S. overseas libraries—not because there is anything political about it but because Kay refused to cooperate with the House Committee on Un-American Activities, which called her to testify in 1953.[2]

As the daughter of Russian immigrants who supported the Bolshevik revolution, Kay had been an activist since childhood. Self-educated, she began her writing career at a young age. She wrote the stories in *Battle in the Barnyard* as a teenage member of the Young Pioneers, and the book was published a few years later, when Kay was a Pioneer leader and editor of the group's magazine, the *New Pioneer*.

Prior to having children, Kay had been a Communist Party activist and a labor journalist, writing for union publications as well as various left-wing periodicals. In her twenties, she worked for the Communist Party as a courier, taking supplies and funds into Nazi Germany in support of the resistance. This work, combined with travel to the Soviet Union and membership in a variety of communist-affiliated organizations, put Kay under suspicion by the FBI, which made repeated but unsuccessful attempts to link her to notorious "spy ring" figures like Elizabeth Bentley and Whittaker Chambers.[3]

Although Kay's refusal to cooperate with the House Committee on Un-American Activities brought her national attention, she still managed to salvage a career as a children's author, publishing over thirty books. She never again published work that was as political as *Battle in the Barnyard*, but she remained proud of this book, and read it to her children and grandchildren.[4] In the 1950s and 1960s, she was active in the Loose Enders, a group of left-wing children's authors that included Eve Merriam (see pages 187–88).

Kay's work organizing Pennsylvania miners earned her a place in Lauren Gilfillan's roman-à-clef, *I Went to Pit College* (1934). Her antifascist work in Germany may have inspired Lillian Hellman's memoir, *Pentimento* (1973), which was later made into the movie *Julia* (1977).[5]

Juanita Preval was born in Milwaukee and studied at the Milwaukee Institute of Art and Design. She left Milwaukee to pursue a fellowship at the McDowell art colony in New Hampshire and later moved to New York City, where she began to contribute artwork to communist publications such as the *Workers Monthly* (1924–1927).[6] She was probably involved with the John Reed Club in New York City, which promoted the work of aspiring radical writers and artists.[7] She illustrated Myra Page's *Gathering Storm: A Story of the Black Belt* (1932), a novel based on the Gastonia strike (see Page, page 106). She became distinguished as a painter, her work appearing at major museums in New York and the Midwest. Marrying the Italian Girolamo Piccoli, a painter, sculptor, and fellow radical, Preval made her home in Rome, Italy. She continued to paint and exhibit her work in Italy and in the United States.[8]

NOTES

1. Jean Simon, "Which Books for Your Children?" *New Masses*, 24 Dec. 1935, 23, 24.

2. *New York Times*, 22 June 1953, 8. The transcript of her testimony is available online. See http://www.senate.gov/artandhistory/history/resources/pdf/Volume2.pdf#search=%22Helen%20Goldfrank%22.

3. See FBI file for Helen Colodny Goldfrank, FOIPA No. 0990202-000. The file, incidentally, makes no mention of *Battle in the Barnyard*.

4. Joan Goldfrank, interview with Julia Mickenberg, 14 July 2006.

5. Joan Goldfrank, interview with Julia Mickenberg, 22 Dec. 2003.

6. Virginia Hagelstein Marquardt, "Art on the Political Front in America: From *The Liberator* to *Art Front*," *Art Journal* 52:1 (1993): 75.

7. In 1930, she signed a statement sponsored by the John Reed Club of New York City protesting civil liberties violations and wrongful arrests of radicals. "'Red Scare' Protest Issued by Liberals," *New York Times*, 19 May 1930, 18.

8. Additional biographical information on Juanita Preval Piccoli from exhibition pamphlet, Galleria Selene Cortina, 1965. Courtesy of Lewis Golfrank, with translation by Dolora Chapelle Wojciehowski.

Out in the country where the fields are green and the sunshine is golden, an old farm stands between two groves of tall poplar trees. On this farm there lived at one time a happy colony of healthy chickens.

Now the yard where these chickens lived was filled with very fertile soil. The rich ground contained a plentiful amount of worms upon which the chickens lived. There were long skinny worms, short stubby worms, and big fat worms. There were as many kinds of worms as there are people. Besides worms a great variety of caterpillars and bugs helped these chicks lead a healthy well-nourished life.

In a corner of the yard where the chickens scratched away their time ran a refreshing spring. This spring was used by the chickens to quench their parched throats in the hot summer days.

Many a happy day was passed by these roosters and hens. The chickens would rise with the sun, scratch for worms, drink water from the spring, cackling and crowing merrily all the while. The hens would lay eggs—and then tell the world about it in delight.

"Cut-cut-cut-ca-dah-cut!" they would cry. Just as if they were trying to say, "I've laid an egg, the loveliest white egg!"

The little downy chicks would play tag and leapfrog between their eating times, to while away the time until they in turn would grow up and become hens and roosters.

The cocks would strut about the farm in their conceited manner, crowing and asking the world if it had not noticed their handsome plumage. "Cock-a-doodle-do!" "Am I not a handsome bird. Am I not. Am I not!"

Then at the setting of the sun the chicken farm would become dark and silent—closed in the embrace of slumber.

On this farm, however, there was one very sly ugly rooster, who had lost most of his fine feathers in his quarrels and fights with the other more sociable inmates of the farm. He would always take advantage of the young chicks. Being a very lazy fellow he would try to get out of doing his own scratching for worms.

For instance, when a younger cock would dig up a dainty morsel from the rich loam, such as a lively young earthworm, this ugly monster would immediately pounce upon his comrade's dinner and gobble it all up. Yes, every single bit of it. This nasty habit made him very much hated by all the others on the farm.

One day the entire colony was amazed. They were in fact so astonished at the sight before their eyes that words actually failed them. Even some of the more talkative hens who always had something to cackle about, couldn't find their tongues.

Dear little comrades, it actually was an unusual sight, for there before their eyes, they saw for the first time this nasty rooster scratching away for worms! But what surprised them even more was that this greedy creature did not eat the worms he unearthed. He put them away. As many worms as he dug up he would lay in a pile on the ground.

The inhabitants of the colony became nervous. Such a state of affairs was impossible. They were unable to understand it. Something had to be done about it.

One evening at the setting of the sun, a huge mass meeting was called. It was advertised far and wide by the young cocks, who would perch themselves on high fences and, flapping their wings, would crow the order for the meeting.

At this gathering the rooster was asked by the patriarchs and industrious hens of the colony, what the meaning of the huge pile of luscious worms meant.

The rooster promptly answered. "Here, I have a huge pile of tasty bugs, caterpillars, and worms . . ." He paused cleverly to let the audience take in the sight. "If you will give me the corner of this yard where the spring runs—and allow me to keep it all to myself— I will give you in return that huge pile of food."

Without further thought the chicken community decided to do as the rooster bargained. His food was evenly divided among all the members of the village and in return he received that section of the yard where the cool spring ran.

The chickens gossiped among themselves—telling each other how stupid the old rooster was to desire that bit of land in return for the delicious pile of eatables.

After an hour or so everyone retired for the night. The sun set and the farm was dark and silent.

The next morning the chickens arose as usual. The sun was up and shining brightly. The. day became very hot and uncomfortable. The inmates of the farm grew very thirsty and as was their habit they strolled over to the spring to quench their thirst. However, as they came within reach of the precious water, the mean rooster arose and said:

"Cock-a-doodle-do!
This spring does not belong to you
It's mine, you cannot drink here!"

The thirsty chickens exclaimed, "What do you mean yours! It is everyone's."

The cock immediately answered, "Didn't you sell it to me yesterday in return for the food that you have already eaten?"

A young rebellious cock cried out, "But we are thirsty You cannot keep the water from us. We wish to drink."

The rooster replied, "For every drink of water that you take out of my spring, I will in return take two worms!"

Since the chickens were very thirsty they consented to this arrangement.

The pile of worms which the old miserly cock reaped from the toil of the chickens began to grow by leaps and bounds. As a matter of fact it grew so large that he alone could not care for it. So he hired ten of the strongest young roosters on the farm to be his policemen.

Their job was to take care of and to protect his hoard of worms. In return, he promised to give them enough water and food to live on, no more nor no less. No less—because he had to have strong husky well-nourished policemen to take care of and guard the surplus that he now lived upon. He would give them no more—because this wicked rooster wanted more and more for himself.

This state of affairs went on for a long time. The chicken colony lost its usual happy satisfied expression. They did not crow as joyously as they did before. The young chickens were afraid to be merry. They were underfed and undernourished. They could no longer play without fear of disturbing the selfish cock. The hens could no longer lay good eggs, because they lacked food, and entertainment. They now had to labor from sunrise to sunset so that they could have enough food to live on, and enough food to give to the cruel rooster in return for the water that they so badly needed.

The chicks who were born during this period were generally not strong enough to live. Most of them died

and the tragic part was that those who did survive took the condition that now existed for granted. They thought it was impossible to live any other way.

On the other hand the rooster grew bigger and fatter. His daughter also grew bigger and fatter. Neither had to work. They merely ate and played all day. They lived off the toil and sweat of their fellow chicks.

Now, on the farm there was a duck, a very hand-some graceful duck. He would waddle and quack all through the chicken farm. One day the rooster decided to marry his daughter to the duck, in order that she would become a duchess, and so be one of the nobility.

The rooster went up to the duck and said, "If you marry my daughter, and so make her a duchess, I will give you a share of my grounds and make you a partner in my food association. You will not have to scratch for your worms, but will live off the worms that the other chickens scratch up. You will lead a life of luxury and play, if you do this."

The duck agreed. And so they were married. They had little aristocratic duck-chicks born to lead lives of idleness.

One day one of the roosters was tired of feeding the mean cock, and going hungry himself. He ran up single handed to the old miser and started to fight him. Of course, he was immediately killed by the police. This incident added to the suffering and to the downtrodden conditions of the other chickens. But they always remembered the brave young cock.

Soon after this occurred, the ugly miser got another idea. He called over some more chickens. He told them that he would pay them more than the policemen if they would act as preachers.

"Your duty," he said, "is to tell the chickens to be submissive and obey me, the apostle of the lord in the heavens above. If they are submissive and do everything I and my family order them to do, when they die they will go to heaven, and there lead happy lives. But, if they rebel they will go down to the fires of hell and burn forever. The harder they work here on earth, the better time they will have in heaven."

As time went on the chickens slaved harder and harder, and the rooster grew richer and richer. They began to believe whatever the preacher chickens told them. They thought that conditions must always be as they are. That the greater amount of chickens should be poor and that a privileged few must live off the wealth that the poor chickens scratched up.

One young and energetic cock who was deeply impressed by all the goings on, began to think. He thought and planned, and others helped him. Then they all decided that the only way to save the chickens of the farm, and themselves, from endless slavery was by driving out the selfish rooster, his daughter, the duchess, her husband, the duck, and the aristocratic duck-chicks, also their protectors, the policemen, and especially the preachers.

Secret leaflets were printed and spread over the colony for the chickens to read and to learn the truth. Huge mass meetings were called and the exploited chicks were organized into battalions to drive out their oppressors.

The chicken colony was in a state of excitement. If they won the battle, they would again be free chickens. If they lost—no one wanted to think of that. They must win.

And dear little comrades, they did win. They certainly were victorious. They drove the old rooster and his protectors, out of their lives forever. The mean cock and his lazy good-for-nothing family were killed. The preachers and policemen fled from the farm. No one has ever heard of them since. Perhaps the wolves ate them.

Now in the summer when the fields are green and the sunshine is golden in the country you can see the hens happily laying eggs, and the other chickens scratching away for worms. They have learned their lesson, and never again will anyone be able to trick them into slavery. The little chicks play tag and leap frog in their merry way. You can hear them go "Peep-peep-peep!" The roosters strut around the farm and crow, "Cock-a-doodle-do!" The hens cry, "Cluck-cluck-cluck!" They are all contented and equal.

18

"Pickets and Slippery Slicks," from
New Pioneer Story Book (1935)

Written by Myra Page
(Dorothy Gary Markey,
1897–1993), Illustrated by
Lydia Gibson (1891–1969)

EDITORS' INTRODUCTION

Dorothy Gary Markey, who used the pseudonym Myra Page, grew up in Newport News, Virginia, where her father was a prominent physician. While studying at a small women's college in Virginia, Page became active in the YWCA, at that time a significant player in social reform, especially in the area of race relations. Page began graduate work at Columbia University in 1919, taking classes from educator and philosopher John Dewey at Teachers College; studying anthropology with Franz Boas and Melvin Herskovitz, both of whom challenged the prevailing theories about racial hierarchies; and sitting in on courses at Union Seminary with the radical theologian Harry Ward (father of Lynd Ward—see *North Star Shining*, pages 175–82). She also attended the socialist Rand School, where she met the radical intellectual Scott Nearing and journalist Anna Louise Strong, who had recently returned from the Soviet Union. Becoming increasingly political, Page became active in the Amalgamated Clothing Workers Union in Philadelphia, where she worked in a sweatshop and participated in a strike. In the early 1920s, she joined the Communist Party in Minnesota, where she had moved to pursue a Ph.D. in sociology at the University of Minnesota. Page taught briefly at Wheaton College in Massachusetts but then decided to devote her time to writing and "the movement."

In "Pickets and Slippery Slicks," the white and black children playing "slippery slicks" by the creek recreated an incident from Page's childhood: she and her brother often played this game with an African-American boy, Tom, whose grandmother worked for Page's family. Their friendship ended suddenly when the children were told they could no longer play together. Page recalled later, "our friendship with Tom and the terrible way it ended left a deep impression on me. It created

a drive in my life to find a solution to the race problem so that people could live together as brothers and sisters."[1]

The story also recalls the wave of strikes in southern textile mills in the late 1920s and the Communist Party's efforts to use the strikes, especially the militant struggle in Gastonia's Loray Mill, to press for racial equality.[2] Page had conducted her doctoral research in this region and, in addition to writing her dissertation (published in 1929 as *Southern Cotton Mills and Labor*), Page used this research as the basis of *Gathering Storm: A Story of the Black Belt* (1932), one of at least six novels inspired by the Gastonia strike. The conclusion of "Pickets and Slippery Slicks" implies that the interracial friendship was resumed thanks to a strike that joined blacks and whites in common cause. In actual fact, the communist push for equality in the National Textile Workers' union stopped short of a push for social equality between blacks and whites, and Page's portrait was clearly idealized.[3] Moreover, despite Page's strong commitment to fighting racism, her portrait of Pa Morgan as a banjo-picking teller of Uncle Remus stories betrays some of the stereotypes that she absorbed during her southern childhood.

Page edited the communist children's magazine *New Pioneer*, which published this story, and she wrote for a range of left-wing publications. Besides *Gathering Storm*, Page wrote two other novels, *With Sun in Our Blood* (1950) and *Moscow Yankee* (1935), the latter based on her experiences visiting the Soviet Union. During the Red Scare of the 1950s, Page published two biographies for children using her real name, Dorothy Markey, because no one would publish work by "Myra Page." She worked actively for civil rights and collaborated with the famed Rosa Parks through their shared involvement with the Highlander Folk School. Page remained committed to the radical movement all her life, although she gradually moved away from the Communist party.[4]

For information on Lydia Gibson, see the introduction to "The Teacup Whale," pp. 151–52.

NOTES

1. Christina Looper Baker, *In a Generous Spirit: A First-Person Biography of Myra Page* (Urbana: U of Illinois P, 1996), 113.

2. As Draper recalls, the Gastonia strike became the testing ground both for the Comintern's "third period" thesis, which insisted that a revolutionary resurgence beginning in 1928 would continue the gains of the 1917 Russian revolution,

and for the Resolution on the Negro Question, which insisted that "[e]very effort must be made to see that all the new unions organized by the left wing and the Communist Party should embrace the workers of all nationalities and of all races." Theodore Draper, "Gastonia Revisited," *Social Research* 38 (Spring 1971): 20.

3. Draper, 22.

4. Baker, 194, 191.

PICKETS AND SLIPPERY SLICKS

"Come on, Charlie, let's go to the crik." Myrtle's tightly braided pigtails popped up and down in an excited way.

The creek flowed through a shaded lane of overhanging trees. Birds trilled lazily as Charlie and Myrtle sat on the bank, and contemplated the cool mud oozing up between their dusky toes. The South Carolina sun danced across their mahogany-tinted arms and legs.

"Look," Charlie pointed, "there's two lil' white kids a-comin' this way." He had spied Billy and Sam on their daily trip for a wade in the creek.

"Uh-huh," and Myrtle pushed the wooden craft she had fashioned out of a stick, with its twig mast and scrap of pink cotton sail, further out into the stream.

For a while the four paddled around in the water, in opposite directions. Billy and Sam eyed Myrtle's small craft enviously. Theirs had no sails. "Mebbe we kin make sails, too," and Billy tore a square from his ragged shirt sleeve, and set to work.

Following their crafts as they floated down-stream the four children came alongside one another.

Presently, Charlie, tiring of this sport, had a bright idea. "Say, Myrtle, look at that thar bank. Le's play slippery slicks." In a flash they were carrying water in old tins or broken bottles they found nearby, to wet the slope's side. Then solemnly they stood at the top of the bank, and quickly slid to the water's edge. Giggling, they started back up.

Fascinated, Billy and Sam followed suit. This was a new game to them. Myrtle hit upon the plan that one must earn a slide down, by crawling up the slippery slope on hands and knees. There were many slips, tumbles, and laughs before the top was reached. But now the slide down seemed twice as sweet.

This was the beginning of the friendship between Charlie and Myrtle and Billy and Sam. Every day, unknown to their elders at work in the mill, two tow heads and two kinky ones would spend happy hours along the creek's bank, floating boats, on its muddy waters or sliding down its inviting slopes. For children, like nature, know no color line.

Humans are humans to them. Of race and class they know nothing and care less, until their elders, trained in the ways of a world divided into classes, take them in hand.

Billy and Sam were sitting, very uncomfortable, on the stiff-backed bench in the Baptist Sunday School of the village church, owned and operated by the company for its white mill hands. The teacher, a poor third-cousin-once-removed of Mr. Haines, who made her living by teaching in the village grammar-school week days and all year round in Sunday School, was now holding forth on the Fatherhood of God and the Brotherhood of Man. Her text was "Little Children, Love One Another." She had explained how the mill owners and workers were really one big family, of elder and younger brothers.

"Miss Houghton, is black and white folks brothers, too?" Billy interrupted to ask.

Miss Houghton gave him a suspicious glance over her spectacles. It was clear, however, that the child was not trying to trap her, but was in earnest.

"Of course not. That is, in the sight of God, but not—Billy, what makes you ask such a question?"

"Wal," Billy squirmed, suddenly self-conscious. "I dunno. I just—"

Sam tried to help him out. "You see, Charlie 'n' Myrtle's colored 'n' I guess—"

"Who," demanded Miss Houghton, scenting trouble, "are Myrtle and Charlie?"

"They live over to Back Row, 'n' their Ma 'n' Pa work at the mill. 'N' we-uns play slide together."

"What! You two play with little niggers?" Her scorn withered the two boys. All eyes were on them; some one sniggered. Miss Houghton, very red in the face, said a good deal more, about Anglo-Saxon purity and white supremacy and a lot of words that Billy and Sam couldn't understand. But one thing she did make clear. They were in disgrace. They had done a shameful thing by playing slide with Charlie and Myrtle.

Miss Houghton lost no time in making a trip to the Crenshaws, and informing Sal, their mother, of what had happened. Sal, in tears, gave them a good talkin'-to, and had Uncle Nat administer a sound thrashing. For weeks Billy and Sam never went near the creek.

Myrtle and Charlie, puzzled at first by the absence of their friends, wondered if they had fallen sick. The yearly epidemic of typhoid fever was raging on the hill. Maybe Billy and Sam were sick, dying, maybe dead? So Charlie and Myrtle took their courage in their hands,

and ventured into the forbidden land of Row Hill. Going around to the back door of the Crenshaws, they knocked timidly on the door. Sal came to the screen.

"Please, ma'am, is Billy 'n' Sam sick or dyin'?" they queried.

"No," she shouted raising a broom at them, "'n' if you lil' niggers come around here again I'll skin ye alive." There was a sputter of dust from four flying heels.

Once out of sight of Sal's wrath, Charlie and Myrtle slackened their pace.

"The ol' hag," Myrtle gasped. Tears of anger and shame coursed over their brown cheeks.

Charlie and Myrtle, like Billy and Sam, had been taught their first lesson in race prejudice. Never again was the shaded lane of over-hanging trees to be a care-free place in which to play. Part of the glamor of the creek was gone forever.

* * * *

"What's troublin' my young'uns?" Pa Morgan put an arm around each slight body as Charlie and Myrtle crouched, one against each knee. Little by little the story came out, between muffled sobs. Pa Morgan's face grew stern, while his pipe, forgotten, smouldered and died.

The story ended, he patted their shoulders gently.

"Thar—thar—doan you care. Plenty of good friends to play with in Back Row. Best not git mixed up with white folks 'n' their children. Stay on your own side the fence."

"But why, Pappy? What we done?"

Pa Morgan sighed. "It's hard tellin' why, sonny. De debil's done sown seeds of hate in the white folks' hearts. They hate us 'cause we're black."

"But what we done to 'em?"

"Nuthin',—chile, nuthin'. It's they what done us wrong. Stealin' 'n' makin' us slaves, 'n' now robbin' us of our rights. Seems like folks always hates the ones they wronged, worse than t'other way round. White folks is scairt, I guess. Jest plain scairt." He drew a little unsteadily at his dead pipe, then rummaged his pockets for a match.

"I'se sorry this come to you like this. But you's black 'n' you's got to larn, sooner or later. Black is black, 'n' white is white, 'n' this here is a white man's world. He gives us a lil' piece 'n' say, 'stay thar.' So long as we says 'Yas-sir' to what he tells, 'n' works hard for him, it's all right. But move a foot, 'n' he'll clove you on the head."

A mist rose from the creek and crept slowly over the fields toward the shacks. Myrtle shivered.

Pa, shaking himself, asked, "How 'bout I tell you some stories tonight?"

The children's sad faces lit up. "Oh, Pappy, Uncle Remus stories; about the Tar Baby!"

But new circumstances brought the separated friends together again.

The mill where their parents worked from six to six, and where in a few more years Billy and Sam would be spinning cotton and Myrtle and Charlie would be sweeping lint along the floor, announced a wage-cut of fifteen per cent. There was a walk-out of five-hundred indignant mill hands and the arrival of white and Negro organizers from the National Textile Union's office in Greenville, who'd received word, "Come over and help us."

Enthusiasm ran high. There was a new sentiment on the hill, everywhere talk of Union, Strike, Solidarity.

"Ma," Pa Morgan's face shone like Myrtle and Charlie had only seen it do, before, when he was picking his banjo, "Ma, us 'n' the white mill-hands all gonna picket the mill tomorrow, to keep them scabs away."

"What! Us 'n' the white mill-hands . . . together? You must be crazy in the head!"

"No, I ain't. That's what the organizers said. Thar's been a lot of talk, I hear, goin' on over in the white section, 'n' arguin' 'n' explainin'! The organizers say, 'Divided, the Boss wins; United, We wins' . . .

'n' what's more Ma, the white mill hands 'n' us gonna be in the same organ-i-za-tion, on an equal basis!"

Ma Morgan threw out her hands. "It jest doan seem possible. . . . Myrtle and Charlie, watch yourself!" for they were whirling about the room, in their glee knocking into chairs and table.

The next morning, they joined with Pa and Ma in the line of pickets that tramped from Back Row to the mill gates. Charlie and Myrtle were carrying a banner between them, which Ma had made from a strip off an old sheet and lettered with stove-blacking, "We've Slaved Long Enough for You, Mister Murphy."

The street before the mill entrance was crowded with white operatives who'd gathered from their part of the hill. Among them, Charlie and Myrtle spied Billy and Sam also holding a banner. Theirs read, "All Mill-hands Stick Together for More Wages."

As the two lines merged, Billy and Sam called out, "Hello, Myrtle; hello, Charlie!"

"Hello, yourself!" they answered shyly.

The pickets marched back and forth in front of the mill. "No scab'll get in there today!" Home-made banners rippled in the breeze; the strikers sang their new song, "Solidarity Forever."

As the four children came alongside, Billy whispered hoarsely, "Say, kids! Me 'n' Sam wants to know, as soon as this here picketin's over, how 'bout we go down to the crik, 'n' have a game of Slippery Slicks?"

19

"The Beavers" (1936)

Written by Oscar Saul
(Oscar Saul Halpern, 1912–1994)
and Lou Lantz (1913–1987),
Illustrated by Jack Herman
(dates unknown)

EDITORS' INTRODUCTION

The *New York Times*' Brooks Atkinson called it "Mother Goose Marx": "Many children now unschooled in the technique of revolution now have an opportunity, at government expense, to improve their tender minds. Mother Goose . . . has been studying Marx; Jack and Jill lead the class revolution."[1] And the *Saturday Evening Post* implied that Saul and Lantz's *Revolt of the Beavers* would encourage poor children to attack rich children.[2] The play, which opened in May of 1937, provoked such controversy that Federal Theatre Project officials canceled it in June, after only twelve performances. Though *Revolt of the Beavers* was not the only play charged with having "red" content, uproar over its alleged message dogged Federal Theatre director Hallie Flanagan until 1939, when Congress finally ended America's four-year experiment with national theater. (Founded in August 1935 as a division of the Works Progress Administration, the Federal Theatre Project provided work for unemployed theater professionals and established regional theaters across the country.) In August 1938, when Flanagan testified before Martin Dies's House Committee on Un-American Activities, Flanagan devoted thirteen pages of her brief to this play, which she considered a simple fairy tale for children, nothing more.[3] Or, as playwright Lou Lantz later observed, "This had been written by people who were reading Marx. But it was not in any important aspects Marxist." It was, he said, "a real classic kind of Robin Hood— good guy versus bad guy—story."[4]

In *Revolt of the Beavers*, the wind blows Paul and Mary to Beaverland, where they meet the Professor in the scene (reproduced here) included in the communist children's magazine *New Pioneer* from December 1936. The beavers are sad because, though they work all day, only the Chief and his gang have plenty to eat and "a

blue sweater and a pair of skates"—no other beavers do. The Professor, the children, and the beavers form "a club for sad beavers to get glad," bringing the worker beavers' exiled leader—Oakleaf—back to Beaverland. Led by Oakleaf, the beavers unite, deposing the Chief and his henchmen. In their newly liberated Beaverland, each beaver gets enough to eat, along with a sweater and skates. Just before the children return home, the happy beavers sing, "We'll be building every day, / Each one helps in his own way. / Every beaver has his say / In building our new land."[5]

Overthrowing a government and redistributing the wealth could, of course, be understood as revolutionary. However, children in the audience did not see parallels to contemporary social ideas. When a professor of psychology at New York University interviewed hundreds of child audience members, they told him the messages they learned were "never to be selfish," "that it is better to be good than bad," and that "beavers have manners just like children."[6]

Brooklyn native Oscar Saul, who had also written for radio, cowrote one other play before turning to screenwriting in the 1940s. Starting with the Cary Grant picture *Once Upon a Time* (1944), Saul wrote or adapted over twenty movies, including the Frank Sinatra film *The Joker Is Wild* (1957). He may be best known for his film adaptation of Tennessee Williams's *A Streetcar Named Desire* (1951), directed by Elia Kazan. (Kazan had also been *The Revolt of the Beavers'* original director, but left when the production was in rehearsal.) In later years, Saul taught screenwriting at UCLA and, in 1990 won the Morgan Cox Award for his teaching in the Writers Guild Open Door School.

Louis Lantz also worked as a screenwriter, but the blacklist cut his career short. Lantz (or at least his name) disappears from movies after 1954. His last screen credit is for the story to Otto Preminger's *River of No Return* (1954), a film that starred Robert Mitchum and Marilyn Monroe.

NOTES

1. Brooks Atkinson, "'The Revolt of the Beavers,' or Mother Goose Marx, under WPA Auspices," *New York Times*, 21 May 1937, 19.

2. "Once upon a Time," *Saturday Evening Post*, 26 June 1937, 22.

3. Lowell Swortzell, *Six Plays for Young People from the Federal Theatre Project (1936–1939): An Introductory Analysis and Six Rep-

resentative Plays, ed. Lowell Swortzell (New York: Greenwood, 1986), 13; Hallie Flanagan, Arena: The History of the Federal Theatre (New York: Benjamin Blom, 1965 [1940]), 200–201.

4. Qtd. in Free, Adult, Uncensored: The Living History of the Federal Theatre Project, eds. John O'Connor and Lorraine Brown (Washington, DC: New Republic Books, 1978), 199.

5. Oscar Saul and Lou Lantz, The Revolt of the Beavers, in Six Plays for Young People, 141, 155, 172.

6. Jane DeHart Matthews, The Federal Theatre, 1935–1939: Plays, Relief, and Politics (Princeton, NJ: Princeton UP, 1967), 117.

ACT I. SCENE II.

The curtain rises on the deep recess of a vast wood of chaotic knots of trunks and branches. Jagged silhouettes of mangled trees make an impassable forest wall in the background. From above, a dim light streams down through the thicket of trees. It is hard to tell whether it is night or day, but since it does not matter we will simply ignore the problem and go on to other important elements that grace the scene. Stage right there is a very surprising thing. A blue marble pedestal, with ornamental grooves and cornices in the best Greek manner, stands calm and quiet amidst the forest's disorder. A little to the left of the pedestal is (of all things) a mail box on which is clearly engraved, "B, Professor." Where is the Professor? He is detected by the only noise that mars the serene quiet. He is lying curled up, fast asleep, upon the pedestal, and he is snoring a gentle and insistent snore. Nothing else is happening and so, for a brief moment, the audience watches the Professor as he sleeps. Suddenly the sound of footsteps is heard and Paul and Mary enter none the worse for the hurricane. They examine the surroundings intently but fail to notice the professor on the far side of the stage.

"I think we gotta wake him up to warn him!"

Paul (looks about and sees the Professor): Wow! Look, Mary!

Mary (awed): A real live beaver!

Paul: You think he'll talk?

Mary: Sure! This is the middle of the woods.

Paul: Gee, he's sleepin'. Maybe he doesn't want anybody to wake him up.

Mary: Yeah, he looks so peaceful and quiet, he might be angry.

Paul: I know, we'll be very quiet and just wait, and when he wakes up we'll talk to him. Shhhhh!

(A loud blatant noise of whistling intrudes upon the quiet and startles the children. The noise stops but the beaver still sleeps on.)

Mary: I wonder what the whistling is about.

Paul: I bet something is happening. I think we gotta wake him up just to warn him (knocks on pedestal). Hey, beaver, wake up, will ya, hey Beaver, wake up, wake up (the beaver stirs drowsily, lifts his head and speaks quietly).

Beaver: Don't you know I'm the beaver who loves peace and quiet?

Paul: But I think something is happening.

Beaver: Something is always happening. (He buries his head in his arms. Paul is fazed for a moment. He stands there irresolutely. Mary nudges him.)

Mary: Tell him you wanna ask him something.

Paul: Hey, I wanna ask you something. How can we have a good time?

Beaver: No more good times. The chief is making everybody sad.

Paul: What chief? What is he talking about, Mary?

Mary: Ask him again! Tell him what Windy said!

Paul (in a single breath): Listen, Windy said he had to go up to the North Pole and he couldn't take us all the way . . .

Beaver (interrupting): I don't care if Windy did say it. Stop bothering me. (Changes his tone) Listen! I'll tell you what I'll do. If you'll be a good beaver and go away I'll sing you a song.

Paul (in a whisper to Mary): Hey, Mary, he thinks we're beavers.

Mary: Maybe he's under a magic spell, don't say anything . . . let him sing.

Paul: All right. Sing a song.

Beaver (clears his throat and sings plaintively):

My favorite instrument is a fife,
But I'm also fond of the fiddle,
I sit on the left and I sit on the right
But my favorite spot is the middle.

I like to get up in the early dawn,
I'm fond of the morning light,

There's nothing I like as much as the morn
But the beautiful, beautiful night.

Oh, I was out in the woods one day
And the sights are fair to see,
On either side was a gay array
Of sights a-calling me.

On the sight an the right was a gorgeous view,
And there I would have sped
But the cleft on the left was lovely too
So I sat right here instead.

Here I sit,
Here I sit,
With a heart as heavy as lead;
I could only see one
So I didn't see none,
Give me eyes in the back of my head.

It's a pity,
It's a pity,
it's a terrible, terrible shame;
It's a pity,
It's a pity,
And I don't know whom to blame.

(The beaver finishes his song with a flourish, the children applaud.)

Beaver: I sang you a song, didn't I?

Paul: And it was a nice song, too. Did you make it up yourself?

Beaver: What's the matter with you, don't you know I'm a professor?

Paul (to Mary): What a funny place . . . how Can he be a professor. He's only a beaver, right, Mary?

Mary: Shhhh! He must be a Beaver professor.

Beaver: You woke me up, see! And it's very hard for me to fall asleep—so take a letter out of my mailbox.

Paul: Mailbox?

Beaver (pointing): Yeah, right over there. Take it out and read it and then I'll fall asleep. (Paul goes to the mailbox and takes out a piece of bark and looks at it in amazement.)

Beaver: You read! (Buries his head in his arms.) All right . . . start reading.

Paul: I can't read this . . . I don't understand it.

Beaver: What!

Mary (to Paul): Let me see it. . . . (She tries) We can't read this. This must be beaver writing.

Beaver (slowly, suspiciously): Say that doesn't sound like a beaver. . . . Wait a minute. (He dips into his pocket and pulls out a pair of glasses which he adjusts on his nose. Then he turns around and surveys his visitors. He is stunned. His hair stands on end. He emits a yowl of surprise.) Wow! Human beings. (He falls off the pedestal. The children run to help him.)

Mary (excitedly): Don't be afraid . . . we're not gonna take you to the zoo.

Paul (as he helps the beaver up): Yeah . . . don't be so scared.

Beaver (having climbed up to his pedestal where he pants with surprise): Wow, human beings . . . wowo . . . human beings in Beaverland. How'd you get here?

Mary: Windy blew us here.

Beaver: Get out of Beaverland. You better get out right away.

Paul: Why?

Beaver: Because there's a lot of trouble in Beaverland. And you might get right in the middle of the trouble.

Paul: I'm not scared. Are we, Mary?

Mary: No, We came to have a good time, Mr. Beaver.

Beaver: Good time! I can see right away you don't know what's happening in Beaverland. I'm telling you for your own good. You better get out.

Paul: We ain't got no place to go, We gotta hang around till Windy comes.

Professor: Wow! Then it's your own hard luck. Well, if you're staying, tell me your name so I can put it in a story book. (Takes out book and pencil.)

Paul: My name is Paul and her name is Mary.

Beaver: How old are you?

Paul: We're both nine years old.

Beaver: That's very good because everybody in Beaverland is nine years old . . . only, except the babies, but they grow up very, very fast.

Paul: What's your name?

Beaver: Can't you read?

Paul: Is that your name? B. Professor. How can you be a professor if you're only nine years old?

Beaver: Because I'm smart.

Paul (dubious): Yeah!

Beaver (pugnaciously): Yeah! I'm the biggest professor in Beaverland, the best story teller too. I could

tell you a million stories, that could last forever, almost . . . besides that, I'm smarter than a teacher . . . that makes me a professor . . . right, Mary?

Mary: Sure . . . that's right.

Paul (unconvinced): Have you got a school! If you're a real professor you *would* be in school right now. What are you doin' here?

Professor: That's part of the trouble. The chief closed all the schools in Beaverland.

Paul: So what's the use if you're a professor and you're smart?

Professor: No use . . . I might just as well be dumb. And that's why I'm very sad.

Paul: (sincerely sympathetic): You see, Mary . . . we're sad . . . and we come to Beaverland and see a sad beaver . . . it looks like everybody in the whole world is sad. (To the professor.) Did the chief make you sad?

Professor: Sure he did.

Paul: Didn't you get sore?

Professor: Sure I got sore.

Paul: So what did you do?

Professor: So I went to sleep, (The noise starts again . . . the whistling, loud and blatant.)

Mary: What's that noise, Professor?

Professor: That's the trouble . . . it's getting worse and worse . . . soon I won't be able to sleep at all.

Paul: You ought to be glad you don't live near the car barns. Then you'd never be able to sleep.

Professor: Yeah, this is even worse than the car barns.

Paul: Aw, you're a wise professor. Come on, Mary, let's take a walk in the woods and look for some other animals. (The children are about to go forward when the noises grow louder.)

Professor: Wait! You'll get hurt in those woods. (The whistling grows louder.)

Mary: Maybe . . . we better get out of Beaverland, Paul.

Paul: Don't be scared. (To the professor.) Who's whistlin' so loud?

Professor: The whistling clubs.

Paul: Wow . . . you got them in Beaverland, too . . . gee whiz, what a country.

Professor (agitated): Mary, get off the rabbit's house.

Mary: I'm not standing on anybody's house.

Professor: C'mon . . . move over. Suppose some one wants to come out. (Mary moves over, mystified. A knock is heard.) There, you see . . . some one wants to come out right now. (A trap door, the rabbit's house opens and a beaver sticks his head out.)

Beaver: Any whistling clubs around?

Professor: No. C'mon out. Why did you come by the secret passage, Beaver Oakleaf? Who's chasing you?

Beaver Oakleaf: The whistling clubs. (To Paul by way of explanation.) That's the chief's gang. They are chasing me out of Beaverland. They're the toughest beavers in the woods and they're right behind me.

Paul: Yeah . . . I'm sorry I left my Zippo gun home.

Oakleaf (aghast): What! A Zippo gun! What do you want to do . . . start a regular war? C'mon everybody, in the rabbit's house, I hear the whistling clubs comin'.

Mary: I can't fit in the rabbit's house.

Oakleaf: Sure you can . . . this is Beaverland. C'mon on, everybody hide. Here they come. (One after another they drop into the rabbit's house as the noise of the whistles and hoots grows louder and louder. . . . No sooner are they hidden than the whistling clubs break in upon the scene. They are beaver police. They carry clubs, wear caps and shiny buttons . . . they dance a heavy stylized dance of pursuit and threat, their clubs waving in rhythm to the dance and the song they sing.)

Whistling Clubs:

Ruff!
Tuff!
Ruff and Tuff and Gruff!

We're always in a terrible huff
Whenever we're out to do our stuff.

Huff!
Puff!
Ruff and Tuff and Gruff!

Now you may think we're crazy
But we're not a bit insane,
Yes, our heads are kind of hazy
But we really have a brain
And it
Says Ruff!
Tuff!
Ruff and Tuff and Gruff!

We're always in a huff
When we're out to do our stuff,
With a huff and a puff
And a ruffety, tuffety, gruff,
And a huff
And a puff
And a puffety, ruffety, huff.

(They stop short and posture.)

Ruff: You see him?

Tuff: No.

Gruff: Looks like he give us da slip.

Ruff: C'mon.

Whistling Clubs:

Ruff!
Tuff!
Ruff and Tuff and Gruff!
We're always in a huff
When we're out to do our stuff.
Ruff!
Puff!
Ruff and Tuff and Gruff!

(They are gone.)

(The trap door opens and the Professor's head appears . . . he looks about.)

Professor: Okay, the coast is clear.

Everybody out of the rabbit's house. (They all climb out, looking cautiously about.)

Professor: What's the matter, Oakleaf?

Oakleaf: The chief told them to chase me out of Beaverland . . . and you know what else he said; if you catch him, hit him till he cries.

Professor: That's against the rules.

Oakleaf: He doesn't care about the rules . . . you know why?

All: Why?

Oakleaf: I'll tell you the whole story. All the beavers were very sad . . . and me too, so I said why don't you make a club for sad beavers to become glad. So all the beavers say Yayy! But when the chief heard about it he said, Oakleaf, you're trying to destroy Beaverland, get out, and you know what else he said? He said I could never come back, not even in a million years. And just because I didn't want the beavers to be sad.

Paul: You hear that, Mary? The chief is making all the beavers sad. Listen, if he makes all the beavers sad, why don't you punch him on the nose?

Professor: You can't punch him on the nose . . . he's got a big gang.

Oakleaf: But some day the beavers will all get very, very sore and they'll wanna do something big against the chief . . . and then they'll call me back because I'm on their side and I got lots of schemes. (To Paul) And

you're gonna tell them how to get me back.

Mary: We don't know how to get you back.

Paul: We don't even know where you're going.

Oakleaf: I'm going to Owl Land now and when the beavers want me back you gotta tell them to send a snoop owl.

Paul: Oh, boy, you don't have to worry. . . . I'll tell the beavers, 'cause we're sad, too, and we're for the beavers because the beavers are sad.

Oakleaf: You wouldn't believe how sad they are. Y'know, not a single beaver has a blue sweater and a pair of skates except the chief and his gang. And now I'm going out of Beaverland . . . so long . . . so long.

All: So long!

Professor (sadly): Poor Oakleaf . . . one of the best beavers in Beaverland . . . chased out forever.

Paul: I'm gonna go right into Beaverland and punch the chief right on the nose . . . and his whole gang too.

Professor: I told you, you can't do that.

Paul: No! I'm the best fighter in my school. Right, Mary?

Mary: Sure! They always send him down to the principal.

Professor: Don't start any fights. I'm gonna do something, I'm gonna tell the chief a story . . . not a plain story . . . but a story with a moral . . . and then that'll show him how mean he is and then he'll turn into a good chief.

Paul: All right, you go ahead and tell him the story . . . but just let him get smart.

Professor: All right, everybody quiet . . . we gotta start. . . . (He lifts the trap door.) Down to the rabbit's house. All right, Mary.

(She disappears, Paul goes down. The Professor follows him . . . the trap door bangs shut.)

CURTAIN

20

"Mary Stays after School or— What This Union's About" (1939)

Amalgamated Clothing Workers of America (1914–)

EDITORS' INTRODUCTION

"Mary Stays after School" is a fairy tale, complete with a fairy that grants wishes (as long as they are "sensible"). But this fairy's real magic is allowing young Mary to appreciate her parents, their work, and, most importantly, their union activity. Mary gets in fights on the playground with children who tease her for wearing shabby clothes; for bringing meager lunches to school; and for having a father who is a foreigner, factory worker, and striker. Thanks to the fairy, Mary learns to be proud of her parents and of her father's union—clothing workers who want to grant their children's basic wishes such as: "to live in a better house, and have nicer things . . . a dress as pretty as Gladys' and . . . a big lunch like Henry's. . . ."

Published for "members' children," "Mary Stays after School" represents one element of a far-reaching worker-education movement that had strong ties to the clothing trades in general and the Amalgamated in particular. The Amalgamated Clothing Workers of America (ACWA) began with the great Chicago strike of 1910. What started with one shop's protest against intolerable working conditions quickly encompassed thirty-five thousand clothing workers who mounted a five-month general strike. Although strikers were forced to return to their jobs by the conservative leadership of the United Garment Workers (UGW, an arm of the American Federation of Labor), the strike galvanized militant workers in their rejection of the UGW's compromises and inspired similar rebellions in New York, Boston, Baltimore, and Cincinnati. By 1914, radicals had become a majority in the UGW, and they broke off to form the ACWA.

Within fifteen years, the Amalgamated had organized "every major clothing market in the country."[1] Its success in raising wages and improving working conditions showed what could be achieved through peaceful collective bargaining. Its pioneering social programs—including cooperative housing, pension plans, and medical care, as well as educational and cultural activities—made the ACWA a model for the "new unionism" that would gain widespread support under the New Deal. This new unionism showed that poverty and exploitation were not merely moral and political issues but were destabilizing to industry, proving that businesses and government had a stake in unions' success.[2]

Under the leadership of Sidney Hillman, a participant in the 1905 Russian revolution, the union maintained a close relationship with organized socialism. The major Jewish presence among garment workers, and within the garment unions, also brought both a tradition of messianic socialism and a commitment to education to these unions.[3]

The ACWA showed an interest in education from its earliest years and established a special education department in 1920. J. B. S. Hardman, a leader in its education program, emphasized that the goal of worker education was not simply to make workers better union members but also to help them transform society.[4] The ACWA sponsored lectures, summer institutes, and classes on a range of subjects; it also published newspapers, pamphlets, and books. By 1950 its book club was the "largest self-sustaining labor book club in the country."[5]

Although the worker education movement focused on adults, this story shows that children were part of that vision as well. The American Federation of Labor promoted labor education in the public schools, and, historically, radical labor leaders protested not just the lack of schooling available to working-class children but also the tenor of that schooling, which tended to be hostile to labor. Around the time that the ACWA set up an education department, there were calls for Junior Amalgamated Clubs, and other unions sponsored "junior unions" for members' children.[6] Labor unions never became major producers of children's literature, but this story suggests that at least some union activists viewed children's literature as a tool for attaining a "Bright Future."

The ACWA merged with the Textile Workers Organizing Committee in 1976. In 1995, they joined with the International Ladies Garment Workers Union to form UNITE. Later, merging with the Hotel and Restaurant Employees Union, they became UNITE HERE!, a strong force in organized labor today.

NOTES

1. Hyman H. Bookbinder and Associates, *To Promote the General Welfare: The Story of the Amalgamated* (Amalgamated Clothing Workers of America, 1950), 28.

2. See Steve Fraser, "Dress Rehearsal for the New Deal: Shop-Floor Insurgents, Political Elites, and Industrial Democracy in the Amalgamated Clothing Workers," *Working-Class America*, ed. Michael H. Frisch and Daniel J. Walkowitz (Urbana: U of Illinois P, 1983), 241.

3. Ibid., 234. Also see Robert Schaffer, "Educational Activities of the Garment Unions, 1890–1948," Ph.D. thesis, Columbia University, 1951, 51.

4. Quoted in E. E. Cummins, "Workers' Education in the United States," *Social Forces* 14:4 (May 1936): 604–5.

5. Bookbinder, 150.

6. Schaffer, 150; Frances Liscomb, writing for the left-wing *Woman Today*, urged progressive parents to encourage their children to join junior labor unions, where they could learn the lessons in labor education that were not taught in schools. Liscomb, "What Shall We Tell Our Children?" *Woman Today*, Mar. 1937, 27.

This story is about Mary, a little girl of nine, or perhaps ten, or older. And about a fairy she met and what came of it. But if you'll read the story carefully you'll find that what happened to Mary might have happened to a much older girl or boy, and that it all is of real importance.

"Little girls must not pull other little girls' hair," Mary's teacher said. "You will write that on the blackboard one hundred times. Then you may go home."

Mary was a very plain-spoken girl.

"I don't care," she said, "Phyllis was mean . . . and it's worth it!"

"You will write it two hundred times," Mary's teacher said, angrily, "I really don't know what to do with you, Mary. You are very naughty. Last week you pulled Gladys' hair. And the week before you scratched Henry Butler's face. Is that the way a good little girl behaves?"

Mary wanted to say that she thought it was a very good way to behave . . . with Gladys, Henry, and Phyllis. But two hundred times was hard enough. She went to the blackboard quietly, and began to write.

ON THE PLAYGROUND

"I can't understand it," Mary's teacher said. "When I spoke to your mother about it, she told me that you always behaved at home. Well, Mary, unless you behave at school I shall have to keep you in the classroom while the other children are eating their lunch in the playground."

Mary's teacher left the room, and Mary went on with her writing.

Such a hair-pulling had never before been seen

"I hate Phyllis," she said to herself, "and I hate Gladys. And I hate Henry Butler, and I hate . . ." but that was too awful, ". . . well, I don't like my teacher today, anyway. No, I don't!" Mary picked out a fresh piece of chalk. "And I'll scratch Henry's face again, if he makes fun of my lunch! It isn't as nice as his, I know, but mother says I'm a lucky girl to have any lunch at all, the

way things are. And what if my dress is made over from mother's old bathrobe? It's a nice dress, and Gladys had no right to giggle about it with all the girls, even if her dress does come from New York and costs a lot of money. And that Phyllis . . . ! Always talking about her father and mother! Always putting on airs! 'My father is a big lawyer!'" she mimicked Phyllis' high voice, "'My father made a wonderful speech in the courtroom yesterday! My father is very rich; we have a big house, and a new car! And my mother knows so many nice people! Her clothes are so beautiful, especially when she goes with my father to a banquet, or a ball, or something grand like that!'"

It always made Mary feel a little ashamed of her own father and mother when Phyllis talked that way. It made her feel poor and . . . dirty.

And today in the playground, Phyllis, looking very sly, said to Mary: "What does YOUR father do?"

What does he do? Mary thought: He works in a factory. . . a clothing factory. That's nothing to be ashamed of, is it? Might as well be ashamed of eating, or skipping rope, or sleeping. But with all the other girls and boys listening, she did feel ashamed. And she wished that Phyllis would keep quiet. But Phyllis had more to say.

"I know what your father is," she said excitedly, one word biting at the heels of another, "your father is a striker! My father told me! And yesterday he was a-RRES-ted! My father had him appear in the court with the policeman!"

Mary walked over to Phyllis and got as close to her as she could.

"So what if he was?" she asked.

"My father says that strikers are bad people. They have things called unions, and unions are very bad. They are un-American! And my father says that your father is the worst striker of all! He is the leader, and he has wrong ideas about things, and he's not a good American!"

"He is too! He is!" Mary shouted, in tears. "He's as good as your father! He's an American just like anyone!"

"He isn't! He's a striker and a foreigner, and he ought to be sent back where he came from! My father said so," Phyllis insisted.

So Mary got both her hands into Phyllis' hair and pulled with all her might. It was the worst hair pulling Phyllis ever got, or the school ever saw. You could hear Phyllis three blocks away, the children said. They were proud of Mary and wished they could help her write her sentence on the blackboard.

"You may go home now," said Mary's teacher when she returned. "But won't you promise never to quarrel with Phyllis again?"

Mary was an honest girl.

"I can't promise! But I'll try not to," she replied.

THE FAIRY IN THE PARK

Mary didn't go home right after school. She knew her mother would be worried about her being late. But if mother didn't worry about that, she'd find something else to worry about. She worried all day and cried all night. It made her ugly, but she didn't seem to care. And anyway she had no pretty clothes to wear, her shoes were run down

Mary didn't like the place they lived in

at the heels, her stockings were thick, black cotton and hung like bags. And when Mary's father would come home he would be tired—too tired—and eat without saying a word. Besides, Mary didn't like the place they lived in, with the long, dark halls that scared her so at night. Her room was too small to do anything in. Its plaster was coming off in chunks, the wallpaper was peeling everywhere. She never liked coming home.

Mary went to the park instead and found a bench in a lonely spot under a huge oak tree where it was quiet, and she could think. But the more she thought things over, the messier they got. She felt miserable. Mary loved her father but she did wish he too were a lawyer, or a judge, or something, and had a lot of money, like the other girls' and boys' fathers. And she wished that her mother. . . .

But what good was wishing! She sighed, and said out loud, "I guess only a good fairy could help me out!"

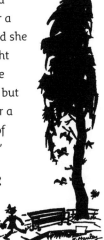

Mary found a bench under a tree

Mary was a sensible girl. So when she suddenly realized that there was a woman sitting with her, she was not startled. She must have come, Mary thought, when I was thinking about things and I didn't hear her. And as she turned to look more closely at her unexpected neighbor Mary said, "How do you do? It's a lovely afternoon, isn't it?"

"And how are you, Mary?" the woman replied in a very round, clear voice, "Yes, it's very fine."

"But I don't think I know you," Mary said. It all sounded like the grammar lesson she had in school that morning. Mary was tempted to go on with the next sentence, "Was it you whom I met at my dear cousin's birthday party last week?" People say and do the strangest things in grammar books, Mary reflected. But what the woman said next was much stranger.

"You wanted a kind fairy to help you with a problem. I am answering your wish."

And the woman, smiling brightly at Mary, took a powder-puff from her bag and patted her nose with it as calmly as you please.

THREE SENSIBLE WISHES

Mary didn't believe in fairies. So she immediately decided that this lady had overheard her, and was trying to be polite in the way grownups are with children.

"I am afraid that only a real fairy could help me," Mary said.

"But I AM a real fairy."

It was awfully annoying but Mary felt it would be rude just to get up and go away. After all, it was only good manners to humor your elders. And she was such a lovely woman too. Bright red hair, small round face with red cheeks and lips, large smiling eyes—just like a movie queen.

"Fairies have butterfly wings," Mary reminded her, "and their clothes are made of spider's silk. They always carry a silver wand with a shining gold star on it. There are little diamond stars sprinkled all over their hair that sparkle even when it's pitch dark. And fairies always tell you who they are right away and then they give you three wishes."

"My name is Bright-Future" said the woman, "and now that you mention it, I remember reading in some of the old fairy books about wings and wands and the other quaint fashions. But of course we have changed with the times. There were dragons in those books too. Now wouldn't a dragon look ridiculous if he went snorting down the city streets today, tying up all the traffic? It would serve the old-fashioned monster right if nobody believed in him! And you could never believe in me, either, if I went about with a pair of mouldy, useless wings. Why, it would be as bad as wearing a bustle!"

But I don't believe in you, Mary wanted to say. Yet Mary wasn't quite so sure of that now. So she said:

"What about the three wishes? I didn't hear you say anything about them. Even if there are fairies, what good are they if they don't grant three wishes?"

"You're quite right about that," the woman said.

"Wouldn't a dragon look ridiculous snorting down the street?"

"Then you can give me three wishes? And you can make them come true?"

"That depends."

"On what, please?"

Mary was more respectful now that she was beginning to believe in her.

"It depends on what your wish is," said the fairy.

"Aren't you supposed to make any wish come true?"

"Of course not," said the fairy, "you can't wish for just anything. You must wish for something that's sensible. Make your three wishes, and if they're sensible, I will grant them."

"Then," Mary said, "I wish my mother would be beautiful, like Phyllis' mother is. I wish I could be proud of my father, and I wish we would live in a better house, and have nicer things and I could go to school with a dress as pretty as Gladys' and with a big lunch like Henry's . . . and we would all be happy again . . . and . . ."

Did she make seven wishes instead of three? Mary hoped not. But above all, she hoped the wishes were sensible.

LOOKS AT YESTERDAY

"This will be an easy day's work for me," said the fairy. "The first thing we'll do is go back to Yesterday."

"Is that easy?" Mary wondered, but while she was wondering the park melted away, there was a great noise, she couldn't see, and she was frightened . . . But in another moment it was quiet again, and they were standing in the kitchen of her own home. Her mother and father were sitting at the dinner-table, and it was Yesterday just as the fairy said, because there were her school-books exactly as she had left them before going to bed.

"I'm like Scrooge, in the Christmas Carol," Mary thought.

The fairy pointed to her father and said: "Listen!"

"We went to see the bosses again today," her father was saying, "but they won't even talk to us. The bosses think that they need only hold out a few weeks more, and then the strike will be broken. Maybe they are right. The strike is ten weeks old now. Everybody is discouraged and there is a lot of talk about going back to work. What can I do? Ten weeks is a long time to be without work when there is no money in the bank.

Going back to Yesterday

The men say that if they had only themselves to think about it wouldn't matter so much. But the women and children are suffering the most. They actually haven't enough to eat, and the children go to school in rags. The other children poke fun at them. . . ."

"Listen!"

"Our own Mary has the same trouble with her schoolmates," Mary's mother interrupted.

"So she knows!" Mary cried. But the fairy said "Hush . . . and listen!"

"Maybe they are right," her father continued. "Yes, it would be a wonderful thing to have a union of the clothing workers . . . but must the women and the children pay for it? Must you go without enough food? Not have a decent dress and stockings to put on? When I come home at night, I am afraid to look my own daughter in the face because there is so much pain in it."

"I don't like to hear you talk like that," Mary's mother said, and Mary could not believe it was her mother's voice, it was so clear and strong. "You

"What can I do?"

are their leader. They depend on you. You knew that all this would happen before you began this fight for the union. But you thought, and they all thought, that it was worth making almost any sacrifice for a chance to live with a little security, a little hope in this world. And you shouldn't change your mind now because the women and children are suffering. I am not different from the other women, and Mary is not different from the other children. They all can stand it and so can we. Are we suffering more than before the strike? I had the same worries then that I have now . . . always trying to make ends meet on your earnings . . . trying to make a home that we could live in with a little decency . . . that Mary could play in. Now at least we have something better to look forward to. And if Mary can have all the things that the other girls have, she will be happy again. No, John, if we lose the strike then we can go back to the old days. But I wouldn't have you go back otherwise."

"Your mother," said the fairy, "is very beautiful, don't you think?"

"Yes," said Mary. And she remembered her mother's words like a fresh, strong, Spring wind.

"That," said the fairy, "is your first wish come true."

SEES A MEETING

"Now," said the fairy, "we will go back to Today."

And that was a lot easier, Mary thought, as they were walking into a large hall where there were hundreds of people at a meeting. Mary didn't know the place, but she felt that the people were familiar. They looked like her father and mother, it seemed to her. The fairy pointed to a man on the platform in the front of the room who was hammering on a block of wood and demanding: "Order! Order!"

Everybody in the room was listening

The fairy said, "That's your father . . . Listen."
Everybody in the room was listening.

"We have just learned from the newspapers that our bosses will not consider our latest demands, or any demands that we care to make," Mary's father said in a firm voice. "They say they will not recognize our union." There was a lot of murmuring. "The bosses also say," Mary's father continued, "that they will deal with anyone of us, individually. They promise to put you back to work, if you will give up the union." There was silence. "I know there has been talk of giving up the strike." Mary's father paused for what seemed a long time before speaking again. "If there is anyone here who feels that way about it, let him speak up now. You have the right to speak!"

A little man in the back of the room, right near Mary, jumped to his feet and yelled, "No!" And

A little man jumped up

men and women in all parts of the room got up and shouted, "No! No! We won't give up!" Then the whole roomful of people were on their feet, shouting, clapping their hands, stamping their feet, and singing, until the windows rattled. Mary's father hammered the table again and after a while it was quiet enough for him to speak.

"I know now that some of you were getting worried and downhearted. That's all right. I know it's been hard on you. It's been hard on me and at times I was getting shaky, too. But in our hearts we all have always known that there is just one answer for our bosses: We'll stick it out! We are Americans and are fighting for decent pay for our work. Our children have a right to a bit of happiness, and we won't stop the fight until we win this union or until it snows in July!"

There was twice as much shouting, and singing started in several parts of the hall, but Mary heard the fairy say: "Your father is an important man."

"They are all important people," Mary thought.

"They are all workers and fathers of little boys and girls like you, Mary. Because they didn't get enough money for the work they were doing from early morning to late at night, they went on strike. They will go back to work again when they are assured that they will get more money to buy food and pretty clothes for you. When they win they will have more time to spend at home or in the park with you. This is what 'Strike' means. You have your second wish, now."

"BRIGHT-FUTURE"

Mary wondered where her third wish was likely to take her.

But the fairy said: "You won't need me any more. You can reach Tomorrow by yourself and your parents will help. And I think you know what tomorrow will bring."

"I will have pretty clothes!" Mary cried. "I can talk about my father and mother too, and be proud of them!"

"Yes," said the fairy. "The strike will be won, and your father will go back to work. There will be more money

"Don't thank me"

for everything. You will be happier."

"Oh, thank you! thank you!" Mary cried. "You are very kind!"

But the fairy said, "You mustn't thank me. I simply showed you what your father and mother were doing for you. You, and all children, must thank your parents, because it is they who make your wishes come true. I have only helped you see the truth."

"You are so beautiful!" Mary cried.

"Yes," said the fairy, "my name is Bright-Future . . . your Bright-Future."

And before Mary could say a word, she was gone.

Everything seemed different the next day. Phyllis made a nasty remark again, but Mary just looked at her and smiled. Because Bright-Future had told her . . .

It was only three days afterwards that Mary came running to school with the grand news. As soon as lunch hour started, she ran to tell Phyllis.

"Your father called my father on the telephone," she shouted. "Your father wants to see dad. He's got to give in, he's got to give in," Mary sang the words and danced around Phyllis. She danced all the way around the playground to tell the other boys and girls. Phyllis threatened to pull her hair but Mary hardly heard her.

She never told anyone about the fairy. She wasn't quite sure they'd believe it, and besides, it's fun having a secret with your own Bright-Future.

The End

21

Mr. His: A Children's Story for Anybody (1939)

A. Redfield (Syd Hoff, 1912–2004)

EDITORS' INTRODUCTION

Bronx native Syd Hoff wrote or illustrated over one hundred books, of which *Danny and the Dinosaur* (1958) is his best-selling and best-known. He went on to write and illustrate many other titles in Harper's "I Can Read" series, including such classics as *Sammy, the Seal* (1959), *Julius* (1959), *Chester* (1961), *Stanley* (1962), and *The Horse in Harry's Room* (1970). Equally successful as a cartoonist, Hoff published 571 cartoons in the *New Yorker* between 1931 and 1975 and created the syndicated strips "Tuffy" (1939–1949) and "Laugh It Off" (1958–1977).

Few people know that Syd Hoff also published under the name A. Redfield. Contrary to what official biographies say, his first collection of cartoons was not Hoff's *Feeling No Pain* (Dial, 1944) but Redfield's *The Ruling Clawss* (Daily Worker, 1935), and his first "children's book" was not Hoff's *Muscles and Brains* (Dial, 1940) but Redfield's *Mr. His* (New Masses, 1939). Hoff's first attempt at writing children's literature may have been tongue-in-cheek: although *Mr. His* looks like a children's book, one intended audience is clearly adults. Nevertheless, the timing suggests that the story started Hoff's celebrated career as a juvenile author.

A gifted artist but an indifferent student, Sydney Hoff dropped out of high school at age sixteen and enrolled in the National Academy of Design. During his two years at the academy, the Depression hit and a classmate introduced him to the communist movement.[1] Throughout the 1930s, Hoff created cartoons for both the workers and the wealthy. He was a regular contributor (as Hoff) to the *New Yorker* and (as Redfield) to the *Daily Worker* and *New Masses*. In "Social Satire," an afterword to *The Ruling Clawss*, Redfield criticized fellow *New Yorker* cartoonists Peter Arno and Otto Soglow for writing escapist cartoons: when "they bite the bourgeoisie," they "use only their lips, but not their teeth."[2] Satire, he wrote, should be "used, not as a medium of escape, but as an amusing and educational means of improving the cultural level of the masses."[3] If Hoff's

New Yorker cartoons do not meet this satirical standard, Redfield's *Daily Worker* cartoons do: in one "Ruling Clawss" panel, a wealthy couple are walking by a legless veteran who sits on a board, cup in hand. The wife says, "Give him a nickel, sweetheart. After all, you made a couple of million on the war."[4]

Hoff's *Danny and the Dinosaur* sold over ten million copies, but *Mr. His* sold only a tiny fraction of that number. Its limited audience derives in large part from the fact that the book's publisher, *New Masses*, could not afford a large print run: the communist weekly magazine was in dire financial straits from 1939 until it ceased publication in 1948. Whether the tale's dual audience (adults and children) would have enhanced or further curtailed its readership is hard to know. However, it's worth noting that *Mr. His*—subtitled *A Children's Story for Anybody*—is both a social fable in the guise of a children's book and a children's book containing a social fable. On the one hand, Redfield seems interested in using the children's genre to satirize adult problems: the tale of Histown neatly reduces society to a struggle between one greedy fat oligarch (Mr. His) and the hardworking people. On the other hand, Redfield remains mindful of potential child readers, explaining that while you might like "to own everything," it "wouldn't be much fun" to "own everything while everybody else had nothing."

Though Hoff retired the A. Redfield pseudonym in the early 1940s, he later wrote a more successful political children's book, *Boss Tweed and the Man Who Drew Him* (1978), which shows the role Thomas Nast's cartoons played in ending the reign of the corrupt William Marcy Tweed in nineteenth-century New York. As Hoff writes in his *Editorial and Political Cartooning: From Earliest Times to the Present* (1976), an effective political cartoonist can "play on readers' emotions, . . . causing them to feel shock, fear, anger, amusement, despair and moral indignation, so that they might want to take to the streets, brandish placards, and maybe march on Washington."[5] Perhaps the citizens in *Mr. His* see just such a cartoon before they unite to make Histown into Ourtown.

NOTES

1. Syd Hoff, letter to Philip Nel, 1 Aug. 2000.

2. A. Redfield [Syd Hoff], *The Ruling Clawss*, with an introduction by Robert Forsythe [Kyle Crichton] (New York: Daily Worker, 1935), 180.

3. Ibid., 178.

4. Ibid., 107.

5. Syd Hoff, *Editorial and Political Cartooning: From Earliest Times to the Present* (New York: Stravon, 1976), 13.

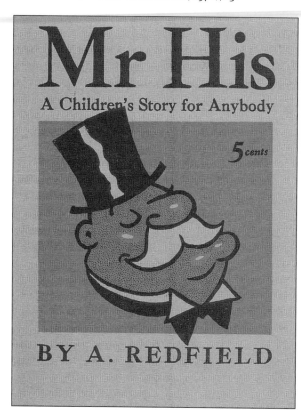

Once upon a time there was a fat little man whose name was Mr. His. He was a very rich little man and he lived in a little town which was called Histown because everything in it was his. The fields of wheat and corn, the fruit trees, the great mines—everything was his. Was the sky his, too? It didn't matter because hardly anyone in Histown ever looked up to see if it was a blue sky, a gray sky, or any old sky.

There were lots of houses in Histown but they weren't nice places at all. They were old and tumble-down and fire could break out in any one of them at a minute's notice. No one of them was fit for a human being.

O, yes! There was one house in Histown fit for a human being. It was a very lovely house made of marble and glass and steel. No fire could break out here! No disease, no vermin! Here, indeed, was a house fit for a human being. Any human being? No. Only one. A very special human being. Mr. His.

Would you like to own everything? Sure you would! Then you could buy anything you wanted and have so much fun! But would you like to own everything while everybody else had nothing? That wouldn't be much fun, would it? Well, maybe it wouldn't be fun for you because you'd worry about others. But not Mr. His. He didn't even know there were any.

Every day he would skip through the street with a paper and pencil in his hands, figuring up profits, and singing as loud as he could. "Do! Re! Me! Fa!" he would sing. "Sol! La! Ti! Do!" The poor people of Histown would hear him coming and would run into their houses and lock the doors. For though Mr. His had everything there was one thing he had not—friends.

O, yes. He did have two friends. But they weren't persons. They were animals. One was a wise old owl who lived in a tree. The other was a little frog who lived in a brook. Every day Mr. His would stand under the tree and say: "Whose is Histown?" And the wise old owl would say: "His is Histown." Then Mr. His would call into the brook: "Ain't it grand?" And the little frog would croak: "Sure, His. Sure, His."

Then Mr. His would go skipping along again, paper and pencil going a mile a minute, and singing louder than ever. And the poor people would peep through their windows and shiver. They didn't know it made Mr. His very happy to see they were afraid of him and that they were doing nothing to improve their lot. For there were no strikes in Histown—and no picketlines and no unions. The newspapers, which Mr. His owned too, said that these things were wicked.

Every night for supper Mr. His had enough food on his table for all the people in Histown. But, of course, it was all for him. Mr. His never cut his own food because his hands would be busy with paper and pencil, figuring up profits. The butler, Thorndyke, would cut his master's food and hold it up to his mouth on a fork. Thorndyke would be very careful because sometimes Mr. His became so entranced in his figures he'd bite the butler's wrist instead.

By and by Mr. His would eat so much he couldn't move. Then Thorndyke would carry him upstairs and put him to bed.

One morning Mr. His was dreaming of a way to get all the air in Histown into cans so the people would have to buy it from him, when he was awakened by a strange commotion. Putting on his robe, Mr. His rushed to a window and looked out. To his surprise it was the people. They were holding signs which read: "Mr. His is unfair." "Mr. His gives us a pain." "Mr. His is a scoundrel."

With a roar Mr. His put on his clothes and ran out of the house to get advice from his two friends. Down the road he sped. But how different Histown was today.

As he passed his factory Mr. His saw all the men standing outside. "Build the union!" the men were yelling. "Build the union!"

By this time Mr. His was sweating terribly, and it wasn't all from running. Presently he reached the woods. Here too things

were different. The squirrels were running up and down with signs: "Phooey on Mr. His." "We're tired of nerts—we want nuts!"

He stood under the tree where the wise old owl lived, and cried:

"Whose is Histown?" And the owl replied: "His is Histown." Mr. His was about to sigh with relief when the wise owl added: "But not for long."

Mr. His turned purple with anger, fear, surprise, and amazement. He called into the brook where lived the little frog: "O, what shall I do?" Croaked the frog: "You can die like me." "What?" cried Mr. His: "Croak," said the frog. "Haw! Haw!"

Disgusted with his friends, Mr. His sat down on a rock.

He thought and thought. Finally he leaped up, saying: "I got it!" Quick as he could he hurried to his printing office. In hardly any time a newspaper was rolling off the presses. Mr. His picked up a bundle and ran into the street.

"Wuxtry!" he shouted. "Read all about it! Blondes —your real enemy is

brunettes! Brunettes, your real enemy is redheads! Baldheads —take your choice." Sales were pretty good for a while. People came up to where Mr. His stood, smiling at each other.

They bought papers, read them, and walked away separately, giving each other dirty looks.

Just when Mr. His was congratulating himself on outsmarting the people, he heard a noise of approaching footsteps. "Wuxtry!" he shouted. But

the noise was growing louder and louder and Mr. His could hardly hear himself. "Wuxtry!" he shouted, but an ocean of voices drowned him out completely. He looked up the block and saw them coming. There was no end to them, and now Mr. His could make out what they were saying: "We're tired of being stepped on! Now we're stepping forward!"

"Speaking of steps," thought Mr. His to himself, "I better step on it." He took to his feet and ran as fast as he could, the great crowd right behind him. Mr. His didn't stop running till he was out of Histown.

And now if Mr. His ever comes back, he'll find a new Histown. The fields of wheat and corn, the fruit trees, the great mines—everything belongs to the people. And O, yes—it's now Ourtown.

22

Oscar the Ostrich (1940)

Written by Jerome Schwartz (Jerome Lawrence, 1915–2004), Illustrated by Mark David (1898?–1973?)

EDITORS' INTRODUCTION

Ohio native Jerome Lawrence Schwartz is better known as Jerome Lawrence, the coauthor (with Robert E. Lee) of the plays *Inherit the Wind*, *Auntie Mame*, and *The Night Thoreau Spent in Jail*. He legally changed his surname to Lawrence in the 1940s.

His father was a printer and his mother an unpublished poet, but Lawrence always wanted to be a professional writer. After graduating from Ohio State University in 1937, he worked for newspapers and in broadcasting. He left journalism for theater because he saw the latter as a "public forum" where he could more effectively reach people.[1]

With writing partner Lee, Lawrence grabbed audiences with plays that used history to comment on the present. *Inherit the Wind* (1955), a fictionalized version of the 1925 Scopes trial, served as a commentary on McCarthyism, which—to Lawrence and Lee—was an attack on American freedoms of speech and thought. In *The Night Thoreau Spent in Jail* (1970), the authors' opposition to the Vietnam War found expression in Henry David Thoreau's act of civil disobedience against the Mexican-American War. Celebrating its heroine's unconventional behavior in the 1920s and 1930s, *Auntie Mame* (1956, revised as a musical 1966) echoed contemporary critiques of conformity, such as William H. Whyte's *The Organization Man* (1956).[2] As Lawrence said, "Almost . . . all of our plays share the theme of the dignity of every individual mind, and that mind's life-long battle against limitation and censorship."[3]

Before meeting Lee, Lawrence created the anti-isolationist parable *Oscar the Ostrich*, published in February 1940. A direct echo of Americans who opposed U.S. involvement in the expanding world war, Oscar prefers to ignore the growing threat of the loud-voiced ostrich, a thinly disguised spoof of Adolf Hitler—the tyrannical ostrich's followers even march in a Nazi-style goose-step. If the ostriches' "yelling" at the dictator ostrich represents Allied nations fighting Hitler's fascist ambitions, then perhaps *Oscar the Ostrich* endorses the advice, earlier in the book, of the ostrich at the conference: "We must be prepared!"[4]

Lawrence and Lee, who met a month after Pearl Harbor, enlisted and cofounded the Armed Forces Radio Service, writing radio plays for the troops. In their long career, they cowrote thirty-nine plays, several movie scripts, and hundreds of radio and TV plays. Lawrence and Lee's works have been translated into dozens of languages, and their plays continue to be performed around the world.

Of the five "Mark Davids" listed on the Social Security Death Index, only one was born early enough to have illustrated this book. Born April 1893, this Mark David registered with Social Security in New York State, and he died in 1973 in Rooseveltown, Saint Lawrence, New York. We do not know if this is the same Mark David who illustrated the book, nor could we discover anything further about him.

NOTES

1. Richard L. Coe, "Jerome Lawrence," *The Playwright's Art: Conversations with Contemporary American Dramatists*, ed. Jackson R. Bryer (New Brunswick, NJ: Rutgers UP, 1995), 169.

2. Alan Woods, "Jerome Lawrence," *Dictionary of Literary Biography*. Vol. 228, *Twentieth-Century American Dramatists, Second Series*, ed. Christopher J. Wheatley (Detroit: Gale, 2000).

3. Nena Couch, "An Interview with Jerome Lawrence and Robert E. Lee," *Studies in American Drama 1945–Present* 7:1 (1992): 14.

4. Dr. Seuss began to publish with Random House in 1939, the year before that publisher brought out *Oscar the Ostrich*. Although he never mentions *Oscar*, Seuss caricatured isolationists as ostriches in his political cartoons. After the war, Seuss represented Hitler as Yertle the turtle, building his throne on the backs of other turtles. Just as this stack of sand dune topples when Oscar speaks out, so Yertle's stack of turtles topples when Mack speaks out.

Any similarity to ostriches, living or dead, is purely coincidental

There was once an ostrich named Oscar.

Oscar was a good ostrich.
He always minded his own business.

He would race around his own little sand dune.

He liked to see his reflection in the oasis.

But Oscar didn't like

NOISE!

NOISE was

wicked.

So every time he heard NOISE,

Oscar would hide his head
in
the
sand.

The sand was warm and comfortable.
With his head in the sand, he didn't bother
anybody—and nobody bothered him.

When the NOISE went away, Oscar took his
head out of the sand.
Oscar was happy.

Putting his head in the sand was surely the
    right thing to do
He had caused no trouble.

HE WOULD SURELY GO TO HEAVEN!

Over the next sand dune was an ostrich with
    a LOUD VOICE.

Of course Oscar had nothing to do with him.
That was a different tribe of ostriches
    altogether!
To be sure Oscar could hear that LOUD VOICE.
But, then again, there was always the warm
    sand.

All he had to do was to
            poke
            his
            head
            in . . .
And he could forget all about the NOISE.

The LOUD-VOICED ostrich frightened all the
    ostriches of his own tribe.
Then he lectured them all about the glory of
    their sand dune.

This impressed the ostriches.
    One ostrich told another.

They flocked to hear the LOUD-VOICED one.

The crowd surrounding him just
            grew
            and
            GREW!

"Why," bellowed the LOUD-VOICED one,
    "can't we have that sand dune to the east?"

The ostriches agreed.
So the LOUD-VOICED one taught them all
    how to march.

The ostriches from all the neighboring dunes
   saw this going on.

It worried them.
   They decided to call a conference.

The ostriches from all the dunes came running. . .
There were old ostriches, ones who had a great
   deal of experience.
There were young ostriches, ones who were
   still damp behind the ears.
There were long-legged ostriches.
There were short-legged ostriches.
There were bow-legged ostriches.
There were dull-colored ostriches.
There were multi-colored ostriches.
There were fat ostriches.
There were thin ostriches.
There were ostriches from the north.
There were ostriches from the south.
There were ostriches from the west.
As a matter of fact, all the ostriches were there . . .
   except the ostriches
   from the sand dune to the east . . .

and Oscar.

But none of them knew what to do.
They looked at each other.
"What shall we do?" they cried.

"We too must learn how to march!"
   one of them exclaimed.

"We must be prepared!"

They all agreed to act at once.

So they quickly put their heads together. . . .
AND GAVE THE LOUD-VOICED OSTRICH

THE SAND DUNE TO THE EAST.

The LOUD-VOICED one strutted about the
   sand dunes.

His voice was LOUDER than ever.

You might think that two sand dunes would be
   enough to satisfy anybody.
But not this LOUD-VOICED ostrich.
He promised
   threatened
   blustered
   robbed
   shouted
   cajoled
   yelled
   plundered
   roared
   pirated
   snatched
   flattered
   tricked
   grabbed
   until he had a whole STACK of sand dunes.

But Oscar didn't care.
He could always

> poke
> his
> head
> in
> the
> sand.

He was more certain than ever
that it was the right thing to do.

He dreamed of the time he would play a harp.
Ah, heaven would be so wonderful!
But then the LOUD-VOICED ostrich noticed
the sand dune with Oscar's head in it.
"Why should that chicken-livered ostrich have
that sand dune?" he cried.
"We need the room!"

So they took Oscar's sand dune too, and left
him—

Without a dune to stand on!

Suddenly Oscar discovered that he had no
place to poke his head.

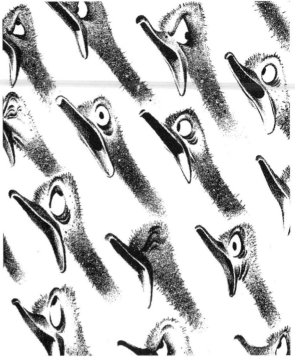

Then Oscar was

SORE!

For the first time, Oscar began to look around
  him—not having anything else to do with
  his head.
He saw all the other duneless ostriches,
  wandering around without a place to poke
  their heads.
Then Oscar had an idea—they would join
  forces.
"Yelling," he told the other ostriches, "seems to
  be the secret of success. Let us yell too!"
So they set up a mighty clamor.

  It was *TERRIFIC!*

It was SO terrific that no one could hear the
  LOUD-VOICED ostrich.
He couldn't even hear himself.
He felt very silly with his mouth open.

The LOUD-VOICED one began to tremble.
His followers began to tremble.
The stack of dunes began to tremble.

Until they all
toppled
down.

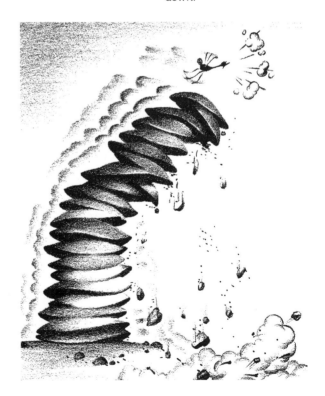

The ostriches all got back their sand dunes.
And so did Oscar.

Oscar was very happy. He determined that
   never again would he poke his head in the
   sand when there there was NOISE.

Not on your plume tip!

He would

STOP
THE
NOISE!

23

"Doria Ramirez," from
small hands, big hands:
Seven Profiles of Chicano
Migrant Workers and
Their Families (1970)

Sandra Weiner (b. 1922)

EDITORS' INTRODUCTION

The thing that most struck Sandra Weiner in doing the research for *small hands, big hands: Seven Profiles of Chicano Migrant Workers and Their Families* was "the sheer crushing irony of the whole experience. Here are people; men, women, and yes, children, under the open sky on the rich earth, doing what today comes closest to God's work—harvesting nature's bounty. And yet they reap little or nothing for themselves."[1]

The direct inspiration for *small hands, big hands*, which the *New York Times* named as one of the best books of 1970,[2] was the widely publicized struggle of Mexican-American migrant farm workers, organizing under the leadership of Cesar Chavez and the United Farmworkers Union (UFW). Between 1967 and 1970, the UFW organized several major strikes among farmworkers, an international grape boycott, and smaller boycotts of citrus, lettuce, and other products. In the context of other social justice movements of the 1960s, these actions brought sympathy to migrant workers' basic demand for a stake in the American dream—for safe working conditions, a decent standard of living, and respect.

Discussing the idea for a picture story about California migrant farmworkers with her editor, Fabio Coen, Weiner insisted that her story not be about Cesar Chavez or the strike but about the workers themselves: "I don't want to go where they are picketing, I want to go where they are working," she told Coen.[3] Through Volunteers in Service to America (VISTA, created by Lyndon Johnson's administration), Weiner found her subjects on a central California garlic farm. She stayed in a local motel, and at 6:00 each morning joined her subjects in the fields or in labor camps. She spent six intense weeks with the people whose lives she documented in the book. What emerges is a portrait not only of their struggles but of what Weiner described as the "unbreakable" human spirit.

In her introduction to the book, Weiner notes some of the ugly facts of agricultural labor: "a system of usurious credit frequently imposes conditions of almost life-long slavery; opportunities for education are for all practical purposes non-existent; housing, sanitary and medical facilities are inadequate." And she makes explicit that "union organization and recognition" represent the only hope in a "never-ending battle against the growers and, perhaps most important of all, against the indifference on the part of the rest of the country."[4]

Yet small hands, big hands is no political diatribe. As one reviewer noted, "Her subjects are very much individuals, and in their brief space for telling their lives they speak with composure and style. Mrs. Weiner's photos are similarly unmelodramatic, nonpropagandistic, memorable—a rarity of photo-journalism in these days of jarring, dismissible images."[5]

small hands, big hands was the second book for children that Weiner created using tape recordings and her photographs. Among her other books, It's Wings That Make Birds Fly (1968) documented the life of a Harlem boy, and They Call Me Jack: the Story of a Boy from Puerto Rico (1973) chronicled another New York boy's experience.

Born in Poland, Weiner escaped with her family during the Nazi invasion, moving to the United States. She studied photography with noted photojournalist Dan Weiner at the Photo League, a photographers' cooperative established as an offshoot of the radical Film and Photo League. She married him and joined the Photo League, likewise taking up a career as a photojournalist. (In 1947 the Photo League was placed on the attorney general's list of subversive organizations, and it was forced to close down in 1951, after having trained some of the most important photographers of the twentieth century.)

Dan Weiner's untimely death in a plane crash while on assignment in 1959 was a devastating blow. This loss and Sandra Weiner's personal confrontation with the Nazi threat gave her an instinctive sympathy for society's victims. In small hands, big hands, Weiner strove to let her subjects speak for themselves and to show images that capture the truth of their experience. A heartfelt work, it suggests why Weiner has won international acclaim as a photographer.

As for Doria Ramirez and her coworkers, thanks to Chavez, the UFW, and their allies, major gains have been made, but today efforts continue, and agricultural workers—many of them undocumented and Spanish-speaking—still face difficult conditions.

NOTES

1. Sandra Weiner, introduction to small hands, big hands (dated March 1970) (New York: Pantheon, 1970).

2. New York Times Book Review, 6 Dec. 1970, 58.

3. Qtd. in "Authors and Editors," Publishers' Weekly, 26 Oct. 1970, 18.

4. Weiner, 1.

5. Peter Nabokov, "Human Beasts of Burden," New York Times Book Review, 8 Nov. 1970, pt. 2, p. 2.

I am Doria Ramirez and I am eighteen years old. I went to school when I was ten years and got out when I was thirteen because I had to help my parents. We used to get up at 3:30 in the morning to pick potatoes and I didn't like it. Always I didn't like it. It was very cold. Another reason I had to leave—I didn't have any shoes with me and I didn't have any sweater and it was in the winter time.

I knew we didn't have any money so I couldn't say, "Poppa I need shoes for my feet." But when I saw all the other children with shoes I knew that there had to be a way to change that life. The way I was feeling I didn't want my sisters to feel the same thing. It was then I started thinking that this was not a life for the migrant worker or any worker. Without shoes and warm clothes all these Mexican children could not go to school. My father did not feel it this way but when I used to see my younger brothers working so hard and feeling so tired at age thirteen years, I wanted to see them in a different position in their life.

We are nine in our family and we were being paid piece rate. With a big family you can work a long day and think you are making some money. But in the winter time when there is no work it doesn't help to have such a large family. My father would never go to the Welfare. He always told us that he didn't like to go to the Welfare because you had to let the Governor's office know what size shoe he was wearing and what

size underwear—and he didn't like it. It was too private. My mother tried to sew our clothes but when you don't have any money you have the time, but you can't buy the material to sew.

The growers give us the jobs because we are a large family. I am not afraid to ask the growers for more money because I used to see families just starving. My father asked, "Why do you always have to argue with the grower?" But always in a family there has to be one member that asks. There has to be one that talks too much. And I was the one. My father would say, 'Don't ask for more or they will not let us work and take all the money away." To him it always has to be the way they gave us. I said, "No, that's not enough, I don't want to live that way." He would answer, "My father lived that way and we can live the same way."

We do whatever each farm needs, either thinning, or tying, or hoeing, or picking. We have picked almost every fruit and vegetable growing, but the hardest job that I know, as a woman, is sugarbeets. Even the men say it is hard. After thinning you leave each plant five inches apart from the other. That's very hard because always you have to be bent over on your knees with a small hoe, maybe twelve hours and this makes you sick with the kidneys or back. You must thin it while it is still a young plant. If you try sitting it doesn't work and you do not get the work done.

There was this man, he was a labor contractor for the ranchers, and he hired about 200 people and I made about 33 or 32 rows that day. You have to be a fast person. I had gone with shoes and socks into the field but I came out without the shoes or socks because the blisters on my feet they were paining me. So I went back to the car to lie down because I couldn't stand or move. I was already half with fever from tiredness. The labor contractor didn't want to pay my father and he was saying, "Well, your daughter has to come out and

get the money, she knows how to sign her name." And even though I was feeling so sick I was happy because I thought we were going to have so much money for the family. And all we got was seven dollars for nine people working twelve hours.

I always had to work to help my parents because I love my parents. We just stick together. This is why it's good to have a big family because together we make our own home. A small home but it's my home and I don't need any other home because I have my family. We have two rooms, a kitchen and another room, and we sleep like hot dogs.

I get up when my mother starts preparing the lunches for the day in the field. She bakes bread and makes tacos and tortillas. At night when we return home she washes the clothes and hangs up just pants on the clothes wire, and the neighbors say, "You have only boys," and my mother said, "No, we are six girls and three boys." In the evenings parents are tired and do not talk very much.

Another time I saw my father crying. That day had been a bad day for us. We had arrived in the field at 4:30 in the morning and they had to put big lights on the tractors so we could see how to pick the potatoes. And we picked all day until 5 o'clock in the evening. There were six of us and we earned only twelve dollars. And that was when my father wanted to cry. It was then I started to think again that I must make a change. My father, he said, "Now I understand you and why you are so angry at the growers."

Once I got really mad when I was working with one of the growers and we were organizing and he fired all the people that were organizing or interested in a union. When we walked from the fields everybody walked with us. But the next day the farmer found other people to work for him and we knew it would take a long time

before all the migrant workers understood about the union. It took my father a long time. Now I spend a lot of time helping to organize farm workers and we hope the dream of a union will come true. It's just like Martin Luther King when he said, "I have a dream too."

I am much happier now because I am learning so much. When I was in school I didn't learn anything. I had to rush from school to pick cotton and I would forget the English and arithmetic. I never learned to speak English but I learned English real good when I started walking on the picket lines asking people not to buy grapes in the stores that sold them. At the first boycott they wouldn't take me because I didn't speak the language. So I had to learn fast to speak English. Everybody helped me who knew how to speak it. I still don't know how to read or write but I will learn.

It is hard to believe now that I had lived the way we did for so long. I remember at home on Saturday we would all take baths and eat together and then my father would play the trumpet. My sister and my brother-in-law played the guitar and my little sister played the guitar and we would sing and dance. Even though our life is with so much work we love to have fun and have some happiness. You have to carry some happiness in your heart.

Part 5

Imagine

JULIA MICKENBERG & PHILIP NEL

The idea that the imagination can be transformative—even revolutionary—has had many advocates, from the Romantics to progressive educators, from nonsense poets to student radicals. In his "Defence of Poetry" (1821), Percy Bysshe Shelley considered the imagination "the greatest instrument of moral good" and felt that poetry—a vital aid to imagination—heralded "the awakening of a great people to work a beneficial change in opinion or institution."[1] Echoing Shelley's claim that poetry "awakens and enlarges the mind" and "makes familiar objects be as if they were not familiar," Celia Catlett Anderson and Marilyn Fain Apseloff write that "[n]onsense literature uses the spirit of playfulness to rearrange the familiar world. It thereby reveals that the rules we live by are not inevitable." As they say in their *Nonsense Literature for Children: Aesop to Seuss* (1989), nonsense "teach[es] the young that the world constructed by their elders is an artificial thing."[2] Such a realization allows children to question the rules of adult behavior, freeing them to form their own ideas. From Lewis Carroll's *Alice's Adventures in Wonderland* (1865) to Dr. Seuss's *On Beyond Zebra!* (1955), writers have seen the imagination as a realm in which children can at least imagine another world, if not actually realize it. Student radicals of the 1960s recognized the revolutionary power of the imagination when they proclaimed, "All power to the imagination."[3]

Imagination is not always a force for good, but it is undeniably powerful—and its basic capacity to "tolerate images that oppose the laws of nature"[4] suggests that imagination is what allows people—including, or perhaps especially, children—to recognize that what exists is not necessarily what ought to exist, or what might exist. As an art educator put it in the 1960s, "Because of its amorality, the imagination is basically subversive. By that we do not mean it is entirely destructive but that it undermines beliefs and the religious, social, aesthetic, and intellectual structures, built upon those beliefs."[5] In the first story in this section, Herminia Zur Mühlen's "Why?" (1925), a boy's persistent question—"Why?"—prompts most to criticize him, but a dryad encourages him to keep asking. According to her, he must ask why the poor have so little and the idle rich have so much, and he must ask "so long and so often that they [the poor] will fall on the structure of injustice like a hammer and smash it." The story supports the child's impulse to question adult naysayers and, by extension, the social order itself.

In *Exile's Return*, a memoir of the 1920s, Malcolm Cowley describes Greenwich Village bohemians' belief that children with liberated imaginations would create a better future: "If a new educational system can be introduced, [they believed,] one by which children are encouraged to develop their own personalities, to blossom freely like flowers, then the world will be saved by this new, free generation."[6] Embracing this spirit, lyrical leftists of the 1910s and 1920s—including children's authors Carl Sandburg, Wanda Gág, and Alfred Kreymborg—supported children's right to dream. As many of Sandburg's *Rootabaga Stories* do, Kreymborg's *Funnybone Alley* (1927) figures the imaginative and playful traits of childhood as liberating. In Kreymborg's "Long Words and Short Ones," reproduced here, a school principal tells his students that he has much to learn from them, and that "we're all equals here." In his school, "[n]othing was discouraged," and teachers encourage students to use their imaginations and pursue their dreams. Indeed, if students' attention wanders during class, they receive not demerits but encouragement "to attempt what the Principal called 'expressing themselves.'"

As these early twentieth-century writers did, many children's authors from later in the century valued children's imagination as a powerful and ameliorative force, encouraging children to imagine alternatives to adult institutions and practices. For instance, in many of Dr. Seuss's books, children challenge the alleged wisdom of adults. In *Bartholomew and the Oobleck* (1949), Bartholomew insists that King Derwin apologize for miring his kingdom in toxic goo; in *The Butter Battle Book* (1984), a child invites us to ask why two nations of similar people would seek to destroy each other. Here and in many of his books, Seuss suggests that children have better ideas than adults. In Crockett Johnson's *Harold and the Purple Crayon* (1955) and its six sequels, Harold's crayon-created world invites readers to envision worlds of their own. While he draws his way in and out of adventures, Harold conveys the idea that all we need is a crayon to create a universe. Leo Lionni's *Frederick* (1967) describes a group of mice who diligently gather food for the winter—except for Frederick, a mouse who spends all his time thinking and dreaming. When the food supply runs out, instead of blaming Frederick for his laziness, the other mice turn to him as their savior. His imagination, and especially his poetry, sustains them—the mice live on the hope supplied by his art. As in *Harold and the Purple Crayon*,

Jon Agee's *The Incredible Painting of Felix Clousseau* (1988) posits that what we imagine can become real. Clousseau's painting of a duck actually quacks, his portrait of a cannon lets loose a cannonball, and his rendering of a dog catches a criminal. Likewise, in Faith Ringgold's *Tar Beach* (1991), Cassie's vision helps her soar above the prejudice and economic limitations faced by her family. When she imagines herself flying over the city, Cassie feels free, powerful, and hopeful. Perhaps most famously of all, Maurice Sendak's *Where the Wild Things Are* (1963) shows Max dreaming his way to and from the wild things, mastering unruly emotions through his imagination. By suggesting that creativity can alter reality, these works send an empowering message to children.

Other works rely upon more subtle representations of a child's hopes and dreams. In Lydia Gibson's *The Teacup Whale* (1934), included here, a boy finds a baby whale in a puddle and continues to believe that it *is* a whale when his mother insists that it's only a polliwog. In the end, the whale grows huge, vindicating his judgment. Similarly, in Ruth Krauss's *The Carrot Seed* (1945), a boy continues to water his carrot seed, despite the fact that his mother, father, and brother doubt that it will ever grow into a carrot. In the final pages, a carrot as large as the boy himself *does* come up, verifying his belief in himself and his project. In both works, the item named in the title—the carrot seed or the whale—serves as a metaphor for believing in something, which not only grows larger through the child's belief but also compels others to believe in it. While there is no guarantee that a child with an active imagination will become a politically progressive adult, there is at least the possibility that he or she may be willing to "think outside of the box" and to consider alternative social arrangements.

As "Why?" does, some stories harness the imaginative faculty to suggest specific changes to those social arrangements. In I. Kaminski's *A Hen Goes to Brownsville* (1937), a hen travels to Brooklyn's Brownsville neighborhood upon hearing that its children don't have enough to eat—she will feed them with her eggs. She "pays" her way there with eggs and feels bewildered by people's requests that she pay with money. This thinking, socially conscious hen stops traffic, questions the law, and refuses to be stopped from her mission of feeding hungry children. While the story is obviously a fantasy, this silly hen is up to serious business.

Revised or adapted fairy tales often (though not always) argue for a particular political agenda. As do several other stories in *Little Rebels*, Jay Williams's *The Practical Princess* (1969) takes a different approach to stories of knights and princesses. Intelligent and quick-witted, Williams's "practical" princess is quite capable of rescuing herself *and* her prince. In questioning gendered assumptions, the story prefigures other feminist fairy tales, like Robert Munsch's *The Paper Bag Princess* (1980), Jeanne Desy's "The Princess Who Stood on Her Own Two Feet" (1981) (see pages 243–49), Ellen Jackson's *Cinder Edna* (1994), and Cornelia Funke's *The Princess Knight* (2003). Some fairy tale revisions go further, playing with the very form of the book itself—notably Jon Scieszka and Lane Smith's *The Stinky Cheese Man and Other Fairly Stupid Tales* (1992) and David Wiesner's *The Three Pigs* (2001). Not content merely to alter a tale's message, these works bend the boundaries of the picture book form.

As Daniel Pinkwater's *The Big Orange Splot* (1977) and Sam Swope and Barry Root's *The Araboolies of Liberty Street* (1989) do, the stories in this section celebrate nonconformists and dreamers. (Both books feature protagonists who, in disregarding the aesthetic norms of the neighborhood, inspire rebelliousness in their neighbors, who in turn repaint their houses in wild colors.) Anticipating Louse Fitzhugh's nonconformist *Harriet the Spy* (1963), Sandra Scoppettone and Fitzhugh's *Suzuki Beane* (1961) (which we were unable to reprint) unites the title character (a daughter of beatniks) and Henry Martin (a son of squares) in a skeptical look at the different social orders to which each belongs. When the Martins mock Suzuki for her beatnik appearance and the Beanes criticize Henry for his square-ness, the free-thinking Suzuki declares that "CHILDREN ARE PEOPLE" and decides that she and Henry "understood more about love and life" than their parents. At the story's end, the two children set off to "get other kids who weren't allowed to be people" and to form a community where children are free to be themselves.

Though "Imagine" is comprised of only five stories, we might include some of the many other stories that value creativity and unconventional thinking. To be a child is to be subject to the rules of others; fostering imaginative engagement with the world may show children how and why they might challenge these rules. True, placing too much faith in the imagination may seem quixotic, but, if children can maintain their willingness to question and to dream, perhaps they will sustain a cognitive agility often lost in adulthood. Perhaps, through her or his imaginative flexibility, a child "creates anew the universe," to borrow Shelley's phrase.[7] In dreams begin possibilities.

NOTES

1. Percy Bysshe Shelley, "A Defence of Poetry" (1821), *Shelley's Poetry and Prose*, eds. Donald H. Reiman and Sharon B. Powers (New York: Norton, 1977), 488, 508.

2. Celia Catlett Anderson and Marilyn Fain Apseloff, *Nonsense Literature for Children: Aesop to Seuss* (Hamden, CT: Shoe String Press and Library Professional Publications, 1989), 94.

3. This was the slogan of French student radicals, but it captures the spirit of many young radicals in the United States as well.

4. Mary J. Reichling, "Images of Imagination," *Journal of Research in Music Education* 38:4 (Winter 1990): 283.

5. Robert J. Saunders, "The Ethics of the Imagination," *Art Education* 15:6 (June 1962): 12.

6. Malcolm Cowley, *Exile's Return: A Literary Odyssey of the 1920s* (New York: Viking Press, 1951), 60.

7. Shelley, 505.

24

"Why?" from *Fairy Tales for Workers' Children* (1925)

Written by Herminia Zur Mühlen (1883-1951), Translated by Ida Dailes, Illustrated by Lydia Gibson (1891-1969)

EDITORS' INTRODUCTION

This story comes from *Fairy Tales for Workers' Children* (1925), a collection translated from the German by Ida Dailes and published with new illustrations by Lydia Gibson (see pages 151–52). In her foreword to American readers ("Little Comrades"), Dailes notes,

> You have read many fairy tales, some of them very beautiful and some that frightened you with their horrible giants and goblins. But never, I am sure, have you read such lovely stories about real everyday things. You see poor people suffering around you every day; some of you have yourselves felt how hard it is to be poor. You know that there are rich people in the world, that they do not work and have all the good things of life. You also know that your fathers work hard and then worry about what will happen if they lose their jobs.
>
> Comrade Zur Mühlen, who wrote these fairy tales, tells us in a beautiful way how these things can be stopped. All of us who work must learn that we can make the world a better place for workers and their children to live in if we will help one another. She shows us that the rich people who do not work but keep us enslaved are our enemies; we must join together, we workers of the world, and stop these wrongs.[1]

Zur Mühlen, also known as the "runaway Countess" (the English title given to the translation of her memoirs), came from Austrian nobility. At a young age she developed a hatred of her own class. As a twelve-year-old she founded "a society for the betterment of the world," enlisting two cousins and several friends as members, and issuing a monthly bulletin featuring fiery editorials that condemned the nobility and the government.[2] The daughter of a diplomat, Zur Mühlen

traveled widely in Africa and Asia as a child and attended an elite girls' boarding school in Dresden. After her schooling she spent time in Geneva, studying the art of bookbinding and meeting revolutionaries from the unsuccessful 1905 uprising in Russia.

In her midtwenties she married the wealthy Count Zur Mühlen, a German baron who had a large estate in the Baltic, but the couple's political differences led to their divorce in 1913. Moving to Switzerland because of a lung disease, Zur Mühlen met the Hungarian Communist Stefan Klein, who became her lover, companion, and fellow traveler, as she too joined the Communist Party. Moving with Klein to Germany, Zur Mühlen became involved in the proletarian literary movement there and supported herself as a translator of authors including Upton Sinclair and Sinclair Lewis; as a journalist for newspaper and radio; and as a writer of novels, thrillers, memoirs, and political propaganda. Most significantly, she became Weimar Germany's "leading writer of revolutionary fairy tales for children."[3] Because of her political activities, Zur Mühlen was forced to leave Germany in 1933, and in ill health she lived in exile in various European countries, ending up in England. She remained a committed antifascist but renounced Stalinism and espoused leftist Catholicism in the 1930s.[4]

The proletarian bard Mike Gold hailed publication of this American edition of Zur Mühlen's stories as a significant event, noting, "The book is not a collection of the usual feeble-minded bedtime stories with which children are lulled to sleep, and their minds lulled to sleep, too, but it partakes of the nature of the best of the new workers' art: it stirs the child's mind to questioning, and it answers some of his questions."[5] Gold, like Dailes in her foreword, singled out "Why?" as a reminder that children should be constantly asking why injustice continues to exist. Gold hoped that "some American writer [in the communist movement] will turn his mind to children's stories, too," stories that could counter "the reactionary myths that are now pumped into children's minds—the Cinderella, Prince Charming, and King and Queen stories that have come to us from the old feudal world, and that still influence the children of workers."[6]

NOTES

1. Ida Dailes, foreword to Herminia Zur Mühlen, *Fairy Tales for Workers' Children*, trans. Ida Dailes, illus. Lydia Gibson (Chicago: Daily Worker Publishing Co.), 1925, n.p.

2. Hermynia Zur Mühlen, *The Runaway Countess*, trans. Frank Barnes (New York: Jonathan Cape & Harrison Smith), 15–24. (Zur Mühlen's first name sometimes appears as "Hermynia.")

3. Jack Zipes, ed. and trans., *Fairy Tales and Fables from Weimar Days* (Hanover, NH: UP of New England, 1989), 204.

4. Mererid Puw Davies, review of *Hermynia Zur Muhlen: Eine Biographie*, by Manfred Altner, *Journal of European Studies* 29:3 (Sept. 1999): 334.

5. Mike Gold, review of "Fairy Tales for Workers' Children," *The Worker's Monthly* 4:12 (October 1925): 571.

6. Ibid., 572.

Once upon a time there was a little boy, who had neither father nor mother, who lived in the poorhouse in a little village. He was the only child in the whole house; all the others were broken-down old people who were always gloomy and cranky, who liked best to sit quietly in the sun, and who would become angry whenever the little boy, while at play, would bump against them or make too much noise.

A sad life it was for little Paul. He never heard a kind word, no one loved him, and no one petted or comforted him whenever he was unhappy. Instead of that he was scolded every day and often he was even spanked. One peculiarity of his particularly irritated the supervisors of the poorhouse: at every occasion he used to ask, "Why?" always wanting to know the cause for everything.

"You mustn't always ask why," angrily declared the stout Matron who was in charge of the poorhouse. "Everything is as it is, and therefore it is right."

"But why have I no parents like the other children of the village have?" insisted little Paul.

"Because they are dead."

"Why did they die?"

"Because the good Lord willed it so."

"Why did the Lord will it so?"

"Keep quiet, you good-for-nothing! Leave me alone with your eternal questions." The fat woman was quite red with anger, because she knew no answer to Paul's questions, and nothing angers ignorant persons more than to be forced to say, "I don't know."

But no one was able to keep little Paul quiet. He looked right up into the angry red face and asked further, "Why are you so impatient with me?"

Slap! and he got a box on the ears. He began to cry, ran away, and while running asked, "Why do you hit me?"

He came to the chicken yard. There stood a big hen with many-colored feathers, cackling aloud, proudly strutting. "I have laid an egg! I have laid an egg!" And from all sides of the yard there sounded in chorus: "I have laid an egg! I have laid an egg!" The rooster, however, was angry because the hens were so proud of having done something which he could not do, and cried scornfully, "I am the rooster, you are only hens!" Along came Mary, the little blond servant of the poorhouse, gathered the eggs carefully into her blue apron, and carried them into the house.

"Where do all your eggs go to?" Paul asked the speckled hen.

"To the city," she cackled.

"Who eats them there?"

"The rich people, the rich people." Thus spoke the hen proudly, as though it were a special honor for her.

"Why don't I ever have an egg?" complained Paul. "I am always so hungry, you know."

"Because you are a poor Have-nothing." And the hen spread her plumage with dignity, and cocked her eye defiantly at Paul over her crooked beak.

"But why am I a poor Have-nothing?"

"Why Didn't I Ever Get An Egg?" Asked Paul

Now the hen became angry as had the stout Matron, and raged:

"Get off with you! You make me tired with your questions."

Disappointed, Paul slipped quietly away. The garden door stood open, and he stepped out onto the road, strolling along aimlessly until he came to the entrance of a cowshed. The shed belonged to a rich farmer.

Many sleek cows, white and reddish brown, stood in a row and gazed before them with large, soft eyes. Paul, feeling very hungry, stepped up to the most friendly looking cow, and begged, "Dear Cow, will you give me some of your milk to drink?"

"I dare not do that," replied the Cow. "The milk belongs to the farmer."

The little boy looked with astonishment at the Cow, then over the entire shed, slowly counting the animals: "One, two, three." Upon reaching twelve he stopped, for although there were many more cows, he stopped because the counting was too hard for him. In the poorhouse he was taught to be gentle and obedient, but nothing else. "Twelve cows," he said thoughtfully. "Is it possible that the farmer can drink the milk of twelve cows?"

"Oh no," the friendly Cow informed him. "He sells the milk in the city."

Paul remembered the words of the speckled hen, and he asked, "Do the poor children there get any of the milk?"

"Good gracious, Paul," sighed the Cow, "how stupid and inexperienced you still are! From the milk they make delicious whipped cream, which then goes on cakes and puddings, and these are bought by rich people."

"Why not by the poor—don't they like to eat good cakes?"

"You shouldn't ask me so many questions, little boy," replied the Cow. "I am only a dumb Cow, and do not know what to answer you. Besides, you had better go away. This is the time when the farmer comes to the barn, and should he see you it might mean a good beating for you."

Paul stroked the shining hide of the friendly Cow, and pursued his way. On and on he went, until he reached a great big wheat field through which the wind was blowing. It looked like softly moving golden waves. The ears sang with soft voices, sounding very sad, and Paul distinguished the words: "Soon the reapers will be here with their scythes, z-z, and will cut us down, z-z-z. Then the people will bake us into fine white bread, z-z-z."

"Who eats the white bread?" asked Paul, who had never in his life tasted a piece of white bread.

"The rich people, the rich people," sang the ears of wheat, swaying to the rhythm of the wind.

"Ah, again the rich people!" exclaimed Paul. "Does everything in this world belong to the rich people?"

"Everything, everything," buzzed the ears.

"Why?"

This question seemed to amuse the ears very much and almost doubling with laughter, they sang, "How silly, how stupid you are!" However, they failed to answer Paul's question. Paul was near to tears; he stamped angrily on the ground with his foot, and cried loudly, "I demand an answer to my questions. Is there no one to give me an answer?"

Just then a Porcupine crept slowly across the road and said, "The wisest creature I know of is the Owl who lives in the great oak forest. Why don't you go to her, you question mark."

"Can't you tell me why . . . ?"

The Porcupine did not permit Paul to finish; impatiently he drew in his head, shot out his quills, until he looked like a ball covered with spikes.

"I do not associate with people," he said, and his voice became as sharp as his quills. "They are too stupid for me. Go to the Owl, but be sure not to irritate her or she will gouge her eyes at you."

Night fell, sending out its black shadows, and covered all the land. It was dark in the forest and Paul became somewhat uneasy, yet this mysterious forest seemed more pleasant to him than the terrible poorhouse, and he walked on further.

The further he went the thicker and closer were the trees. Soon there was no longer a path; but Paul pushed on over the soft carpet of green moss. The fragrance of the forest was pleasant. Beneath the tall trees grew delicious strawberries and the little boy picked them and refreshed himself as he went along.

At last he came to a great oak, and saw the owl perched on one of the branches. The Owl wore a large pair of spectacles and studied attentively a green sheet which she held in her claws.

Paul halted beneath the tree and shouted, "Mrs. Owl! Mrs. Owl!"

But the Owl was so deeply absorbed in her studies, that she did not hear, and only after he had repeated his call several times did she look down. Uttering an angry cry, she glared down at Paul with fierce round eyes.

"Well, what is it you want?" she asked. "How dare you disturb me in my studies?"

"Excuse me, Mrs. Owl," begged Paul. "The Porcupine sent me to you. He told me that you are the wisest creature he knows of. Surely, you will be able to answer my questions."

"What matter the opinions of the Porcupine to me? What have I to do with your questions?" growled the Owl. "Why should I waste my precious time on such a stupid child as you? You know very well that I can see only at night and the summer nights are so short

that I have hardly time enough for my studies. I, too, think over all kinds of questions. One in particular has bothered me for countless years; I have grown old and grey over it, and yet no science in the world has helped me to solve it." The Owl sighed deeply and her countenance became sorrowful.

"And just what is this question of yours?" Paul inquired anxiously.

"Do you think, perhaps, that YOU can answer it, you young saucebox?" sneered the Owl. "Around this question hang all the other questions of the world; it is: Why are all people so stupid?"

"Are all people really so stupid?" asked Paul, astonished.

"Yes, and if you don't know that, why do you disturb me? Is it because you have never seen anything that you are so idiotic?"

"Very little," replied the little boy shamefacedly. "You ought to know, dear Mrs. Owl, that I live in a poorhouse, where there are only old folks, and naturally they are all wise."

"Ha, ha, ha," laughed the owl. It sounded most awful in the dark forest. "Ha, ha, ha! You are certainly another splendid example of the stupidity of mankind. So it is in the poorhouse that all people are wise? Well, we will see if you are right. Who is it that you like best in the poorhouse?"

"Mary."

"Who is Mary?"

"The maid."

"What does she do?"

"She works all day long. She gets up at five o'clock in the morning, and is the last one to go to bed."

"Then she most likely earns lots of money, wears beautiful clothes, and eats good food?"

"Oh no, she's as poor as a beggar, she patches her clothes over and over, and eats what other people leave."

"H-m-m. Well, why then does she work so hard if she gets nothing out of it?"

Little Paul thought a while, finally he said, "I don't know."

"But I know—it is because she is stupid. Mary knows, too, that there are fashionable ladies who don't move a hand, who wear gorgeous clothes, eat costly food, live in luxury. Hasn't Mary ever asked herself: How is it that I, who work all day long have nothing, and they, who do nothing, have everything?"

"I believe not."

"Well then, your Mary is stupid, very stupid. Whom do you still consider wise, you little sheep?"

"Old Jacob."

"Who is this Old Jacob?"

"He is an old laborer, he is eighty years old. He worked until his seventieth year. Now he can't do anything more, and has his hands and feet and legs crippled by rheumatism."

"He worked sixty years for others! A pretty long time. I suppose that Old Jacob is treated like a prince, everybody is terribly anxious to serve him? He has a wonderful soft bed for his tired limbs, gets a special kind of food every day, lives well and happily?"

"Oh no, the old matron always curses at him when he complains that the bread is too hard for his old teeth. And if he asks for a little tobacco, she gets angry and cries that he is unreasonable."

"Why then did Old Jacob work until he was seventy years old, if now when he's old he doesn't even live well?"

"I don't know."

"Because he is stupid. He knows also, just like Mary, that there are fine young gentlemen who do nothing at all and yet live like kings. Do you see now, little imp, that people are stupid?"

"Yes," said Paul sadly. "But I would like to ask you something, dear Mrs. Owl. Why are there rich people in the world?"

"You really ought to be able to answer this question yourself after our talk, little stupid head: Because the poor people are stupid."

"But why are they stupid?"

But now the owl became angry, the same as the fat matron and the brightly speckled hen.

"Didn't I tell you, little imp, you stupid little person, that I have been thinking about this question for years and years? Come back again eighty years from now, perhaps I will answer you then."

"But why . . . ?"

"Quiet!" the owl commanded little Paul. "You have stolen enough valuable time from me already. Go to the Cuckoo!"

"Where does she live?" asked the frightened little boy.

But already the Owl had adjusted her spectacles, become absorbed in the green leaf, and gave no answer.

"Oh, poor me!" little Paul thought sadly. "Now I am to go to the Cuckoo, and I don't even know where he lives. Will the Cuckoo know more than the Owl? And I am already so tired, my feet hurt me."

He sank down upon the soft green moss at the foot of a slender young birch. Little by little he became very depressed. He was thinking how he was altogether abandoned and alone, how nobody was good to him, and all at once he began to weep bitterly. Thereupon he became aware of a thin small voice coming from somewhere high up; it sounded like little bells of pure silver.

"Why are you crying, little child?" the silvery voice asked.

Paul looked upward and he saw the most wonderful little creature he had ever beheld in his life. Upon a branch of the birch sat a fairy. She had long golden-blond hair, which reached down to her feet, her little face was pale and delicate as moonlight, and her big eyes shone green like the leaves of the birch. She fluttered down toward Paul very lightly, alighted on his shoulder, it was as though a light leaf touched him, and stroked his face with her tiny white hands. Paul's heart warmed. How good it was to be touched by tender hands! His tears stopped, he stared at the little creature, and asked at last, "Who are you?"

"I am a Dryad, I am the soul of the birchtree," declared the little creature. "All day long I must sit in my tree, but when night comes I am free, I walk about on the earth, play with the other Dryads, my sisters. But tell me, for what reason are you sad?"

Paul told the Dryad of his unhappiness, saying at the end, "I must always ask why. The question burns in my heart, hurts me, and I believe if I ever receive an answer I will be happy. But now this question stands between me and all other people who do not ask the question like a big wall and this makes me so lonesome."

The little Dryad laughed and her pretty face became sweeter and more tender than before.

"You are mistaken, little Paul, she said softly. You are not alone. Hundreds and thousands ask the same question, sad and troubled. Put your ear down to the earth and tell me what you hear."

Paul obeyed. At first he heard only an indistinct sighing and whispering, then he thought he heard a terrible weeping and crying, and at last he heard words.

"Mother, I am hungry, why is there nothing to eat?" cried a child's voice.

"I am stifling in this hot city, why can't I go to the country like my rich schoolmates?" murmured a boy's voice.

"I work all day, why are wages so low that I scarcely have enough to live on?" sobbed a woman's voice.

"Why have the idlers everything and the workers nothing?" said a man's voice threateningly.

And then all the voices rang together, crying, murmuring, sobbing, threatening, "Why? Why?"

Paul sat up, looked at the little Dryad who sat very quietly near him and asked, "Who are these people whom I heard?"

"They are your people," replied the little Dryad. "That is your family. You have heard all the languages in the world, you will hear questions from all mouths, angrily, anxiously, threateningly. Every day new voices join the chorus, and when the thousands of voices become millions and billions, then there will be an end to the misery and poverty and to those lazy parasites."

"When will that be?" asked Paul eagerly.

"That I cannot tell you, I know only this—every time I put my ear to the earth, I find new voices added and that is how I know that the day is not far distant."

"And can nothing be done to make the day come sooner?"

"Of course. There are many, many people who do not know yet how good it is for other people and how bad their lives are; who work like beasts and never ask why their honest labor brings a starvation wage. These poor blind people must be shown the truth, and this is not at all easy, because the poor are so tired from the day's work that they can hardly think; and the rich do everything not to awaken questions in the minds of the workers. That is why they punish every one who asks, 'Why?' You have already learned from your own experience, little Paul."

"Then I must continue asking questions?"

"Yes, little Paul, but do not ask the rich, they will not answer you because if they did they would have to say, 'The world is such a bad place for poor people because we, the rich, are greedy, selfish, vile,' and no person

likes to say that about himself. But go to the poor people, ask them, 'Why do you eat dry bread though you work hard, while the idle rich eat cake? Why are your children pale, thin and ill while the rich children are rosy, fat and healthy? Why does your long life of toil end in the poorhouse, whereas the lazy grafters are well taken care of in their old age, resting luxuriously from their lives of idleness?' Ask the poor people these questions so long and so often that they will fall on the structure of injustice like a hammer and smash it. Will you do it, little Paul?"

"Yes," replied the boy with eyes alight.

The little Dryad kissed his forehead and said earnestly, "Your life will be hard, little Paul. The rich, who are afraid of losing what they have robbed, will punish you. They will try to choke the question in your throat, they will throw you into jail, that no one may hear your voice. But you must not lose courage, for the question was not born in you in vain, you are destined to speak before many thousands who are today still dumb. And you will find comrades, friends—you will not be alone."

The little Dryad nodded laughingly to Paul, swept lightly upwards, and sat on a branch of the birch.

"Are you going already?" asked little Paul, worried.

"You must go home, little Paul. But you must always come back and I will comfort you and help you."

"Wait a little," begged Paul. "The Owl said in eighty years, not until eighty years from now, she will be able to answer my question. That is a long time. Did the Owl speak truly?"

"That depends on you people," replied the light, silvery voice of the tiny Dryad. "Perhaps it will take you eighty years to become wise, perhaps if you, you and your comrades, do not stop asking questions, it may only take fifty years. The great day of freedom may come in twenty, in ten years. Yes, perhaps even tomorrow.

The tiny Dryad disappeared into the tree, but all the trees called in light, joyous voices to little Paul:

"Tomorrow! Tomorrow! Tomorrow!"

25

Excerpt from *Funnybone Alley* **(1927)**

Written Alfred Kreymborg

(1883-1966), Illustrated by

Boris Artzybasheff (1899-1965)

EDITORS' INTRODUCTION

Funnybone Alley, from which Kreymborg's book takes its title, is a crooked street in Ballyboo, an imaginary neighborhood in New York City. The people on Funnybone Alley have no head for business (they refuse to charge more for their goods than they are worth "and often charge less"), and the people in town instinctively look out for one another. Children—like Lonesome Sam Pumpernickel, Bolivar Bill, and Strawberry Sue—take imaginary adventures and roam through the real world of the city, delighting in all it has to offer. Reviewing *Funnybone Alley* for the *New York Post*, Newbery award–winning children's author Rachel Field proclaimed, "No more beautifully made or artistically inspiring book could be put into the hands of children today. Such decorations should do much to stimulate a new interest in skyscrapers, city lamp-posts, in streets and parks, in sandwich men and brokers of silk hats and other personages and familiar sights of here and now."[1]

Field's mention of "here and now" was probably a reference to a major trend in progressive education, popularized by educator and author Lucy Sprague Mitchell's "Here and Now" stories. Influenced by the philosophy of John Dewey, Mitchell and others held that children learned best through direct experience of the world around them. The section of the book included here, "Long Words and Short Ones," shows Kreymborg's interest in a new kind of school that would liberate the child's imagination and stimulate learning. Its serious ideas are punctuated by Kreymborg's distinctive "comic spirit," which the *New York Times* described as "detached and gay and gallant, perceiving life as fantasy and tragedy."[2]

At the center of the modernist literary movement, Kreymborg wrote dozens of works (primarily poetry and drama), but his greatest contribution was probably his ability to recognize literary talent. He founded and edited or coedited several of the most important modernist literary magazines, including *Glebe*, *Others*, and *American Caravan*.

Born in New York City, Kreymborg was educated in public schools and raised Roman Catholic. Before establishing himself as a writer Kreymborg made a living as a professional chess player. He was a regular at photographer Alfred Stieglitz's famous "291" gallery in New York City. Along with painter and photographer Man Ray and other artists, he helped found an anarchist art colony in Ridgefield, New Jersey.[3] Kreymborg's verse play, *Lima Beans*, was performed by the Provincetown Players, and with his wife, Dorothy, Kreymborg traveled the country performing puppet plays.

Kreymborg once wrote that his "political convictions embrace any leader or average person who never loses sight of the social under-dog and who does his utmost toward making democracy a really living process for everyone concerned."[4] His growing preoccupation with economic inequality and war emerge in "The Economic Muse," a series of poems written from 1929 to 1938, and in "Arms and Armageddon," pacifist poems written between 1939 and 1944.

Funnybone Alley was made into a record album in 1945, in collaboration with radical composer Elie Siegmeister.

Boris Artzybasheff was born in Kharkov, Russia, and was the son of Michael Artzybasheff, a well-known Russian novelist and playwright. He attended Prince Tenishev's school, which Artzybasheff described as "an extremely liberal and progressive school for the sons of the rich and powerful."[5] At school, Artzybasheff's work in art class was so far above the work of his peers that his teachers did not even try to grade it. When his father could not afford the school's high fees, school officials offered a scholarship so that he would continue. Artzybasheff completed the equivalent of a year at college before revolution and civil war forced him into the military and then on a series of travels, which ultimately landed him in New York City. Although he barely subsisted at first, he decorated his apartment in a fifteenth-century Russian style so striking that a 1921 issue of *House Beautiful* published a story on it.[6] His murals for the interior of a Russian restaurant around this time attracted the attention of the publisher E. P. Dutton. After that his career as an illustrator took off, although he continued designing interiors, stage sets, and even clothing. Artzybasheff designed and illustrated dozens of books, as well as writing and illustrating several of his own. He also did commercial work, including numerous covers for *Time* magazine.

In his masterwork of collected drawings, *As I See* (1954), now a cult classic, Artzybasheff proclaimed,

> I dislike every form of tyranny and control of thought including communism, fascism, jingoism and spread eagleism. All these should be remitted to hell from which they sprung. It would seem to me there is very little human about men at times, except their shapes. However, since the scientists, through many experiments on laboratory mice, have proven that it is possible to accumulate enough experience to negotiate a simple maze, I have much hope for our future. We still have time to learn. After all, as a race, we are much younger than mice.[7]

NOTES

1. Rachel Field, review of *Funnybone Alley*, *New York Evening Post*, 24 Sept. 1927, 10.

2. Lloyd Morris, "History of American Artistic Revolt in an Autobiography" (review of "Troubadour"), *New York Times Book Review*, 29 Mar. 1925, 7.

3. *American National Biography* (New York: Oxford UP, 2004), accessed online; Christine Stansell, *American Moderns: Bohemian New York and the Creation of a New Century* (New York: Henry Holt, 2000), 99–100.

4. Autobiographical note taken from *World Authors* (New York: Wilson, 1966). Accessed online.

5. Qtd. in *Current Biography* (New York: Wilson, 1945).

6. Ibid.

7. Boris Artzybasheff, *As I See* (New York: Dodd, Mead, 1954), n.p.

XVI. LONG WORDS AND SHORT ONES

The finest feature about the school the youngsters attended was this: it always contained something or other they loved so much they hated to leave it. The school had grown mellow and kindly with age. Its very appearance gave this impression. It was as hazily yellow as the first foliage of autumn and as lazily yellow as the renewal of shoots in spring. Its outer walls formed a tall hexagon. Not a perfect hexagon—since nothing was perfect here. Not even the teachers. Or the Principal—Dr. Isosceles. But a figure composed of six long backs, joining arms at the sides without making angles, and reaching up to small towers or heads bending over something between them: a playground shaded with trees. It was all very simple and quiet. No fuss or feathers. Nothing elaborate.

The wrinkles on the face of old Dr. Isosceles were not only wise, but as gentle as the creases in a pillow case. Though the teachers under his care had wrinkles too, they were not yet so numerous. But they held a similar wisdom—or tolerance. The Principal was fond of long words. Especially at the morning assembly. He would have used "tolerance" in preference to "wisdom." Doubtless because he had beheld so many things. And grown modest with the years.

"I have much more to learn than to teach," he sighed one morning as he gazed at the rows of faces, like so many apples on a fruit-stand gazing at him. "You little shavers down there think otherwise. Or your parents think otherwise for you. And send you here to learn otherwise. But I say to you and to them—I have lots to learn too. I can get it from you—providing you love me as much as I do you—or something in between —something like it. No, don't applaud—it's disturbing —and now I've forgotten what I wanted to add.

"You laugh? That's an interruption too. You're glad I've forgotten something. I don't blame you. It proves I'm not above you. That I can blunder much faster than you. It's nice to hear others making mistakes for a change. It makes one feel so much lighter. And less reprehensible.

"Who's raising his hand over there? Raspberry Red? Don't stand up—it'll make you blush. And we're all equals here. You want to know what it means? Reprehensible? It means nothing here. And don't look it up in the dictionary. When you're grown up, perhaps —but not now.

"The assembly is dismissed. I've lost my dignity again. I always do on a platform. So let me step down among you. And endeavor to find it there. You may go to your classrooms now. Don't let mistakes upset you. Or teachers trip you. Don't worry—be happy— that's all."

Similar care-free methods obtained in the class-rooms. With the teachers, who were called—not Miss Jones, Mr. Prism and so on—but Aunt Jones, Uncle Prism and so on. Aunt Jones taught spelling, Uncle Prism arithmetic, Aunt Syntax grammar, Uncle Wayfair geography, Aunt Crotchet drawing, Uncle Doodle music, Aunt Noble history.

Lonesome Sam had a mighty poor head for arithmetic, but an excellent ear for spelling. Right and wrong created a balance which nobody praised or censured. If Sam stuttered that four times thirteen are forty-two and forgot to carry one—and Bolivar carried it and corrected him—no one blamed Sam or praised Bill. Bill could spell a word doe when it should have been dough, or coff when it should have been cough. And stumbled over other words throughout the language left by our ancestors. Sam rarely made such mistakes. Nor did Aunt Jones laud him or scold Bill. Not really.

And if Raspberry Red—who had never been anywhere beyond his imagination—declared that an island is a body of water surrounded by land-nobody laughed. And if they did, not at him, but at what Uncle Wayfair said as he drew a fancied picture of Raspberry's

answer. "If the island we live on were water, our houses would float and we'd need boats to reach them." The boys almost wished it were true. It would have been similar to living in Holland.

Nothing was discouraged in the school—not even the arts. If the youngsters wished to paint things, write things, sing things, no one held them back. "Go to Aunt Crotchet, Aunt Noble, Uncle Doodle," was the move the teachers suggested.

Sam's mind, meaning no harm, might wander from multiplication toward the nearest window and his eye catch sight of the toy-balloon man passing by. Bolivar might have just spelled laugh with two 'fs because of a steeplejack crawling the side of a skyscraper with a flag in his hand which would soon be flying from the Chewing Gum Steeple. Raspberry might be dreaming of the flapjacks he saw on the way to school and see the cakes turn to islands as they bounced up and down on the pan of the girl who stood in the window of a lunch room. Strawberry, who was very very strict with herself —even when the teachers were not—might suddenly recall the horns of petunias opening up at the florist's that morning. And Christopher long for the letter the letter-carrier always failed to bring him from Sue.

The school had been made to meet such problems. Right in the middle of a spelling bee, blackboard exercise, lesson on peninsulas, teachers would have to ask—"Where are *you* off to now?" This meant that those who were threatened with dreams must leave the room. Not in disgrace. There were no such demerits here. They were sent out in order to attempt what the Principal called "expressing themselves."

If Sam felt like writing what he had seen, Bolivar like modeling, Christopher like composing—there was a private room for these needful activities. And now-a-days, this call of the wild to capture fleeting impressions had taken on the prelude of a definite direction. Still led by Sam in the desire to write and put on a play of their own, the group was moving closer and closer to the actual product and production. The final outline was still as vague as a shifting cloud. But certain details were as plain and radiant as they could be.

Sam had determined to write the lines of the play if he could. The bits he committed to scraps of paper continued to gather in the happiest profusion. And not a few actually began to fit together. As his chums hastened to assure him. Any whittling or carving of properties fell to the lot of Bolivar, any painting of scenes to Raspberry. For these two had shown the most consistent talent in that direction. The main rôle in the play, with lines to be sung as solos, would obviously be assumed by Sue. And since, in the general excitement, past scores were forgotten in favor of conscripting every available talent, Christopher was appointed to compose any music he possibly could on the mandolin his father, the pawnbroker, had given him. Cris buried his jealousy with joy and, prompted by the vision of hearing Sue sing while he played, burst A strings and E strings galore in his mounting enthusiasm.

Although the idea had been kept a secret so far from the rest of the school and the alley, the teachers had been confided in. And they used this trust as it deserved to be used—by hovering in the background and helping the budding artists whenever they requested it. Not

otherwise. And all that the youngsters had to be careful about in leaving class-rooms for the studio—as the Principal pronounced it—was not to make a noise. This the old doctor called "consideration." And those who stayed behind with the arithmetic and irregular verbs were requested to be quiet too. Not to look startled or even surprised. This he called "understanding."

The same leniency was shown to those who came a little late in the morning. Or left a little early in the afternoon. While such things were not encouraged, there were times they could not be helped. And so they were excused. The boys and girls were not obliged to say they wanted to go home before the dismissal bell. There was a word for such a need. Dr. Isosceles had invented it. He called it "the snickerbitties."

It meant that certain dark insects had begun to infect the patient with an itching complaint termed drowsiness. There was no quicker cure for this than fresh air, the streets or the home. The youngsters were honorable about the symptoms. They never made believe they had them. Nor did they have to say "snickerbitties." A yawn was usually sufficient. And the teacher would nod and the pupil leave. Without a sound.

The Principal called this "harmony." And when he said harmony he never meant music. But a word of four letters he used more often than any other. Much as he was fond of the longer words he always came back to this short one. Right in the heart of a complicated sentence, he would stop—repeat the word —and hesitate. And he would not continue. As a rule, he would repeat—"No, don't applaud—it's disturbing. And now you've made me forget what I wanted to add."

THE DOCTOR SWALLOWS THE DICTIONARY
When man began to express what he felt
On a stone or a tree or a pelt,
To us the signs that he made seem absurd
But to him each mark meant a word.
Now some are as old as the boldest cliffs
He carved into hieroglyphs,
While others are fresh as the day they were born
And it's many a tongue they adorn.
Some have come down from the Hebrew, the Greek,
And joined the great language we speak,
Some are more recent, the Roman or Latin—
And others were coined in Manhattan.
The latest come out of the streets in a gang—

Don't turn a deaf ear to such slang—
We'll learn to employ them and then before long
They'll join Noah Webster's throng.

Some flare up in a fountain and fall
In a spray with a whisht for a call,
Some move in rivers and twirl around nooks
And then they meander in brooks.
Others have feathers and fly into birds
And sing to the sun without words,
While others expand to immense balloons
And go sailing as silent as moons.
Some are as light as the night butterflies
With sorrow in front of their eyes,
Others are shiny or slimy or squirmy
And ever so fond of the wormy.
Finally some have to go back to bed,
Broken or shrunken or dead,
But some come to birth again, some rise to earth again,
Under the glance of the rain.

Some are as crooked as cobble-stones
With rumbles and bumps in their bones,
Some are as smooth as a boulevard
And sniff upon those in a yard.
Some have no speech but a groan or a sigh
And others are blind of one eye,

Some are as agile as tumbling clowns
And some prefer wrinkles and frowns.
Some are so short that they stub their toes
Over those with a foot out for foes,
Some trot about with their nose in the air
And buttercup curls in their hair.
Others run round in a rigmarole
With nothing but that for a soul,
While some mean all you can feel in a touch,
And some you can never clutch.

None mean as much by themselves as in groups
And some mean still more in troops.
Some in a line can stir up tragedies
None of the others can ease.
Most, as soon as they grow to a crowd,
Want the first place and exclaim aloud
For hatchets, arrows, daggers and darts
To pierce all their enemies' hearts.
Some are composed of the swiftest hate
Because the lucky ones live in state,
While those who have much must have a bit more—
They soon send the rest to war.
And as they elbow and hammer and squeeze,
Stumble and tumble and fall to their knees,
Rise but to scramble for one more shove,
It's time for that tiny peacemaker—love.

26

The Teacup Whale (1934)

Lydia Gibson (1891–1964)

EDITORS' INTRODUCTION

One of three daughters of the English-born architect Robert W. Gibson, Lydia Gibson was a child of privilege who became an advocate for the less privileged. Her affiliation with politically progressive causes probably began in the 1910s, when she was marching for women's suffrage and publishing her poetry and artwork in *The Masses*, a radical magazine that "owed allegiance to no single sectarian dogma and often combined Freudianism, feminism, socialism, syndicalism, anarchism, and bohemianism in a heady but gregarious blend."[1]

Contributors to *The Masses*, all of whom were unpaid, included poets Carl Sandburg, Amy Lowell, and Louis Untermeyer; political cartoonists Art Young and Boardman Robinson; and Ashcan School artists John Sloan, George Bellows, and Robert Henri. Through her *Masses* connections, Gibson met defenders of Tom Mooney, the labor leader framed for a 1916 bombing in San Francisco. Among the group advocating Mooney's release was Robert Minor, then an anarchist and political cartoonist, whose work also appeared in *The Masses*. Minor fell in love with Gibson, but she, then twenty-five years old, turned down this 32-year-old divorcé.[2]

President Wilson's Espionage Act shut down *The Masses* in December 1917, but Gibson continued creating art for radical publications such as *The Daily Worker* and *The Masses'* successor, *The Liberator*. Meanwhile, Minor traveled to the Soviet Union, where he became a Bolshevik. After Minor returned, Gibson, having undergone a change of heart, sought him out, and they married in 1923. As Joseph North notes, Gibson "was not a Communist," and Minor "spent much of their honeymoon reading to her the works of Lenin."[3] With Minor, Gibson visited Bartolomeo Vanzetti, the indicted Italian anarchist and cause célèbre, in Charleston Prison, drawing a sketch of him for *The Liberator*. In 1926, Gibson traveled to the Soviet Union with Minor.

After their return, Gibson continued her involvement with radical politics by joining the New York John Reed Club, one of several communist clubs created to nurture leftist talent, and by contributing to the new communist children's magazine, *The Pioneer*.[4] In 1933–1934, she created *The Teacup Whale*, the sole children's book that she both wrote and illustrated. Gibson's tale features a young boy who is sure the small creature he finds in a puddle is a whale (not a polliwog, as his mother keeps calling it), and he has no doubt that it will grow until it really is "enormous." And it does. If *The Teacup Whale* is not explicitly radical, Gibson's politics invite us to read the story as encouraging children to believe in their big dreams, to discount the advice of doubters, and to follow their own sense of what feels right and true. Or it could simply be a story about a boy who brings home a whale. Certainly, contemporary reviews of *The Teacup Whale* neither mentioned the politics of the book's author nor hinted at a political subtext. The *New York Times Book Review* considered it a "pleasantly nonsensical story," and the *Boston Evening Transcript* predicted that it would "delight children."[5]

Gibson and Minor had no children, instead dedicating their lives to leftist activism. Along with William Gropper, Lynd Ward, and others, Gibson called for an American Artists Congress against fascism, which had its first meeting in 1936. Minor went to Spain to help organize the Abraham Lincoln Brigade, fighting against Franco. Minor ran unsuccessfully for several offices (including mayor of New York City and governor of New York) and served as the American Communist Party's general secretary when Earl Browder was imprisoned, 1941–1942. During the postwar Red Scare, Gibson frequently posted bail for arrested communist leaders. Even after Minor's death in 1952, she continued to lend her support, contributing five thousand dollars' worth of U.S. Treasury Bonds to bail out Gus Hall (then general secretary of the Communist Party) in 1962.[6]

Despite decades of art and activism, Gibson remains relatively unknown today.

NOTES

1. Leslie Fishbein, introduction to *Art for the Masses: A Radical Magazine and Its Graphics*, by Rebecca Zurier (Philadelphia: Temple UP, 1988), 3.

2. Biographical data on Lydia Gibson is scarce, and most of it comes through her connections to Robert Minor. Dee Garrison's *Mary Heaton Vorse: The Life of an American Insurgent* (Philadelphia: Temple UP, 1989) mentions, in passing, that Gibson met Minor in 1916, at which time he "had fallen in love with Gibson . . . , but had been spurned by her" (174). Joseph North's five-page chapter on Lydia Gibson in *Robert*

Minor: Artist and Crusader (New York: International Publishers, 1956) places the date of their meeting in 1915 (152).

3. North, 153.

4. "New Children's Magazine," *New Masses*, May 1931, 22.

5. A. T. Eaton, "The New Books for Boys and Girls," *New York Times Book Review*, 25 Nov. 1934, 10; Jean West Maury, "Books of the Christmas Season for Children," *Boston Evening Transcript*, 31 Oct. 1954, 2.

6. "Hall and Davis Free in $5,000 Bail Each," *New York Times*, 17 Mar. 1962, 6.

One day early in spring David was going along the road, splish splash, squish squash. In spring when the snow has melted, the road is very muddy. David came to a big puddle in the middle of the road. He had to walk around it because it was too big to jump over. Walking around took longer than jumping, so David got interested in the puddle on the way round, and he stopped to look in. He saw pebbles and he saw bubbles and he saw mud. He saw some sticks floating and he saw an early angleworm coming out for a springtime walk around the edge of the puddle. He saw a tiny river running in one end of the puddle and another tiny river running out the other end, made of wheeltracks in the muddy road.

Then all of a sudden he saw a little black SOMETHING in the middle of the puddle. It wiggled. It blew a little tiny fountain. Then it went down out of sight under the muddy water. David crouched down to see better and leaned over so far he almost fell in. For a minute all he could see in the puddle was himself, as if he were looking in a mirror, and the white clouds overhead in the blue sky. Then the little tiny black thing came up to the top of the water and flopped its little tiny black tail—kersplash!

"Why, my goodness gracious me!" said David with his eyes bulging out. "It's a WHALE!"

He had a map of Nantucket on the wall beside his bed at home, with a picture of a whale on it. He knew exactly what a whale was like, from the spout that came out of his blowhole to the flukes of his spreading tail fully an inch away.

David luckily had his little tin bucket with him. He hardly ever went out without his little red tin bucket, it was so very useful for carrying all sorts of things home. This time he worked hard and splashed and puffed and caught the whale in his hands and put it in the bucket with enough water to swim in, and he carried it home.

The bucket was quite deep and dark for such a tiny whale, and you couldn't see him very well, so David went and climbed on a chair, and reached on the shelf, and got a white teacup and filled it with water before he put in the whale. The whale showed up very black and shiny and handsome in the nice white teacup. Then he carried it to his mother.

"Whatever have you got there?" asked David's mother. "Another polliwog?"

"No," said David, "that is a whale."

"Nonsense," said his mother. "Whales are enormous."

"What is a nor-mouse?" asked David.

"Whales are," said his mother; it didn't make sense, but then very few things did.

She went on: "It means very big indeed. Bigger than a horse. Bigger than a car. Bigger than an elephant. Whales are enormous. But what a VERY funny polliwog this is!"

Every day the whale grew. David fed him bits of chopped meat and he got bigger and bigger and he got stronger and stronger. One morning when David came down to breakfast the teacup was smashed into bits and the whale lay flopping in the saucer in a few drops of water. He had grown too big and too strong for the little white teacup. So David went to the kitchen and got a strong yellow bowl, the kind they mix ginger cookies in. The whale swam in that and it fitted him nicely. He went round and round and round to the left side and admired the scenery, and then he turned and went round and round and round to the right side and admired the scenery. He never seemed to get tired of doing it. For a good many days the whale swam in the yellow mixing bowl. But he was growing all the time. He ate boiled rice—at first ten grains a day and then more and more. He got bigger and bigger and he got stronger and stronger. One day he gave a JUMP, and landed on the floor. He was too big for the yellow bowl.

David sat down and put his elbows on his knees and put his chin in his hands. That was to make thinking easier. Then he thought what to do. The watering can was too small. The soup kettle was too small. The brass fruit bowl was too small. The wash basin was too small,

and, besides, they couldn't wash their hands if there were a whale in it. So he asked his mother if he could borrow the wash boiler. She said yes, if he would be careful of it. So the whale lived in the wash boiler. All the time he was getting bigger and bigger and stronger and stronger, and the little fountains he blew through the blowhole in the top of his head were getting bigger too, and he couldn't turn around.

"I do declare," said David's mother. "I never in all my born days saw a polliwog blow fountains through the top of his head! What a VERY funny polliwog!"

The whale lived in the wash boiler about a week. He knocked over the wash boiler one day and made a big puddle on the floor. So David had to move him again. He thought and he thought. There wasn't any place in the house now big enough for the whale to turn around in but the bath tub. So David moved the whale into the bath tub. By this time he was about as big as a big cat or a smallish dog, and a very pretty shiny black like patent leather shoes. He was getting so tame that he used to come swimming up to the top of the water and blow a fountain whenever David whistled for him.

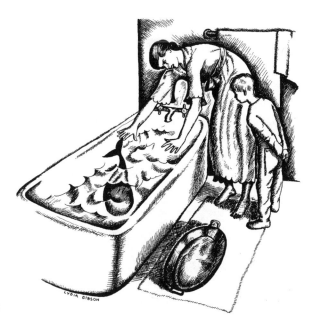

But you can see that it wasn't very convenient to keep the whale in the bath tub, because whenever anybody wanted to take a bath, they had to bring the dish pan up from the kitchen to put the whale into, and it was hard to keep him from jumping out of the dish pan. He was so impatient to get back into the big tub where he could swim around in comfort, he simply wouldn't lie still long enough for anyone to take a bath. And every day the whale grew. By this time he was eating left-over tea biscuits, toast and vegetables. He got bigger and bigger and stronger and stronger. At last one day David's mother said, "I simply cannot and will not be bothered lifting out this great big clumsy heavy polliwog every time anyone in this house takes a bath!"

So David and his father got into the car and they drove down the hill to the Village. They went past the Grocery Store and the Butcher Store and the Drugstore and the Post Office and the Railroad Station till they came to Mister Barlow's Hardware Store.

"Good morning, Mister Barlow," said David.

"Good morning, David, fine weather we're having and what can I do for you this fine morning?" said Mister Barlow.

"I have a whale which is growing very fast," said David, "and I must have a tank to keep him in. Perhaps you keep tanks in your store?"

"Yes, indeed," said Mister Barlow proudly, and showed him several tanks. But they were goldfish tanks.

"Oh, dear no," said David, "these aren't NEARLY big enough! Show me some bigger tanks, please."

But Mister Barlow didn't have any bigger tanks. David had to order one made four times as big as the bath tub and twice as deep and all lined with tin to make it water-tight.

In two or three days the tank was finished and Mister Barlow brought it up to David's house. They put it in the garden right beside the porch so they could watch the whale easily, and they filled it with water. It was summertime now, so the whale enjoyed living in the garden. He grew very fast from being out in the sun. He got bigger and bigger and stronger and stronger. Pretty soon he got as big as a pony.

All the children in the neighborhood used to come to visit David's whale. They got sardines at the Grocery Store and threw them to the whale one at a time for a treat. They brought the whale ice cream cones, because whales come from the polar regions and they thought he must miss the icebergs. But the whale didn't like ice cream cones which melted and made the water horrid and cloudy; so the children took turns changing the water in the tank, with the garden hose.

One day some visitors came a long way to see the whale. There was Mister Queebus and Missis Queebus and their little boy Alexander. They came in their car all the way from Woodstock, ninety miles away, and they were all dressed up in their Sunday-go-to-meeting clothes. They stood in a row on the porch and looked down on the whale in his tank, and admired him. The whale was so pleased with all this admiration that he blew an especially splendid fountain in honor of the Queebus family, when David whistled. It was his only way of thanking them. But now he was so big that his fountain was like the smoke that you see coming out of the smokestack of a locomotive, when you sit in the car at the railroad crossing gate and watch the express go

roaring by. So the fountain blew all over the Queebus family and their best visiting clothes got soaking wet and it made them very cross. David's mother said, "REALLY we can't keep that ridiculous polliwog of David's any longer. It's MUCH too big. And I don't believe it will ever be a frog anyway!"

David was getting quite tired of changing the water in the big tank with the garden hose every few days, and of running around the Village with his red bucket collecting bread and scraps from all the neighbors to feed the hungry whale, who ate a great deal. And the whale was growing all the time. Day by day he was getting bigger and he was getting stronger.

So David telephoned to Tony, the Express Man, to bring up his truck. And he telephoned to Nick, the Garage Man, to bring his wrecking car, and all together they hoisted the whale onto the truck by means of the derrick on the wrecking car, with wet bath towels pinned around his head to keep him from drying out on the ride.

David climbed up on the driver's seat beside Tony the Express Man and they went down the hill to the Village. They went past the Grocery Store and past the Butcher Store and past the Drugstore and past the Post Office and past the Railroad Station till they came to Mister Barlow's Hardware Store. There David bought a very long strong chain, and then they drove the whale down to the wharf that stuck out into the river. They hooked

the whale to the wharf with the chain around his tail because he hadn't any neck, and David promised to come down every day to visit him.

Every day David's father drove him down to the wharf and David whistled to his whale. The whale came up close alongside the wharf and blew lovely fountains for David. He was a very happy and comfortable whale, swimming around the wharf and eating fresh fish right out of the river, and sleeping under the wharf at night like a dog in his kennel. He was a great pet with all the people in the Village. The Grocer brought his three little boys to see him, and the Butcher brought his little girl, and the Postman brought his twins, and the old Station Agent who sold railroad tickets for train rides brought his little golden-haired grandchild. They all admired the whale and some of them brought him sardines out of a can.

But catching fresh fish out of the river had spoiled the whale for sardines out of a can, and he would spit them out for the crabs and fish to eat.

People used to come out from the City on Sundays just to see David's whale. The man who owned the wharf was planning to charge ten cents admission from everyone, to pay him for his trouble. But David couldn't see what trouble the man had; David took care of the whale, David had tied him up, and David had collected food for him in his bucket all the while he was growing! But all the time the whale was getting stronger and stronger.

One morning David went down the wharf to visit the whale as usual. He whistled and whistled for the whale. But the whale didn't come to blow him a fountain. Then David noticed that the wharf was all broken at the end; planks were ripped apart, and the big heavy plies were pulled sidewise.

The whale had broken the wharf in the night. He had broken loose and had swum majestically down the river to the sea, a mighty full-grown whale, towing a piece of the chain behind him.

David went home and told his mother the whale had gone, and his mother said, "Well, David, it WAS a whale after all!"

27

Geyt a hindele ken Bronzvil [*A Little Hen Goes to Brownsville*] (1937) Written by Yehoshua Kaminski (1883–1958), Illustrated by Nota Koslowsky (Note Kozlovski, 1906–?), Translated by Jerold C. Frakes

INTRODUCTION BY JEROLD C. FRAKES

Yehoshua Kaminski was an important educator and writer of Yiddish children's literature.[1] Born near Malin, in the Kiev district of the Ukraine, Kaminski received formal education in traditional Jewish schools, the *kheyder* (elementary level) and *yeshive* (intermediate and advanced study), while he gained a more secular and general education through self-study, as was common for Eastern European Jewish intellectuals of the period. From the age of sixteen, he was an itinerant educator and labor organizer in Russian towns. He was ultimately arrested for such activities, and after serving time in prison, in 1906 he departed for the United States, where he settled in New York and supported himself for several years by factory work. In 1913 he founded the first of the Jewish schools that was to develop into the widespread system of secular Jewish (and initially also Yiddish-language) schools named for the "father of modern Yiddish literature," Sholem Aleykhem (Shalom Aleichem). Kaminski also founded two presses for children's books: Matones ("gifts") and Kinder-ring ("children's circle") and edited the monthly *Kinder-zhurnal* ("children's newspaper/ journal") for twenty-five years. Additionally, in 1923 he was one of the founders of Camp Boyberik, a secular Yiddish-culture summer camp associated with the Sholem Aleykhem school system. In the course of several decades of his own writing for children, he produced hundreds of stories, songs, poems, riddles, and anecdotes, published under his own name, as well as under various pseudonyms. His work is characterized both by the inspiration that it so clearly draws from traditional Ashkenazic (Eastern European Jewish) life and customs, and by a commitment to socialist ideals of equality. He died in New York.

His story of Hindele, the little hen, embodies the central themes of his work: in a general sense the notion that the human enterprise must be a cooperative one in which everyone can at one time or another lend a helping hand to one's fellows; and more concretely that urban poverty strikes most brutally at children, often in terms of the most basic needs, such as nutrition, which can be ameliorated by rather simple, humane acts. There is also a direct admonition that justice is best served by a system that is not defined by the strict and inflexible administration of a legal code but rather by a human and humane application of the principles of that code. While the story could appeal to a broad children's audience, its verbal style is difficult enough that it might present difficulties for beginning readers, although the plot might be somewhat too simplistic for more accomplished early readers. It seems thus most akin to what we now think of as the "read aloud" genre.

Not surprisingly, the book conforms to the orthographical practice of the Arbeter-ring (Workmen's Circle) during the period, in spelling Yiddish words of Semitic origin phonetically rather than according to the traditional Hebrew spelling. A similar practice was enforced in the Soviet Union and is often cited as an indicator of Soviet antisemitism (by erasing the traces of Jewish religious culture from the "people's" vernacular); alternatively, the practice has been explained as a (non-Soviet) socialist attempt to level out an exclusionary, class-defined orthography that prevents those who do not know Hebrew (and thus do not belong to traditional Ashkenazic society's elite) from recognizing and pronouncing common Yiddish words. The orthographical practice of the Arbeter-ring and the Sholem Aleykhem schools (of which *Geyt a hindele ken bronzvil* is an example), which adhered to what is conventionally termed the "right wing" of Ashkenazic socialism, had more of a pragmatic than an overtly political function: to render common words more readily legible to readers who were not necessarily literate in traditional Jewish texts.

The book's illustrator, Nota Koslowsky (Note Kozlovski), was born in Porozowa, Poland, and studied art in Warsaw and New York. In addition to numerous exhibitions and work that appeared in the Yiddish-language press, he illustrated many important children's books, especially during the period of the 1920s–1940s.

NOTES

1. On Kaminski, see Yekhezkel Lifshits, in *Leksikon fun der nayer yidisher literatur* (New York: Alveltlekher yidisher kultur-kongres, 1981), 8: coll. 62–63; I. Mlotek, "Di yidishe kinder-literatur in di fareynikte shtatn," *Algemeyne entsiklopedye*, Yidn h (New York, 1957), 227 ff.; Uriel Ofek, in *Leksikon ofek le-sifrut yeladim* (Tel Aviv: Zemorah, Bitan, 1985), 2: 563.

Little Hen continues on her way, strides on for a long time, until she comes to loud and noisy Times Square. In the meantime a desire to lay an egg has come over her. She doesn't wait around, but puts down her little basket right in the middle of Times Square, where so many streets come together, climbs in and starts singing:

> Kvo-kvo-kvo-kvo-kvo!
> Here I sit myself down
> And close my eyes,—
> And one, and two, and three
> And start laying eggs.

In the meantime, cars, buses, wagons, streetcars and pedestrians come barrelling up from all sides, more by the second, and they all come to a halt and can go not a step farther—the traffic is blocked for miles. The horns of the buses are honking impatiently; the bells of the streetcars are ringing, all making a fuss and a racket; people are shoving each other in the crowd; everyone wants to move on. But they cannot, for right in the middle of Times Square there sits a little hen in a little woven basket who is about to lay an egg.

Meanwhile a tall, smooth-talking policeman comes running up to see who has blocked his traffic. He sees the little hen in the little basket. The policeman begins to shout: "Hey, how dare you, and how can you obstruct my traffic here? For a deed like this you have to go to court and pay a heavy fine."

Little Hen answers from her little basket:

> Ku-dakh-takh, ku-dakh-takh,
> Oy, I'm in a big hurry,—
> Because I'm going to Brownsville
> To lay eggs for children.

The policeman explodes: "What's Brownsville to me!? Who cares about eggs?! You've fouled up the traffic here. Look what's going on for miles around! Here's a ticket for you, and now we're off right away to court." And he takes the little basket with the little hen and heads off to court.

The judge sits in the courtroom with a very serious expression on his face and waits for defendants to be brought before him. The policeman does his duty and carries the little basket with the little hen up to the judge's desk.

So, a little hen goes to Brownsville to lay eggs. She had heard that in Brownsville there are children who are small and pale, thin and weak, because many of the mothers there often have no money to buy fresh eggs for the children. For this reason she set out to go there to lay white eggs for the children and took a little woven basket under her wing, in case a desire came over her to lay eggs while she was on the way there. For Little Hen was able to lay as many eggs as she wanted and whenever she wanted.

So she walks along the narrow sidewalks and long avenues and streets, and so that the way seems easier and the path quicker to her, she sings a little song to herself, like this:

> Ku-dakh-takh, ku-dakh-takh,
> Oy, I'm in a big hurry,—
> Because I'm going to Brownsville
> To lay eggs for children.

(In addition to the fact that she liked laying eggs at all times, she could also sing songs.) So when the people see how a little hen is striding along with a little basket under her wing singing a little song, they look in amazement and step out of her way.

Little Hen has a look at the thick book along with the judge and sees that it is indeed written in the book, in black and white: a two dollar fine or two days and nights locked up behind bars.

Little Hen replies to the judge: "Your honor, I don't have two dollars, but

Kvo-Kvo-Kvo-Kvo-Kvo
Here I sit myself down
And close my eyes,—
And one, and two, and three
And start laying eggs.

And she sits down on the book (on the very page on which was written the paragraph about obstructing traffic), lays a white egg, stands up, takes the little basket under her wing, and flies with a whoosh out the window of the courtroom and goes along Delancey Street to the Williamsburg Bridge, the long one. And just as she goes up onto the bridge, she hears a yell from down below: "Throw the ball! Catch the ball! Throw it to me! No, to me!" She is curious about what's going on, climbs up on the steel railing, looks down and sees: boys are playing ball on the street right next to the bridge. One is throwing the ball and the others stand ready to catch it with their outstretched hands. Little Hen thinks for a moment and sings her song, and then white eggs begin to fall into the outstretched hands of surprised boys.

"This one right here, that you see before you, your honor, obstructed traffic and caused me trouble. A desire came over her to lay an egg on Times Square of all places." The judge reached the verdict that for such a crime the fine was two dollars. She asked him: "Your honor, even for a little hen that is going to Brownsville to lay eggs for children?" The judge was not happy: "What, you don't want to believe me? Come here, and I'll show you." And he takes down a heavy volume from the desk, opens it up in the middle and shows her: "Have a look at this very page, in this very paragraph it is specifically written that if one obstructs traffic, one pays a fine of two dollars. And if you have no cash, then you get locked up for two whole days and nights."

Meanwhile Little Hen jumps down from the steel railing, crosses the Williamsburg Bridge loudly singing her song:

> Ku-dakh-takh, ku-dakh-takh,
> Oy, I'm in a big hurry,—
> Because I'm going to Brownsville
> To lay eggs for children.

All the way to the end of the bridge, where she sees a man standing and waiting.

"Hm, what?" the man responds to her. "You want to know the way to Brownsville? You turn right, then you turn left; you go up, and then you go down. And that is the way to Brownsville. But it's a long way to go on foot. It's better if you take that bus over there; it'll take you straight to Pitkin Avenue, right in the middle of Brownsville."

She thanks him with an egg, a white one. She jumps into the bus that has just pulled up.

"Fare, please!" the driver calls politely and holds out the palm of his hand. Little Hen is silent and looks for a seat. "Fare, please!" the driver reminds her again. Little Hen sits still, as if he were not talking to her. "Nickel, please!" the driver is becoming impatient. "Look at this," thinks Little Hen, "Everyone wants money from me. The judge, two dollars; the bus driver, a nickel. Where am I supposed to get money for them all the time?" And she tosses an egg into the outstretched hand of the driver. In the meantime, the bus flies along on its six rubber tires, until it reaches Brownsville.

"Pitkin! Pitkin Avenue!" the driver calls loudly and opens the door for the passengers. Little Hen jumps down from the bus and stops in front of an open window to a little cellar room. She sees a mother sitting by a crib and looking lovingly at her child, who is just waking up. Little Hen sings to herself:

> Kvo-kvo-kvo-kvo-kvo
> Here I sit myself down
> And close my eyes,—
> And one, and two, and three
> And start laying eggs.

And indeed she soon lays a white egg on the window sill. When the mother sees the fresh, white egg on the window sill, she quickly picks it up, strokes the egg on her child's face and says the following words:

> Just as the little egg is pure,—
> So should my child's eyes be pure.
> Just as the little egg is round,—
> So should my child's face be round.
> Just as the little egg is fresh,—
> So should my child's face be fresh.

When Little Hen hears such words from the mother, she is delighted beyond measure and sets out to lay eggs on the window sills of the other cellar rooms. The mothers take the fresh, white eggs, roll them on the faces of their little children, and while they're doing it, they say the following words:

> Just as the little egg is pure,—
> So should my child's eyes be pure.
> Just as the little egg is round,—
> So should my child's face be round.
> Just as the little egg is fresh,—
> So should my child's face be fresh.

So be it!

28

The Practical Princess (1969)

Written by Jay Williams
(1914-1978), Illustrated by
Friso Henstra (b. 1928)

EDITORS' INTRODUCTION

Born in Buffalo, New York, Jay Williams (né Jacobson) was the son of a vaudeville producer. In his early career, Williams followed his father into the entertainment business, performing comedy or acting as a master of ceremonies in vaudeville shows and in nightclubs in the Catskill Mountains. In the mid-1930s Williams was a social director at left-wing summer camps for adults, and he worked as a press agent for the radical Group Theater. A theater actor in the 1940s, he also played the Pony Ride Man in the Academy Award–nominated feature film, *Little Fugitive* (1953), directed by his friend Raymond Abrashkin (under the pseudonym Ray Ashley).

Williams published nearly one hundred books, including sixty for children, among them mysteries, historical fiction, and fantasy. He is probably best known for the Danny Dunn science fiction series, coconceived with Abrashkin and published between 1956 and 1977. Like all Williams's stories, they were written to make children think. As Williams put it, "the stories look as though they are pretty simple—about a kid who gets mixed up in scientific adventures—but they really deal with the necessity of thinking for yourself, of asking certain key questions about the universe, of trying all the time to get at the truth."[1] From the 1940s, when he began his career as a children's writer, he was keenly aware that this literature "feeds . . . youngsters their ideology and patterns of thinking." He also warned other progressive writers (as well as critics) that to ignore children and their literature was a kind of "adult chauvinism as detrimental to our own future as any other kind of discriminatory practice."[2]

The Practical Princess was one of his several feminist fairy tales, beginning with *Philbert the Fearful* (1966). That story featured a knight who used his brains instead of his brawn. Of Williams's fairy tales, *The Practical Princess* gained the most recognition, earning the *School Library Journal*'s Best Books citation and the Golden Apple Award at the Biennale of Illustrators festival in Bratislava, Czechoslovakia. Many reviewers praised "the gutsy, independent, and practical Bedelia,"[3] the heroine of *The Practical Princess*. But some felt this and Williams's other feminist fairy tales went too far. One reviewer, for instance, complained that all the men in *The Practical Princess* are "incompetent and ignorant,"[4] and another wondered whether better mates might be found for all the "clever, practical, and courageous" women in *The Practical Princess and Other Liberating Fairy Tales* (1977), which collected six of Williams's stories.[5] On the other side of the coin, Williams was chided for the stereotypes he still perpetuated: all his heroines are beautiful, and he has "the irritating habit of calling his adult heroines 'girls,' but his heroes 'young men,'" as one reader noted.[6]

Friso Henstra was already an established artist in the Netherlands when he illustrated the Dutch edition of Jay Williams's historical novel, *Tomorrow's Fire*, in 1968, but the job helped him break into the American marketplace. The son of an artist himself, Henstra studied drawing and sculpture in Amsterdam, becoming an illustrator and comic artist. He began teaching at the academy of visual arts in Arnhem in 1968. After he sent one of the original illustrations for *Tomorrow's Fire* to Williams as a gift, Williams stopped in Amsterdam during a family vacation, beginning a friendship and fruitful collaboration. After *The Practical Princess*, Henstra illustrated eight more of Williams's stories. Given almost full control over layout, Henstra relished the opportunity to use his pictures to call upon "the dream world, the story behind the story."[7] Of his approach to art Henstra has said, "I like to draw extremes. Good must be really good and bad terribly bad; if the wind is blowing your face should feel it, and if it's raining, the fish should be able to swim in the sky."[8] Henstra has received several awards for his book illustrations, and his art has been featured in museums.

NOTES

1. Qtd. in Aidan Chambers, interview with Jay Williams, *The Horn Book Magazine* 53:1 (Feb. 1977): 92–96. Qtd. in *Children's Literature Review*, vol. 8, ed. Gerard J. Senick (Detroit: Gale, 1985), 220.

2. Jay Williams, "What Do Kids Read?" *New Masses*, 10 June 1947, 10.

3. Margherite Girard, review of "The Practical Princess," *School Library Journal*, an appendix to *Library Journal* 15:8 (Apr. 1969): 109.

4. Masha Kabakow Rudman, "The Female: 'The Practical Princess,'" *Children's Literature: An Issues Approach* (Lexington, MA: Heath, 1976), 354.

5. Ruth Macdonald, "The Tale Retold: Feminist Fairy Tales," *Children's Literature Association Quarterly* 7:2 (Summer 1982): 18.

6. Enid Davis, "Maidens with Spunk: Books by Jay Williams," *The Liberty Cap: A Catalogue of Non-Sexist Materials for Children* (Chicago: Academy Press, 1977), 14.

7. Friso Henstra, "Friso Henstra," translated from the Dutch by Jennifer Gage, *Something about the Author Autobiography Series* 14, ed. Joyce Nakamura (Detroit: Gale, 1992), 139.

8. Ibid.

Princess Bedelia was as lovely as the moon shining upon a lake full of waterlilies. She was as graceful as a cat leaping. And she was also extremely practical.

When she was born, three fairies had come to her cradle to give her gifts as was usual in that country. The first fairy had given her beauty. The second had given her grace. But the third, who was a wise old creature, had said, "I give her common sense."

"I don't think much of that gift," said King Ludwig, raising his eyebrows. "What good is common sense to a princess? All she needs is charm."

Nevertheless, when Bedelia was eighteen years old, something happened which made the king change his mind.

A dragon moved into the neighborhood. He settled in a dark cave on top of a mountain, and the first thing he did was to send a message to the king. "I must have a princess to devour," the message said, "or I shall breathe out my fiery breath and destroy the kingdom."

Sadly, King Ludwig called together his councillors and read them the message.

"Perhaps," said the Prime Minister, "we had better advertise for a knight to slay the dragon. That is what is generally done in these cases."

"I'm afraid we haven't time," answered the king. "The dragon has only given us until tomorrow morning. There is no help for it. We shall have to send him the princess." Princess Bedelia had come to the meeting because, as she said, she liked to mind her own business and this was certainly her business.

"Rubbish!" she said. "Dragons can't tell the difference between princesses and anyone else. Use your common sense. He's just asking for me because he's a snob."

"That may be so," said her father, "but if we don't send you along, he'll destroy the kingdom."

"Right!" said Bedelia. "I see I'll have to deal with this myself."

She left the council chamber. She got the largest and gaudiest of her state robes and stuffed it with straw, and tied it together with string. Into the center of the bundle she packed about a hundred pounds of gunpowder. She got two strong young men to carry it up the mountain for her. She stood in front of the dragon's cave and called, "Come out! Here's the princess!" The dragon came blinking and peering out of the darkness. Seeing the bright robe covered with gold and silver embroidery, and hearing Bedelia's voice, he opened his mouth wide.

At once, at Bedelia's signal, the two young men swung the robe and gave it a good heave, right down the dragon's throat. Bedelia threw herself flat on the ground, and the two young men ran.

As the gunpowder met the flames inside the dragon, there was a tremendous explosion.

Bedelia got up, dusting herself off. "Dragons," she said, "are not very bright."

She left the two young men sweeping up the pieces, and she went back to the castle to have her geography lesson.

The lesson that morning was local geography.

"Our kingdom, Arapathia, is bounded on the north by Istven," said the teacher. "Lord Garp, the ruler of Istven, is old, crafty, rich, and greedy."

At that very moment, Lord Garp of Istven was arriving at the castle. Word of Bedelia's destruction of the dragon had reached him.

"That girl," said he, "is just the wife for me."

And he had come with a hundred finely dressed courtiers and many presents to ask King Ludwig for her hand.

The king sent for Bedelia. "My dear," he said, clearing his throat nervously, "just see who is here."

"I see. It's Lord Garp," said Bedelia. She turned to go.

"He wants to marry you," said the king.

Bedelia looked at Lord Garp. His face was like an old napkin, crumpled and wrinkled. It was covered with warts, as if someone had left crumbs on the napkin. He had only two teeth. Six long hairs grew from his chin, and none on his head. She felt like screaming.

However, she said, "I'm very flattered. Thank you, Lord Garp. Just let me talk to my father in private for a minute." When they had retired to a small room behind the throne, Bedelia said to the king, "What will Lord Garp do if I refuse to marry him?"

"He is rich, greedy, and crafty," said the king, unhappily. "He is also used to having his own way in everything. He will be insulted. He will probably declare war on us, and then there will be trouble."

"Very well," said Bedelia. "We must be practical."

She returned to the throne room. Smiling sweetly at Lord Garp, she said, "My lord, as you know, it is customary for a princess to set tasks for anyone who wishes to marry her. Surely, you wouldn't like me to break the custom. And you are bold and powerful enough, I know, to perform any task."

"That is true," said Lord Garp, smugly, stroking the six hairs on his chin. "Name your task."

"Bring me," said Bedelia, "a branch from the Jewel Tree of Paxis."

Lord Garp bowed, and off he went. "I think," said Bedelia to her father, "that we have seen the last of him. For Paxis is a thousand miles away, and the Jewel Tree is guarded by lions, serpents, and wolves."

But in two weeks, Lord Garp was back. With him he bore a chest, and from the chest he took a wonderful twig. Its bark was of rough gold. The leaves that grew from it were of fine silver. The twig was covered with blossoms, and each blossom had petals of mother-of-pearl and centers of sapphires, the color of the evening sky.

Bedelia's heart sank as she took the twig. But then she said to herself, "Use your common sense, my girl! Lord Garp never traveled two thousand miles in two weeks, nor is he the man to fight his way through lions, serpents, and wolves."

She looked more carefully at the branch. Then she said, "My lord, you know that the Jewel Tree of Paxis is a living tree, although it is all made of jewels."

"Well, of course," said Lord Garp. "Everyone knows that."

"Well," said Bedelia, "then why is it that these blossoms have no scent?"

Lord Garp turned red.

"I think," Bedelia went on, "that this branch was made by the jewelers of Istven, who are the best in the world. Not very nice of you, my lord. some people might even call it cheating."

Lord Garp shrugged. He was too old and rich to feel ashamed. But like many men used to having their own way, the more Bedelia refused him, the more he was determined to have her.

"Never mind all that," he said. "Set me another task. This time, I swear I will perform it."

Bedelia sighed. "Very well. Then bring me a cloak made from the skins of the salamanders who live in the Volcano of Scoria."

Lord Garp bowed, and off he went. "The Volcano of Scoria," said Bedelia to her father, "is covered with red-hot lava. It burns steadily with great flames, and pours out poisonous smoke so that no one can come within a mile of it."

"You have certainly profited by your geography lessons," said the king, with admiration.

Nevertheless, in a week, Lord Garp was back. This time, he carried a cloak that shone and rippled with all the colors of fire. It was made of scaly skins, stitched together with fine golden wire. Each scale was red and

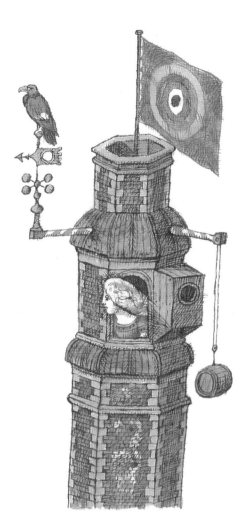

her breath and look about her, she found herself in a room at the top of a tower.

Bedelia peered out of the window. About the tower stretched an empty, barren plain. As she watched, a speck appeared in the distance. A plume of dust rose behind it. It drew nearer and became Lord Garp on horseback.

He rode to the tower and looked up at Bedelia. "Aha!" he croaked. "So you are safe and snug, are you? And will you marry me now?"

"Never," said Bedelia, firmly.

"Then stay there until never comes," snarled Lord Garp.

Away he rode.

For the next two days, Bedelia felt very sorry for herself. She sat wistfully by the window, looking out at the empty plain. When she was hungry, food appeared on the table. When she was tired, she lay down on the narrow cot and slept. Each day, Lord Garp rode by and asked if she had changed her mind, and each day she refused him. Her only hope was that, as so often happens in old tales, a prince might come riding by who would rescue her.

But on the third day, she gave herself a shake.

"Now, then, pull yourself together," she said, sternly. "If you sit waiting for a prince to rescue you, you may sit here forever. Be practical! If there's any rescuing to be done, you're going to have to do it yourself."

She jumped up. There was something she had not yet done, and now she did it. She tried the door.

It opened.

Outside, were three other doors. But there was no sign of a stair, or any way down from the top of the tower.

She opened two of the doors and found that they led into cells just like hers, but empty. Behind the fourth door, however, lay what appeared to be a haystack.

From beneath it came the sound of snores. And between snores, a voice said, "Six million and twelve . . . *snore* . . . six million and thirteen . . . *snore* . . . six million and fourteen . . ."

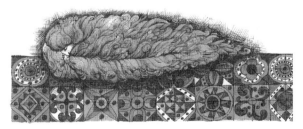

orange and blue, like a tiny flame. Bedelia took the splendid cloak. She said to herself, "Use your head, miss! Lord Garp never climbed the red-hot slopes of the Volcano of Scoria."

A fire was burning in the fireplace of the throne room. Bedelia hurled the cloak into it. The skins blazed up in a flash, blackened, and fell to ashes.

Lord Garp's mouth fell open. Before he could speak, Bedelia said, "That cloak was a fake, my lord. The skins of salamanders who can live in the Volcano of Scoria wouldn't burn in a little fire like that one."

Lord Garp turned pale with anger. He hopped up and down, unable at first to do anything but splutter.

"Ub—ub—ub!" he cried. Then, controlling himself, he said, "So be it. If I can't have you, no one shall!"

He pointed a long, skinny finger at her. On the finger was a magic ring. At once, a great wind arose. It blew through the throne room. It sent King Ludwig flying one way and his guards the other. Bedelia was picked up and whisked off through the air. When she could catch

Cautiously, she went closer. Then she saw that what she had taken for a haystack was in fact an immense pile of blond hair. Parting it, she found a young man, sound asleep.

As she stared, he opened his eyes. He blinked at her. "Who—?" he said. Then he said, "Six million and fifteen," closed his eyes, and fell asleep again.

Bedelia took him by the shoulder and shook him hard. He awoke, yawning, and tried to sit up. But the mass of hair made this difficult.

"What on earth is the matter with you?" Bedelia asked. "Who are you?"

"I am Prince Perian," he replied, "the rightful ruler of —oh, dear, here I go again. Six million and . . ." His eyes began to close.

Bedelia shook him again. He made a violent effort and managed to wake up enough to continue, "—of Istven. But Lord Garp has put me under a spell. I have to count sheep jumping over a fence, and this puts me to slee—ee—ee—"

He began to snore lightly.

"Dear me," said Bedelia. "I must do something."

She thought hard. Then she pinched Perian's ear, and this woke him with a start.

"Listen," she said. "It's quite simple. It's all in your mind, you see. You are imagining the sheep jumping over the fence—No! Don't go to sleep again!

"This is what you must do. Imagine them jumping backwards. As you do, *count* them backwards, and when you get to *one*, you'll be wide awake."

The prince's eyes snapped open. "Marvelous!" he said. "Will it work?"

"It's bound to," said Bedelia. "If the sheep going one way will put you to sleep, their going back again will wake you up."

Hastily, the prince began to count, "Six million and fourteen, six million and thirteen, six million and twelve . . ."

"Oh, my goodness," cried Bedelia, "count by hundreds, or you'll never get there."

He began to gabble as fast as he could, and with each moment that passed, his eyes sparkled more brightly, his face grew livelier, and he seemed a little stronger, until at last he shouted, "Five, four, three, two, ONE!" and awoke completely.

He struggled to his feet, with a little help from Bedelia.

"Heavens!" he said. "Look how my hair and beard have grown. I've been here for years. Thank you, my dear. Who are you, and what are you doing here?"

Bedelia quickly explained.

Perian shook his head. "One more crime of Lord Garp's," he said. "We must escape and see that he is punished."

"Easier said than done," Bedelia replied. "There is no stair in this tower, as far as I can tell, and the outside wall is much too smooth to climb down."

Perian frowned. "This will take some thought," he said. "What we need is a long rope."

"Use your common sense," said Bedelia. "We haven't any rope."

Then her face lighted, and she clapped her hands. "But we have your beard," she laughed.

Perian understood at once, and chuckled. "I'm sure it will reach almost to the ground," he said. "But we haven't any scissors to cut it off with."

"That is so," said Bedelia. "Hang it out of the window and let me climb down. I'll search the tower and perhaps I can find a ladder, or a hidden stair. If all else fails, I can go for help."

She and the prince gathered up great armfuls of the beard and staggered into Bedelia's room, which had the largest window. The prince's long hair trailed behind and nearly tripped him.

Perian threw the beard out of the window and braced himself, holding the beard with both hands to ease the pull on his chin. Bedelia climbed out of the window and slid down the beard.

But suddenly, out of the wilderness came the drumming of hoofs, a cloud of dust, and then Lord Garp on his swift horse.

With one glance, he saw what was happening. He shook his fist up at Prince Perian.

"Meddlesome fool!" he shouted. "I'll teach you to interfere."

He leaped from the horse and grabbed the beard. He gave it a tremendous yank. Headfirst came Perian, out of the window. Down he fell, and with a thump, he landed right on top of old Lord Garp.

This saved Perian, who was not hurt at all. But it was the end of Lord Garp.

Perian and Bedelia rode back to Istven on Lord Garp's horse. In the great city, the prince was greeted with cheers of joy once everyone had recognized him after so many years and under so much hair.

And of course, since Bedelia had rescued him from captivity, she married him. First, however, she made him get a haircut and a shave so that she could see what he really looked like.

For she was always practical.

part 6

History and Heroes

JULIA MICKENBERG & PHILIP NEL

Over the course of the twentieth century, leftists called upon history and tradition to challenge contemporary power relations and to unearth from the past seeds of a more liberatory future. They did so by rewriting master narratives and by recovering the histories of marginalized groups, particularly the working class, ethnic minorities, and women.[1] In general, whether they were recovering or interpreting the past, their project was to show what they believed to be the truth of history, on the assumption that "truth is revolutionary."[2] At the same time, history seemed a safer realm than the present when it came to social critique, because writers could avoid "bumping into the controversial issues of the contemporary scene."[3] Children, symbolic of both the past (as precitizens) and the future (as citizens-to-be), were an especially significant audience for the Left's lessons in history. These portraits of the past were formulated to be directly relevant to contemporary concerns, as the "prehistory to the present."[4]

American history and traditions proved especially useful for offering a critique of present conditions in the United States. A series on the "History of Our Country" in the *Little Socialist Magazine for Boys and Girls* (1909–1912) emphasized "truths" about American history not taught in schools, and debunked "myths" that were propagated as history. In the *Little Socialist*'s version of American history, Thomas Paine—an outspoken critic of slavery, defender of the poor, and advocate of reason over religion—was the real father of our country, not George Washington. For his part, George Washington could, and did, tell lies. And the American Revolution was inspired not by the masses but by those in power, since "the masses of any nation never made war on any other nation."[5]

In the early 1930s, the *New Pioneer*, a communist magazine for children, ran a series on "American History through Pictures," from which the first selection in this section is taken. The editors' introduction to the series very explicitly articulated a radical communist position on history. As they note,

> There are two ways of looking at history. One is the way the textbooks and public schools go at it. This is history as Wall Street and the owning class want you to see it. Facts and events are set forth in a false way and other facts are left out, so that wrong ideas are given you of times in the past, the present world, and what the future holds.

The other way of looking at history, our way, is from the standpoint of the workers and toiling masses. This is the only true, scientific way of studying history and finding out what will happen in the future.[6]

The declaration of a Popular Front against fascism in the mid-1930s led to significant changes in the ways in which Communists discussed history and influenced a broad spectrum of the Left, from independent radicals to New Deal liberals. Communist Party leader Earl Browder's 1936 presidential campaign slogan, "Communism is Twentieth-Century Americanism," pointed to a view of history in which revolution was as American as apple pie. Popular Front Americanism sought to recover a usable past for radicals and progressives, typically by reframing well-known historical figures as "people's heroes" and by spinning well-worn historical narratives as heroic epics of the working class. Whereas the *New Pioneer* series excerpted here sought to *debunk* the usual cast of American heroes, the histories written during the period of the Popular Front strove to *reclaim* those figures for the working class. Folklore and folksong, thought to embody the spontaneous expression of the masses, could likewise be employed in this way. Keeping the tune but changing the words, a radical message could be made familiar and unthreatening.

Left-wing folk music groups like the Almanac Singers transformed Appalachian ballads into union anthems, and familiar figures like Abe Lincoln became people's heroes—and the subject of at least ten juvenile biographies by left-wing writers. As an unofficial alliance among Communists, independent radicals, and New Deal liberals, the American Popular Front was relatively short-lived. Even so, a Popular Front "structure of feeling" remained evident in children's books published up through the 1950s.[7] Thus we find a similar pattern in books such as Esther Forbes's Newbery Medal–winning *Johnny Tremain* (1943), William Cunningham's *The Real Book about Daniel Boone* (1952), and Meridel Le Sueur's *River Road: the Story of Abraham Lincoln* (1950), among dozens of others.

Although one strand of leftist history emphasized Anglo, male, and ostensibly working-class "people's heroes," another strand recovered radical traditions within the histories of ethnic and racial minorities and in women's history. Secular Yiddish schools empha-

sized the Jewish heritage of struggle, and small outfits like the Hebrew Publishing Company printed Herbert Kruckman's *Joey Meets His People* (1940), about a boy who falls asleep in Hebrew school and, in his dreams, witnesses great moments in (radical) Jewish history. Howard Fast's *Haym Solomon: Son of Liberty* (1941), the story of a Jewish financier of the American Revolution, and Eve Merriam's *The Voice of Liberty: The Story of Emma Lazarus* (1959) would bring progressive or radical aspects of Jewish history to a somewhat wider audience.

By the late 1940s, African-American history increasingly gained the attention of people on the Left. During the Second World War, the struggle against fascism and its racist doctrines highlighted the problem of racial discrimination within the United States. African-American history very quickly became a source of inspiration for those active in the struggle for civil rights. Hildegarde Hoyt Swift cited World War II as the direct inspiration for *North Star Shining* (1947), a poetic history (excerpted here) that evokes the everyday as well as the spectacular heroism of past and contemporary African Americans. Like Arna Bontemps's *Story of the Negro* (1948), the book was groundbreaking. Despite a growing trend of more inclusive literature, especially after the 1954 *Brown* decision mandating school desegregation, the floodgates would not open until the late 1960s. Indeed, as late as 1965, children's literature specialist Nancy Larrick would comment upon the "All White World of Children's Books," noting the dearth of African-American characters in American children's books, and blaming publishers' fears of losing southern markets.[8] Of the works that existed, many focused on history. And of the authors who wrote such works, liberals (like Swift and Bontemps) and radicals (especially Communists and former Communists) played an important role.

In the years following World War II, the Communist Party placed particular emphasis on the African-American fight for civil rights and the hidden history of African Americans, whose struggles evoked the repressed history of all oppressed peoples. Communist historian Herbert Aptheker called "Negro History" an "Arsenal for Liberation," maintaining, "from their history a people may gain sustenance, guidance, courage, dignity, maturity."[9] Writing in the radical African-American newspaper *Freedom* in 1955, Lorraine Hansberry pointed to history's importance for African-American children, noting, "from the time he is born the Negro child is surrounded by a society organized to convince him that he belongs to a people with a past so worthless and shameful that it amounts to no past at all."[10] *Freedom's* historically oriented "stories for children" and sketches of "Heroes in Our History," reprinted here, represent a direct response to the gaps in black history that characterized American history textbooks and children's books.

Among Communists and their allies, attention to African-American issues also brought attention to the "woman question" and the problem of "male chauvinism." This emerging critique, along with the feminist impulses that arose from women's participation in the Second World War, helped turn some radicals' attention to women's history. The trend would accelerate in the 1960s and 1970s with the rise of the New Left and second-wave feminism, both of which were greatly influenced by the civil rights movement.[11] Dorothy Sterling's books on black history and women's history —including juvenile biographies of Harriet Tubman (1954) and Lucretia Mott (1964)—illustrate one writer's movement from an interest in African-American history to an interest in women's history (particularly black women's history).

Eve Merriam, whose portrait of Lucretia Mott from *Independent Voices* (1968) is included here, was a pioneer in feminist children's literature. Merriam was part of the Popular Front generation of radicals, but by the time *Independent Voices* was published, a new generation would likewise be mining history. Julius Lester's *Black Folktales* (1969), a selection of which is included here, was directly inspired by the civil rights and Black Power movements, in which Lester was an active participant.

Members of the 1960s' New Left helped dramatically transform children's literature. Thanks largely to the efforts of activists in the 1960s and 1970s, children's books exploring the histories of African Americans, Mexican Americans, American Indians, Puerto Rican Americans, Japanese Americans, and other groups—as well as the history of labor struggles and of women's rights activism—are now in the mainstream. In creating these books, New Left and feminist historians issued a dramatic challenge to "consensus" historians, whose picture of the American past was narrowly limited to the history of powerful white men.

Progressive and radical authors of books for children continue to find lessons in the past that speak to contemporary concerns. Milton Meltzer (also from the Popular Front generation) has written dozens of histories for children about people who fought for unpopular causes or who spoke for society's most marginal people—figures like Langston Hughes, Carl Sandburg, Lydia Maria Child, and Dorothea Lange. The "If You Lived" series for young children includes texts like Ann McGovern's *If You Lived in Colonial Times* (1992), Anne Kamma's *If You Lived When There Was Slavery in America* (2004), and Ellen Levine's *If You Traveled on the Underground Railroad* (1988) and *If You Lived at the Time of Martin Luther King* (1990), all of which are informed by a progressive sensibility. Contemporary historical fiction likewise encourages children to critically examine contemporary conditions. Angela Hubler has discussed several stories in the popular "Dear America" series: Patricia McKissack's *A Picture of Freedom* (1997) offers a fictionalized portrait of an enslaved girl who joins the Underground Railroad; and Kathryn Lasky's *Dreams in the Golden Country: The Diary of Zipporah Feldman* (1998) comments on immigration, discusses a sweatshop fire modeled on the Triangle Shirtwaist Fire of 1911, and positively depicts the struggles of the trade union movement. "Importantly," Hubler notes of these books, "the 'path to liberation' [Lukacs 340] suggested by Lasky's treatment of racism, unionization, is collective and political, as are the strategies suggested in McKissack's novel."[12] Addressing more recent history, Angela Johnson and Eric Velasquez's *A Sweet Smell of Roses* (2005) follows two African-American girls as they watch and then participate in a 1960s civil rights march. They hear racist whites oppose them, but draw inspiration from the other marchers, and from Dr. Martin Luther King, Jr., who addresses the crowd.

On a lighter note, Lane Smith's *John, Paul, George, and Ben* (2006) brings the Founding Fathers off their pedestals to depict them as real human beings—and as children—in a way that also teaches young people to separate history's truths from its myths. (As Smith notes, Ben Franklin may have invented bifocals but it is sheer myth that he invented Playstation.)

Rescuing ignored histories is looking back in order to look forward—just as asking questions of the past invites children to likewise question arrangements in the present. These writers and illustrators have sought to recover the past not to repeat it, but to examine how it has shaped the present, and to discover how it may help young people envision a better tomorrow.

1. Much of the material for this introduction comes from Julia Mickenberg, *Learning from the Left: Children's Literature, the Cold War, and Radical Politics in the United States* (New York: Oxford UP, 2006). See especially chapter 7, "Ballad for American Children: History, Folklore, and Leftist Civic Education," 231–72.

2. Michael Gold, "Daniel Boone Belongs to Us," *New Masses*, 28 Aug. 1934, 26. Gold is quoting Henri Barbusse here; George Orwell (an opponent of communism) also once said, "In times of universal deceit, telling the truth will be a revolutionary act."

3. Mary Lapsley, "Socially Constructive Literature for Children," transcript of speech given to Juvenile Writers panel of League of American Writers, June 1941. League of American Writers papers, Bancroft Library, University of California at Berkeley.

4. George Lukacs, *The Historical Novel*, trans. Hannah and Stanley Mitchell (Boston: Beacon, 1963). Qtd. in Angela Hubler, "Girl Power and History in the Dear America Series Books," *Children's Literature Association Quarterly* 25:2 (2000): 98.

5. Frederick Krafft, "History of Our Country for Boys and Girls: Twelfth Chapter," *Little Socialist Magazine for Boys and Girls* 3:2 (Feb. 1910): 5–6; Krafft, "History of Our Country . . . Eleventh Chapter," *Little Socialist Magazine* 3:1 (Jan. 1910): 5–6; Krafft, "History of Our Country . . . Thirteenth Chapter," *Little Socialist Magazine* 3:3 (Mar. 1910): 5–6.

6. *New Pioneer* 1–2 (June 1931): 6.

7. Michael Denning has drawn upon the work of Raymond Williams to characterize a Popular Front "structure of feeling." See Michael Denning, *The Cultural Front* (New York: Verso, 1996), 9.

8. Nancy Larrick, "The All-White World of Children's Books," *Saturday Review*, 11 Sept. 1965, 63–65+.

9. Herbert Aptheker, "Negro History: Arsenal for Liberation," *New Masses*, 11 Feb. 1947, 11–12.

10. Lorraine Hansberry, "Life Challenges Negro Youth," *Freedom* 5:3 (Mar. 1955): 7.

11. On the "woman question" and its relationship to interest in "white chauvinism," see Kate Weigand, *Red Feminism: American Communism and the Making of Women's Liberation* (Baltimore, MD: Johns Hopkins UP, 2001). Daniel Horowitz has described Betty Friedan's initiation to women's issues via the labor movement: see *Betty Friedan and the Making of the Feminine Mystique* (Amherst: U of Massachusetts P, 1998).

12. Hubler, 104. See note 4 for Lukacs reference.

29

"American History Retold in Pictures" (1931)

Written by Jack Hardy (1901–?), Illustrated by William Siegel (1905–?)

EDITORS' INTRODUCTION

"American History Retold in Pictures" ran in the communist children's magazine, the *New Pioneer*, between June of 1931 and February of 1932—a period in which the U.S. Communist Party was in its most radical phase. The magazine's editors told children to read this series "with a great purpose in mind. . . . You are striving to understand America's past, so that you can do your share in bringing about a new history in the future."[1]

Jack Hardy's commentary in this episode, covering the period from Columbus's landing to the aftermath of the American Revolution, reflects a cynical view of the revolution, described as a revolt of the wealthy that failed to serve the interests of working people. Subsequent episodes in the series, still illustrated by Siegel (but with text by another author), tracked various moments, phenomena, and figures in American history: readers learn about Shay's rebellion; Thomas Jefferson (said to be a "militant atheist"); the development of industry; Fanny Wright (who "defended the rights of women and spoke about the class struggle"); the abolitionists (whose greatest supporters were "the working masses"); and immigrants (who were lured by employers but found only "misery and persecution"). The series describes the bloodshed and terror that characterized the opening of the West; it presents labor heroes Bill Haywood and Gene Debs; it describes U.S. imperialism in the Spanish-American War; and, finally, it celebrates the founding of the Communist Party in the United States in 1919.

Like "ABC for Martin" (pages 19–21), the lesson we can take today from "American History through Pictures" is probably very different from its authors' original intent. The unintended lesson, for today's readers, is that ideology can obscure the quest for truth. Still, this sampling of "American History through Pictures" offers a fascinating and at times amusing example of how history might be written from the perspective of the working class.

Jack Hardy (the name may have been a pseudonym) was born in New York and "studied at two eastern universities, in one of which he served on the faculty for one year," according to a biographical sketch published with one of his books.[2] He was the author or coauthor of several books and pamphlets, including (with Scott Nearing) *The Economic Organization of the Soviet Union* (1927), *The Clothing Workers* (1935), and *The First American Revolution* (1937). Jack Hardy published work primarily with the communist press.

William Siegel was born in a small village near Riga, Latvia. After emigrating to the United States, he studied at the National Academy of Design in New York City and began illustrating books, among them children's stories such as *Boy's Ghengis Khan* (1930) and Siegel's own adaptation of a Soviet story, *Around the World in a Mail Bag* (1932). In the late 1930s, he also illustrated several stories for children produced through the Works Projects Administration (WPA) under the direction of the New York City Board of Education.[3]

Siegel's work appeared regularly in *New Masses*, and his paintings were part of a 1932 exhibition at New York's ACA Gallery showcasing Twenty John Reed Club Artists on Proletarian and Revolutionary Themes (his work was among the pieces that "impressed reviewers as 'tirades or homilies'").[4] He signed the call for an American Artists' Congress, held in 1936 with the purpose of uniting artists in solidarity around issues such as "fascism and war; racial discrimination; preservation of civil liberties" and more bread-and-butter issues such as preservation of the Federal Art Projects.[5]

His *The Paris Commune: A Story in Pictures* (1932), which appeared as part of a pamphlet series published by International, is similar in form to the selection included here. As Alexander Trachtenberg, head of International Publishers, notes in an introduction to Siegel's booklet, "this is a medium in which little working class literature has previously been done. It is graphic, dramatic and simple and should give to the reader the story of the Commune."[6]

NOTES

1. *New Pioneer* 1–2 (June 1931): 6–7.

2. "Biographical Note," *The Economic Organization of the Soviet Union*, by Jack Hardy and Scott Nearing (New York: Vanguard Press, 1927), vi.

3. Thanks to Blair Mosner for identifying the Reading Materials collection at Columbia University.

4. Andrew Hemingway, *Artists on the Left: American Artists and the Communist Movement, 1926–1956* (New Haven, CT: Yale UP, 2002), 56.

5. Call for an American Artists' Congress, reproduced in Gerald M. Monroe, "The American Artists' Congress and the Invasion of Finland," *Archives of American Art Journal* 15:1 (1975): 16.

6. Alexander Trachtenberg, "The Lessons of the Paris Commune," introduction to *The Paris Commune: A Story in Pictures* by William Siegel (New York: International Pamphlets [No. 12], 1932), 10.

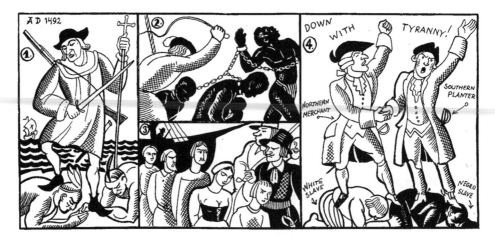

1. In the fifteenth century the chief source of trade and new markets for the trading classes was with the Orient, but in 1453 the Turks captured Constantinople and closed the last of the trade routes to Europeans. Various expeditions were sent out to find new routes. One such expedition, headed by Columbus, accidentally landed in America in 1492.

2. The planters sent expeditions to Africa which captured Negroes and brought them as slaves to America. The first shipload arrived in 1619. By 1765 there were over 100,000 slaves whose lot was a deadly one.

3. More than 20,000 whites, known as indentured servants, were kidnapped in European seaports and shipped to America for many years of forced labor. Many of these were children. All lived and worked under the worst conditions.

4. Northern merchants exploiting white labor, and southern planters exploiting Negro slaves came to be rich and powerful, but English lords of trade were determined to exploit the American colonies for their own profit. With this idea in mind, the British sought to prevent the economic development in the colonies. There was continuous conflict between the colonial merchants and England, while the masses in the cities and on the land were doubly oppressed by their native masters and their foreign rulers.

5. In 1775 open war resulted and the thirteen colonies won their freedom from British rule. This marked a forward step. Although it was a war mainly in the interest of the colonial merchants, slave holders and traders, the workers in the cities and the farmers eagerly took up arms against their hated British oppressors, in the hope that they also would improve their lot. However, as we shall see, they were to be disappointed. The British rulers could not recruit enough British workers to fight against the brave colonists; so paid troops known as Hessians were sent over from the continent.

6. The American merchants became fabulously wealthy after independence from England was secured. Molasses, rum and Negro slaves were their chief items of trade.

7. So long as the colonies belonged to England, English factory owners kept a monopoly on factory production. They closely guarded their industrial inventions and would not permit any machinery to be exported for fear that it might be copied. The War for Independence cleared the way for the development of the factory system in the United States. In 1790, a young Englishman, Samuel Slater, who had worked in English textile mills and then migrated to America, constructed some of the machines from memory. This was the beginning of the American factory system. Hours in these early mills were from 5:00 A.M. to 7:00 P.M. and conditions of work were almost unbelievable. A large part of the workers were children from seven to twelve years of age. So it is clear that the American workers, slaves, and other toilers had not rid themselves of their terrific conditions by the War of Independence. They were still exploited by slaveholders, factory owners, and robbed by landlords.

30

Excerpt from *North Star Shining: A Pictorial History of the American Negro* (1947)

Written by Hildegarde Hoyt Swift (1890–1977), Illustrated by Lynd Ward (1905–1985)

EDITORS' INTRODUCTION

When *North Star Shining* was published in 1947, one reviewer called it "the most exciting book" published that month. Another review called *North Star Shining* "the type of book not often found—a really significant theme developed in a truly distinctive manner."[1]

At a time when African Americans could be found in children's literature primarily as racist caricatures, the work of Hildegarde Hoyt Swift—herself white —showed strong sympathy for the plight of African Americans. Swift's first book, *Railroad to Freedom* (1933), was one of the earliest juvenile biographies of Harriet Tubman (and a Newbery Honor book). Interest in the subject undoubtedly came from Swift's childhood in Auburn, New York, where Harriet Tubman lived out her final years. According to Swift, she wrote both this story and *North Star Shining* "with the idea of giving the white youngster some knowledge of the Negro's fine contribution to our history, and to the Negro child an increased sense of racial pride."[2]

Designed to showcase the history of African Americans in verse and image "from slave ship to the fighting chaplain of today," *North Star Shining* was very consciously written with "the cause" of a burgeoning civil rights movement in mind, along with the "rising tide of discrimination" that followed World War II.[3] The book's title invokes the *North Star*, the antislavery newspaper published by Frederick Douglass in the 1850s.

Swift's maternal grandmother, Louise Woodcock, was one of the founders of the Bank Street College of Education, which had a major impact on American children's literature. Swift's father was a professor at Hamilton College and Auburn Seminary. Early losses may have contributed to her great sensitivity as an author: her brother died at twelve; her mother, a classically trained musician, died when Hildegarde was sixteen.

Swift graduated from Smith College, studied at the New York School of Social Work, and then lived at Union Settlement, where she worked with children. Her husband, Arthur L. Swift, Jr., was a professor of sociology and religion at Union Theological Seminary and was dean and vice-president at the New School for Social Research.

Both Arthur and Hildegarde were "particularly interested in race relations and civil rights."[4] The direct inspiration for *North Star Shining* was the combat death of a close family friend, Chaplain (Captain) Clarence W. Griggs, to whom the book is dedicated. Griggs, an African American, had been Arthur Swift's student and, in the 1920s, had tended Arthur and Hildegarde's nine-year-old son when he was ill for months; thus Griggs's death was a great blow to the family.

Hildegarde Hoyt Swift wrote seven books, the best-known of which is *The Little Red Lighthouse and the Great Grey Bridge* (1942), also illustrated by Ward. That book tells a story about the Jeffreys Hook Lighthouse, which sits under the George Washington Bridge and which Swift and Ward's book made "the most beloved lighthouse in America." When the lighthouse was deactivated in the late 1940s and scheduled for demolition, the children of New York City, who had read the book in school, helped save the lighthouse from destruction.[5]

When she came up with the idea for *North Star Shining*, Swift had Lynd Ward in mind as an illustrator: "You, who are much more sensitive than I am to the social struggle, could make [the pictures] significant," she wrote him.[6]

Lynd Ward came to activism through his father, Harold Ward, who was a professor at Union Theological Seminary with Arthur Swift, Hildegarde's husband. Harry Ward had been active in the settlement house movement of the early twentieth century, and his concern for the poor made him increasingly radical: he traveled to the Soviet Union, wrote glowingly about what he saw, and was involved with many political causes in the United States. He was a founding member of what became the American Civil Liberties Union in 1917.

Lynd Ward, who moved frequently as a child but attended high school in New Jersey, decided to pursue art as a career when, in first grade, he realized that "Ward" was "draw" spelled backward.[7] He would take seriously the legacy of his name, as a call both to produce art and to be an activist like his father.

One of the most distinguished illustrators of the

twentieth century, Ward won many awards for his work. He authored ten books, including several novels-in-woodcuts that are today considered forerunners of the contemporary graphic novel. His children's book, *The Biggest Bear*, won the Caldecott Medal in 1953. Ward also illustrated close to one hundred books for children and adults, including at least twenty by May McNeer (his wife) and two Newbery Award–winning books, *The Cat Who Went to Heaven* (1930) and *Johnny Tremain* (1943).

Ward was outspoken in his politics, and he tried, when possible, to mix his passions for art and activism. He led the call for an antifascist American Artists Congress in 1936; he supported Progressive Party candidate Henry Wallace in 1948; and he strongly criticized McCarthyism in the 1950s. Ward's passion gives vitality to the illustrations in *North Star Shining*, and both text and illustration reflect the urgency that World War II brought to the racial situation in the United States.

In a sketch on "The Book Artist: Today and Tomorrow," published the same year as *North Star Shining* (1947), Ward noted,

> We have a world without Hitler, but we need a world without those cancerous ideas that were not his alone and still live, shared by his friends and counterparts in many countries: ideas of enslavement and exploitation, of master races and inferior peoples, of special privilege and individual enrichment at the expense of others. Those ideas, and the complicated social and economic practices that stem from them, stand between us and the future. Only in a world completely free shall we be able to fulfill the promise of our heritage from the past. It is our great responsibility, weighted now with the heavy secret of the atom, to win that world.[8]

NOTES

1. Beatrice Murphy, "New Books," *Pulse*, Mar. 1947; "Significant and Lovely," *Junior Books* (Mar.–Apr. 1947). Reviews retyped by William Morrow, in Lynd Ward/May McNeer papers, Georgetown University, Box 19, folder 4.

2. Hildegarde Hoyt Swift, letter to Lynd Ward, dated 7 June 1945, Ward/McNeer papers, Box 7, folder 27. Subsequent references to correspondence from same folder.

3. Ibid. Letter from Swift to Ward dated 3 July 1946.

4. Email message from Barbara Brauer (Swift's granddaughter), 25 Aug. 2006.

5. Http://www.hudsonlights.com/littlered.htm, accessed 22 Aug. 2006. Information about New York City school children from Barbara Brauer, telephone interview with Julia Mickenberg, 26 Aug. 2006.

6. Letter from Swift to Ward, dated 3 July 1945.

7. May McNeer, "Lynd Ward," *Horn Book Magazine*, Aug. 1953, 291.

8. Lynd Ward, "The Book Artist: Yesterday and Tomorrow," *Illustrators of Children's Books, 1744–1945*, comp. Bertha E. Mahoney, Louise Payson Latimer, and Beulah Folmsbee (Boston: Horn Book, 1947), 262.

My name was legion,
    I came in every slave to the Colonies,
        In every slave ship.

Mine was the long horror of the middle passage,
The cruel kiss of the whip, the darkness, the burden of
        chains.
Mine the stench of the hold, the groans of the dying.
Mine the queasy lurch of the ship, the hungry roar of
        the sea.
Mine the long, long horror and the hope of death,
    But still I endured.

I came in every slave ship to the Colonies,
    Through the loss of my own freedom
        To build a world for the free.

I came to the New World empty-handed,
    A despised thing, to be used and broken,
Yet I brought immeasurable gifts.
I brought the gentleness of the Bantu,
    The Dahomian's arrogance and courage.
I brought devotion—and wisdom—
    The knowledge of jungle ways and jungle rhythms,
    Wind-magic and moon-magic,
The knowledge of communion with the mystery men
        call God.

I stood in the water of the rice fields,
    I bent beneath the sun of the cotton lands,
I mined the ore hidden in the earth,
    I laid the ties of the railroads,
I swung the axes and cleared the forests
    And served in the white man's kitchen.

I built your world, Oh white man, but in the building
    It became mine too.

I brought to the New World the gift of courage.

I was Crispus Attucks—bold, intrepid, daring,
Wild and unpredictable.
In life infamous, I was called
Beggarly wretch, runaway, ne'er-do-well, rapscallion;
Yet in death I became immortal.

I was the first to fall on that memorable night of March
In the year of our Lord seventeen hundred and seventy,
 When the English Redcoats shot at an unarmed
  people.
Mine was the first blood to stain the snow of Boston.
Though the sober citizens called us "rioters,"
 My death, and the death of the men around me,
 Roused the staid freeholders of Massachusetts,
 Shocked the men of the Colonies into final action,
So that long afterwards, in cold blood, John Adams
  wrote,
 "On that night the formation of Independence was
  laid."

My blood was the first to be shed for freedom;
I was Crispus Attucks—wild and unpredictable—
 Who died under a young moon.

I brought to the New World the gift of devotion.

I was Harriet Tubman, who would not stay in bondage.
I followed the devious, uncharted trails to the North,
I followed the light of the North Star,
 I ran away to freedom in 1849.
I was Harriet Tubman who could not stay in freedom,
 While her brothers were enslaved.
"Go down, Moses," back into Egypt,
 Back to the land of the bloodhound and the
  pateroller,
"Tell old Pharaoh, let my people go!"

Everywhere they waited for my coming,
 Tiny treasures hid against my coming—
I was the lone call of an owl in the darkness,
I was the blurred line of a Spiritual under a slave-cabin
  window,
I was the last, faint tremor of hope upon the wind.
 I was Harriet Tubman,
 Who "never run my train off the track,
 And never lost a passenger."

I brought to the New World the gift of endurance.

My name was Carney,
I was the standard-bearer for the Fifty-fourth
      Massachusetts,
In the War between the States.
I carried the colors for Colonel Robert Shaw.

For three nights we had been without sleep,
    For two days without an issue of rations,
But when the word came that we were to support the
      Union fleet and take Fort Wagner,
    We led the attack, boys, we led the attack!

On one side the treacherous, bottomless marsh,
    On the other the sea;
Before us the sweeping line of Rebel fire—
I climbed the walls of Hell that night,
    To plant Old Glory on the very parapet
    Before I fell to a nameless grave.

I was Carney—and I planted the red-blue flower of
    courage at Fort Wagner.

Our name is legion;
    There are thirteen million of us now.
We are a potent force in America,
    We are America.

    I am the man in the ranks,
    I am a taxi driver,
    I am a Pullman porter,
    I am a mailman,
    I stow freight;
    I paint ships.
You may not know our names, but we know you,
    Oh yes, we know all about you!
We do the hard, dull work that needs to be done.
Why not—it's there to be done, isn't it?
It's there to be done.

We are the names high on the scroll of honor,
   We have achieved education, fame—and power.
No avenues are closed to us; we have blazed the trails
      for others; we are still blazing them.
We have followed the North Star, Oh yes, we have
      followed the Star!
   We are musicians, writers, teachers,
   Doctors, lawyers, scientists,
   Artists, college presidents,
   Ministers, actors, statesmen.
   Booker T. Washington, James Weldon Johnson,
   George Washington Carver, Paul Robeson,
   Channing Tobias, Shelby Rooks, Walter White,
   William H. Hastie, Louis T. Wright, George Haynes,
   Max Yergan, Mary M. Bethune,
   William Lloyd Imes, Charles S. Johnson,
   Richard Harrison, Roland Hayes,
   Marian Anderson, Dorothy Maynor,
   Joe Louis, W. E. B. DuBois,
   Augusta Savage, Arna Bontemps,
   Richard Wright, Langston Hughes, Countee Cullen.

These—and many others.

I am Joe Louis, the champion of all time.
   I don't say that—you say it to me.
   I don't tell you, you tell me!
I am Joe Louis, the Brown Bomber;
   I fight hard, and I fight clean.

When Schmeling kayoed me in the twelfth,
   They said I was done for, they said I'd never come
      back.
Brother, that's the time to fight!
I put Jim Braddock. out in the eighth,
   I knocked Schmeling cold in a single round.

When the Navy needed a show "for relief," they turned
      to me.
   "You pack 'em in, Joe," they said.
I put all my skill into that bout for the Navy.
   I put all my strength into that fight to kayo want and
      need.

They sent me to Europe to box for the boys—
In an army tent, in a converted sheep-fold, under the
      open sky,
   In the opera house at Naples, or the Vittore Emanuel
      Stadium at Rome,
Before fifty—or five thousand—what did it matter?
A man's best skill belongs to his country.
   I'm Joe Louis, the lightning Brown Bomber.

I am Dorie Miller, mess-boy of the *Arizona*,
  Dorie Miller, who wasn't asleep at Pearl Harbor
When the Rising Sun shone in infamy from December
    skies,
  I stood unwavering under its brutal rays.

"Yes, I was just collecting laundry when the alarm for
    General Quarters sounded,
And I headed for my battle station.
No, I'd never shot an antiaircraft gun before,
  But I'd watched others shoot 'em,
So I pulled the trigger and she worked just fine."

I went to my captain on the bridge when he was
    mortally wounded;
I rescued the wounded, and tended the dying,
  But I went back to that gun.

Admiral Nimitz himself pinned the Cross of Bronze on
    my breast.
Now I have long since gone to a nameless grave,
  But I'll never be nameless while America stands,
    No, I'll never be nameless.
I am Dorie Miller, mess-boy of the *Arizona*.

Our name was Legion,
  We came in every slave ship to the Colonies,
    In every slave ship,
      Bringing unpredictable gifts.
We brought the agony of the dispossessed,
  The Judas-gold of the slave block,
    The long horror of fratricidal strife,
The bitter, writhing fruit of the lynching tree,
And the clear beauty of a Spiritual rising to the moon.

We were the named,
  And the nameless,
Carney—and Carver, Douglass—and Dorie Miller.
  These, and more than these.

No longer to be shackled and enslaved,
  No longer to be dispossessed and denied,
    We have become a mighty race,
      Dreaming your dreams, Oh America—
Our genius has become your genius,
  And your pride has become our pride.

I am Clarence Griggs, who died at Okinawa.
   I died for freedom, too.
Oh yes, I knew what freedom meant.
I knew the long, slow struggle up to win an education—
   And hold it—
     I knew.

I was a chaplain, gentle, kindly—keen.
I would have led my people in the paths of peace;
Instead, I served them in the wrack of war.

I died for freedom—for a different world,
Where men forget to hate and stand as brothers,
   Yellow and white and black, together—one.

I died for you—and you—and you—
   Oh do not fail me! Build a world united,
   Out of the shadows
   Turning toward the sun!

31

"Stories for Children," from *Freedom* (1950–1955)

Written by Linda Lewis, Elsie Robins, and Others

EDITORS' INTRODUCTION

Freedom newspaper was published intermittently from 1950 to 1955 under the aegis of the United Freedom Fund, a group organized by the African-American activist, singer, and actor Paul Robeson. Part of a long tradition of black newspapers that have played an important role in fostering social change, *Freedom* highlighted its place in this tradition by carrying on its front page the motto of Frederick Douglass's *North Star*: "Where one is enslaved, all are in chains."

Freedom covered civil rights issues, African-American culture, and black athletes. But the newspaper also gave extensive coverage to international affairs, particularly anticolonial struggles and organizing efforts among black workers.[1] Paul Robeson's support for communist causes also helped distinguish his newspaper from others. According to historian Lawrence Lamphere, "*Freedom*'s positions on both domestic and international affairs were often similar to those of the Communist Party: opposition to American involvement in Korea, support for Communist-led labor unions, support for decolonization in Asia and Africa, opposition to McCarthyism, and support for Soviet foreign policy."[2] So *Freedom* had a mixed legacy: it offered a black, internationalist perspective that consistently countered American Cold War ideology during a period when few voices openly challenged the status quo; but it also tended to unquestioningly put forth a Soviet position on current affairs.

Major figures in the African-American Left contributed to *Freedom*. In addition to Paul Robeson, who published a column in every issue, contributors included Lorraine Hansberry, who would win acclaim for her play *A Raisin in the Sun*; Alice Childress, who would win acclaim as a playwright, novelist, and children's author; and sociologist W. E. B. Du Bois, who wrote occasional columns about African-American history. "Stories for Children" (or cartoon sketches on "Heroes in Our History") appeared in nearly every issue. Their authorship was usually uncredited; however, two of the pieces reproduced here are credited to Linda Lewis and Elsie Robins (about whom we have no information). These pieces were part of an ongoing effort on the part of the communist Left to reach children, and in this instance, to instill in black children a sense of pride in the historic struggles and achievements of African Americans.

The children reading these sketches in *Freedom* may have encountered for the first time figures such as Josiah Henson, Henry "Box" Brown, Peter Poyas, Harriet Tubman, Ellen Craft, and Ida Wells Barnett, some of whom are better known by children today. Josiah Henson, the model for Uncle Tom in Harriet Beecher Stowe's *Uncle Tom's Cabin*, reminds us that the figure most associated with African-American submissiveness and white loyalty was actually an outspoken abolitionist who escaped from slavery. Henry Box Brown, whose history (and name) will surely intrigue children, likewise was an outspoken critic of slavery after his escape from bondage with the aid of a white shoemaker, who shipped him as dry goods to the offices of the Philadelphia Anti-Slavery Society.[3] After publishing his autobiography in 1851, Brown fled to England to escape the Fugitive Slave Act. A moving scroll of scenes depicting slave life and Brown's unusual escape, which he called "Mirror of Slavery," helped foster antislavery sentiment in England. The story of Peter Poyas, hanged for participating in Denmark Vesey's foiled plot to free South Carolina's slaves, most likely appeared here because it resonated with the situation of Julius and Ethel Rosenberg, who at the time this story was published were awaiting their execution for passing "atomic secrets" to the Soviet Union. Poyas's refusal to name his coconspirators was similar to the stance taken by the Rosenbergs, who could have avoided death if they had "named names." Ida Wells Barnett's outspoken stance against lynching was even more timely than *Freedom* recognized here: lynching remained an issue in 1953, when the sketch was published. In fact, the brutal murder of fourteen-year-old Emmett Till in Mississippi in 1955 would be a rallying point in the movement for African Americans' civil rights.

The sketches of Harriet Tubman and Ellen Craft, published under the "Heroes in Our History" banner, mirror the graphic style of Ripley's *Believe It or Not*, one of the longest-running comic panels in history. Robert Ripley's comic strip first appeared in the New York *Globe* in 1918, and he traveled the world collecting strange tidbits for the strip. Putting the "Heroes in Our History" sketches in Ripley's style emphasized the amazing heroism of people like Harriet Tubman and Ellen Craft in the context of their times. The pieces also show us how leftists used popular forms to attract a child audience.

Freedom folded in the summer of 1955, most likely for financial reasons. Published at the height of the McCarthy era, the paper's radical stance scared off most advertisers, and few newsstands were willing to stock *Freedom* on their racks.[4] Gifts, subscriptions, and income from Robeson's concert tours kept the paper in existence for five years, but it was almost always in the red.[5] *Freedomways*, an African-American journal published from 1961 to 1985, took its inspiration from *Freedom* and attempted to extend its contributions to radical black culture and thought.

NOTES

1. Lawrence Lamphere, "Paul Robeson, *Freedom* Newspaper, and the Black Press," Ph.D. thesis, Boston College, 2003, 143.

2. Ibid., 131.

3. For more on Brown, see *Narrative of the Life of Henry Box Brown*, written by himself, available at http://docsouth.unc.edu/brownbox/menu.html.

4. Lamphere, 136.

5. Rebeccah Welch, "Black Art and Activism in Postwar New York, 1950–1965," Ph.D. thesis, New York University, 2002, 206.

JOSIAH HENSON — KEPT RIGHT ON TRAVELING TO FREEDOM

BY LINDA LEWIS

One hundred years ago —in 1851—the story, "Uncle Tom's Cabin" first appeared as a serial in a newspaper. Everybody knows about that famous book and its author, Harriet Beecher Stowe, who did so much to arouse the American people against slavery.

But not very many people know about Josiah Henson, who inspired Mrs. Stowe's novel.

Josiah was born a slave in Maryland. His master put him in charge of the other slaves and even sent him to travel through the South to take care of the owner's business. Though he was a favored slave, Josiah wanted to be free. So one day when his master sent him on a trip he kept right on traveling to Freedom in the North.

Now he was free—but his people were still in chains. Josiah did not forget them. "I won't feel free," he said, "until all Negroes are free." He joined the Abolitionists and made many secret trips back to the South and led other slaves to Freedom.

He became a public speaker and made many lecture trips across the free states to tell the people the truth about slavery. He took up collections—not for himself but to buy slaves from their masters. In this way he freed 118 Negroes.

He told his story in a book, "The Life of Josiah Henson, as Narrated by Himself." When she heard his story and read his book Harriet Beecher Stowe got the idea for her novel, "Uncle Tom's Cabin." Josiah Henson was the model for her hero, Uncle Tom.

Actually, of course, the Uncle Tom of the book was not at all like Josiah. As you can see from his real life, he was no Uncle Tom at all. He was not meek and humble. He had no love or loyalty for the slave masters.

Mrs. Stowe's book made such a stir that one day during the Civil War, when President Abraham Lincoln met the author he said: "So you're the little lady who started this big war."

We don't know whether she told the President about Josiah Henson and how she got the idea for the book from him. But we do know that it is not fair that Harriet Beecher Stowe's name is in all the school books while they never write anything at all about Josiah.

Real-life heroes, like the brave Josiah Henson who fought for his people, are better models for us to follow than any old Uncle Toms.

HOW HENRY BOX BROWN WAS EXPRESSED FROM SLAVERY

BY ELSIE ROBINS

Once there was a slave named Henry Brown. He lived when every slave who could find a way was running away from the Southland, from slavery. Some slaves ran through the woods for miles and

miles; others swam under water in the rivers; and some stowed away on Northbound river boats without food. However they did it, it was always hard. But getting away from slavery was just that important to them. So Henry Brown thought and thought, how could he escape from Richmond, Virginia?

Finally he hit on the idea—to send himself away in a box! He would be express-delivered from slavery! And that is just what he did.

He had a box made 32 inches deep and 24 inches wide and 36 inches long and lined with a soft, cushiony material. He put in it a few biscuits and some water and a tool to make air holes, and he climbed in. Then he had a friend seal up the box with wooden hoops and deliver it to the station. He kept very quiet in the dark box, and still, though his heart pounded very loud. And hour after hour he was chugged along on his way to freedom.

The next day a friend of his in Philadelphia received a telegram that said: "Your case of goods has arrived and will be delivered tomorrow morning." And so the next morning a driver was sent to pick up the box at the station and deliver it to the Anti-Slavery Society.

When the box finally got to the Anti-Slavery Society four men stood around it. Their hearts were pounding too as they wondered if the precious "goods" was safe and sound. Finally one of them tapped on the lid and asked, "All right?" And the box answered fast, "All right!" And as soon as the hoops were ripped away and the nails pried loose, up stood the ex-slave Henry Brown, alive—and free.

"Gentlemen!" he greeted them with dignity, "I resolved that if I reached safety I would give thanks to the Lord." And, still standing in his box, he sang the psalm: "I waited patiently for the Lord and He heard my prayer."

And ever after that he was known as Henry Box Brown.

PETER POYAS SAID: 'DIE SILENT AS YOU SHALL SEE ME DO'

Forty years before the Civil War was fought and the slaves were made free by the Emancipation Proclamation a great man named Denmark Vesey went among the slaves saying: "As the children of Israel were delivered out of the bondage of Egypt—we must deliver ourselves."

Denmark Vesey was brought to this country when he was about 15 years old and his real African name was Telemaque.

When he was 34 years old he bought his freedom from his master and began to make plans for a great revolt that was to free all the slaves in South Carolina and then spread throughout the South.

He began an organization of slaves, men like Peter Poyas and Rolla Bennett and Gullah Jack and Frank Ferguson and Mingo Harth and Batteau Hammett. They were very brave and worked very hard.

By 1822 they had secretly organized 9,000 Negroes. Two hundred and fifty spike heads and bayonets and 300 daggers had been made and hidden in the earth. Maps of gun powder storehouses and arsenals were made and carefully studied. All the available horses in the district were in readiness for the appointed hour when the great revolt was to begin: 12 o'clock Sunday night, June 16, 1822.

A traitor who accidentally learned of the plans went to his master and told him of Denmark Vesey and his followers. Two days before the revolt was to begin 135 leaders were arrested and tried. Thirty-eight of them were sentenced to death.

As they sat in prison waiting to die, they were told that they could save their lives and win their freedom by telling the names of the slaves whose names had been on the lists they had destroyed before they were arrested.

It was then that the young leader Peter Poyas passed before them on his way to death and said: "Die silent, as you shall see me do."

The other men died as he did, and because of their bravery hundreds of other Negroes lived to plan and take part in many other revolts right up to the Civil War.

IDA BARNETT FOUGHT FOR EQUAL RIGHTS

One day in March, 1898, a group of congressmen were ushered into the office of William McKinley, who was then President of the United States.

The group was led by a famous Negro woman whose name was Mrs. Ida B. Wells-Barnett. She and the congressmen had been sent to see the President by the Negro people of Chicago. These were the times when terrible crimes of murder called lynchings were being committed against Negroes all over the country. So in Chicago they had called a great mass meeting to protest, and the people had elected Mrs. Barnett to go and present their complaints to the President.

One of the congressmen, whose name was Senator Mason, introduced Mrs. Barnett and she stepped forward and spoke to the President. Even though she was quite angry about the murder of her people, she spoke calmly and clearly and told the President exactly what the Negro people expected him to do to put an end to lynching. She told him that more than 10,000 people had been killed by lynch mobs since slavery was abolished 33 years earlier. She said that the United States government had always made statements against other countries for treating their citizens badly. Then she asked why the President and the government didn't make laws which would punish people who committed such terrible crimes right in our own country. Mrs. Barnett said, "We refuse to believe this country is unable to protect its citizens."

The President listened and promised that he and the Department of Justice, which is supposed to handle such things, would do everything they could to stop lynching.

But the President did not tell the truth, because he did not do anything and the Department of Justice did not do anything, and Negro people continued to be murdered throughout the country.

And Mrs. Barnett continued to write and to speak against lynching. She had once been the editor of a newspaper in the South, the Memphis Free Press. The stories and articles that Mrs. Barnett wrote in her paper against lynching and discrimination made those white people who mistreated Negroes so angry that they formed angry mobs outside of her office and her home and threatened her life. But Mrs. Barnett was truly a brave woman, and once she bought two pistols and wore them through the streets of Memphis, and continued to write her articles.

Years later whenever there was a meeting or an organization being formed to fight for the rights of the Negro people, Mrs. Barnett was there.

For a long time she toured the country lecturing for equal rights for all people and her writings appeared in many Negro papers and magazines until she was known as one of the most outstanding leaders of the anti-lynching movement.

Today in the city of Chicago, on the Southside, there is a big housing project covering many blocks, where hundreds of Negro families live. This project is named in memory of this great woman. It is called the Ida B. Wells Homes.

32

"Lucretia Mott," from

Independent Voices (1968)

Written by Eve Merriam (1916–1992)

EDITORS' INTRODUCTION

In "A Note to the Reader," published as the prologue to *Independent Voices* (from which this selection is excerpted), Merriam explains why she chose the heroes and heroines portrayed in her book, including Benjamin Franklin, Elizabeth Blackwell, Frederick Douglass, Henry Thoreau, Lucretia Mott, Ida B. Wells, and Fiorello Laguardia. "What appealed especially was their gumption—not hesitating to look and act like a fool—and the pinch of mischief along with the high purpose and morality in each of their personalities," she writes. "All were drop-outs from Graceful Social Behavior Under Any and All Boring Circumstances. . . . Daring for their own times, they would be equally daring today."[1]

That combination of a "pinch of mischief" along with "high purpose and morality" aptly describes Merriam herself, whose work mixes poetry and passion in equal measures. Best known for her children's poetry, for which she won the National Council of Teachers of English award for excellence in 1981, Merriam also published fiction and biographies for young people, as well as nonfiction, poetry, and plays for adults. Born Eve Moscowitz but later Americanizing her name, Eve Merriam grew up in Philadelphia, where her immigrant parents owned a chain of women's clothing stores. Merriam began to write poetry at a very young age, and in high school she published in the school literary magazine. She studied at Cornell University, the University of Pennsylvania, Columbia University, and the University of Wisconsin. Her first book of poetry, *Family Circle* (1946), won the Yale Younger Poets prize.

In her early career, Merriam worked as a copywriter, as host of a radio show about poetry, and, later, as a fashion editor. In 1945 she wrote a verse column for the left-liberal news magazine PM.[2] Around this time she also began to publish poetry and journalism in left-wing and liberal magazines, including *New Masses*, *Jewish Life*, the *Nation*, and *Masses and Mainstream*, as well as in the mainstream *New York Times* and the *Ladies Home Journal*. A series of articles that ran in the *Nation* in the late 1950s on American women anticipated many of the arguments that Betty Friedan would make in the *Feminine Mystique* several years later.

Merriam supported Benjamin Davis in his (successful) run on the communist ticket for New York City Council in the 1940s as well as Henry Wallace's unsuccessful run for president on the Progressive Party ticket in 1948.[3] She was a member of the National Council of the Arts, Sciences, and Professions, which was often pegged as a "communist front," and she taught at the Jefferson School of Social Science, participating in its 1949 conference on "Marxism and the Woman Question." She protested the war in Vietnam and the buildup of nuclear weapons, and actively supported the civil rights movement.[4] She became a major figure in the women's movement of the 1960s and 1970s.

Merriam brought a social conscience to her books, highlighting issues related to feminism, gender roles, the struggle for racial equality, urban poverty, and ecology. These concerns are evident in writings for children such as *Mommies at Work* (1961), *Boys and Girls; Girls and Boys* (1972), *Male and Female under Eighteen: Frank Comments from Young People about Their Sex Roles Today* (coedited with Nancy Larrick, 1973), and *Project 1-2-3* (1971), as well as in works for adults such as *Montgomery, Alabama, Money, Mississippi, and Other Places* (1956), *After Nora Slammed the Door* (1964), and *The Inner-City Mother Goose* (1969), a book of poetry for adults that was later adapted into a Broadway play.

Merriam may well have chosen the figures in *Independent Voices* for their "gumption," but she also very deliberately gave prominence to African Americans and women (black and white) at a time when writers and scholars were just beginning to recognize the imbalances and biases in children's literature and school textbooks.[5] She clearly had current politics in mind when writing: she suggested to her editor that students might want to compare the abolitionist movement described in the Mott sketch to "the non-violent movement of today"—that is, the civil rights movement—considering "freedom slogans, then and now." She also urged teachers to call attention to the Motts' "unorthodox" childrearing, and suggested they ask students, why was the "theory that children should be taught humanely in schools" a "radical" one?[6]

As for reception, feminist groups gave *Independent Voices* high praises, and *Book World* listed it as one of the best children's books of 1968.[7]

NOTES

1. Eve Merriam, "A Note to the Reader," *Independent Voices* (New York: Atheneum, 1968), ix–x.

2. Above information taken from Terrie M. Rooney, "Eve Merriam," *Something about the Author*, Vol. 73, 153–59, and from Laura M. Zaidman, "Eve Merriam," *Dictionary of Literary Biography*, Vol. 61, *American Writers for Children since 1960: Poets, Illustrators, and Nonfiction Authors*, a Bruccoli Clark Layman Book, ed. Glenn E. Estes, Graduate School of Library and Information Sciences, University of Tennessee (Detroit: Gale, 1987), 224–33. "Eve Moscowitz" as birth name appears in Merriam's FBI file, FOIPA #0991305-000.

3. There are several flyers and other materials supporting Davis in Merriam's papers in the Schlesinger Library, Radcliffe College. The fliers are undated, but Davis ran in 1942 and 1945. There is also a flier in these papers from a group called "Writers for Wallace" with Merriam's name on it. See Box 1, folder 3.

4. Merriam papers, Schlesinger Library; FBI file.

5. See Fred Hechinger, "Textbooks and the Negro Stereotype," *New York Times*, 20 Nov. 1966, E9. In Merriam papers, Box MF 1166, folder 5, University of Minnesota.

6. Merriam, notes to editor Jean Karl, 11 June 1968, Merriam papers, Box MF 1166, folder 5, University of Minnesota.

7. For praise from feminist groups see reviews in Mary Ellen Siegel, *Her Way: A Guide to Biographies of Women for Young People*, 2d ed. (Chicago: ALA, 1984); Feminists on Children's Media, *Little Miss Muffet Fights Back: A Bibliography of Recommended Non-Sexist Books about Girls for Young Readers* (New York: Feminists on Children's Media, 1974).

What sort of tether
could hold them together:
impulsive Lucretia
and halting James?
Sea captain's daughter from Nantucket Island,
salty, adventurous all of her days,
and young Mr. Mott
with his set mainland ways.

What was the bonding,
strong as steel, supple as leather,
to keep such an unlikely couple together?

So unlike in every trait:
slate-eyed and dark-haired, tiny Lucretia;
towering, tow-headed, blue-eyed James.

Lucretia whose tongue could never be still;
James for whom all speech was always uphill.

With quick-as-a-trick Lucretia,
with James
so
ploddingly
slow—
what sort of life could the two of them share?

As if the tortoise and the hare
were to make a married pair!

Upon their April wedding day,
Lucretia garbed in sober gray,
just a flicker of white for her kerchief and cap.
The ceremony plain as could be
with Quaker phrasing of *thy* and *thee:*
on the meeting house bench they sat
side by side, gazing straight ahead;
then, at a simple command, they rose
hand in hand, faced each other
and pledged their future life:
sat down again as husband and wife.

It couldn't last,
they were so wrongly matched
from the very start;
temperamentally
poles apart.

The parade of nay-sayers
brayed and nayed:
Lucretia's fire would have to damp down,
for the coolness of James could never change.
Or the rock of James would be chipped away
by the snip of a needle-sharp girl.

One of them would have to give in:
which of the two would win?
Stubborn Lucretia or stalwart James?
Stalwart Lucretia or stubborn James?
All that they shared was their pairing of names.

Darting Lucretia, deliberate James:
opposite natures, identical aims.
Bride and groom
from the very start
sharing a unified will and heart.

> *Oppose injustice by every non-violent means.*
> *Simple as a song,*
> *that was their refrain life-long.*

A test came soon.
They scarcely had a honeymoon
before a time of trial.

James was due to take his turn at military service.
It was merely routine,
a harmless chore;
the country in no way threatened by war.

He was a Quaker, a pacifist.
He would not go.

But wasn't it quixotic to resist?

Advice came to James from every side.
Why risk imprisonment and blacklist?
Even throughout the Quaker Society of Friends,
not every member kept harmony between all means
    and ends.
Be a man of peace—but not fanatically.

Only James could not be satisfied.
Stubbornly, he held to his creed,
and stalwartly, Lucretia agreed.

His jail sentence lasted a mere two days.
The principle clear for always.
> *Beyond the laws*
> *there could come a more sacred cause.*
> *If need be,*
> *he would break the laws of men again.*
> *And so would she.*

Conscience that called with an inner voice
bound them also to love and rejoice.

Mother Lucretia, Father James:
blessed with babies abundantly
babbling, reaching, crying and cooing,
crawling, falling, chewing, *doing.* . . .

> In an age when parents rarely smiled,
> the Motts delighted in every child.
> Unorthodox in everything,
> they taught their children to pray—and sing.

> What a heretic household
> where it was understood
> that children weren't always
> expected to be good!

> How strange not to treat children
> like objects on display,
> not to serve them up for company
> like teacups on a tray,
> and then when you had had enough—
> to order them away.
> What a peculiar family,
> that family of Mott
> caring more for one another
> than a broken toy or spot;
> a most peculiar family,
> caring more to keep their consciences
> clear of any blot.

James was selling cotton cloth,
a good livelihood;
while they didn't bask in riches,
they did moderately well
till Lucretia had to ask:
> How was cotton grown?
> Wasn't the answer only too well known?

White white cotton in the Southern sun
black seeds in the cotton in the golden sun
deeper and deeper the blood-red sun
tighter and tighter the cotton thread spun. . . .

They must give up their ill-gotten trade,
and never again deal in anything slave-made.
This time it was stubborn Lucretia who decreed
and James who stalwartly agreed.
Furthermore, they took a vow:
from now on there would not be
anything in their own home
that came from where
people were held as property.
That meant no more sugar from the canefield South;
molasses instead from islands far away at sea,
and calico cloth from Quaker farms on North Carolina
     land—
all else was contraband—
when the family Mott
began to boycott
they did it totally:
the only products that they would buy
must all be "free."

Nothing slave-made ever use:
exhorting others to share their views,
Lucretia spoke up more and more in meeting.
(Among the Quakers, women did not have to be
shyly retiring or retreating.)

Lucretia moved steadily forward.
Became an official preacher.
Before her passionate voice and piercing eyes,
it was hard to maintain a sanctimonious guise:
that the law is the law . . . rules are made to be
     obeyed . . .
Lucretia thundered: humanity comes first,
thou durst not be afraid!

Spoke until her voice grew hoarse,
then turned the force of her argument
to silent picketing or writing;
engaging in every form of non-violent fighting.
Looking gentle, demure in her Quaker gray,
she used every minute of every day;
if sitting, she'd be knitting—a scarf with a freedom
     slogan,

and every birthday card, greeting, invitation
that busy little body sent
went intertwined with abolitionist sentiment.

Her deeds were trivial and great,
silly and superb.
Did housework, hackwork, holy work,
believing truly that all men were her brothers,
and women of every color and kind her sisters,
this little lady preacher,
this most belligerent of non-resisters.

With all her activity,
she needed a sanctuary,
a place of deliberate calm,
some haven for the heart
where she could be apart from outside claims.
Remember James?
Supporting Lucretia in all her public acts,
abetting her passion with logic and with facts.
Lucretia was ready to speak anywhere;
James would carefully drive her there.
In their Dearborn wagon the duo would go;
he'd cover her up with a laprobe of fur
and watch out for the road, for the weather, for her.
She was still gabby, nimble, and spry.
He was still gawkily solemn and shy.
They didn't change much as the years went by.
They still thought as *we* and never *I.*

He knew how hard it was for her to hide
her natural angry pride.
She knew that though her opinions could be swayed,
once James had made his mind up, there it stayed.
Most of all, she knew he kept her unafraid.
In letters she spoke of "James and self"
as if the two were an integer.

Darting Lucretia, deliberate James:
opposite natures, identical aims;
sharing a unified will and heart,
though by temperament still wide apart.
Out in the garden, he'd hoe and weed;
she'd rather sew by the fire and read.
He preferred a straightback chair;
it was hard for her to sit still anywhere,
but at least a rocker could go to and fro. . . .

So unalike in every way,
their marriage could hardly last a day—

—enduring all kinds of emotional weather
together for fifty-seven years.

On their golden anniversary,
what a merry Mott time was had by all!
James, though white-haired and bent, still tall,
and Lucretia, though fragile, so *powerfully* small.
Children, grandchildren, friends by the score,
and a sense of what life was worth living for:
always the sacred cause
above any man-made laws.

    James and Lucretia,
    unquenchable flames,
    indelibly linked
    their lives and names.

Whichever of the two died first:
worse to be the one living.

Lucretia was left. . . .
inconsolable, bereft.
James was gone.
James was gone.
Her heart and soul were dead;
if only her body had also fled.
James was gone!

    But nature, as it has to,
    comes yearly to renew.
    Spring was coming on,
    time of their April wedding.
    Flowers began to appear:
    yellow forsythia,
    crocus,
    jonquil golden as
    their golden fifty years.
    A granddaughter had planned to be wed
    on just that anniversary date.
    (But that was before Grandfather James was dead.)
    Now it would be blasphemous;
    their wedding must wait
    for a less heartbreaking day in late summer or fall.

Lucretia dried her tears.
The wedding should take place
on exactly the date as planned.
James and self would have it so.
Let there be no doubt about it.
The color came back to her face
as the preacher in her took over:
let their long-lived years together
be an omen of clear and sunny weather
for this new bride and groom.
There was nothing about the past to mourn;
time for rejoicing, time to be reborn.

After the wedding,
Lucretia came home and took off her bonnet and
    cheerful smile.
The world seemed so quiet since James had died.
She glanced outside.
There was a rustling breeze blowing across those two
    trees
he had planted from acorns years before.
Lucretia sighed. Like James, they had rooted deep and
    true.
Suddenly, there was something she wanted to do.

James had helped to found a different kind of school
that went not by the flogging stick and rule,
but by the radical theory
that children should be taught humanely.
Lucretia had the trees transplanted to the school nearby.
She was pleased to see them grow strong and high,
not a dead statue,
but a living memorial to James.
Stalwart oaks, in autumn their leaves
holding on long after the scarlet and gold
of maples and birches had gone.
Their copper tones
Like James. Not flamboyant, but stalwart.
Not easily swayed.

How dear were the years they had had!
Suddenly, she could live more easily
with memory
and face the dark and winter cold
alone.

Later, after Lucretia died,
was it only a dazzlement
made by the sun and shade,
or could it be so
that the twin trees
planted side by side
had come to grow
into one arching splendor against the sky?

33

"High John the Conqueror," from *Black Folktales* (1969)

Written by Julius Lester (b. 1939), Illustrated by Tom Feelings (1933–2003)

EDITORS' INTRODUCTION

Julius Lester wrote this version of "High John the Conqueror" for a small booklet called *Our Folktales*, which the Student Non-Violent Coordinating Committee (SNCC), a civil rights organization, published in 1967. He expanded the collection and republished it in 1969, this time under the title *Black Folktales*, with pictures by Tom Feelings. The stories drew upon oral narratives from African-American folklore, some of which Lester originally found in Zora Neale Hurston's *Mules and Men* (1935), an important book that had gone out of print.

Lester also drew upon tales from his childhood. The version of "High John the Conqueror" reprinted here brings together several stories about High John, a few of which Lester heard from his father, a minister. "He's a hero figure who comes out of slavery," Lester notes, "and basically shows how foolish white people could be." High John recognizes that white people don't see blacks as individuals, and he uses white stereotypes to his advantage.[1] A reviewer for the *New York Times* praised Lester for proving that "black resistance to white oppression is as old as the confrontation between the two groups" and said Lester's versions of these folktales "bring a fresh, street-talk language" to familiar narratives.[2] Other readers, however, took offense. Prominent children's book critic Zena Sutherland called *Black Folktales* "a vehicle for hostility," noting that "there is no story that concerns white people in which they are not pictured as venal or stupid or both."[3] As to whether the violence in a story such as "High John" is appropriate for children, Lester himself says, "the stories really reflect the violence that was in the life of being a slave; the violence they were surrounded with, and the violence I grew up with. And it reflects the violence that a lot of black and Hispanic kids face today in urban areas. Not much has changed. In some ways it's gotten worse."[4]

Of the more than forty books Lester has published since 1965, many are children's books, and several of those have won major awards. Nearly all of his books draw upon history and folklore. Writing for the *New York Review of Books* in 1972, Eric Foner and Naomi Lewis suggested that the purpose of Lester's historical and folkloric reworkings is "not merely to impart historical information, but to teach moral and political lessons," that is, to provide his readers, especially his young readers, with a "usable past."[5] However, Lester himself resists the idea that children's literature has to have lessons. "Primarily I want kids to take joy from the stories. If anything else, I want kids to value the stories they hear from their parents or grandparents," he says.[6]

According to a sketch in *Contemporary Authors*, "Lester has distinguished himself as a civil-rights activist, musician, photographer, radio and talk-show host, professor, poet, novelist, folklorist, and talented writer for children and adults."[7] In the 1960s, Lester was involved in the civil rights movement as a photographer and musician. He recorded two albums of traditional and original songs for Vanguard Records. He served on the board of the Newport Folk Festival and also produced and hosted a live radio show on New York's WBAI called *The Great Proletarian Cultural Revolution*. From 1971 until his retirement in 2003, he taught at the University of Massachusetts at Amherst, first as professor of Afro-American Studies and then as professor of Near Eastern and Judaic Studies, with adjunct appointments in the English and History departments. He converted to Judaism in 1982.

Illustrator Tom Feelings is likewise a major figure in children's literature. Three of his books have received the Coretta Scott King Award; two were runners-up for the Caldecott Medal; and his illustrated autobiography, *Black Pilgrimage* (1972), received numerous awards and citations. He also illustrated Lester's collection of historical fiction, *To Be a Slave* (1968), which received a Newbery Honor Book citation in 1969. Feelings grew up in Bedford Stuyvesant, in New York City, and from a young age began sketching the people in his neighborhood. He attended art school with the goal of becoming a professional illustrator, but his focus on African-American subjects made it difficult to find work. For several years he drew a comic strip called "Tommy Traveler in the World of Negro History," which he sold to a Harlem newspaper. Designed to showcase black heroes, the strip featured a boy who read books about African Americans from the past and dreamed about their exploits.

Feelings published his "drawings from life" in the radical African-American periodicals *The Liberator* and *Freedomways* (the latter a successor to *Freedom*—see page 183). His breakthrough into the mainstream media came when an editor at *Look* magazine sent him to New Orleans to depict members of the African-American community for a feature on "The Negro in the USA." Returning to New York, Feelings wished to recapture some of the warmth and hope he saw in the faces of southern blacks, and he began to focus on children as subjects "because they had less time to be exposed to the pain of being Black in a white country, and because they reflect the best in us before it is changed or corrupted."[8]

In the early 1960s, Feelings moved to the West African nation of Ghana, at that time the only independent black republic. There he worked as staff illustrator for the Ghana Government Publishing House. Feelings's time in Africa had a profound impact on his art. When he returned to the United States he found a growing African-American consciousness, and a greater market for books on black themes, but he still believed that too many of these books were written by white writers, who "didn't know anything about the black experience."[9]

In the conclusion to *Black Pilgrimage*, Feelings proclaims,

I say to our young people: while you are young, travel if you can. See as much of the Black world as possible. Go to the Caribbean. Go to Africa, the source of the spiritual force that helped us survive 400 years of forced labor and oppression, where Black is not only beautiful, but natural. America is not the world, and American values are not the only ones, as young people who go to Africa will see.[10]

NOTES

1. Julius Lester, telephone interview with Julia Mickenberg, 17 Jan. 2006.

2. John A. Williams, review of *Black Folktales*, *New York Times Book Review*, 9 Nov. 1969, 10.

3. Zena Sutherland, review of *Black Folktales*, *Bulletin of the Center for Children's Books*, Feb. 1970, 101.

4. Lester, interview with Julia Mickenberg, op. cit.

5. Qtd. in "Julius Lester," *Contemporary Authors*, Gale Literary Databases, updated 9 Feb. 2006.

6. Lester, interview with Julia Mickenberg, op. cit.

7. "Julius Lester," op. cit.

8. Tom Feelings, *Black Pilgrimage* (New York: Lothrop, Lee & Shepard, 1972), 36.

9. Ibid., 62.

10. Ibid., 72.

Way back during slavery time, there was a man named John. High John the Conqueror, they called him. And he was what you call a man. Now some folks say he was a big man, but the way I heard it, he wasn't no bigger than average height and didn't look no different than the average man. Didn't make any difference, though. He was what you call a be man—be here when the hard times come, and be here when the hard times are gone. No matter how much the white folks put on him, John always survived.

John lived on this plantation in Mississippi. I'm not quite sure whereabouts in Mississippi, but it must've been on one of them cotton plantations up in what they call the Delta. John lived on one of them bad plantations. They had plantations so bad up in there, and the white folks was so mean, that the rattlesnakes wouldn't even bite 'em. 'Fraid they'd poison themselves. Snakes only bit niggers. White folks was so mean up there, they'd shoot a nigger just to bet on whether the body would fall frontwards or backwards. And then they'd go whup the dead nigger's mama if the body fell the wrong way.

That's the kind of plantation John lived on. But it didn't bother John none. He was a be man. Wasn't no disputing that. High John loved living, and, although he was a slave, he made up in his mind that he was gon' do as much living and as little slaving as he could. He used to break the hoes—accidentally, of course. Set ol' massa's barn on fire. Accidentally, of course. He always had a hard time getting to the field on time, and when he did get there, somehow the mule would accidentally tromp down a whole row of cotton before the boss man knew what was happening.

Ol' massa was never sure, though, whether or not John was doing all this on purpose, because John would work real hard some years and make a good crop. The next year, though, it seemed like everything he touched got destroyed. But the following year, he'd pick more cotton than anybody ever thought possible. So the white folks were never sure just whose side John was on. And you better believe that that was the way John wanted it.

Well, it was after one of those seasons when John had really worked, and ol' massa decided he would reward John for it. Maybe it would encourage him to do good work all the time, massa thought. So he gave John an ol' mule and a patch of ground so John could raise a few vegetables of his own. John thanked massa, but the last thing John wanted was a mule of his own. Why should he have to raise his own vegetables when he could take massa's? Stealing was what you did if you took something from another black person. Anything you took from white folks was yours to begin with, because everything they had they got because of your work.

So John really didn't want the ol' mule. All it meant was that massa would expect to see him out there plowing up that little patch of ground, and John had had enough of work for a while. With all the work he'd done this year, he figured on not working hard for the next five. So he started thinking how he was going to get rid of the mule massa had given him.

Bright and early the next morning, John went down to the barn to hitch up his mule. He decided to hitch up massa's best mule to his mule to make the plowing easier, and he went on out to the field and began plowing. Now you know how stubborn mules are. There're some niggers like mules. Won't do right for doing wrong. Well, these were some sho' nuf nigger mules, and every time the mules would balk, John would take his whip and hit massa's mule, WHACK! "Get up there, Miss Anne!" He'd nicknamed massa's mule Miss Anne and he'd hit that mule as hard as he could, whack! "What's wrong with you, Miss Anne! Act like you got some sense!" WHACK! But he never would hit his own mule. If John's mule acted like it was having a hard time, he'd stop, and fan it, and give it a sip of Kool-Aid.

Well, one of them ol' Uncle Tom niggers come by. You know the kind I mean. One of them house niggers who wore massa's hand-me-down clothes. Them was the kind of niggers that would sell their grandmama if it meant they'd get a word of praise from the white folks. Them was the kind of niggers that just loved white folks. They wanted to be white folks so bad that they always tried to walk in the shade. Walking in the shade wouldn't make 'em white, but at least they wouldn't get no blacker. Them kind of niggers loved ol' massa so much that if massa's house caught on fire, the house nigger would say, "Massa, our house is on fire." House nigger barely had a house. If massa was sick, house nigger would come 'round and say, "Massa we sick, ain't we?" And you know that's how they are, 'cause I couldn't make up nothing like that.

From what I've heard, we got some house niggers with us today. If the people are talking about black power, it's the house nigger who runs down to the white folks and says, "Boss, Tom, Sally, Bob, and James are up there talking about this here black power!" If the folks are talking about getting them some guns to defend themselves from the police, the house nigger goes and tells the police. Living with a house nigger is worse than picking up a hungry rattlesnake and putting it inside your shirt.

At any rate, it was one of them house niggers who came by and saw High John beating on massa's mule. Great God a-Mighty! He took off for the big house. "Massa! Massa!"

"Roy, what's wrong with you?"

"Oh Lawd, massa! Oh Lawd! You oughta see what I just seen. Oh Lawd, massa!"

"Well, nigger, stop all this nonsense and tell me what it is."

"Massa, John is down there in the field with your best mule, and he's whipping it like whipping is going out of style. Massa, you got to do something before John kills our mule."

You have to understand that John was a field nigger. John had never set foot in massa's house and wouldn't have if he'd had the opportunity. Only way John would've gone in the big house was through the window one night with a knife in his hand. John worked in the fields, and if massa's house caught on fire, you could be sure that John had set it afire and was down behind the barn praying for a big wind. And if massa got sick, John was praying he'd die. I understand, too, that we got some field niggers running around today. Praise the Lord!

Well, ol' massa went marching down to the fields to see if what Roy was saying was true. He got there, and ol' John was trying to carve his initials on that mule's backside, WHACKITY, WHACK, WHACK, WHACK, WHACKITY! John was making that whip talk like Martin Luther King, Jr. preaching.

Ol' massa turned right red in the face. You know how white folks look when they get mad. "John! What you think you doing?"

"Massa, I'm glad you come by, 'cause I'm just plumb wore out trying to beat some sense into this mule of yours. I say 'Gee,' and he go 'Haw.' I say 'Haw,' and he go 'Gee.' I just can't do a thing with your mule, boss."

Massa didn't know what to say for a minute, 'cause he'd expected John to be apologizing, "Well, J-J-John, what're you doing with my mule, anyway? You didn't ask me if you could use it."

"Well, I figured you wouldn't mind a bit once you saw the vegetables I was gon' be bringing you to put on your table."

For a minute, ol' massa was sorry he'd ever laid eyes on a nigger. They were Excedrin Headache Number One. Wasn't no doubt about it. "Well, John, if I catch you beating on my mule one more time, I'm going to kill your mule."

"What's that, massa?"

"I said, you beat mine, I'm going to kill yours."

"Well, massa, if you do, I bet I'll beat you making money."

Massa just looked at John, thinking he must've lost his mind. "I don't know what nonsense you talking about, John, but hit my mule one more time, and your mule is going to be dead."

Massa wasn't out of sight when ol' John started in on Miss Anne one more time, whackity, WHACK, WHACK, WHACKITY, WHACKITY, WHACK! I mean John

just laid it on her that time. Massa came tearing back to the field.

"I told you, John. I told you." And he pulled out his knife and cut John's mule's throat.

John shrugged his shoulders. "Well, I guess I got to beat you making money."

Now what massa didn't know was that John was a conjure man. I mean John could conjure anything. He was even better than Aunt Caroline Dye, and you know she was one of the best. John could cast spells and cast 'em away. He could tell when a man was gonna die and a baby be born. He could tell when a woman was doing what she wasn't supposed to and a man was doing what he wasn't supposed to. And, if John had a good reason, he could make the birds sing at midnight and the dew fall at noon on a hot summer day. High John was so famous that they even got a root named after him now, called the John-the-Conqueror root, and it's the most powerful root there is. Only thing more powerful than the John-the-Conqueror root is a Black Cat Bone, and John had one of them.

Well, John cut off the mule's skin, dried it, and went into town to make some money. He sat down on the lawn around the courthouse and started shaking his muleskin. "Fortune telling! Fortune telling!"

A white man came up and said, "Nigger, can you tell fortunes?"

"Yes, suh."

"If you tell mine, I'll give you ten dollars." John shook the muleskin three times, held it up to his eye, shook it again, threw some dust on it, shook the dust off, and looked at the muleskin again. "Oh Lawd!"

"Nigger, what're you moaning about?"

"Naw. It can't be."

"Nigger, what're you talking about? What do you see on that muleskin?"

John shook his head. "Let me examine this real close." And he turned the muleskin upside down. "Say the same thing this way, too."

John slowly folded the muleskin. "Boss, I just can't tell you. You wouldn't like it."

"Nigger, if you don't tell me, I'll kill you."

John chuckled. "You can do that if you want to, but then you never would find out."

"I'll give you a hundred dollars."

John thought for a minute. "Boss, I'm just telling you what I saw on the muleskin. This is the muleskin talking, not me."

"O.K. O.K. Now what'd that muleskin say?"

"Well, the muleskin said that you shouldn't go home early today. The muleskin say if you don't go home early, you won't see your wife and best friend sitting in the house all by themselves. And the muleskin say they ain't reading the Bible to each other."

The white man pulled out his gun. "Nigger, you lying, and I'm gon' blow your head off."

John just looked at him. "I knew it. White folks don't want to hear the truth. Just want to hear what they want to hear. You asked me and I told you. Now you want to blame me for what your wife is doing."

The white man slowly put the gun away. "Nigger, if you lying, I'm coming back here and kill you."

"Just be sure you bring a hundred dollars with you when you come."

Well, the white man took off for home, and, just like John said, his wife and his best friend were there not reading the Bible. The white man shot both of 'em and came back and gave John the money.

John went on back to the plantation after telling a few more fortunes, and, as he was going to his house, he saw ol' massa. "Hey there, massa!"

"What you so happy about, John?"

"I told you if you killed my mule, I'd beat you making money." And John pulled out enough money to paper a house with. Of course, there was a whole lot of inflation then, so he didn't have more than fifty dollars, but it looked good, anyway.

Massa's eyes got real big. He had more money than he knew what to do with, but you know how greedy some white folks are. They got cash registers instead of souls. "Uh, John. You think if I kill my mule, I could make some money?"

"Oh, massa. I know you could."

Massa ran down to the barn, killed his mule, and skinned it. Next morning, he was in town bright and early. "Muleskin for sale! Muleskin for sale!"

"Give you two bits for it," one man said.

"Two bits! This muleskin is worth a hundred dollars."

All day, massa went around yelling, "Muleskin for sale," and folks thought he had lost his mind. When sundown came, massa threw the muleskin in a ditch and came home, angry at John.

"Well, massa, I didn't tell you to go try to sell no muleskin for a hundred dollars. Why, anybody knows a muleskin ain't worth more than two bits. What's wrong, massa? These niggers about done drove you crazy.

That's what it is. These niggers would drive St. Peter to sin. You need a rest. You ain't thinking straight."

Well, massa was so mad he could've killed John, but he couldn't see a way he could do it and make a profit, so he let him live. A week or so later, massa just happened to be talking to another slave-owner.

"I got a nigger on my plantation that can whup any nigger in the world," this slave-owner said.

"Can't whup my nigger John."

"I got twenty-five thousand dollars say he can."

"It's a bet," John's owner said. "We'll have the match in town a month from today."

Massa couldn't wait for the match. He knew that John was probably going to get killed, and massa didn't mind losing $25,000 for the pleasure of seeing it.

Well, the news spread around the state quicker than hoof-and-mouth disease. It was going to be a match between the two baddest niggers in Mississippi. All the white folks was planning on coming. The Governor had announced he was coming and bringing his family. White folks didn't like nothing better than to see two niggers in the ring, fighting each other until they both fell out.

"Well, John," massa said one day, "you getting ready for the match?"

John was stretching out on the grass eating some chicken. "I'm ready, massa."

"John! Where'd you get that chicken leg from?"

"Strangest thing, massa. Last night, this chicken just walked in my house, and I was trying to chase it out, you know, and that chicken got so scared that it jumped in this skillet of hot grease I had on the fire. And before I could do a thing, it was all fried. So I thanked the Lord for sending a chicken to a poor, honest, colored man. You know something, massa?" John asked, throwing the chicken bone on massa's hat brim. "The Lord sure takes care of you when you live right."

Massa didn't say a word, but stalked off angrily. He couldn't wait to see John get a good beating.

Well, the day of the match came, and white folks were there from everywhere. There were white folks there from Hang-a-Nigger, Mississippi. And there were white folks there from Cut-a-Nigger, Alabama, and Burn-a-Nigger, Georgia, and even some white folks from Co-opt-a-Nigger, New York. The Governor and his wife and daughter were there. The Lieutenant Governor and his family was there. The Sergeant Governor and his family. The Corporal Governor and his family. There was so many white folks there, it looked like a lynching party.

About an hour before the match was to start, in come the plantation owner with his nigger Andy. Now, let me tell you, this was one big nigger. He was so big and strong, they had him tied with chains. He was snorting and growling and carrying on so that they had to chain him to one of the pillars of the courthouse. He was so big that he had to stoop down at nights to let the moon go by. Four white ladies fainted when they saw him. When John's massa saw him, he began to feel sorry he'd made the bet. He looked at that nigger Andy and could just see John getting pulverized. John deserved a good beating, but nothing like what he was going to get.

Well, about ten minutes before match time, in come John. And John was dressed like he was going to his own funeral. I mean, he was clean! Had him on a pair of black patent leather shoes with spats. Some red trousers with a red coat, a white shirt, and a black string tie. Over his arm was a hand-carved cane studded with diamonds. He was wearing a Stetson hat and walking real slow, tipping his hat to everybody. John diddy-bopped down the aisle speaking to all the white folks. "How you do, boss. It's good to see you. Haven't seen you since you sold my mama." "How you do, suh? Last time I saw you was the time you whipped my sister and rubbed the cuts with vinegar. That was to keep her from getting lockjaw." John was as polite as he could be. A perfect gentleman.

After John had finished greeting all the white folks, he stepped out in the center and looked around. He pretended like he hadn't even seen Andy, who was snorting like he had swallowed a box of snuff. John looked around until he spied the Governor and walked over to him as fast as he could go, looking mean, mean, mean. John crawled over the Governor's wife, stepped on the Governor, and hauled off and slapped the Governor's daughter, pow! He hit that white girl all upside the head. He hit that girl so hard that her blonde hair turned brown. He hit her so hard she was cross-eyed for the rest of her life, POW! He smacked her again! "Girl, didn't I tell you to stay at home and not come out here today! What do you mean disobeying me?" POW! He smacked her one more time.

Well, when that nigger Andy saw John hit that white girl, he started getting away so fast that he pulled the courthouse down, broke his chains and, from what I

heard, he didn't stop running until he got to Canada. Andy knew he couldn't whup John, 'cause if John was bad enough to slap a white woman, John was bad enough to whup him.

The white folks were kind of upset about John slapping that white woman until they realized that he'd simply outsmarted everybody. Then they fell out laughing. Especially the ones who had bet on John. Massa wasn't mad, 'cause the Governor's daughter had said one time that his son wasn't good enough for her to marry. But the Governor was kind of ticked off until ol' massa slipped him half of the $25,000, at which point the Governor told his daughter t` shut up all that screaming and hollering, or he was going to smack her one time himself.

John went on back to the plantation, and, even though he'd won massa all that money, he still had to get out in the fields and work the next day. John couldn't see why, so he went in the barn and broke all the plows, the hoes, poured water in the cotton seed, broke the mules' legs, told the house nigger to go tell it, and then stretched out under a big sycamore tree, put his hat over his face to keep the flies off, and went to sleep.

"John! You went too far this time!" massa hollered. "You just went too far this time, and I'm going to kill you!"

John didn't even take the hat off his face. "Kill me, and I'll beat you making money."

"Not this time, nigger."

Massa shoved John in a gunny sack and drug him down to the river to throw him in. But he'd forgotten his weights and had to go back to the big house to get them. While he was gone, some of the other field niggers, who'd been watching all along, came out of the woods, untied the sack, and let John out. They filled the sack with stones, and when massa came back with his weights, he threw a sack of stones in the river. By that time, though, John was home, finishing his nap.

Later that afternoon, he got up, grabbed his muleskin and went into town to tell fortunes. Long about six that afternoon, he came back to the plantation, money just jingling in his pocket.

"John? Is that you?" massa said when he saw him.

"I told you if you killed me, I'd beat you making money."

"John?"

"Yes, massa."

"John, you think if I let you kill me, I could make some money?"

John's face was very serious as he said, "Massa, I *know* you could."

John shoved ol' massa in a gunny sack and tied it up. John called to the other field niggers, and they didn't forget their weights. They carried the sack down to the river, and, just as they were getting ready to throw it in, massa called out, "You sure I'm gon' make some money, John?"

"Massa, I *know* you is," John called back, as ol' massa hit the water and sank.

And that's the story of High John the Conqueror.

part 7

A Person's a Person

JULIA MICKENBERG & PHILIP NEL

The title of this section comes from Dr. Seuss's *Horton Hears a Who!* (1954), which one reviewer called "a rhymed lesson in protection of minorities and their rights."[1] In that book, smallness stands for an arbitrary mark of difference for which the Whos are mistreated —be that difference a matter of race, creed, sex, or nationality. So, when Horton says, "A person's a person, no matter how small," he defends the rights of all individuals, irrespective of their differences. We have borrowed his motto to name this section because each of its stories comments in some way upon discrimination. In addition to the six stories that follow, many pieces in this book could have been included here—we note some of these below.

These texts participate in a tradition of American children's literature dating back to nineteenth-century abolitionists, who challenged discrimination against African Americans with children's periodicals like *The Slave's Friend*, a monthly pamphlet published by the American Anti-Slavery Society. In the twentieth century, circles around the National Association for the Advancement of Colored People (NAACP, established in 1909) helped produce children's stories encouraging African-American children to take pride in themselves and their heritage, from Socialist and NAACP founder Mary White Ovington's *Hazel* (1913) to the *Brownies Book* (1921–1922), edited by W. E. B. Du Bois. Children's "proletarian literature" written and illustrated by American Communists in the 1930s often featured black and, to a more limited degree, American Indian and Hispanic characters.[2] This work reached a limited audience, but it speaks to an ongoing concern among Communists with the problem of "white chauvinism."

Despite this longer tradition, prior to the 1940s, very few popular children's books (or school textbooks) offered any open comment on racial discrimination; indeed, it was difficult to find books that portrayed African-American children in terms other than caricature. In 1932, Langston Hughes suggested that overcoming a "racial inferiority complex" was "one of the greatest tasks of the teachers of Negro children. To make their little charges feel that they will be men and women, not 'just niggers,' is a none too easy problem when textbooks are all written from a white standpoint."[3] As we note elsewhere, Hughes at this time had become involved in many left-wing causes and, as evidenced by his publication in the communist *New Pioneer*, had seen an important connection between his radicalism and his interest in writing for children. Hughes and Arna Bontemps's *Popo and Fifina* (1932), a story of two Haitian children, is not openly critical of racial discrimination, but it does offer subtle critiques of U.S. colonial interests in Haiti and the conditions of poverty. Most importantly, it portrays sympathetic, autonomous black characters. This story earned critical acclaim and remained in print for decades. "The need today," Hughes would insist, "is for books that Negro parents and teachers can read to their children without hesitancy as to the psychological effect on the growing mind, books whose dark characters are not all clowns, and whose illustrations are not merely caricatures."[4]

World War II and the fight against fascism helped make emphasizing diversity a national priority. Suddenly there were more books featuring ethnic and racial minorities. Those by radicals distinguish themselves in subtle ways: for instance, illustrations by Ernest Crichlow in Jerrold and Lorraine Beim's *Two Is a Team* (1945) show a black child and a white child who are best friends, a situation that was basically taboo in children's literature. Giving Terry a white friend in *The First Book of Negroes* (excerpted in this section) was likewise a radical gesture. Several of the texts in *Little Rebels* speak to the changing racial climate around World War II—Hildegarde Hoyt Swift's *North Star Shining* (1947) (see pages 175–82), Ruth Benedict and Gene Weltfish's *In Henry's Backyard* (1948) (see pages 267–73), and Alex Novikoff's *Climbing Our Family Tree* (1945) (see pages 37–39), to name a few.

During the Cold War, challenging racial discrimination was often seen as a form of communist agitation. For instance, Georgia governor Herman Talmadge attributed the victory for integrationists in the 1954 *Brown* decision to "vicious and dangerous brain washing" by communist propagandists.[5] The pieces for children published in *Freedom* (included in "History and Heroes") do, in fact, attest to the ongoing efforts of African-American radicals to build a sense of racial pride in black children. Likewise, juvenile biographies of African Americans published in the 1950s by radicals such as Shirley Graham, Ann Petry, Dorothy Sterling, and Emma Gelders Sterne continued this work for a wider audience. In the 1940s and 1950s, John R. Tunis and Florence Crannell Means also wrote realistic children's fiction that featured minority characters: African Americans, American Indians, Japanese Americans, Jewish Americans, and others.

Within the context of Cold War paranoia, these three works gain particular significance: Dr. Seuss's "The Sneetches," a selection from Langston Hughes's *First Book of Negroes*, and Walt Kelly's "Who Stole the Tarts." Hughes wrote *The First Book of Negroes* (1952) after McCarthyism shut him out of other work. Walt Kelly's 1954 adaptation of *Alice's Adventures in Wonderland* offered an unusually bold satire of Senator McCarthy, then a still powerful figure. The original version of Seuss's "The Sneetches" appeared in 1953, over a decade before antiracist children's stories became prominent in children's publishing.

Open challenges to racial discrimination became relatively mainstream by the mid-1960s, as the civil rights movement gained strength and influence. Still, as late as 1962, Nancy Larrick offered a searing critique of children's book publishing in "The All-White World of Children's Books," noting how rare were any representations of people of color, positive or negative, in children's books. The publication of Ezra Jack Keats's *The Snowy Day* (1962) and the founding of the Council on Interracial Books for Children (in 1965) helped pave the way for the black children's writers and illustrators of the 1970s and later—among them Alice Childress, Lucille Clifton (whose *The Black BC's* is included in our collection; see pages 22–25), Rosa Guy, Muriel and Tom Feelings, Margaret Musgrove, and Leo and Diane Dillon (Leo is black, Diane is white).[6] Authors who had addressed racial issues in children's books published in prior decades now felt free to be more open in their critique. For instance, Hughes's *Black Misery* (1969), published posthumously with the help of Arna Bontemps, grapples directly with stereotypes of African Americans: "Misery is when you find out you are not supposed to like watermelon but you do." Or, "Misery is when you start to help an old white lady across the street and she thinks you're trying to snatch her purse."

Julius Lester's *Black Folktales*, illustrated by Tom Feelings (see pages 192–99), came out of Lester's involvement with the civil rights movement. Sandra Weiner's *small hands, big hands* (1970) depicted migrant workers (see pages 133–36), and Frank Bonham's *Viva Chicano* (1970) spoke to discrimination against Mexican Americans. In the past several decades there has been an explosion in multicultural children's literature—which can be traced back to radical agitation during the civil rights movement. African Americans' central place in the struggle for civil rights resulted in a greater output of children's literature, and other marginalized groups followed this lead, taking their own struggles into the realms of children's literature.

Feminism and the gay rights movement have likewise brought us radical children's stories concerned with undermining gender stereotypes. Perhaps the most famous text in this realm is *Free to Be You and Me* (1972–1974), by Marlo Thomas and friends. That book is still in print, which kept us from using it in our collection, but we have included two stories from *Ms.* magazine's "Stories for Free Children," out of which the idea for *Free to Be* emerged: Lois Gould's *X* and Jeanne Desy's "The Princess Who Stood on Her Own Two Feet." Feminists on Children's Media formed to monitor sexist stereotypes in children's literature, and other feminists sponsored ventures such as Lollipop Power Press, which published children's books that "portrayed non-sexist and non-stereotypical role models to empower and instruct children in very diverse life situations."[7]

When thirty-eight children's literature editors responded to a 1970 query from *Publishers Weekly* on how the women's movement was affecting their editorial thinking, nearly half said it had definitely made an impact. Several editors cited books that they had launched in direct response to the movement, such as Marijean Suelzle's *What Every Woman Should Know about the Women's Liberation Movement* (1971).[8] Likewise, Random House reissued Eve Merriam's *Mommies at Work*, ahead of its time when first published in 1961. Both *Mommies at Work* and Norma Klein's *Girls Can Be Anything* (1973) (see pages 87–94) represent the many different jobs that women do. Charlotte Zolotow's *William's Doll* (1972) shows children and their parents that it's okay for boys to play with dolls. Anthony Browne's *Piggybook* (1986) teaches a chauvinist dad and sons not to take mom for granted.

Fairy tales and retellings of fairy tales have been popular for challenging gender stereotypes. In the 1960s and 1970s, feminists looked back to the resourceful heroine Molly Whuppie, whose story of the same name first appeared in the late nineteenth century. Advocates for women's equality also updated traditional tales or wrote new ones of their own, including Jay Williams's *The Practical Princess* (1969) (in "Imagine," pages 161–67), Jeanne Desy's "The Princess Who Stood on Her Own Two Feet" (1981), Robert Munsch's *The Paper Bag Princess* (1980), and the many tales collected in

Jack Zipes's *Don't Bet on the Prince* (1986). Others have examined masculine gender roles, whether explicitly in Williams's *Philbert the Fearful* (1966) or implicitly in Munro Leaf's *Ferdinand* (1936).

Lois Gould's *X* may be the first children's book sympathetic to transgendered people, but, generally speaking, children's books that speak to nontraditional gender identifications and sexual orientations emerge in the 1980s and 1990s. Jane Severance's *Lots of Mommies* (published by Lollipop Power in 1983), about one child with four female caregivers who share a house, shows successful child rearing with no fathers present, and so can be interpreted as friendly to lesbian parents. Leslea Newman and Diane Souza's *Heather Has Two Mommies* (1989) is perhaps the most famous children's book featuring same-sex couples, but others have ventured into this territory, notably Johnny Valentine's *One Dad Two Dads Brown Dad Blue Dads* (1994), Linda de Haan's *King and King* (2003), and Justin Richardson, Peter Parnell, and Henry Cole's *And Tango Makes Three* (2005), a true story about two male penguins in New York's Central Park Zoo and the baby penguin they raise together. Although books for adolescents (which our anthology is not focused on) feature children struggling with their own sexuality, most such books for younger children (the focus of our anthology) highlight the parents' situation. The message in these books is that, as one character says in Valentine's *Two Moms, the Zark, and Me* (1993), "real families come in all forms and sizes."

As different groups have fought for justice, children's literature has documented that fight. Although there are battles not yet fully won and others not yet joined, literature for children today is much more inclusive and more conscious of treating difference with respect. The stories that follow—along with many others in this anthology—reflect the movements to honor each member of the diverse group of people who comprise humankind.

NOTES

1. Judith and Neil Morgan, *Dr. Seuss and Mr. Geisel: A Biography* (New York: Random House, 1995), 151.

2. See "Primers for Revolution," in Paul C. Mishler, *Raising Reds: The Young Pioneers, Radical Summer Camps, and Communist Political Culture in the United States* (New York: Columbia UP, 1999), 111, 117.

3. Langston Hughes, "Books and the Negro Child," *Children's Library Yearbook* 4 (1932): 108.

4. Ibid., 109.

5. Mary Dudziak, *Cold War Civil Rights: Race and the Image of American Democracy* (Princeton, NJ: Princeton UP, 2000), 117.

6. Michelle H. Martin, *Brown Gold: Milestones of African-American Children's Picture Books, 1845–2002* (New York: Routledge, 2004), 53.

7. For collections relating to Carolina Wren Press (of which Lollipop Power was an imprint), see Duke University's Special Collections: <http://library.duke.edu/specialcollections/bingham/guides/beyond/lollipop.html>.

8. *The Spokeswoman: A Twice-Monthly Information Service for All Women*, 30 July 1970, 7–8. In Eve Merriam papers, University of Minnesota.

34

"A Little Boy in a Big City," from *The First Book of Negroes* (1952)

Written by Langston Hughes (1902–1967), Illustrated by Ursula Koering (1921–1976)

EDITORS' INTRODUCTION

The First Book of Negroes was an important contribution to the nonfiction series of "First Books" and "Real Books" put out by the publisher Franklin Watts in the years following World War II. A number of left-wing authors, including Franklin Folsom, Mary Elting Folsom, Rose Wyler, Harold Coy, Jane Sherman, and Eve Merriam published with Watts. His wife, Helen Hoke Watts, was very liberal and may have consciously sought to help writers and artists who were subject to blacklisting during the McCarthy era. Hughes himself was beginning to suffer the consequences of his radical activism when he obtained a contract to write *The First Book of Negroes*, and in the midst of the book's production he was called to testify before the House Committee on Un-American Activities.

Although Watts did publish books by leftists, two of his more prolific authors, Franklin Folsom and Mary Elting (she wrote under her maiden name), complained that there were no African Americans who were either the authors or the subjects of Watts's books. Finding their complaint reasonable, Watts offered to do a "First Book of Negroes." The Folsoms insisted that Watts find an African American writer to do the book, and they suggested Langston Hughes, whom they knew from the antifascist League of American Writers, of which Franklin Folsom was secretary.[1]

Hughes undoubtedly welcomed the opportunity to write a children's book when Watts contacted him in the early 1950s. The American Legion had begun a smear campaign against Hughes in the 1940s, and by 1950 the right-wing publication *Red Channels* had compiled four pages of Hughes's left-wing associations. Around this time, the publisher Henry Holt canceled all of Hughes's contracts and fired most of the employees who had worked with him, and Hughes found much of his income from speaking tours drying up as high school administrators balked at the idea of exposing students to a "red."[2]

Although the invitation to write *The First Book of Negroes* came as Hughes was trying to distance himself from his radical associations, the Wattses—with prodding from Mary Elting—urged Hughes not to downplay contemporary racial dynamics in the book and to be explicit about segregation, housing discrimination, colonialism, and other highly charged issues.[3] At the time, segregation was in full force in the South (but beginning to be challenged), and fear of losing southern markets made children's book publishers reluctant to print texts with black subjects, let alone those that showed blacks and whites cooperating or that openly discussed segregation.[4]

Written as a series of vignettes about historical and contemporary Africans and African Americans, *The First Book of Negroes* is held together by stories about a boy named Terry, who lives in New York. The selection reprinted here depicts Terry as attractive and intelligent; it explains and openly condemns segregation; and it emphasizes the varied racial inheritance of those classed together as "Negroes" (the term of choice in the 1950s). Elsewhere, the book shows Terry's family to be educated and cosmopolitan, and the illustrations depict Terry with white friends. It does, however, rather conspicuously omit figures such as Paul Robeson and W. E. B. Du Bois (both radicals) from the section on "Famous American Negroes," and a picture of Josephine Baker in the first edition of the book was taken out after a New York columnist threatened to attack the book.[5] Although Franklin Watts did demand that Hughes publicly clear his name as attacks against him became increasingly hard to ignore,[6] Hughes continued working with the Wattses for another decade, and the firm published several more of his books, including *The First Book of the West Indies* (1956) and *The First Book of Africa* (1960).

Ursula Koering was born in Vineland, New Jersey, and lived in that area for most of her life. She came from an artistic family: her father and grandfather did glassblowing, and her mother was a painter. During grade school, her mother took her to the Philadelphia Museum of Art every Saturday for their children's drawing class. After high school, Koering enrolled full-time at the Philadelphia College of Art, intending to be a sculptor. However, she discovered there was not much of a market for "lady sculptors," and so she began illustrating children's stories, first working for the magazine *Jack and Jill*, and gradually getting book assignments as well. Her illustrations can be found in more than two hundred books, among them a number by Franklin Folsom or Mary Elting. Koering taught art for nine years at a New Jersey girls' school, and later in life she became a sculptor for the Franklin Mint, creating at least sixteen coins.[7]

NOTES

1. Mary Elting Folsom, interview with Julia Mickenberg, 22 Jan. 1998; Franklin Folsom, *Days of Anger, Days of Hope: A Memoir of the League of American Writers, 1937–1942* (Niwot: UP of Colorado, 1994).

2. On the cancellation of Hughes's contracts with Holt see Arnold Rampersad, *The Life of Langston Hughes.* Vol. 2, 1941–1967 (New York: Oxford UP, 1988), 230. On the cancellation of speaking engagements see Langston Hughes papers, Beinecke Library, Yale University, Box 186, folder "Common Ground."

3. There is correspondence relating to this book in Hughes's papers, box 163, folder "Franklin Watts." For further discussion, see Julia Mickenberg, *Learning from the Left: Children's Literature, the Cold War, and Radical Politics in the United States* (New York: Oxford UP, 2006), 152–58.

4. See Nancy Larrick, "The All-White World of Children's Books," *Saturday Review*, 11 Sept. 11 1965, 63+.

5. Rampersad, 230.

6. Hughes was asked to make a statement affirming his patriotism that Watts could send to anyone critical of the firm's decision to publish his work. Rampersad, 191.

7. "Ursula Koering" (autobiographical sketch), *More Junior Authors*, ed. Muriel Fuller (New York: Wilson, 1963); "Ursula Koering . . . a Lifetime in Art," *The Franklin Mint Almanac*, April 1976, 18–22.

A LITTLE BOY IN A BIG CITY

Terry Lane is a little boy whose skin is brown as a walnut and whose hair is black and beautifully crinkly. He lives in Harlem, a section of New York City where many colored people live. It has been the home of famous folks like Joe Louis, world champion boxer; Adam Powell, pastor of the largest Baptist Church in the world and a member of Congress; and of many musicians like Duke Ellington, maker of happy music.

Terry does not know these famous men, but he knows the "A" train on the subway, about which Duke Ellington wrote a song. The "A" train rushes full speed underground through a long tunnel. Sometimes Terry's father and mother take him downtown on the subway to Broadway or Radio City where some of the tallest buildings in the world are. They take Terry to a show or into a fine restaurant or to see the ice skating at Rockefeller Plaza.

If Terry lived in the South where his great-grandfather was once a slave, he could not go into a downtown theater or restaurant, since it is against the law in Southern cities for colored people to sit next to white people or eat with them in public. Negroes must ride on the back seats of busses and streetcars, and they must sit in a separate train coach unless they are rich enough to afford a Pullman. This is legal segregation, but Negroes call it "Jim Crow," and they do not believe it is legal because it does not follow our Constitution or the Declaration of Independence which says all men are free and equal.

Such divisions of the races in the South come from the time when Negroes were slaves and white people were free. Now the division lies in what people can do and where they can go. There are many things in the South Negroes are not permitted to do. For example, in many towns a Negro cannot read a book at the public library, and if he is sent there on an errand he must go in the back door. This is true of railroad and bus stations, too, where the entrances to the barren rooms set apart for Negroes are usually at the back or on the side.

If Terry lived in the South he could not go to school with white children, nor could they go to school with him. That is one reason why Terry's father and mother prefer to live in New York where children go to any school. Some of Terry's teachers are white and some are colored. Some of his classmates are white and others are as brown as Terry. Some are Puerto Ricans who are just now learning English, since their island home once belonged to Spain and they spoke Spanish. But all of these children are good friends, learning and playing together.

Perhaps Terry's great-great-grandfather was an explorer who came to America from Portugal or Spain. Perhaps Terry's great-great-grandmother was an Indian who married an explorer. Maybe another great-great-grandfather was a slave, perhaps another was a free Negro. Like most Americans, Terry's ancestors had the blood of many races in their veins.

African Negroes are almost all very dark people, handsome in their blackness, but American Negroes are of many colors. Some American Negroes are ebony, some a warm cinnamon brown, some tan, some the color of ginger, others golden as peaches, and some are the color of ivory. Some are coffee-and-cream. There is a reason for such differences in color. A long time ago the Indians, the French in Louisiana, the Spanish, the Negroes from Africa, and people from many other countries met in the New World and their children's children became the American Negroes of many colors and types today.

TERRY'S ANCESTORS MAY HAVE
COME FROM MANY PLACES

35

"The Sneetches" (1953)

Dr. Seuss (Theodor Seuss Geisel, 1904–1991)

EDITORS' INTRODUCTION

Born Theodor Seuss Geisel in Springfield, Massachusetts, Dr. Seuss first gained national recognition in the 1930s for "Quick, Henry, the Flit!"—an advertising catchphrase that was the "Got Milk?" of its day. Concerned that isolationism left the United States vulnerable, Seuss took a break from writing children's books in 1940 (he had written only four at the time) and began a 21-month career writing political cartoons for PM, New York's Popular Front newspaper. The fight against fascism galvanized Seuss's political commitment and led him, after the war, to write political children's books. Though his Cat in the Hat (1957) and Green Eggs and Ham (1960) have taught generations of American children to read, Seuss also wrote many stories designed to teach children to think. Yertle the Turtle (1958) is an antifascist fable, How the Grinch Stole Christmas! (1957) criticizes commercial exploitation of the holiday, The Lorax (1971) advocates environmental conservation, The Butter Battle Book (1984) satirizes nuclear proliferation, and The Sneetches (1961) shows the folly of bigotry.

Inspired by his opposition to antisemitism, Seuss wrote "The Sneetches" for Redbook in 1953. Two experiences in his early life made him sympathetic to victims of social injustice. Americans' responses to the First World War fueled anti-German sentiments, and he recalled being "chased home from school, being clobbered with brickbats" because "I was a kid with a German father. When they clobbered me, they yelled, 'Kill the Kaiser.'"[1] (His paternal grandparents were German, and his maternal grandparents—Seuss—were Bavarian.) Later, during his freshman year at Dartmouth, not a single fraternity invited him to pledge. As he said, "With my black hair and long nose, I was supposed to be Jewish. It took a year and a half before word got around that I wasn't. I think my interest in editing the Dartmouth humor magazine [Jack-o-lantern] began . . . that Pledge Week."[2] Picked on for his ethnicity and appearance, Seuss grew up to attack prejudice in books like Horton Hears a Who! (1954) and The Sneetches.

But *The Sneetches* nearly did not become a Dr. Seuss book. When a respected friend told him that the tale "was anti-Semitic," Seuss abandoned plans to expand the page-long *Redbook* piece into a full story. Random House sales manager (and, later, president) Robert Bernstein persuaded Seuss to finish the book.[3]

The earlier version of the tale, reproduced on the following page, offers a glimpse into the creative processes of Dr. Seuss. Still a little rough around the edges, the *Redbook* "Sneetches" offers greater detail and less hope than the familiar story. In their 1953 genesis, the Sneetches are "birds" from "Aw-WawHoo," possibly an allusion to the Yahoos, those "most unteachable of all brutes" in *Gulliver's Travels* by Jonathan Swift, whose satire Seuss admired. In their 1961 incarnation, the Sneetches could be from anywhere, and they clearly represent people—the revised story does not identify them as "birds" and *does* call their offspring "children." In changing birds to people, Seuss more closely aligns the characters with the book's readers, and his altered conclusion suggests that experience can teach us to shed our prejudices. At the end of the Random House book, "the Sneetches got really quite smart": they now understand "that Sneetches are Sneetches / And no kind of Sneetch is the best on the beaches." In contrast, the *Redbook* tale offers no sense that the Sneetches have learned to abandon their bigotry. However, when readers look at the illustration, they will understand not to judge by appearances alone—as the narrator explains, "except for those stars, every Sneetch is the same."

NOTES

1. Judith Morgan and Neil Morgan, *Dr. Seuss and Mr. Geisel* (New York: Random House, 1995), 276.

2. Ibid., 27.

3. Ibid., 173.

If you go to Aw-WawHoo
And walk down the beach,
You'll notice a sort-of-a-bird called the Sneetch.
In fact, there are *two* sorts of Sneetches you'll find:
The Star-Belly kind, and the Plain-Belly kind.
The Star-Belly Sneetches have bellies with stars.
The Plain-Belly Sneetches don't have them on thars.

Now those stars . . .
They're not big. They are really so small
You'd think such a thing wouldn't matter at all.
But, because of their stars, all the Star-Belly Sneetches
Believe *they're* the best kind of Sneetch on the beaches.
Won't talk to the others! They pass them right by
With their snoots high-and-mighty, stuck up in the sky.
Won't ask them to go to their parties or sleigh rides,
Their ball games, their marshmallow roasts or their hay
    rides.
And the Plain-Belly Sneetches . . .
Well, *they* get so mad
That they sometimes do things that are really quite bad,
And they throw dreadful things at the Star Bellies'
    heads . . .
Like oysters and clams and the springs of old beds!

How they fight on those beaches,
Those unfriendly Sneetches!
And all because Sneetches whose bellies have stars
Think they're better than Sneetches with none upon
    thars.
(And, really, it's sort of a terrible shame.
For, except for those stars, every Sneetch is the same.)

36

"Who Stole the Tarts?" from
The Pogo Stepmother Goose (1954)
Written by Lewis Carroll
(Charles Dodgson, 1832–1898),
Adapted and Illustrated by
Walt Kelly (1913–1973)

EDITORS' INTRODUCTION

Born in Cheshire, England, in 1832, Charles Lutwidge Dodgson became at twenty-four an Oxford don and lecturer in mathematics, a position he held until resigning in 1881. Dodgson became friends with the daughters of Oxford dean Henry George Liddell. He photographed the girls, took them on picnics, and invented stories for them. After a particularly memorable tale, ten-year-old Alice Liddell "started to pester him to write down the story."[1] He did, giving her *Alice's Adventures Under Ground* (1864), which he next revised and expanded, publishing *Alice's Adventures in Wonderland* (1865) as Lewis Carroll.

Alice and *Through the Looking-Glass and What Alice Found There* (the sequel, 1871)—both illustrated by *Punch* cartoonist John Tenniel—are the two most famous titles in children's literature. They have never gone out of print and have been translated into over seventy languages. As Carroll biographer Morton Cohen notes, "Next to the Bible and Shakespeare, they are the books most widely and most frequently translated and quoted."[2]

Dodgson was "a mixture of . . . both liberal and conservative," as when, for example, he voted against the admission of women to Oxford but advocated the formation of a Women's University.[3] Carroll's *Alice* novels, however, were radical in many ways. They broke with the conventions of children's literature by refusing to offer moral homilies, by trusting the child's imagination, and by treating the child as both resourceful and intelligent.

Since *Alice's Adventures in Wonderland* fell out of copyright in 1907, more than a hundred artists have reillustrated it. Of those who bring politics to the fore, Peter Blake depicts the Mad Hatter languishing in a prison cell, a ball chained to his ankle. Ralph Steadman draws the cards as gruff union members, blackening each other's faces with dripping paintbrushes. Others have

changed more than the illustrations. Saki's *The Westminster Alice* (1900–1902) sharply criticized Britain's failure to end the Boer War. In E. Nesbit's *Justnowland* (1912), the "Alice" character disenchants a kingdom whose people have been turned into crows as punishment for mistreating workers. Henry T. Schnittkind's *Alice and the Stork: A Fairy Tale for Workingmen's Children* (1915) advocated socialism and women's suffrage.[4] In the 1930s, several polemically Marxist adaptations ran in the *New Pioneer*, and in 1954 Kelly introduced his own political *Alice*.

Born in Philadelphia, Walter Crawford Kelly, Jr., moved to Bridgeport, Connecticut, with his family when he was two. After high school, he worked "at almost every job in the art and editorial departments" of the *Bridgeport Post*.[5] As an editorial cartoonist, Kelly supported his paper's endorsement of socialist Jasper McLevy for mayor in 1932. (McLevy won, and served as mayor until 1957.)

In 1936, Kelly left for California. There, he worked at the Disney studios as an animator for *Pinocchio*, *Fantasia*, and *Dumbo*. Following the May 1941 Screen Cartoonists Guild strike, Kelly and his wife moved back east, settling in Darien, Connecticut. Kelly contributed to comic books, including *Animal Comics*, where some of *Pogo*'s characters first appeared in 1942. As art director for the short-lived liberal newspaper *The New York Star*, Kelly created editorial cartoons and the daily comic strip *Pogo*. After the *Star* folded, the Post-Hall syndicate gave *Pogo* national distribution in May 1949.

By 1954, *Pogo* was appearing in more than five hundred papers, and the first of four dozen *Pogo* books appeared in 1951. The fifth, *The Pogo Stepmother Goose* (1954), included Kelly's adaptation of chapters 11 and 12 from *Alice's Adventures in Wonderland*. An adept nonsense poet, Kelly harnessed the satiric impulses of Carroll's original and directed them at McCarthyism.

Nearly a year before Edward R. Murrow's famous *See It Now* broadcast (March 9, 1954) went after McCarthy, Walt Kelly lampooned the Wisconsin senator in *Pogo*. Kelly began mocking anticommunist witch hunters with a trio of bats who joined Deacon Mushrat's Audible Boy Bird Watcher's Society in a March 1951 *Pogo* strip, making "bird-watching" a metaphor for "Commie-hunting": tellingly, the bird watchers misidentify everything.[6] On May 1, 1953, Mole MacCarony—Kelly's version of Nevada senator Pat McCarran, portrayed as a Bird Watcher undeterred by his near-blindness—invites

Simple J. Malarkey to become a member of the club. Malarkey, Kelly's version of Joseph R. McCarthy, seizes control of the club, renaming it "the Bonfire Boys."[7] The McCarthy *Pogo* sequence ended in June of 1953, when Malarkey and MacCarony proceed to do each other in. As comics scholar R. C. Harvey puts it, the implication is "that the villains destroyed themselves."[8]

Senator McCarthy had not yet destroyed himself, so Kelly revived Malarkey in *Pogo* and in the "Who Stole the Tarts?" episode of *The Pogo Stepmother Goose*. Malarkey plays the King, Deacon Mushrat the Queen, and Mole MacCaroney one of the Guards. (To ensure that readers saw the parallels to his daily strip's characters, Kelly provided a list of dramatis personae, which included Pogo Possum as Alice, Albert Alligator as the Gryphon, Easter Bun as the White Rabbit, and Bun Rabbit as the March Hare.) In the book's afterword, dated March 1954, Kelly praises Carroll's gift for reporting "on the frailties and foibles of the human race" and asks how this novel could attain "an aged air of virtuous profundity in 1954? On these things we can but guess." He continues, "Of one conclusion we can be sure: Such writings are revealed in their true purpose when they tinge with doubting ridicule the present purposes of legalized investigation in ANY country."[9]

Kelly never testified before McCarthy or HUAC, though he did testify at the Senate comics hearings inspired by Fredric Wertham's *Seduction of the Innocent*, a sensationalist exposé of alleged connections between comic books and juvenile delinquency. Kelly weathered both storms, and *Pogo* remained enormously popular. Its title character even became a presidential candidate. With the slogan and theme song "I Go Pogo!" Pogo has run in every election year since 1952—undeterred by the strip's end in 1975 and Kelly's death in 1973.

Reflecting society's failings in the distorted mirror of *Pogo*, Kelly hoped not only to provoke laughter but also to show us that we can change things. In 1959, describing McCarthy as "a *true* comedian" because "he was not pretending for a moment," Kelly indicted the citizens who allowed McCarthyism to happen: "With his uproarious and highhanded disregard of the amenities and established precedent, [McCarthy] became almost a law to himself. Before our eyes, we saw ourselves allowing ourselves to be chumps."[10] Or, as Kelly more famously said in a strip from 1970, "We have met the enemy and he is us."

NOTES

1. Morton N. Cohen, *Lewis Carroll: A Biography* (New York: Knopf, 1995), 123.

2. Ibid., 134.

3. Ibid., 372, 485.

4. Carolyn Sigler's *Alternative Alices: Visions and Revisions of Lewis Carroll's Alice Books* (Lexington: UP of Kentucky, 1997) collects these four *Alices* and others.

5. Richard Marschall, *America's Great Comic-Strip Artists* (New York: Stewart, Tabori & Chang, 1997 [1989]), 257.

6. Walt Kelly, *Pogo Volume 5* (Seattle, WA: Fantagraphics Books, 1996), 65.

7. Kelly, *Pogo Volume 10* (Seattle, WA: Fantagraphics Books, 1998), 23.

8. R. C. Harvey, "Attacking the Attack Dogs: Walt Kelly's Finest Hour," introduction to *Pogo Volume 10* by Walt Kelly, ix. Our analysis of the "Pogo" strips owes a great deal to Harvey's introductions to Fantagraphics' *Pogo* volumes (1992–2000).

9. Kelly, afterword to *The Pogo Stepmother Goose* (New York: Simon & Schuster, 1954), n.p.

10. Harvey, "Attacking the Attack Dogs," viii.

THE QUEEN OF HEARTS

The Queen of Hearts,
She made some tarts
All on a summer's day.

The Knave of Hearts,
He stole those tarts
And took them quite away.

The King of Hearts
Called for the tarts
And beat the Knave full sore.

The Knave of Hearts
Brought back the tarts
And vowed he'd steal no more.

*How was the
trial...?*

*Oh...fair, just fair...
It was like this....*

THE TRIAL
AND
THE TARTS

"There was a little
One-eyed gunner
Who killed all the birds
That died last Summer".*

*"Whether this is so or not is not
verifiable. However, it is known that
such birds as died are indeed dead".

International doctrine.

A Report from Lewis Carroll's
ALICE'S ADVENTURES IN WONDERLAND

WHO STOLE THE TARTS?

The King and Queen of Hearts were seated on their throne when they arrived, with a great crowd assembled about them—all sorts of little birds and beasts, as well as the whole pack of cards: the Knave was standing before them, in chains, with a soldier on each side to guard him; and near the King was the White Rabbit, with a trumpet in one hand, and a scroll of parchment in the other.

In the very middle of the court was a table, with a large dish of tarts upon it: they looked so good, that it made Alice quite hungry to look at them—"*I wish they'd get the trial done*," she thought, "*and hand round the refreshments*." But there seemed to be no chance of this, so she began looking at everything about her to pass away the time.

The twelve jurors were all writing very busily on slates. "*They're putting down their names*," the Gryphon whispered, "*for fear they should forget them before the end of the trial*."

"*Stupid things!*" Alice began in a loud indignant voice, but she stopped herself hastily, for the White Rabbit cried out, "*Silence in the Court!*" and the King put on his spectacles and looked anxiously round, to make out who was talking.

"Herald, read the accusation!" said the King.

On this the White Rabbit blew three blasts on the trumpet, and then unrolled the parchment scroll, and read as follows:

*"The Queen of Hearts, she made some tarts,
All on a summer day:*

*"The Knave of Hearts, he stole those tarts,
And took them quite away!"*

"Consider your verdict," the King said to the jury.
"Not yet, not yet!" the Rabbit hastily interrupted, *"There's a great deal to come before that!"*

"Call the first witness," said the King; and the White Rabbit blew three blasts on the trumpet, and called out, *"First witness!"*

The first witness was the Hatter. He came in with a teacup in one hand and a piece of bread-and-butter in the other. *"I beg pardon, your majesty,"* he began, *"for bringing* these in, but I hadn't quite finished my tea when I was sent for." *"You ought to have finished,"* said the King. *"When did you begin?"*

The Hatter looked at the March Hare, who had followed him into the court, arm-in-arm with the Dormouse. *"Fourteenth of March, I think it was,"* he said.

"Fifteenth," said the March Hare.   *"Sixteenth,"* added the Dormouse.

"Write that down," the King said to the jury, and the jury eagerly wrote down all three dates on their slates, and then added them up, and reduced the answer to shillings and pence.

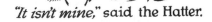

"Take off your hat," the King said to the Hatter.

"It isn't mine," said the Hatter.

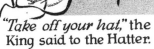

"Stolen!" the King exclaimed, turning to the jury, who instantly made a memorandum of the fact.

"I keep them to sell," the Hatter added as an explanation, *"I've none of my own. I'm a hatter."*

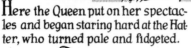

Here the Queen put on her spectacles and began staring hard at the Hatter, who turned pale and fidgeted.

"Give your evidence," said the King; *"and don't be nervous, or I'll have you executed on the spot."*

This did not seem to encourage the witness at all; he kept shifting from one foot to the other, looking uneasily at the Queen,

and in his confusion he bit a large piece out of his teacup instead of the bread-and-butter.

"I'm a poor man, your majesty," the Hatter began in a trembling voice, *"and I hadn't but just begun my tea—not above a*

week or so—and what with the bread-and-butter getting so thin—and the twinkling of the tea—"

"*The twinkling of what?*"said the King. "*It began with the tea,*"the Hatter replied.

"*Of course twinkling begins with a T!*"said the King sharply. "*Do you take me for a dunce? Go on.*"

"*I'm a poor man,*"the Hatter went on, "*and most things twinkled after that—only the March Hare said—*

"*I didn't!*"the March Hare interrupted in a great hurry. "*You did!*"said the Hatter.

"*I deny it,*"said the March Hare. "*He denies it,*"said the King: "*leave out that part.*"

"*Well, at any rate, the Dormouse said—*" the Hatter went on, looking anxiously round to see if he would deny it too; but the Dormouse denied nothing, being fast asleep.

"*After that,*" continued the Hatter, "*I cut some more bread-and-butter—*"

"*But what did the Dormouse say?*" one of the jury asked. "*That I can't remember,*" said the Hatter.

"*You must remember,*" remarked the King, "*or I'll have you executed.*" The miserable Hatter dropped his teacup and bread-and-butter, and

went down on one knee. "*I'm a poor man, your majesty,*" he began. "*You're a very poor speaker,*" said the King.

Here one of the guinea pigs cheered, and was immediately suppressed by the officers of the court.

"*If that's all you know about it, you may stand down*," continued the King.

"*I can't go no lower,*" said the Hatter, "*I'm on the floor, as it is.*" "*Then you may* ***sit*** *down,*" the King replied.

Here the other guinea pig cheered and was suppressed.
"*I'd rather finish my tea,*" said

the Hatter, with an anxious look at the Queen, who was reading the list of singers.

"*You may go,*" said the King, and the Hatter hurriedly left the court ~~~~~~

"*And just take his head off outside,*" the Queen added to one of the officers; but the Hatter was out of sight before the officer could get to the door.

"*Call the next witness,*"
said the King.

The next witness was
the Duchess' cook.

"*Give your evidence,*" said the King.
"*Shan't,*" said the cook.
The King looked anxiously at the

White Rabbit, who said in a
low voice, "*Your majesty must
cross-examine this witness.*"

"*Well, if I must, I must,*" the King
said with a melancholy air, and, after
folding his arms and frowning at

the cook till his eyes were nearly
out of sight, he said in a deep
voice, "*What are tarts made of?*"

"Pepper, mostly," said the cook. "Treacle," said a sleepy voice behind her. "Collar that Dormouse!" the Queen shrieked out. "Behead that Dormouse! Turn that Dormouse out of court! Suppress him! Pinch him! Off with his whiskers!"

For some minutes the whole court was in confusion getting the Dormouse turned out, and, by the time they had settled down again, the cook had disappeared.

"Never mind," said the King, with an air of great relief. "Call the next witness." Alice watched the White Rabbit as he fumbled over the list. Imagine her surprise, when he read out the name, "Alice!"

"*What do you know about this business?*" the King said to Alice. "*Nothing,*" said Alice.

"*Nothing whatever?*" persisted the King. "*Nothing whatever,*" said Alice.

"*That's very important,*" the King said, turning to the jury. They were just beginning to write this down on their slates, when the White Rabbit interrupted;

"*Unimportant, your majesty means, of course,*" he said in a very respectful tone, but frowning and making faces at him as he spoke.

"*Unimportant, of course, I meant,*" the King hastily said, and went on to himself in an undertone. "*important—unimportant—unimportant—important—*"

as if he were trying which word sounded best. Some of the jury wrote it down "*important*" and some of them "*unimportant.*"

"There's more evidence to come yet, please your majesty," said the White Rabbit, jumping up in a great hurry, *"this paper has just been picked up."*
"What's in it?" said the Queen.

"I haven't opened it yet," said the White Rabbit, *"but it seems to be a letter, written by the prisoner to—to somebody."*
"It must have been that," said the King, *"unless it was written to nobody, which isn't usual, you know."*

"Who is it directed to?" said one of the jurymen. *"It isn't directed at all,"* said the White Rabbit, *"in fact, there's nothing written on the outside."* He unfolded the paper as he spoke, and added, *"it isn't a letter after all, it's a set of verses."*

"Are they in the prisoner's handwriting?" asked another of the jurymen. *"No, they're not,"* said the White Rabbit, *"and that's the queerest thing about it."* (The jury all looked puzzled.)

"He must have imitated somebody else's hand," said the King. (The jury all brightened up again.)

"*Please your majesty,*" said the Knave. "*I didn't write it, and they can't prove I did: there's no name signed at the end.*"
"*If you didn't sign it,*" said the King, "*that only makes the matter worse.*

*You **must** have meant some mischief, or else you'd have signed your name like an honest man.*"
There was a general clapping of hands at this: it was the first really clever thing the King had said that day.

"*That proves his guilt,*" said the Queen. "*It proves nothing of the sort,*" said

Alice. "*Why, you don't even know what they're about!*'"

"*Read them,*" said the King. The White Rabbit put on his spectacles. "*Where shall I begin, please your majesty?*" he asked. "*Begin at the beginning,*" the King said gravely, "*and go on till you come to the end: then stop.*"

"They told me that you had been to her,
And mentioned me to him.

"She gave me a good character,
But said I could not swim.

"He sent them word I had not gone
(We know it to be true:)

"If she should push the matter on,
What would become of you?

"I gave her one, they gave him two,
You gave us three or more;

"They all returned from him to you,
Though they were mine before.

"*If I or she should chance to be
Involved in this affair,*

"*He trusts to you to set them free,
Exactly as we were.*

"*My notion was that you had been
(Before she had this fit)*

"*An obstacle that came between
Him, and ourselves, and it.*

"*Don't let him know she liked them best,
For this must ever be*

"*A secret, kept from all the rest,
Between yourself and me.*"

"The most important evidence yet," said the King, rubbing his hands, "so now let the jury—"

"If any one of them can explain it," said Alice, "I'll give him sixpence. I don't believe there's an atom of meaning in it."

The jury all wrote down on their slates. "She doesn't believe there's an atom of meaning in it," but none of them attempted to explain the paper. "If there's no meaning in it," said the King, "that saves a world of trouble, you know, as we needn't try to find any. And yet I don't know," he went on, spreading out the verses on his knee, and looking at them with one eye;

"I seem to see some meaning in them, after all—'said I could not swim'—you can't swim, can you?"

he added, turning to the Knave. The Knave shook his head sadly.

"*All right, so far,*" said the King, and he went on muttering over the verses to himself: "*We know it to be true'*— that's the jury, of course—*'I gave her one, they gave him two'*—why, that must be what he did with the tarts, you know—"

"*But it goes on 'they all returned from him to you,'*" said Alice.

"*Why, there they are!*" said the King, triumphantly, pointing to the tarts on the table.

"*Nothing can be clearer than that. Then again—'before she had this fit'—you never had fits, my dear, I think?*" he said to the Queen.

"*Never!*" said the Queen, furiously.

"Then the words don't fit you," said the King, looking round the court with a smile. There was a dead silence.

"It's a pun," the King added in an angry tone, and everybody laughed. "Let the jury consider their verdict," the King said for about the twentieth time that day. "No, no!" said the Queen, "Sentence first—verdict afterward."

"Stuff and nonsense!" said Alice loudly. "The idea of having the sentence first!" "Hold your tongue!" said the Queen, turning purple. "I wont!" said Alice. "Off with her head!" the Queen shouted at the top of her voice.

Nobody moved.

"Who cares for you?" said Alice, *"You're nothing but a pack of cards!"*

At this the whole pack rose up into the air, and came flying down upon her; she gave a little scream, half of fright and half of anger, and tried to beat them off, and found herself lying on the bank, brushing away some dead leaves that had fluttered down from the trees on to her face.

37

X: A Fabulous Child's Story (1978)

Written by Lois Gould (1931–2002), Illustrated by Jacqueline Chwast (b. 1932)

EDITORS' INTRODUCTION

When *Ms.* magazine made its debut in the spring of 1972, it included the children's feature "Stories for Free Children." That December, *Ms.* printed Lois Gould's "X: A Fabulous Child's Story." The revised version of X, reproduced here, was a controversial success when published as a book in 1978. Some adult readers were troubled by the book's willingness to question gender identity, and one *Village Voice* reviewer thought it evoked "genital mutilation anxiety."[1] However, as that same reviewer noted, the book is "less *against* sexist toys and gender roles than *for* all toys and roles; kids' psyches shouldn't be stupidly restricted by these things."[2]

Gould grew up with an acute consciousness of the restrictions imposed by gender roles. Born Lois Regensburg, she was the daughter of Jo Copeland, the famous New York fashion designer. Having a mother with a successful career, Lois learned early on that "'independent' was not a nice word when it described a woman." As Gould writes in the memoir *Mommy Dressing* (1998), her father's friends teased him, calling him "Mr. Jo Copeland" and asking him who wore the pants in the family.[3] When Gould was three, her parents divorced, and her mother became the primary breadwinner for Lois and her brother Anthony.

Though her childhood had ample material comforts, social expectations often thwarted Lois's ambitions. Jo Copeland had many dinner parties with glamorous guests—Joan Crawford, Tyrone Power, Greer Garson—but insisted that Lois and Anthony stay in their rooms, neither seen nor heard. Though Lois loved horseback riding, her mother put a stop to it because it made her sweaty, and a young lady should not sweat.[4] She enjoyed tap dancing, but, as Gould recalled, she was "wrested" out of it "on the grounds that it was not 'seemly' for a young lady growing up to be doing that sort of thing instead of dancing with fellows."[5]

After graduating from Wellesley, Gould became a journalist, reporting on criminal courts for the Long Island Star-Journal. In 1955, she married *New York Times* reporter and novelist Philip Benjamin, with whom she had two children. In 1967, she married psychiatrist Robert Gould. The previous year, when her first husband died unexpectedly, Lois Gould found among his papers a diary written in code. Breaking the code, Gould learned of his extramarital affairs with her friends. The experience inspired *Such Good Friends*, a bestselling novel (1970) and Otto Preminger film (1971) that starred Dyan Cannon in the title role.

Such Good Friends and *Mommy Dressing* remain Gould's best-known works, but in addition to other novels and nonfiction, she wrote the *New York Times* "Hers" column and served as editor at both *Ladies Home Journal* and *McCall's*. X is her sole children's story, but she wrote it with a much broader audience in mind. As she recalled, "I wrote it as if I were talking to my own family, including the adults. . . . I've been told . . . that any age person can read it without feeling that it's for another age group, which is fascinating."[6]

Jacqueline Chwast has illustrated for many audiences, from books for children to periodicals for grownups—such as the *New York Times*, *Gourmet*, and *Ms.* Her distinctive illustrations look like woodcuts, but Chwast creates them by cutting white spaces out of black paper: the remaining black pieces form the lines and shapes of the image. Familiar with Chwast's work, Gould knew she wanted X's pictures to be in precisely that style. She contacted Chwast, who accepted the job.

The daughter of cab driver William Weiner and the former Lillian Averman, Chwast always loved to draw. After high school, she completed a three-year course at the Newark School of Fine and Industrial Arts. Next, she thought she would teach, but just before enrolling in a teaching course at NYU, she decided, "no, I was going to be an artist and that was it."[7] Taking a few courses at the Art Students League and at the New School, she quickly developed a portfolio and found success as a freelance artist.

She married artist Seymour Chwast (pronounced "Quast") in 1953. They had two daughters, and Jacqueline began illustrating children's books, starting with Myra Cohn Livingston's *Whispers and Other Poems* (1958). Although best known for illustrating the works of others (about fifty books in all), Chwast created the words and pictures for two of her own: *When the Baby-Sitter Didn't Come* (1967) and *How Mr. Berry Found a Home and*

Happiness Together (1968). After eighteen years together, Mr. Chwast and she divorced in 1971.

Having been involved in the women's movement of the 1970s, Chwast was interested in the message of Gould's story. As Gould did, Chwast grew up aware that she was treated differently because of her gender. "My brother was younger than I was," she recalls, "and yet he was allowed to go out into the world much more easily than I was. At 8 or 9, he would take buses and go downtown, and I wasn't allowed to cross the street." She also knew that, whenever a new baby was born in the neighborhood, "there was a different feeling about having a girl than a boy": "it was considered something better to have a boy."[8]

Although today she sees more differences between boys and girls, at the time she thought them more similar than different. So, in illustrating X, Chwast found it quite easy to depict a child whose sex is withheld. "Little boys and little girls look very similar," she says. "If you put them in overalls, they look very much alike."[9]

NOTES

1. Eliot Fremont-Smith, "The Secret of the Crotch," *Village Voice*, 10 July 1978, 72.

2. Ibid., 72. Emphasis mine.

3. Lois Gould, *Mommy Dressing: A Love Story, after a Fashion* (New York: Anchor Books, 1999 [1998]), 121.

4. Ibid., 74.

5. Jane S. Bakerman, "An Interview with Lois Gould," *Writer's Digest*, Sept. 1980, 25.

6. Ibid., 28.

7. Jacqueline Chwast, telephone interview with Philip Nel, 2 Mar. 2006.

8. Ibid.

9. Ibid.

This book is for X's brothers, Tony and Roger, for X's best friends, Carole and Bruce Hart, and for the B, who cried when X was born.

Once upon a time, a Baby named X was born. This Baby was named X so that nobody could tell whether it was a boy or a girl.

Its parents could tell, of course, but they couldn't tell anybody else. They couldn't even tell Baby X—at least not until much, much later.

You see, it was all part of a very important Secret Scientific Xperiment, known officially as Project Baby X.

The smartest scientists had set up this Xperiment at a cost of Xactly 23 billion dollars and 72 cents. This might seem like a lot for one Baby, even if it was an important Secret Scientific Xperimental Baby.

But when you remember the cost of strained carrots and stuffed bunnies, and popcorn for the movies and booster shots for camp, let alone 28 shiny quarters from the tooth fairy, you begin to see how it adds up.

Besides, long before Baby X was born, the smart scientists had to be paid to work out the secret details of the Xperiment, and to write the *Official Instruction Manual*, in secret code, for Baby X's parents, whoever they were.

These parents had to be selected very carefully. Thousands of mothers and fathers volunteered. But then the scientists made them take thousands of tests and answer thousands of tricky questions.

Almost everybody failed because, it turned out, almost everybody really wanted either a baby boy or a baby girl, and not a Baby X at all.

Also, almost everybody was afraid that a Baby X would be a lot more trouble than a boy or a girl. (They were right, too.)

There were families with grandparents named Milton and Agatha, who didn't see why the baby couldn't be named Milton or Agatha instead of X, even if it *was* an X.

There were families with aunts who insisted on knitting tiny dresses and uncles who insisted on sending tiny baseball mitts.

Worst of all, there were families that already had other children who couldn't be trusted to keep the secret. Certainly not if they knew the secret was worth 23 billion dollars and 72 cents—and all you had to do was to take one little peek at Baby X in the bathtub to know what it was.

But, finally, the scientists found the Joneses, who really wanted to raise an X more than any other kind of baby—no matter how much trouble it would be.

Ms. and Mr. Jones had to promise they would take equal turns caring for X, and feeding it, and singing it lullabies.

And they had to promise never to hire any baby-sitters. The government scientists knew perfectly well that a baby-sitter would probably peek at X in the bathtub, too.

The day the Joneses brought their baby home, lots of friends and relatives came over to see it. None of them knew about the secret Xperiment, though. So the first thing they asked was what kind of a baby X was.

When the Joneses smiled and said, "It's an X!" nobody knew what to say.

They couldn't say, "Look at her cute little dimples!"

On the other hand, they couldn't say, "Look at his husky little biceps!"

And they didn't feel right about saying just plain' 'kitchy-coo.' In fact, all they could say was that the Joneses were very rude to play such a silly joke on their friends and relatives.

But, of course, the Joneses were not joking. "It's an X" was absolutely all they would tell anyone. And that made the friends and relatives very angry.

The relatives all felt embarrassed about having an X in the family.

"People will think there's something wrong with it!" some of them whispered.

"There is something wrong with it!" others whispered back.

"Nonsense!" the Joneses told them all cheerfully. "What could possibly be wrong with this perfectly adorable X?"

Nobody could answer that, except Baby X, who had just finished its bottle. Baby X's answer was a loud, satisfied burp.

Clearly, nothing at all was wrong. Nevertheless, nobody they knew felt comfortable about buying a present for a Baby X. The cousins who had sent a tiny football helmet would not come and visit any more. And the neighbors who sent a pink-flowered romper suit pulled their shades down when the Joneses passed their house.

The *Official Instruction Manual* had warned the new parents that this would happen, so they didn't fret about it. Besides, they were too busy with Baby X and the hundreds of different Xercises for treating it properly.

Ms. and Mr. Jones had to be Xtra careful about how they played with little X. They knew that if they kept bouncing it up in the air and saying how *strong* and *active* it was, they'd be treating it more like a boy than an X. But if all they did was cuddle it and kiss it and tell it how *sweet* and *dainty* it was, they'd be treating it more like a girl than an X.

On page 1654 of the *Official Instruction Manual*, the scientists prescribed: "plenty of bouncing and plenty of cuddling, *both*. X ought to be strong and sweet and active. Forget about *dainty* altogether."

There were other problems, too. Toys, for instance. And clothes. On his first shopping trip, Mr. Jones told the store clerk, "I need some clothes and toys for my new baby." The clerk smiled and said, "Well, now, is it a boy or a girl?" "It's an X," Mr. Jones said, smiling back. But the clerk got all red in the face and said huffily, "In *that* case, I'm afraid I can't help you, sir."

So Mr. Jones wandered helplessly up and down the aisles trying to find what X needed. But everything in the store was piled up in sections marked BOYS or GIRLS.

There were "Boys' Pajamas" and "Girls' Underwear" and "Boys' Fire Engines" and "Girls' Housekeeping Sets." Mr. Jones went home without buying anything for X.

That night he and Ms. Jones consulted page 2326 of the *Official Instruction Manual*. It said firmly: "Buy plenty of everything!"

So they bought plenty of sturdy blue pajamas in the Boys' Department and cheerful flowered underwear in the Girls' Department.

And they bought all kinds of toys. A boy doll that made pee-pee and cried, "Pa-Pa." And a girl doll that talked in three languages and said, "I am the Pres-i-dent of Gen-er-al Mo-tors."

They also bought a storybook about a brave princess who rescued a handsome prince from his ivory tower, and another one about a sister and brother who grew up to be a baseball star and a ballet star, and you had to guess which was which.

The head scientists of Project Baby X checked all their purchases and told them to keep up the good work. They also reminded the Joneses to see page 4629 of the *Manual*, where it said, "Never make Baby X feel *embarrassed* or *ashamed* about what it wants to play with. And if X gets dirty climbing rocks, never say, 'Nice little Xes don't get dirty climbing rocks.'"

Likewise, it said, "If X falls down and cries, never say, 'Brave little Xes don't cry.' Because, of course, nice little Xes *do* get dirty, and brave little Xes *do* cry. No matter how dirty X gets, or how hard it cries, don't worry. It's all part of the Xperiment."

Whenever the Joneses pushed Baby X's stroller in the park, smiling strangers would come over and coo: "Is that a boy or a girl?" The Joneses would smile back and say, "It's an X." The strangers would stop smiling then, and often snarl something nasty-as if the Joneses had said something nasty to *them*.

By the time X grew big enough to play with other children, the Joneses' troubles had grown bigger, too. Once a little girl grabbed X's shovel in the sandbox, and zonked X on the head with it. "Now, now, Tracy," the little girl's mother began to scold, "little girls mustn't hit little-" and she turned to ask X, "Are you a little boy or a little girl, dear?"

Mr. Jones, who was sitting near the sandbox, held his breath and crossed his fingers.

X smiled politely at the lady, even though X's head had never been zonked so hard in its life. "I'm a little X," said X.

"You're a *what*?" the lady exclaimed angrily. "You're a little b-r-a-t, you mean!"

"But little girls mustn't hit little Xes, either!" said X, retrieving the shovel with another polite smile. "What good does hitting do, anyway?"

X's father, who was still holding his breath, finally let it out, uncrossed his fingers, and grinned back at X.

And at their next secret Project Baby X meeting, the scientists grinned, too. Baby X was doing fine.

But then it was time for X to start school. The Joneses were really worried about this, because school was even more full of rules for boys and girls, and there were no rules for Xes.

The teacher would tell boys to form one line, and girls to form another line.

There would be boys' games and girls' games, and boys' secrets and girls' secrets.

The school library would have a list of recommended books for girls, and a different list of recommended books for boys.

There would even be a bathroom marked BOYS and another one marked GIRLS.

Pretty soon boys and girls would hardly talk to each other. What would happen to poor little X?

The Joneses spent weeks consulting their *Instruction Manual*.

There were 249 ½ pages of advice under "First Day of School." Then they were all summoned to an Urgent Xtra Special Conference with the smart scientists of Project Baby X.

The scientists had to make sure that X's mother had taught X how to throw and catch a ball properly, and that X's father had been sure to teach X what to serve at a doll's tea party.

X had to know how to shoot marbles and how to jump rope and, most of all, what to say when the Other Children asked whether X was a Boy or a Girl.

Finally, X was ready. The Joneses helped X button on a nice new pair of red and white checked overalls, and sharpened six pencils for X's nice new pencil box, and marked X's name clearly on all the books in its nice new book bag.

X brushed its teeth and combed its hair, which just about covered its ears, and remembered to put a napkin in its lunch box.

The Joneses had asked X's teacher if the class could line up alphabetically, instead of forming separate lines for boys and girls. And they had asked if X could use the principal's bathroom, because it wasn't marked anything except BATHROOM. X's teacher promised to take care of all those problems. But nobody could help X with the biggest problem of all—Other Children.

Nobody in X's class had ever known an X before. Nobody had even heard their parents say, "Some of my best friends are Xes."

What would other children think? Would they make Xist jokes? Or would they make friends?

You couldn't tell what X was by studying its clothes —overalls don't even button right to left, like girls' clothes, or left to right, like boys' clothes.

And you couldn't guess whether X had a girl's short haircut or a boy's long haircut.

And it was very hard to tell by the games X liked to play. Either X played ball very well for a girl, or else X played house very well for a boy.

Some of the children tried to find out by asking X tricky questions, like, "Who's your favorite sports star?" That was easy. X had two favorite sports stars: a girl jockey named Robyn Smith and a boy archery champion named Robin Hood.

Then they asked, "What's your favorite TV program?" And that was even easier. X's favorite TV program was "Lassie," which stars a girl dog played by a boy dog.

When X said its favorite toy was a doll, everyone decided that X must be a girl. But then X said that the doll was really a robot, and that X had computerized it, and that it was programmed to bake fudge brownies and then clean up the kitchen.

After X told them that, the other children gave up guessing what X was. All they knew was they'd sure like to see X's doll.

After school, X wanted to play with the other children. "How about shooting some baskets in the gym?" X asked the girls. But all they did was make faces and giggle behind X's back.

"Boy, is *he* weird," whispered Jim to Joe.

"How about weaving some baskets in the arts and crafts room?" X asked the boys. But they all made faces and giggled behind X's back, too.

"Boy, is *she* weird," whispered Susie to Peggy.

That night, Ms. and Mr. Jones asked X how things had gone at school.

X tried to smile, but there were two big tears in its eyes. "The lessons are okay," X began, "but . . ."

"But?" said Ms. Jones.

"The Other Children hate me," X whispered. "Hate you?" said Mr. Jones.

X nodded, which made the two big tears roll down and splash on its overalls.

Ms. and Mr. Jones just looked at X, and then at each other. "Other Children," said Ms. Jones thoughtfully.

"Other Children," echoed Mr. Jones sadly.

Once more, the Joneses reached for their *Instruction Manual*. Under "Other Children," they found the following message:

"What did you Xpect? Other Children have to obey all the silly boy-girl rules, because their parents taught them to. Lucky X—you don't have to stick to the rules at all! All you have to do is be yourself.

"P.S. We're not saying it'll be easy."

X liked being itself. But X cried a lot that night, partly because it felt afraid.

So X's father held X tight, and cuddled it, and couldn't help crying a little, too.

And X's mother cheered them both up by reading an Xciting story about an enchanted prince called Sleeping Handsome, who woke up when Princess Charming kissed him.

The next morning, they all felt much better, and little X went back to school with a brave smile and a clean pair of red and white checked overalls.

There was a seven-letter-word spelling bee in class that day. And a seven-lap boys' relay race in the gym. And a seven-layer-cake baking contest in the girls' kitchen corner.

X won the spelling bee. X also won the relay race.

And X almost won the baking contest, except it forgot to light the oven. Which only proves that nobody's perfect.

One of the Other Children noticed something else, too. He said: "X don't care about winning. And X don't care about losing. X just thinks it's fun playing-boys' stuff *and* girls' stuff."

"Come to think of it," said another one of the Other Children, "maybe X is having twice as much fun as we are!"

So after school that day, the girl who beat X at the baking contest gave X a big slice of her prize-winning cake.

And the boy X beat in the relay race asked X to race him home.

From then on, some really funny things began to happen.

Susie, who sat next to X in class, suddenly refused to wear pink dresses to school any more. She insisted on wearing red and white checked overalls-just like X's.

Overalls, she told her parents, were much better for climbing monkey bars.

Then Jim, the class football nut, started wheeling his little sister's doll carriage around the football field.

He'd put on his entire football uniform, except for the helmet.

Then he'd put the helmet *in* the carriage, lovingly tucked under an old set of shoulder pads.

Then he'd start jogging around the field, pushing the carriage and singing "Rockabye Baby" to his football helmet.

He told his family that X did the same thing, so it must be okay. After all, X was now the team's star quarterback.

Susie's parents were horrified by her behavior, and Jim's parents were worried sick about his.

But the worst came when the twins, Joe and Peggy, decided to share everything with each other.

Peggy used Joe's hockey skates, and his microscope, and took half his newspaper route.

Joe used Peggy's needlepoint kit, and her cookbooks, and took two of her three baby-sitting jobs.

Peggy started running the lawn mower, and Joe started running the vacuum cleaner.

Their parents weren't one bit pleased with Peggy's wonderful biology experiments, or with Joe's terrific needlepoint pillows.

They didn't care that Peggy mowed the lawn better, and that Joe vacuumed the carpet better.

In fact, they were furious. It's all that little X's fault, they agreed. Just because X doesn't know what it is, or what it's supposed to be, it wants to get everybody *else* mixed up, too!

Peggy and Joe were forbidden to play with X any more. So was Susie, and then Jim, and then *all* the Other Children.

But it was too late: the Other Children stayed mixed up and happy and free, and refused to go back to the way they'd been before X.

Finally, Joe and Peggy's parents decided to call an emergency meeting of the school's Parents' Association, to discuss "The X Problem."

They sent a report to the principal stating that X was a "disruptive influence," and demanding immediate action.

The Joneses, they said, should be *forced* to tell whether X was a boy or a girl. And then X should be *forced* to behave like whichever it was.

If the Joneses refused to tell, the Parents' Association said, then X must take an Xamination. An Impartial Team of Xperts must Xamine it physically and mentally, and issue a full report. If X's test showed it was a boy, it would have to start obeying all the boys' rules. If it proved to be a girl, X would have to obey all the girls' rules.

And if X turned out to be some kind of mixed-up misfit, then X must be Xpelled from school. Immediately! And a new rule must be passed, so that no little Xes would ever come to school again.

The principal was very upset. Disruptive influence? Mixed-up misfit?

But X was an Xcellent student! All the teachers said it was a delight to have X in their classes!

X was president of the student council. X had won first prize in the talent show, and second prize in the art show, and honorable mention in the science fair, and won six athletic events on field day, including the potato race.

Nevertheless, insisted the Parents' Association, X is a Problem Child. X is the Biggest Problem Child we have ever seen!

So the principal reluctantly notified X's parents that numerous complaints about X's behavior had come to the school's attention.

And that after the Impartial Team of Xperts' Xamination, the school would decide what to do about X.

The Joneses reported this at once to the Project X scientists, who referred them to page 85769 of the *Instruction Manual*. "Sooner or later," it said, "X will have to be Xamined, physically and mentally, by an Impartial Team of Xperts.

"This may be the only way any of us will know for sure whether X is mixed up-or whether everyone else is."

The night before X was to be Xamined, the Joneses tried not to let X see how worried they were.

"What if—?" Mr. Jones would say. And Ms. Jones would reply, "No use worrying."

Then a few minutes later, Ms. Jones would say, "What if—?" and Mr. Jones would reply, "No use worrying."

X just smiled at them both, and hugged them hard and didn't say much of anything. X was thinking: What if—? And then X thought: No use worrying.

At Xactly 9 o'clock the next day, X reported to the school health office.

The principal, along with a committee from the Parents' Association, X's teacher, X's classmates, and Ms. and Mr. Jones, waited in the hall outside.

Inside, the Impartial Team of Xperts had set up their famous testing machine: the Superpsychiamedicosocioculturometer.

Nobody knew Xactly how the machine worked, or the details of the tests X was to be given, but everybody knew they'd be *very* hard, and that when it was all over, the Xperts would reveal Xactly what everyone wanted to know about X, but were afraid to ask.

It was terribly quiet in the hall. Almost spooky. Once in a while, they would hear a strange noise inside the room.

There were buzzes.

And a beep or two.

And several bells.

An occasional light would flash under the door. (The Joneses thought it was a white light, but the principal thought it was blue. Two or three children swore it was either yellow or green. And the Parents' Committee missed it completely.)

Through it all, you could hear the Impartial Team of Xperts' voices, asking hundreds of questions, and X's voice, answering hundreds of answers.

The whole thing took so long that everyone knew it must be the most complete Xamination anyone had ever had to take.

Poor X, the Joneses thought.

Serves X right, the Parents' Committee thought.

I wouldn't like to be in X's overalls right now, the children thought.

At last, the door opened. Everyone crowded around to hear the results. X didn't look any different; in fact, X was smiling. But the Impartial Team of Xperts looked terrible. They looked as if they were crying!

"What happened?" everyone began shouting. Had X done something disgraceful? "I wouldn't be a bit surprised!" muttered Peggy and Joe's parents.

"Did X flunk the *whole* test?" cried Susie's parents.

"Or just the most important part?" yelled Jim's parents.

"Oh, dear," sighed Mr. Jones.

"Oh, dear," sighed Ms. Jones.

"*Sssh*," ssshed the principal. "The Xperts are trying to speak."

Wiping his eyes and clearing his throat, one Xpert began, in a hoarse whisper. "In our opinion," he

whispered—you could tell he must be very upset—"in our opinion, young X here—"

"Yes? Yes?" shouted a parent impatiently.

"*Sssh!*" ssshed the principal.

"Young *Sssh* here, I mean young X," said the other Xpert, frowning, "is just about—"

"Just about *what*? Let's have it!" shouted another parent.

". . . just about the *least* mixed-up child we've ever Xamined!" Xclaimed the two Xperts, together. Behind the closed door, the Superpsychiamedico-socioculturometer made a noise that sounded like a contented hum.

"Yay for X!" yelled one of the children. And then the others began yelling, too. Clapping and cheering and jumping up and down.

"*SSSH!*" SSShed the principal, but nobody did.

The Parents' Committee was angry and bewildered. How *could* X have passed the whole Xamination?

Didn't X have an *identity* problem? Wasn't X mixed up at *all*?

Wasn't X *any* kind of a misfit?

How could it *not* be, when it didn't even *know* what it was? And why was the Impartial Team of Xperts crying?

Actually, they had stopped crying and were smiling politely through their tears. "Don't you see?" they said. "We're crying because it's wonderful! X has absolutely no identity problem! X isn't one bit mixed up! As for being a misfit—ridiculous! X knows perfectly well what it is! Don't you, X?" The Xperts winked. X winked back.

"But what *is* X?" shrieked Peggy and Joe's parents. "*We* still want to know what it is!"

"Ah, yes," said the Xperts, winking again. "Well, don't worry. You'll all know one of these days. And you won't need us to tell you."

"What? What do they mean?" some of the parents grumbled suspiciously.

Susie and Peggy and Joe all answered at once. "They mean that by the time it matters which sex X is, it won't be a secret any more!"

With that, the Xperts began to push through the crowd toward X's parents. "How do you do," they said, somewhat stiffly. And then they both reached out to hug Ms. and Mr. Jones. "If we ever have an X of our own," they whispered, "we sure hope you'll lend us your instruction manual."

Needless to say, the Joneses were very happy. The Project Baby X scientists were rather pleased, too. So were Susie, Jim, Peggy, Joe, and all the Other Children. The Parents' Association wasn't, but they had promised to accept the Xperts' report, and not make any more trouble. They even invited Ms. and Mr. Jones to become honorary members, which they did.

Later that day, all X's friends put on their red and white checked overalls and went over to see X.

They found X in the back yard, playing with a very tiny baby that none of them had ever seen before.

The baby was wearing very tiny red and white checked overalls.

"How do you like our new baby?" X asked the Other Children proudly.

"It's got cute dimples," said Jim.

"It's got husky biceps, too," said Susie.

"What kind of baby is it?" asked Joe and Peggy.

X frowned at them. "Can't you tell?" Then X broke into a big, mischievous grin. "*It's a Y!*"

38

"The Princess Who Stood on Her Own Two Feet," from *Stories for Free Children* (1982)

Written by Jeanne Desy (b. 1942), Illustrated by Leslie Udry (b. 1950s)

EDITORS' INTRODUCTION

Jeanne Desy grew up in Ohio's Steel Belt. Born in Youngstown, she moved to Akron at age nine, and Columbus at age thirty. Her parents were born in poverty: as she puts it, "all the young men in both families 'worked in the mills' (Youngstown Sheet and Tube)."[1] Thanks to the GI Bill, her father went to college and the family moved into the middle class.

As a child, Desy read fairy tales and Robert Lewis Stevenson's *A Child's Garden of Verses*. Unable to find other children's literature at home or in the sparsely stocked public library, she read the books from the American Literature course her father took as an engineering student. By age eight, she had read through all 712 pages of Louis Untermeyer's *Modern American Poetry*.[2]

Though she primarily writes poetry today, Desy wrote her sole children's story after finishing a novel (for adults) about a cat's plan to rescue an imprisoned princess. Not satisfied with the manuscript, she put it aside and began to write "The Princess Who Stood on Her Own Two Feet," finishing it over a weekend. Deeply influenced by feminism and fairy tales, "The Princess" made its debut in the "Stories for Free Children" section of *Ms.* magazine's February 1981 issue. Since then, the tale has become Desy's best-known work, republished in a half-dozen anthologies, adapted for puppet theater, and even optioned for a motion picture. Widely taught in American college courses on children's literature, "The Princess" also appears in language textbooks from Norway, Africa, Germany, and China. As Desy puts it, the story has become "popular with women around the world who are not in the foreground of the feminist struggle: those who, like me, live ordinary lives, marry, have children, work in menial jobs, women for whom independence from defined roles is a lifelong task."[3]

Often struggling to find time to write while working other jobs, Desy has nonetheless succeeded as an author in a variety of genres. She has won two grants from the Ohio Arts Council, and her *Folk Dancing: Notes for a Comic Novel* (1999) won the Josiah Bancroft Prize. Her articles have appeared in such publications as *Ms.*, *Harper's Weekly*, and *Iris: A Journal for Women*. She has also done scholarly work, notably several studies of vocational education. Inspired to reenter academia, Desy in 1995 earned a Ph.D. from Ohio State University in creative writing and literary theory.[4] Having finished the degree, she decided that she no longer wanted to teach but did want to write. Desy has done just that. Since 1999, she has published three books of poetry, the most recent of which is *Leaving Zen Mountain* (2006).

Like the princess of her story, Jeanne Desy has stood on her own two feet and followed her own path.

Leslie Udry is the daughter of Janice May Udry, author of the Caldecott-winning *A Tree Is Nice* (1956). Her father, Richard Udry, is a professor of sociology at the University of North Carolina at Chapel Hill. Born in California when her father was in graduate school, Leslie "began drawing early and often. . . . I often preferred to stay inside and draw instead of playing outside."[5]

After she finished art school in Philadelphia, *Ms.* magazine gave Udry one of her first major illustration assignments—"The Princess Who Stood on Her Own Two Feet." She became a graphic journalist, freelancing for Philadelphia's *Inquirer Magazine* and *Daily News*, and then becoming art director for the *News* and for *The News Journal* of Wilmington, Delaware.

Recently, Udry has given up her regular paycheck to pursue art, painting in oils and working in clay, but she still does freelance illustration. Examples of her work in various media appear on her website, <http://www.leslieudry.com/>.

NOTES

1. Jeanne Desy, email to Philip Nel, 6 June 2006.
2. Ibid.
3. Ibid.
4. Ibid.
5. Leslie Udry, email to Philip Nel, 19 July 2006.

A long time ago in a kingdom by the sea there lived a Princess tall and bright as a sunflower. Whatever the royal tutors taught her, she mastered with ease. She could tally the royal treasure on her gold and silver abacus, and charm even the Wizard with her enchantments. In short, she had every gift but love, for in all the kingdom there was no suitable match for her.

So she played the zither and designed great tapestries and trained her finches to eat from her hand, for she had a way with animals.

Yet she was bored and lonely, as princesses often are, being a breed apart. Seeing her situation, the Wizard came to see her one day, a strange and elegant creature trotting along at his heels. The Princess clapped her hands in delight, for she loved anything odd.

"What is it?" she cried. The Wizard grimaced.

"Who knows?" he said. "It's supposed to be something enchanted. I got it through the mail." The Royal Wizard looked a little shamefaced. It was not the first time he had been taken in by mail-order promises.

"It won't turn into anything else," he explained. "It just is what it is."

"But what is it?"

"They call it a dog," the Wizard said. "An Afghan hound."

Since in this kingdom dogs had never been seen, the Princess was quite delighted. When she brushed the silky, golden dog, she secretly thought it looked rather like her, with its thin aristocratic features and delicate nose. Actually, the Wizard had thought so too, but you can never be sure what a Princess will take as an insult. In any case, the Princess and the dog became constant companions. It followed her on her morning rides and slept at the foot of her bed every night. When she talked, it watched her so attentively that she often thought it understood.

Still, a dog is a dog and not a Prince, and the Princess longed to marry. Often she sat at her window in the high tower, her embroidery idle in her aristocratic hands, and gazed down the road, dreaming of a handsome prince in flashing armor.

One summer day word came that the Prince of a neighboring kingdom wished to discuss an alliance. The royal maids confided that he was dashing and princely,

and the Princess's heart leaped with joy. Eagerly she awaited the betrothal feast.

When the Prince entered the great banquet hall and cast his dark, romantic gaze upon her, the Princess nearly swooned in her chair. She sat shyly while everyone toasted the Prince and the golden Princess and peace forever between the two kingdoms. The dog watched quietly from its accustomed place at her feet.

After many leisurely courses, the great feast ended, and the troubadours began to play. The Prince and Princess listened to the lyrical songs honoring their love, and she let him hold her hand under the table— an act noted with triumphant approval by the King and Queen. The Princess was filled with happiness that such a man would love her.

At last the troubadours swung into a waltz, and it was time for the Prince and Princess to lead the dance. Her heart bursting with joy, the Princess rose to take his arm. But as she rose to her feet, a great shadow darkened the Prince's face, and he stared at her as if stricken.

"What is it?" she cried. But the Prince would not speak, and dashed from the hall.

For a long time the Princess studied her mirror that night, wondering what the Prince had seen.

"If you could talk," she said to the dog, "you could tell me, I know it," for the animal's eyes were bright and intelligent. "What did I do wrong?"

The dog, in fact, *could* talk; it's just that nobody had ever asked him anything before.

"You didn't do anything," he said. "It's your height."

"My height?" The Princess was more astonished by what the dog said than the fact that he said it. As an amateur wizard, she had heard of talking animals.

"But I am a Princess!" she wailed. "I'm supposed to be tall." For in her kingdom, all the royal family was tall, and the Princess was tallest of all, and she had thought that was the way things were supposed to be.

The dog privately marveled at her naiveté, and explained that in the world outside this kingdom, men liked to be taller than their wives.

"But why?" asked the Princess.

The dog struggled to explain. "They think if they're not, they can't . . . train falcons as well. Or something." Now that he thought for a moment, he didn't know either.

"Who told you?" the Wizard asked. Somebody was in for a bit of a stay in irons.

"The dog." The Wizard sighed. In fact, he had *known* the creature was enchanted.

"It's my height," she continued bitterly. The Wizard nodded. "I want you to make me shorter," she said. "A foot shorter, at least. Now,"

Using all his persuasive powers, which were considerable, the Wizard explained to her that he could not possibly do that. "Fatter," he said, "yes. Thinner, yes. Turn you into a raven, maybe. But shorter, no. I cannot make you even an inch shorter, my dear."

The Princess was inconsolable.

Seeing her sorrow, the King sent his emissary to the neighboring kingdom with some very attractive offers. Finally the neighboring King and Queen agreed to persuade the Prince to give the match another chance. The Queen spoke to him grandly of chivalry and honor, and the King spoke to him privately of certain gambling debts.

In due course he arrived at the castle, where the Princess had taken to her canopied bed. They had a lovely romantic talk, with him at the bedside holding her hand, and the nobility, of course, standing respectfully at the foot of the bed, as such things are done. In truth, he found the Princess quite lovely when she was sitting or lying down.

"Come on," he said, "let's get some fresh air. We'll go riding." He had in mind a certain dragon in these parts, against whom he might display his talents. And so the Prince strode and the Princess slouched to the stables.

On a horse, as in a chair, the Princess was no taller than he, so they cantered along happily. Seeing an attractive hedge ahead, the Prince urged his mount into a gallop and sailed the hedge proudly. He turned to see her appreciation, only to find the Princess doing the same, and holding her seat quite gracefully. Truthfully, he felt like leaving again.

"Didn't anyone ever tell you," he said coldly, "that ladies ride sidesaddle?" Well, of course they had, but the Princess always thought that that was a silly, unbalanced position that took all the fun out of riding. Now she apologized prettily and swung her legs around.

At length the Prince hurdled another fence, even more dashingly than before, and turned to see the

"It's my legs," she muttered. "When we were sitting down, everything was fine. It's these darn long legs." The dog cocked his head. He thought that she had nice legs, and he was in a position to know. The Princess strode to the bell pull and summoned the Wizard.

"Okay," she said when he arrived. "I know the truth."

Princess attempting to do the same thing. But riding sidesaddle, she did not have a sure seat, and tumbled to the ground.

"Girls shouldn't jump," the Prince told the air, as he helped her up.

But on her feet, she was again a head taller than he. She saw the dim displeasure in his eyes. Then, with truly royal impulsiveness, she made a decision to sacrifice for love. She crumpled to the ground.

"My legs," she said. "I can't stand." The Prince swelled with pride, picked her up, and carried her back to the castle.

There the Royal Physician, the Wizard, and even the Witch examined her legs, with the nobility in attendance.

She was given infusions and teas and herbs and packs, but nothing worked. She simply could not stand.

"When there is nothing wrong but foolishness," the Witch muttered, "you can't fix it." And she left. She had no patience with lovesickness.

The Prince lingered on day after day, as a guest of the King, while the Princess grew well and happy, although she did not stand. Carried to the window seat, she would sit happily and watch him stride around the room, describing his chivalric exploits, and she would sigh with contentment. The loss of the use of her legs seemed a small price to pay for such a man. The dog observed her without comment.

Since she was often idle now, the Princess practiced witty and amusing sayings. She meant only to please the Prince, but he turned on her after one particularly subtle and clever remark and said sharply, "Haven't you ever heard that women should be seen and not heard?"

The Princess sank into thought. She didn't quite understand the saying, but she sensed that it was somehow like her tallness. For just as he preferred her sitting, not standing, he seemed more pleased when she listened, and more remote when she talked.

The next day when the Prince came to her chambers he found the royal entourage gathered around her bed.

"What's the matter?" he asked. They told him the Princess could not speak, not for herbs or infusions or magic spells. And the Prince sat by the bed and held her hand and spoke to her gently, and she was given a slate to write her desires. All went well for several days. But the Prince was not a great reader, so she put the slate aside, and made conversation with only her eyes and her smile. The Prince told her daily how lovely she was,

and then he occupied himself with princely pastimes. Much of the time her only companion was the dog.

One morning the Prince came to see her before he went hunting. His eyes fixed with disgust on the dog, who lay comfortably over her feet.

"Really," the Prince said, "sometimes you surprise me." He went to strike the dog from the bed, but the Princess stayed his hand. He looked at her in amazement.

That night the Princess lay sleepless in the moonlight, and at last, hearing the castle fall silent, and knowing that nobody would catch her talking, she whispered to the dog, "I don't know what I would do without you."

"You'd better get used to the idea," said the dog. "The Prince doesn't like me."

"He will never take you away." The Princess hugged the dog fiercely. The dog looked at her skeptically and gave a little doggy cough.

"He took everything else away," he said.

"No," she said. "I did that. I made myself . . . someone he could love."

"I love you, too," the dog said.

"Of course you do." She scratched his ears.

"And," said the dog, "I loved you *then*." The Princess lay a long time thinking before she finally slept.

The next morning the Prince strode in more handsome and dashing than ever, although oddly enough, the Princess could have sworn he was getting shorter.

As he leaned down to kiss her, his smile disappeared. She frowned a question at him: What's the matter?

"You've still *got* that thing," he said, pointing to the dog. The Princess grabbed her slate.

"He is all I have," she wrote hastily. The lady-in-waiting read it to the Prince.

"You have *me*," the Prince said, his chin high. "I believe you love that smelly thing more than you love me." He strode (he never walked any other way) to the door.

"I *was* going to talk to you about the wedding feast," he said, as he left. "But now, never mind!"

The Princess wept softly and copiously, and the dog licked a tear from her trembling hand.

"What does he *want*?" she asked the dog.

"Roast dog for the wedding feast, I'd imagine," he said. The Princess cried out in horror.

"Oh, not literally," the dog said. "But it follows." And he would say no more.

At last the Princess called the Wizard and wrote on her slate what the dog had said. The Wizard sighed. How awkward. Talking animals were always so frank. He hemmed and hawed until the Princess glared to remind him that Wizards are paid by royalty to advise and interpret—not to sigh.

"All right," he said at last. "Things always come in threes. Everything."

The Princess looked at him blankly.

"Wishes always come in threes," the Wizard said. "And sacrifices, too. So far, you've given up walking. You've given up speech. One more to go."

"Why does he want me to give up the dog?" she wrote. The Wizard looked sorrowfully at her from under his bushy brows.

"Because you love it," he said.

"But that takes nothing from him!" she scribbled. The Wizard smiled, thinking that the same thing could be said of her height and her speech.

"If you could convince him of that, my dear," he said, "you would be more skilled in magic than I."

 When he was gone, the Princess reached for her cards and cast her own fortune, muttering to herself. The dog watched bright-eyed as the wands of growth were covered by the swords of discord. When the ace of swords fell, the Princess gasped. The dog put a delicate paw on the card.

"You poor dumb thing," she said, for it is hard to think of a dog any other way, whether it talks or not. "You don't understand. That is death on a horse. Death to my love."

"His banner is the white rose," said the dog, looking at the card intently. "He is also rebirth." They heard the Prince's striding step outside the door.

"Quick," the Princess said. "Under the bed." The dog's large brown eyes spoke volumes, but he flattened and slid under the bed. And the Prince's visit was surprisingly jolly.

After some time the Prince looked around with imitation surprise. "Something's missing," he said. "I know. It's that creature of yours. You know, I think I was allergic to it. I feel much better now that it's gone." He thumped his chest to show how clear it was. The Princess grabbed her slate, wrote furiously, and thrust it at the Royal Physician.

"He loved me," the Royal Physician read aloud.

"Not as I love you," the Prince said earnestly. The Princess gestured impatiently for the reading to continue.

"That's not all she wrote," the Royal Physician said. "It says, 'The dog loved me *then*.'"

When everyone was gone, the dog crept out to find the Princess installed at her window seat thinking furiously.

"If I am to keep you," she said to him, "we shall have to disenchant you with the spells book." The dog smiled, or seemed to. She cast dice, she drew pentagrams, she crossed rowan twigs and chanted every incantation in the index. Nothing worked. The dog was still a dog, silken, elegant, and seeming to grin in the heat. Finally the Princess clapped shut the last book and sank back.

"Nothing works," she said. "I don't know what we shall do. Meanwhile, when you hear anyone coming, hide in the cupboard or beneath the bed."

"You're putting off the inevitable," the dog told her sadly. "I'll think of something," she said. But she couldn't. At last it was the eve of her wedding day, While the rest of the castle buzzed with excitement, the Princess sat mute in her despair.

"I can't give you up and I can't take you!" she wailed. And the dog saw that she was feeling grave pain.

"Sometimes," the dog said, looking beyond her shoulder, "sometimes one must give up everything for love." The Princess's lip trembled and she looked away.

"What will I *do*?" she cried again. The dog did not answer. She turned toward him and then fell to her knees in shock, for the dog lay motionless on the floor. For hours she sat weeping at his side, holding his lifeless paw.

At last she went to her cupboard and took out her wedding dress, which was of the softest whitest velvet. She wrapped the dog in its folds and picked him up gently.

Through the halls of the castle the Princess walked, and the nobility and chambermaids and royal bishops stopped in their busy preparations to watch her, for the Princess had not walked now for many months. To their astonished faces she said, "I am going to bury the one who really loved me."

On the steps of the castle she met the Prince, who was just dismounting and calling out jovial hearty things to his companions. So surprised was he to see her walking that he lost his footing and tumbled to the ground. She paused briefly to look down at him, held the dog closer to her body, and walked on. The Prince got up and went after her.

"What's going on here?" he asked. "What are you doing? Isn't that your wedding dress?" She turned so he could see the dog's head where it nestled in her left arm.

"I thought you got rid of that thing weeks ago," the Prince said. It was difficult for him to find an emotion suitable to this complex situation. He tried feeling hurt.

"What you call 'this thing,'" the Princess said, "died to spare me pain. And I intend to bury him with honor." The Prince only half-heard her, for he was struck by another realization.

"You're talking!"

"Yes." She smiled.

Looking down at him, she said, "I'm talking. The better to tell you good-bye. So good-bye." And off she went. She could stride too, when she wanted to.

"Well, my dear," the Queen said that night, when the Princess appeared in the throne room. "You've made a proper mess of things. We have alliances to think of. I'm sure you're aware of the very complex negotiations you have quite ruined. Your duty as a Princess . . ."

"It is not necessarily my duty to sacrifice everything," the Princess interrupted. "And I have other duties: a Princess says what she thinks. A Princess stands on her own two feet. A Princess stands tall. And she does not betray those who love her." Her royal parents did not reply. But they seemed to ponder her words.

The Princess lay awake that night for many hours. She was tired from the day's exertions, for she let no other hand dig the dog's grave or fill it, but she could not sleep without the warm weight of the dog across her feet, and the sound of his gentle breathing. At last she put on her cloak and slippers and stole through the silent castle out to the gravesite. There she mused upon love, and what she had given for love, and what the dog had given.

"How foolish we are," she said aloud. "For a stupid Prince I let my wise companion die."

At last the Princess dried her tears on her hem and stirred herself to examine the white rose she had planted on the dog's grave. She watered it again with her little silver watering can. It looked as though it would live.

As she slipped to the castle through the ornamental gardens, she heard a quiet jingling near the gate. On the bridge there was silhouetted a horseman. The delicate silver bridles of his horse sparkled in the moonlight. She could see by his crested shield that he must be nobility, perhaps a Prince. Well, there was many an empty room in the castle tonight, with the wedding feast canceled and all the guests gone home. She approached the rider.

He was quite an attractive fellow, thin with silky golden hair. She smiled up at him, admiring his lean and elegant hand on the reins.

"Where have you come from?" she asked.

He looked puzzled. "Truthfully," he replied, "I can't remember. I know I have traveled a long dark road, but that is all I know." He gave an odd little cough.

The Princess looked past him, where the road was bright in the moonlight.

"I see," she said slowly. "And what is your banner?" For she could not quite decipher it waving above him. He moved it down. A white rose on a black background.

"Death," she breathed.

"No, no," he said, smiling. "Rebirth. And for that, a death is sometimes necessary." He dismounted and bent to kiss the Princess's hand. She breathed a tiny prayer as he straightened up, but it was not answered. Indeed, he was several inches shorter than she was. The Princess straightened her spine.

"It is a pleasure to look up to a proud and beautiful lady," the young Prince said, and his large brown eyes spoke volumes. The Princess blushed.

"We're still holding hands," she said foolishly. The elegant Prince smiled, and kept hold of her hand, and they went toward the castle.

In the shadows the Wizard watched them benignly until they were out of sight. Then he turned to the fluffy black cat at his feet.

"Well, Mirabelle," he said. "One never knows the ways of enchantments." The cat left off from licking one shoulder for a moment and regarded him, but said nothing. Mirabelle never had been much of a conversationalist.

"Ah, well," the Wizard said. "I gather from all this—I shall make a note—that sometimes one must sacrifice for love."

Mirabelle looked intently at the Wizard. "On the other hand," the cat said at last, "sometimes one must *refuse* to sacrifice."

"Worth saying," said the Wizard approvingly. "And true. True." And then, because he had a weakness for talking animals, he took Mirabelle home for an extra dish of cream.

39

Excerpts from *Elizabeth: A Puerto Rican–American Child Tells Her Story* (1974)

Joe Molnar (b. 1930)

EDITORS' INTRODUCTION

Inspired by the civil rights movement, Joe Molnar decided to do a series of books on minority groups in the United States. The first of the three books was *Graciela, A Mexican-American Child Tells Her Story* (Watts, 1972). A social worker in Brownsville, Texas, helped him find Graciela and her family, and Molnar traveled to Texas, taking a portable tape recorder and camera. In Graciela's own words, Molnar's first book tells the story of a girl who divides her time between Texas and Michigan, where she and her family are migrant laborers. The book's candidness and the dignity with which it portrayed Graciela and her family earned the book praises from *Commonweal*, *School Library Journal*, and *Saturday Review*. Molnar followed with *Sherman: A Chinese American Child Tells His Story* (1973) and, finally, *Elizabeth*.

Molnar's process was essentially the same for all three of the "photo-and-tape books." He followed the children, shooting photographs of them playing, shopping, helping around the house. Most of the pictures were not posed: "I always tried for the most natural looking pictures, which were fairly easy to get if I just let the kids alone," he notes.[1] Based on conversations he recorded, Molnar constructed a story for each book, pairing text with appropriate images.

Elizabeth's home in East Harlem was surrounded by slums. "The theme of a child having to cope with that type of environment was very much in the forefront of my mind," Molnar says. "I wanted to show the stamina and courage of the kids in dealing with this type of undernourished kind of environment that they were growing up in."[2] Molnar says he would have done more books in the series had the publisher remained interested.

A native New Yorker, Molnar did not seriously take up photography until the 1960s. Working as an elementary school teacher, he bought his first camera hoping only to become a good amateur photographer but quickly discovered he had a talent for the work. He decided to devote himself full-time to freelance photojournalism. Stirred by the social and political upheavals of the 1960s, Molnar documented several significant events of his time, including the infamous Democratic National Convention in 1968, where police beat both demonstrators and members of the press. Molnar was lucky to escape unharmed and afterward sold what became enduring images of that event. Molnar's photographs of children attracted the attention of psychiatrist Robert Coles, who used about a dozen of Molnar's photographs to illustrate his writings on children. Molnar's photography ranged from political work like the Chicago DNC to candid portraits and photographs of New York slums. He also did an extensive series on the Bread and Puppet Theatre. His photographs have been published in over a dozen magazines, including *Saturday Review*, *Ms.*, and *Scholastic*, and in numerous textbooks and encyclopedias.

Besides journalism and books, Molnar did a portion of the photography for a filmstrip, *Families around the World*, which included images of children in Fiji, Japan, Crete, Upper Volta, Jordan, and Iran (he did the Fiji pictures). He also took photographs for a book about sheep herding in Australia.

Molnar gave up photography in the late 1970s, becoming a social worker and a playwright. His plays are in the genres of comedy, farce, and political satire, a carryover from his interests in the 1960s and 1970s.

NOTES

1. Joe Molnar, telephone interview with Julia Mickenberg, 29 May 2006.

2. Ibid.

My name is Elizabeth. I live in New York City in East Harlem. We call it El Barrio because a lot of Spanish people from Puerto Rico live here. I live with my parents, my two brothers, my cousin, and my uncle. My father's name is Manuel, my mother's name is Haidee, and my brothers are Victor and Alberto.

My father is a waiter in a restaurant. He treats the people nice and they sometimes give him big tips. He serves a lot of clams. He's also a good cook and cooks for us when we go on a picnic. In the summer he teaches us how to swim and plays games with us on the beach.

My brother Victor is ten and he likes to play jokes on people. Alberto is nine and I'm the oldest, twelve. Alberto plays with little wooden soldiers all day He has about four hundred of them. When we have nothing else to do we sit on the stoop downstairs and talk.

My mother stays home and takes care of us. She cooks and cleans and makes sure we get up in time to go to school. Sometimes I help her around the house by washing the dishes.

And sometimes I polish the furniture and make the glass on our cabinet shine so clear I can see myself in it.

My room is very small. The bed has a pretty canopy on it. When Christmas comes we take the canopy down and put up a new one. We like the apartment to look clean and new for the holidays.

If my brothers and me want to play together we go down to the street. We play ball near the school building. My father tells us not to go too far from the house, but the school is only a block away. It's the only building in our neighborhood that looks pretty new.

The principal of my school is Puerto Rican. He is a very nice man and speaks in Spanish to some of the children when they are bad, but he uses English when they are good. All the children like him and the parents too. My teachers are nice, too, but they don't know Spanish and sometimes that makes it hard for them to know what the kids are really feeling. But sometimes it's good, because we use Spanish when we don't want the teacher to know something. That doesn't happen too often.

They have a nice big playground in back of the school and it's safe there. So sometimes we go there with my cousin and get on the swings. Victor likes to swing real high, but Alberto is a little afraid. So I help Alberto with a push and make sure he doesn't go too high.

I like to go up high. It makes my head feel light and I think I'm going to fly off into the air. But I hold on tight.

I have girl friends who live in the same building. We make parties and play Spanish music on records. Or we go down to the street and skip rope. I'm good at skipping rope, but I don't like boys to watch because they tease too much and that makes me mad.

On Saturday my father takes me shopping with him to the outdoor market in El Barrio. They sell a lot of things that Puerto Rican people like to eat. Like fish, crabs, rice and beans, avocados, papayas, bananas, oranges, coconuts, and mangos. We buy all our food there. It's like a little village and it's open from seven in the morning to six at night.

The market sells clothing too and jewelry. I like to look at the jewelry but I don't buy too much because I don't have the money. Once in a while my father gets me a pair of earrings for a present. He buys presents there for our relatives, too, when we go to visit them in Puerto Rico.

My father and mother were both born in Puerto Rico. We have to save a lot of money before we can visit there. I remember when we went there two years ago. It was my first time on a plane and I was scared. I buckled my seat belt and I wanted to find out how the airplane went, so I asked a lot of questions. When the plane took off I couldn't hear anything and it felt like a lot of pressure in my ears. I looked out the window and saw the water. It was clear blue. And the clouds looked like fields of cotton.

I like Puerto Rico better than El Barrio. The streets are clean there. But here they're sometimes very dirty and I think that they forget to collect the garbage or wash the dirt off the streets.

El Barrio is big. There are a lot of streets. Some of them, like the ones near where I live, are pretty safe. But I don't like to walk on some others. I'm afraid to walk on those streets unless my father comes with me. Sometimes people drive their cars crazy and all kinds of things happen in the streets.

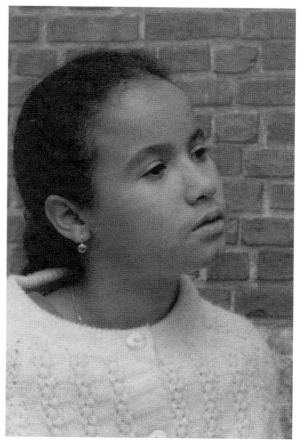

In Puerto Rico they make their houses good, with cement. And they don't have roaches in the walls. Here we live in a six story building on the third floor. The halls are dark at night, the paint is old, and the building is not always too clean. Sometimes the halls smell a little. But I know most of the people in the building. They're not dangerous.

I like the way they build the houses in Puerto Rico. They are no more than one or two floors and most people own their houses. They have big yards with plants and trees and plenty of room to play.

We don t have to play in the streets like we do here. It's a warm country. You don't have to worry about wearing your coat in the winter because you don't need it. You can stay out in the sun and play and eat and take naps, and you never get cold.

I have a girl friend in Puerto Rico. I write letters to her in Spanish and she answers me. When I left her she cried. I cried too, but I told her I might come back. I want very much to live in Puerto Rico. I keep asking my father—when will we go?

I know he is saving up money for a house there. It's a house in the country with lots of grass and trees and fields right next to it. It costs a lot of money. But my father keeps saving a little every month.

I hope we won't have to wait too long.

Part 8

Peace

JULIA MICKENBERG & PHILIP NEL

In America, peace activism dates back to colonial times, when Quakers opposed using violence against Native Americans.[1] During the twentieth century (the focus of this anthology), pacifist activism grew out of the Spanish-American War (in 1898): the Anti-imperialist League and other groups opposed America's empire building and European land grabbing. Outcault's retelling of "David and Goliath" (in the "Buster Brown" story included here) was probably understood by readers of his day as an argument against the Russo-Japanese War (1904–1905), which President Roosevelt described as an "Oriental David" taking on a "Slavic Goliath." While the biblical story of "David and Goliath" may not be antiwar, the moral of Outcault's version echoes the Bible's many strongly pacifist messages, as in Isaiah 2:4, which advises people to "beat their swords into plowshares, and their spears into pruning hooks; nation shall not lift up sword against nation, neither shall they learn war any more."

Although one wing of the Socialist Party supported World War I, another contingent was fiercely opposed to it. Under the Espionage and Sedition Acts (1917 and 1918, respectively), opponents of the First World War faced prosecution and jail. The rift within the Socialist Party and these two acts further weakened the peace movement. After armistice, widespread feeling that the war had been a mistake helped revive pacifism, and people began to discuss "the connection between war and profit making."[2] Carl Sandburg, an active member of the Socialist Party's radical wing until 1919 or so, had an ambiguous position on the war, but his story of the Sooners and the Boomers (1923), included here, clearly rejects war making as a practice of rational people and shows how wars impoverish the people who fight them. Perhaps the most famous children's story thought to advocate pacifism was published during the Spanish Civil War. Though Munro Leaf did not write *The Story of Ferdinand* (1936) as an antiwar tale, many have interpreted the bull's refusal to fight as a pacifist stance, and the book has been both hailed and criticized for its imagined political position.

Making overtly political arguments, James Thurber's *The Last Flower* and Ben Martin's *John Black's Body* were probably influenced by General Smedley D. Butler's *War Is a Racket* (1935), which argued that war creates profit for corporations but misery for common people. Written before the Nazis' invasion of Poland (which prompted many avowed pacifists to support the

Allied cause in World War II), the picture books by Martin and Thurber (both published in 1939) convey the sense that no war is just. *The Last Flower*, which begins after "World War XII" has ended civilization, watches humankind rebuild only to see "liberators" (clearly dictators) goading people to fight a war that proves even more destructive than the last. The book's conclusion leaves room for doubt as to whether civilization will return. With incisive cynicism, *John Black's Body* portrays its title character as the victim of a capitalist war. Though the majority of Americans opposed entry into the war in 1939, the pacifism of both books is striking. (By 1940, Martin has already changed his mind: his *Mr. Smith and Mr. Schmidt*, published that year, contrasts American democracy with German fascism, and suggests that the Americans will fight if provoked.)[3]

The war's end brought renewed hope for a lasting peace. By promoting democratic values and opposing bigotry, some children's books sought to prevent the seeds of future conflicts from being sown. Margret and H. A. Rey's *Spotty* (1945) and, included here, Ruth Benedict and Gene Weltfish's *In Henry's Backyard: The Races of Mankind* (1948) both affirm the idea that—as the latter book puts it—people are not "*born haters.*" They all "have the same aspirations . . . for . . . love and a home . . . a family growing up . . . and the right to worship in their own way." Using spots as a metaphor for ethnic or racial difference, *Spotty* conveys its message of tolerance by showing that spotted bunnies and unspotted bunnies should treat each other fairly and without prejudice. *In Henry's Backyard*, where science advances the same idea, inspired Ruth Krauss to write *The Big World and the Little House* (1949), in which one family's restoration of a little house serves as a metaphor for rebuilding the world. As Krauss's narrator notes of the family that has turned a broken shell of a house into a home, "'Home is a way people feel about a place. These people feel that way about the little house." And "[s]ome people feel that way about the whole world."

As the Cold War overtook the optimism that briefly followed the end of World War II, Erich Kästner's *The Animals Conference* (1949) has the animals of the world, frustrated by world leaders' efforts to attain peace, holding a conference of their own and deciding to kidnap the children of the world in order to convince the world's statesmen to sign a peace treaty. The animals' gambit works in this fictional tale, but, as Robbie Lieberman writes in *The Strangest Dream: Communism,*

Anticommunism, and the U.S. Peace Movement, 1945–1963 (2000), Popular Front liberals who hoped "for a lasting peace built on U.S.-Soviet cooperation" had their hopes dashed by the Cold War's "very different view of peace and freedom—centered on anticommunism and military preparedness."[4] As a result, by the late 1940s and into the 1950s, members of the U.S. peace movement were often accused of being Communists. Indeed, advocating peace could be rather dangerous, as exemplified by the McCarthyite attacks on the March 1949 Cultural and Scientific Conference for World Peace (held at the Waldorf-Astoria Hotel in New York) and on Women Strike for Peace, an organization of mothers who opposed nuclear testing.[5]

In the later 1950s, as McCarthyism waned, concerns about radiation from nuclear testing were on the rise. Founded in 1957, the Committee for a Sane Nuclear Policy (SANE) was an instant success, swiftly growing from a small ad hoc group to a large organization with hundreds of local chapters.[6] That same year, Linus Pauling started a petition calling for a halt to nuclear testing. Gathering the support of eleven thousand scientists in forty-nine countries, Pauling presented the petition to United Nations secretary-general Dag Hammarskjöld in January 1958.[7] Though Munro Leaf's *Three Promises to You* (1957) makes no mention of nuclear testing, it does seek to advance the United Nations' goal of promoting peace and cooperation among the nations of the world. As UN under-secretary Ahmed Bokhári writes in his introduction to the book, the United Nations' attempt "to arrange that there should be no wars" is "a difficult task because the world is very big and people are not always kind or sensible. All the same we cannot give up trying."

In the 1960s, the Cuban missile crisis and escalation of the war in Vietnam gave a new urgency to the peace movement in the United States. In 1963, President Kennedy's administration negotiated a limited nuclear test ban treaty with the USSR. In proposing a "visiting kind of sister-brotherhood day" among children of all nations, Edith Segal's "U.S. Calling UNICEF Friends," published that same year, certainly fits with the spirit of peaceful cooperation among countries. Stressing friendship, the poem provides the word for "friend" in Spanish, French, Yiddish, Hebrew, Japanese, and Russian. Although the title of Segal's "The Work of the World" echoes Marx's call for the "workers of the world" to unite, the poem focuses instead on the different kinds of occupations, representing jobs that, with one or two exceptions (such as astronauts), would be found in nations around the world—factory workers, farmers, engineers, teachers, firemen, architects, scientists, teachers, doctors. Emphasizing jobs people of different nationalities have in common suggests a kinship among peoples, another reason for being friends rather than enemies.

Taking a more satirical angle, Jean Merrill's classic, The Pushcart War (1964), describes a fictional future battle between pushcart peddlers and truck drivers in New York City, following a rash of truck/pushcart "accidents" deliberately caused by the truckers. The pushcart peddlers engage in sabotage, using pin-filled peas in pea shooters to puncture truck tires. After the city's corrupt mayor taxes the pins and prohibits the sale of dried peas, the peddlers march for peace and ultimately gain not just moral high ground but also public sympathy—especially the sympathy of children. Despite being overpowered and outnumbered, the peddlers win. A sentence in the book's foreword sums up its argument: "big wars are caused by the same sort of problems that led to the pushcart war."

Just a few years later, Leo Lionni's The Alphabet Tree (1968) echoes the rising tide of protest against the war in Vietnam. After a group of tree-dwelling letters learn to make words, a friendly caterpillar suggests that they create sentences that "mean something." The letters create "peace on earth good will toward men" and, riding on the caterpillar's back, set off to take this message "to the president."

During the 1970s, 1980s, and 1990s, peace-themed children's books flourished. Prominent subjects addressed in these books included the Vietnam War, its aftermath, the Cold War, and the Second World War. Alexander Crosby's One Day for Peace (1971) tells of a girl who organizes a protest march against the Vietnam War. In John and Faith Hubley's The Hat (1974), adapted from their 1963 cartoon of the same name, when the helmet of one soldier lands on the other side of the border, he and a soldier from the other side debate peace and international law. Trân-Khánh-Tuyêt's The Little Weaver of Thái-Yên Village (1977, revised 1986) addresses the war in Vietnam from the point of view of a Vietnamese child whose village is bombed, and Eve Bunting's The Wall (1992) follows an American father and son's visit to the Vietnam War Memorial in Washington.

In the 1980s, children's books responded to the belligerent policies of British prime minister Margaret Thatcher and U.S. president Ronald Reagan. Raymond Briggs, best known for his gentle The Snowman (1978), produced a scathing critique of the Falklands War in The Tin-Pot Foreign General and the Iron Old Woman (1984). In The Butter Battle Book (1984), Dr. Seuss satirized Reagan's escalation of the Cold War. Though it also ponders issues other than peace, David Macaulay's Baaa (1985) certainly echoes concerns about the results of a nuclear war. Set in a postholocaust world after all people have vanished, Baaa shows the sheep taking over, inhabiting the structures of human civilization, and making the same mistakes, which finally results in their own extinction. To name just one more of many antiwar children's books published during this decade, Toshi Maruki's Hiroshima No Pika (1982) provides a stark portrait of the effects of nuclear weapons in its chronicle of a little girl living in Hiroshima on the day the United States' atomic bomb destroyed the city.

As the Cold War ended, hope for peace emerged in Ann Durrell and Marilyn Sachs's The Big Book for Peace (1990), an anthology featuring the work of thirty-four artists and writers, including Katherine Paterson, Maurice Sendak, Lois Lowry, Jerry Pinkney, Charlotte Zolotow, and Lloyd Alexander. The book won the Jane Addams Book Award, given annually since 1953 by the Women's International League for Peace and Freedom to children's books that promote peace and social justice. Eugene Trivizas's The Three Little Wolves and the Big Bad Pig (1993, illustrated by Helen Oxenbury) tells of three gentle wolves who at first treat a "big bad pig" as an enemy, building ever stronger houses (that the pig still manages to destroy). In the end they build a house of flowers, and the pig, overcome by the beauty and scent, befriends the wolves, and the former foes go on to live together (happily ever after). This radically revised fairy tale makes opponents into allies, stressing peaceful coexistence instead of confrontation.

Strong opposition to the second Iraq War, including protests by millions of people worldwide on February 15, 2003, showed that the desire for peace remained robust. Although the governments of the United States, the United Kingdom, and their allies did not heed these protests (the war began on March 20, 2003), opposition to the war has remained strong—though it has consistently been stronger in Europe and Canada than it has been in the United States. Presently, we are starting to see children's books that depict the effects of the war. Jeanette Winter's *The Librarian of Basra: A True Story from Iraq* (2005) describes a librarian's efforts to save her community's collection of books from the ravages of war. As long as wars continue, those who oppose them will continue to express their wishes through the medium of children's literature.

NOTES

1. Robbie Lieberman, *The Strangest Dream: Communism, Anti-communism, and the U.S. Peace Movement, 1945–1963* (Syracuse, NY: Syracuse UP, 2000), xiv.

2. Lieberman, 9.

3. Such a shift on Martin's part may have reflected initial support for the Nazi-Soviet pact, which Communists and communist sympathizers rationalized as a way to keep the Soviet Union out of an "imperialist war." See Maurice Isserman, *Which Side Were You On? The American Communist Party during the Second World War* (Urbana: U of Illinois P, 1993 [1982]), 32–54.

4. Lieberman, 33.

5. Amy Swerdlow, *Women Strike for Peace: Traditional Motherhood and Radical Politics in the 1960s* (Chicago: U of Chicago P, 1993).

6. Lieberman, 137.

7. Lieberman, 137–38.

40

"Buster Brown Plays David and Goliath," from *Buster Brown Goes Shooting and Other Stories* (1907)

R. F. Outcault
(Richard Felton Outcault, 1863–1928)

EDITORS' INTRODUCTION

Born in Lancaster, Ohio, during the Civil War, Richard Felton Outcault left home at age fourteen to study art at Cincinnati's McMicken University. By age seventeen, he was working as a commercial artist, doing such jobs as "painting pastoral scenes on safes" and, by his mid-twenties, drawing technical diagrams for the inventions of Thomas Edison.[1] Outcault won the job of official artist for Edison's exhibit at the 1889 Paris World's Fair. Edison became a close friend and helped pay for Outcault's art studies in Paris's Latin Quarter.

Returning to New York in 1890, Outcault married and began working in the medium that would make him famous—cartoons. Like his contemporaries, photographer Jacob Riis (*How the Other Half Lives*) and novelist Stephen Crane ("Maggie, a Girl of the Streets"), Outcault specialized in depicting the urban poor.[2]

One such character, the Yellow Kid, starred in Outcault's first famous comic strip, *Hogan's Alley* (1895–1898). Although it was not the first comic strip (as has been claimed), Outcault's Yellow Kid deserves credit for popularizing the medium. People bought not only the newspaper to read his strip but also the myriad "Yellow Kid" products—toys, games, candy, buttons, fans, chewing gum, and cigars. There was even a Broadway musical based on the Kid.

Buster Brown (1902–1921), Outcault's next successful strip, is best remembered for one of the many products associated with it: Buster Brown shoes, which are still manufactured today. There were also Buster Brown clothes, chocolate, coffee, shirt collars, stockings, games, and soap. Outcault published over a dozen *Buster Brown* books, each of which collected three of his Sunday strips, at one panel per page: the story reprinted here, "Buster Brown Plays David and Goliath"

(1905), comes from one such book, *Buster Brown Goes Shooting and Other Stories* (1907). Buster was also the star of a musical, animated cartoons, and, later, both a radio show and a television show. Comics historian Richard Marschall considers Buster's bulldog Tige to be "the first major talking animal of the comics," ancestor of Mickey Mouse and Snoopy.[3] According to comics scholar Maurice Horn, *Buster Brown* is also the source of the popular expressions "Wait a minute, Buster!" and "Who do you think you are, Buster?"[4]

Unlike the Kid, Buster Brown was a well-dressed, angel-faced, rich child. The Kid lived in a slum, but Brown lived in a fancy apartment with servants. What the two comic strips have in common is that both are political. In the run-up to the 1896 presidential election, Outcault's "Yellow Kid" strips mocked Republican candidate William McKinley, Democratic candidate William Jennings Bryan (whom Outcault and his newspaper ultimately endorsed), and the fickleness of voters.[5] *Buster Brown* delivers its political messages at the end of each strip, when Buster, having gotten into mischief, claims to have learned from his behavior and promises never to do it again. The title story of *Buster Brown Goes Shooting* ends with Buster Brown vowing not to shoot "innocent" animals and takes a jab at President Theodore Roosevelt for "going out armed with a gun and a camera and a press agent to shoot helpless and unarmed animals." The morals of *Buster Brown* were so popular that Outcault published one book comprised exclusively of the final "moral" panel from several dozen different strips.

The political context for the moral to "Buster Brown Plays David and Goliath" is probably the Russo-Japanese War (1904–1906), which killed seventy thousand soldiers and fed the discontent that led to the 1905 Russian revolution. When the Japanese were winning, President Roosevelt praised the "Oriental David" for beating the "Slavic Goliath."[6] Writing this cartoon before the war's end, Outcault could not know that Roosevelt would win the Nobel Peace Prize for helping to broker a peace settlement between the victorious Japanese and defeated Russians—an action of which the cartoonist probably approved.

At the time, Outcault was turning more of his attention to business, having established the Outcault Lecture Bureau, the Buster Brown Amusement Company, and the Outcault Advertising Agency. He retired from cartooning in 1921 and died a wealthy man in 1928, hailed by obituary writers as "The Father of the Funnies."[7]

NOTES

1. Richard Marschall, *America's Great Comic-Strip Artists: From the Yellow Kid to Peanuts* (New York: Stewart, Tabori & Chang, 1997 [1989]), 20.

2. Ibid., 21.

3. Ibid., 32. See also Coulton Waugh, *The Comics* (Jackson: UP of Mississippi, 1991 [1947]), 152.

4. Maurice Horn, "Buster Brown," *100 Years of American Newspaper Comics: An Illustrated Encyclopedia* (New York: Gramercy Books, 1996), 74.

5. Bill Blackbeard, "The Yellow Kid, the Yellow Decade," *R. F. Outcault's The Yellow Kid: A Centennial Celebration of the Kid Who Started the Comics* (Northampton, MA: Kitchen Sink Press, 1995), 46–47.

6. "Topics in the News: America, Europe, and Asia," *American Decades: 1900–1909*, ed. Vincent Tompkins (Detroit: Gale, 1996), 210.

7. Marschall, 38.

41

"How Two Sweetheart Dippies Sat in the Moonlight on a Lumber Yard Fence and Heard about the Sooners and the Boomers," from *Rootabaga Pigeons* (1923)

Written by Carl Sandburg (1878–1967), illustrated by Maud Petersham (1889–1971) and Miska Petersham (1888–1960)

EDITORS' INTRODUCTION

"How Two Sweetheart Dippies" is among the second batch of "Rootabaga Stories" that earned Carl Sandburg a distinguished place among authors of children's books. (*Rootabaga Stories* came out in 1922, and *Rootabaga Pigeons*, from which this selection is drawn, followed a year later.) As versions of tales spun for Sandburg's own three daughters, the *Rootabaga Stories* were marketed as children's fare, but Sandburg himself claimed that his imagined audience was "people from 5 to 105."[1]

Rootabaga country is at once a fantasyland and a clearly midwestern milieu of cornfields and prairies—as well as a few cities with skyscrapers. This very American setting, along with the classic Sandburg vernacular, led at least one critic to call *Rootabaga Stories* "the first genuinely American fairy tales."[2] More recently, literary critic Gillian Avery cited Sandburg's *Rootabaga Stories* as marking the emergence of a truly American idiom in children's literature.[3]

The most memorable quality of the *Rootabaga Stories* is the series of nonsense names, locations, and scenarios: characters such as Googler and Gaggler, Eeta Peeca Pie, and Please Gimme; places such as the Village of Liver and Onions and the Village of Cream Puffs; and marvelously mundane circumstances such as The Toboggan-to-the-Moon Dream of the Potato Face Blind Man, and How Bimbo the Snip's Thumb Stuck to His Nose When the Wind Changed. In many ways, the nonsense itself is the message: it is a call to liberate the child's imagination, to imagine a fantasy of possible lives in the child's own world.

Yet the story reprinted here, set in the town of Thumbs Up (sometimes known as Thumbs Down), contains another story, of ridiculous wars waged by sooners and boomers, who were once great friends. Sandburg's tone is lighthearted, but the underlying theme is serious, if somewhat ambiguous. The peaceful, cooperative commonwealth is clearly set forth as an ideal; whether this ideal is attainable—and sustainable—is left open to question. This ambiguity may well reflect the state of Sandburg's own political thinking in the early 1920s.

The son of Swedish immigrants, Carl Sandburg was born in Galesburg, Illinois. From the age of eleven, he worked before and after school, and in his early teens left school to support his family, taking a series of low-wage jobs.[4] After serving in the Spanish-American War, Sandburg worked his way through Lombard College in Galesburg. There, he read the work of English Socialists John Ruskin and William Morris and heard speeches by major critics of the American scene: Jacob Riis, photographer and muckraker; Samuel Gompers of the American Federation of Labor; and Eugene Debs, socialist presidential hopeful.[5] In 1907, Sandburg took a job as an organizer for the Socialist Party in Wisconsin, where he met his soon-to-be wife, Lilian Steichen, sister of the photographer Edward Steichen and a devout Socialist. Sandburg became increasingly radical in the years prior to the First World War, writing monthly reports for the far-left *International Socialist Review* and publishing poetry that embraced elements of literary modernism and revolutionary politics.

Throughout his career, Sandburg would be known as a "people's poet" or the "poet of industrial America," but by 1920 his years as a fiery radical were largely over, thanks to a number of factors: government repression of radicals; Sandburg's growing popularity as a poet; and the fact that "social poetry" had gone out of fashion. Sandburg maintained a warm relationship with Eugene Debs; he appeared on the masthead of the *New Masses* as a "contributing editor"; and he, like other radicals, responded with a mix of rage and despair to the execution of the Italian anarchists Sacco and Vanzetti in 1927. But for the rest of his career Sandburg would publicly play down his radical past.[6]

By midcentury Sandburg would be the most well-known poet in America. He was the recipient of two Pulitzer Prizes, and a friend to several presidents.

Miska Petersham was born Mikaly Petrezselyem

in Toeroekszenmiklos (near Budapest), Hungary. He attended art school in Budapest and in London and emigrated to the United States in 1912, where he met American-born Maud Fuller, daughter of a Baptist minister and an artist herself. The two married and became lifelong collaborators. The Petershams are known for "introducing an international scope to the American picture book, for developing informational books that are attractive as well as informative, and for setting a standard in book illustration through their mastery of the lithographic method, experimentation with printing processes, and emphasis on total book design."[7] Their illustrations for *The Poppy Seed Cakes* (1924) are seen as pivotal in the development of the picture book in the United States. The first book that they authored and illustrated, *Miki*, which describes an American boy (their son) who visits his grandparents in Budapest, inspired other authors and illustrators to portray foreign settings in their work. During World War II the Petershams focused on producing books with American themes. These works, collectively known as the "This Is America" series, included *An American ABC* (1942), a Caldecott runner-up, and *The Rooster Crows* (1946), a Caldecott medal winner. In time, both books drew criticism for their stereotypical representations of ethnic groups and rhymes using black dialect; a revised version of *The Rooster Crows*, eliminating the offending material, was published in 1969.[8]

NOTES

1. Letter to Alfred Harcourt, 29 July 1922, in Mitgang, 211–12.

2. Harry Golden, "In Prose You Say What You Mean," in *Carl Sandburg* (Cleveland, OH: World Publishing Company, 1961), 221–38. Qtd. in *Children's Literature Review*, vol. 67, ed. Jennifer Bause (Detroit: Gale, 2001), 161.

3. Gillian Avery, *Behold the Child: American Children and Their Books, 1621–1922* (London: Bodley Head, 1994).

4. *Something about the Author*, vol. 8, ed. Anne Commire (Detroit: Gale, 1976), 178.

5. Philip R. Yanella, *The Other Carl Sandburg* (Jackson: UP of Mississippi, 1996), 5.

6. Ibid., 155.

7. *Children's Literature Review*, vol. 24, ed. Gerard J. Senick (Detroit: Gale, 1991), 155.

8. Ibid., 156.

Not so very far and not so very near the Village of Liver-and-Onions is a dippy little town where dippy people used to live.

And it was long, long ago the sweetheart dippies stood in their windows and watched the dips of the star dippers in the dip of the sky.

It was the dippies who took the running wild oleander and the cunning wild rambler rose and kept them so the running wild winters let them alone.

"It is easy to be a dippy . . . among the dippies . . . isn't it?" the sweetheart dippies whispered to each other, sitting in the leaf shadows of the oleander, the rambler rose.

The name of this dippy town came by accident. The name of the town is Thumbs Up and it used to be named Thumbs Down and expects to change its name back and forth between Thumbs Up and Thumbs Down.

The running wild oleanders and the running wild rambler roses grow there over the big lumber yards where all the old lumber goes.

The dippies and the dippy sweethearts go out there to those lumber yards and sit on the fence moonlight nights and look at the lumber.

The rusty nails in the lumber get rustier and rustier till they drop out. And whenever they drop out there is always a rat standing under to take the nail in his teeth and chew the nail and eat it.

For this is the place the nail-eating rats come to from all over the Rootabaga country. Father rats and mother rats send the young rats there to eat nails and get stronger.

If a young rat comes back from a trip to the lumber yards in Thumbs Up and he meets another young rat going to those lumber yards, they say to each other, "Where have you been?" "To Thumbs Up." "And how do you feel?" "*Hard as nails.*"

Now one night two of the dippies, a sweetheart boy and girl, went out to the big lumber yards and sat on the fence and looked at the lumber and the running wild oleanders and the running wild rambler roses.

And they saw two big rusty nails, getting rustier and rustier, drop out of the lumber and drop into the teeth of two young rats.

And the two young rats sat up on their tails there in the moonlight under the oleanders, under the roses, and one of the young rats told the other young rat a story he made up out of his head.

Chewing on the big rusty nail and then swallowing, telling more of the story after swallowing and before beginning to chew the nail again, this is the story he told—and this is the story the two dippies, the two sweethearts sitting on the fence in the moonlight, heard:

Far away where the sky drops down, and the sunsets open doors for the nights to come through—where the running winds meet, change faces and come back —there is a prairie where the green grass grows all around.

And on that prairie the gophers, the black and brown-striped ground squirrels, sit with their backs straight up, sitting on their soft paddy tails, sitting in the spring song murmur of the south wind, saying to each other, "This is the prairie and the prairie belongs to us."

Now far back in the long time, the gophers came there, chasing each other, playing the-green-grass-grew-all-around, playing cross tag, hop tag, skip tag, billy-be-tag, billy-be-it.

The razorback hogs came then, eating pignuts, potatoes, paw paws, pumpkins. The wild horse, the buffalo, came. The moose, with spraggly branches of antlers spreading out over his head, the moose came —and the fox, the wolf.

The gophers flipped a quick flip-flop back into their gopher holes when the fox, the wolf, came. And the fox, the wolf, stood at the holes and said, "You *look* like rats, you *run* like rats, you *are* rats, rats with stripes. Bah! you are only *rats*. Bah!"

It was the first time anybody said "Bah!" to the gophers. They sat in a circle with their noses up asking, "*What* does this 'Bah!' mean?" And an old timer, with his hair falling off in patches, with the stripes on his soft paddy tail patched with patches, this old timer of a gopher said, "'Bah!' speaks more than it means whenever it is spoken."

Then the sooners and the boomers came, saying "Bah!" and saying it many new ways, till the fox, the wolf, the moose, the wild horse, the buffalo, the razorback hog picked up their feet and ran away without looking back.

The sooners and boomers began making houses, sod houses, log, lumber, plaster-and-lath houses, stone, brick, steel houses, but most of the houses were lumber with nails to hold the lumber together to keep the rain off and push the wind back and hold the blizzards outside.

In the beginning the sooners and boomers told stories, spoke jokes, made songs, with their arms on each other's shoulders. They dug wells, helping each other get water. They built chimneys together helping each other let the smoke out of their houses. And every year the day before Thanksgiving they went in cahoots with their post hole diggers and dug all the post holes for a year to come. That was in the morning. In the afternoon they took each other's cistern cleaners and cleaned all the cisterns for a year to come. And the next day on Thanksgiving they split turkey wishbones and thanked each other they had all the post holes dug and all the cisterns cleaned for a year to come.

If the boomers had to have broom corn to make brooms the sooners came saying, "Here is your broom corn." If the sooners had to have a gallon of molasses, the boomers came saying, "Here is your gallon of molasses."

They handed each other big duck eggs to fry, big goose eggs to boil, purple pigeon eggs for Easter breakfast. Wagon loads of buff banty eggs went back and forth between the sooners and boomers. And they took big hayracks full of buff banty hens and traded them for hayracks full of buff banty roosters.

And one time at a picnic, one summer afternoon, the sooners gave the boomers a thousand golden ice tongs with hearts and hands carved on the handles. And the boomers gave the sooners a thousand silver wheelbarrows with hearts and hands carved on the handles.

Then came pigs, pigs, pigs, and more pigs. And the sooners and boomers said the pigs had to be painted. There was a war to decide whether the pigs should be painted pink or green. Pink won.

The next war was to decide whether the pigs should be painted checks or stripes. Checks won. The next war after that was to decide whether the checks should be painted pink or green. Green won.

Then came the longest war of all, up till that time. And this war decided the pigs should be painted both pink and green, both checks and stripes.

They rested then. But it was only a short rest. For then came the war to decide whether peach pickers must pick peaches on Tuesday mornings or on Saturday afternoons. Tuesday mornings won. This was a short war. Then came a long war—to decide whether telegraph pole climbers must eat onions at noon with spoons, or whether dishwashers must keep their money in pig's ears with padlocks pinched on with pincers.

So the wars went on. Between wars they called each other goofs and snoofs, grave robbers, pickpockets, porch climbers, pie thieves, pie face mutts, bums, big bums, big greasy bums, dummies, mummies, rummies, sneezicks, bohunks, wops, snorkies, ditch diggers, peanuts, fatheads, sapheads, pinheads, pickle faces, horse thieves, rubbernecks, big pieces of cheese, big bags of wind, snabs, scabs, and dirty sniveling snitches. Sometimes when they got tired of calling each other names they scratched in the air with their fingers and made faces with their tongues out twisted like pretzels.

After a while, it seemed, there was no corn, no broom corn, no brooms, not even teeny sweepings of corn or broom corn or brooms. And there were no duck eggs to fry, goose eggs to boil, no buff banty eggs, no buff banty hens, no buff banty roosters, no wagons for wagon loads of buff banty eggs, no hayracks for hayrack loads of buff banty hens and buff banty roosters.

And the thousand golden ice tongs the sooners gave the boomers, and the thousand silver wheelbarrows the boomers gave the sooners, both with hearts and hands carved on the handles, they were long ago broken up in one of the early wars deciding pigs must be painted both pink and green with both checks and stripes.

And now, at last, there were no more pigs to paint either pink or green or with checks or stripes. The pigs, pigs, pigs, were gone.

So the sooners and boomers all got lost in the wars or they screwed wooden legs on their stump legs and walked away to bigger, bigger prairies or they started away for the rivers and mountains, stopping always to count how many fleas there were in any bunch of fleas they met. If you see anybody who stops to count the fleas in a bunch of fleas, that is a sign he is either a sooner or a boomer.

So again the gophers, the black and brown striped ground squirrels, sit with their backs straight up, sitting on their soft paddy tails, sitting in the spring song murmur of the south wind, saying, "This is the prairie and the prairie belongs to us."

Far away to-day where the sky drops down and the sunsets open doors for the nights to come through —where the running winds meet, change faces and come back—there the gophers are playing the-green-grass-grew-all-around, playing cross tag, skip tag, hop tag, billy-be-tag, billy-be-it. And sometimes they sit in a circle and ask, "What does this 'Bah!' mean?" And an old timer answers, "'Bah!' speaks more than it means whenever it is spoken."

That was the story the young rat under the oleanders, under the roses, told the other young rat, while the two sweetheart dippies sat on the fence in the moonlight looking at the lumber and listening.

The young rat who told the story hardly got started eating the nail he was chewing, while the young rat that did the listening chewed up and swallowed down a whole nail.

As the two dippies on the fence looked at the running wild oleander and the running wild rambler roses over the lumber in the moonlight, they said to each other, "It's easy to be a dippy . . . among the dippies . . . isn't it?" And they climbed down from the fence and went home in the moonlight.

42

In Henry's Backyard:

The Races of Mankind (1948)

Written by Ruth Benedict
(1887–1948) and Gene Weltfish
(Regina Weltfish, 1902–1980),
Illustrated by United Productions
of America (1944–1960s)

EDITORS' INTRODUCTION

To contribute to the U.S. war effort, two Columbia University anthropologists collaborated with artist Ad Reinhardt to create The Races of Mankind (1943), a 32-page pamphlet that debunked racial myths spread by fascists abroad and racists at home. Former students of Franz Boas, authors Ruth Benedict and Gene Weltfish knew the subject well. Dr. Weltfish had studied several Native American groups and began teaching Columbia's Race Relations course in the 1930s. Dr. Benedict was the author of Race: Science and Politics (1940) and coauthor of Race and Cultural Relations: America's Answer to the Myth of a Master Race (1942).

Using science to prove that we are all "one human race"[1] and that culture (not nature) accounts for differences among peoples was controversial in the 1940s. Weltfish and Benedict wrote the pamphlet for the army, to be distributed through the USO. But Kentucky congressman Andrew May objected, irritated by their inclusion of data from World War I army intelligence tests showing southern whites (including those from Kentucky) scoring lower than northern blacks. As Benedict and Weltfish write, "The differences did not arise because people were from the North or the South, or because they were white or black, but because of differences in income, education, cultural advantages, and other opportunities."[2] When May persuaded the army to stop distributing the pamphlet, his act inspired public protests, garnered media coverage, and boosted sales. The Races of Mankind sold nearly a million copies in its first ten years, and was translated into French, German, and Japanese.[3]

In 1945, United Productions of America (UPA) made the book into an animated cartoon, Brotherhood of Man.

UPA was an innovative animation studio founded by Dave Hilberman, Zack Schwartz, Steve Bosustow, and John Hubley, all former Disney employees—and ex-Communists—who took part in the 1941 strike. (Disney's response to the strikers was to fire them.) Hubley and Phil Eastman—another ex-Disney-striker and ex-Communist—animated the cartoon, and future Hollywood Ten member Ring Lardner, Jr., cowrote the script.[4] (The UPA studio would go on to produce the Academy Award–winning cartoon Gerald McBoing Boing and the Mr. Magoo cartoons.) In 1948, Weltfish and Violet Edwards, under the supervision of Benedict, adapted Brotherhood of Man for In Henry's Backyard: The Races of Mankind, illustrating it with images from the cartoon.

The New York Times Book Review both disliked the "flat" illustrations and disagreed with the book's central claim of racial equality: "until much more is known about human genetics it will hardly be possible to lay down the law on heredity vs. environment in measuring racial capability." The review also discredits the authors on the grounds that both work in anthropology, "not a true science at all, but . . . a kind of specialized reportage."[5] In contrast, the New York Herald Tribune praised In Henry's Backyard: "By two members of the Department of Anthropology of Columbia, you might expect it to be scientifically sound; it is not only that but quite explosively funny."[6]

Both white and of Christian upbringing, Benedict and Weltfish were not targets of racism or antisemitism, but the setbacks they experienced—many of which have been attributed to sexism—surely fueled their awareness of social injustice. Benedict, the first woman president of the American Anthropological Association, only became a full professor the year she died —the first woman in Columbia's political science faculty to achieve that rank. Though Weltfish completed her dissertation in 1929, she did not receive the Ph.D. until 1950 because she could not afford Columbia's requirement that she pay four thousand dollars to publish it. As a result, she was employed only as a lecturer at Columbia—until 1953, when Columbia fired her after she was summoned to appear before McCarthy.[7]

From the 1930s through the 1960s, the FBI believed opponents of racism were also Communists. As David H. Price points out, what "were scientists like Gene Weltfish to do" when America's main political parties condoned Jim Crow racism and "the Communist

Party's position on racial equality was in total alignment with the scientific findings of biological and anthropological research"?[8] Benedict was not a party member, and Weltfish's allegiances are unknown—the FBI thought she was a member, but her daughter disputed that claim.[9] In any case, the activism of Benedict and Weltfish was rooted in the empirical methods of scientific inquiry, not in the procrustean confines of ideological doctrine. Ignoring Columbia president Nicholas Murray Butler's 1940 crackdown on academic freedom, Benedict gave talks exposing "America's Racial Myths," and Weltfish spoke out against the American Red Cross's wartime policy of segregating blood plasma donated by blacks—a message included in *In Henry's Backyard*. Both women put science in the service of activism. As Benedict wrote, "I have the faith of a scientist that behavior, no matter how unfamiliar to us, is understandable if the problem is stated so that it can be answered by investigation and if it is then studied by technically suitable methods. And I have the faith of a humanist in the advantages of mutual understanding among men."[10]

NOTES

1. Ruth Benedict and Gene Weltfish, *The Races of Mankind* (New York: Public Affairs, 1946 [1943]), 3, 16.

2. Ibid., 18.

3. Margaret M. Caffrey, *Ruth Benedict: Stranger in This Land* (Austin: U of Texas P, 1989), 298.

4. Michael Barrier, *Hollywood Cartoons: American Animation in Its Golden Age* (New York: Oxford UP, 1999), 513–15.

5. E.B.G., "Why We Behave like Humans," *New York Times Book Review*, 7 Mar. 1948, 23.

6. Herbert Kupferberg, "Going to Judgment," *New York Herald Tribune Weekly Book Review*, 7 Mar. 1948, 8.

7. Stanley Diamond, ed., *Theory and Practice: Essays Presented to Gene Weltfish* (New York: Moulton, 1980), ix. Information also drawn from Philip Nel, telephone conversation with Ann Margetson (Weltfish's daughter), 2 Feb. 2006.

8. David H. Price, *Threatening Anthropology: McCarthyism and the FBI's Surveillance of Activist Anthropologists* (Durham, NC: Duke UP, 2004), 135.

9. Ibid., 119.

10. Ruth Benedict, qtd. in Margaret Mead, *Ruth Benedict* (New York: Columbia UP, 1974), 75.

Everybody has his own dream about what the world is going to be in the future, but we all know that it's steadily shrinking. One of these days we're going to wake up and find that people and places we used to read about are practically in our own backyard.

Henry was a man who was given to dreaming about these things. He was an ordinary, friendly person, who lived in an ordinary house with an ordinary yard in back of it, where he raised tomatoes and petunias—the usual patch. He also did his best to raise hair on his head, but it was a losing battle. Only three surviving hairs grew there, lonesomely, but that didn't worry Henry too much.

"I take after my father, I guess," he would say to himself, "and my grandfather, and probably all the other bald heads in my family going back to Adam, for all I know."

But Henry had common sense enough to realize that it wasn't the hair on one's head that was important, but the thoughts inside it . . . the thoughts . . .

"You know," said Henry to himself, "with this new jet propulsion and atomic energy, a man could really go places . . . maybe a weekend on the Congo . . . or Christmas in Greenland . . ."

One night Henry had a remarkable dream. He dreamed that the whole world became so small that it fitted nicely into his own backyard and all sorts of odd people had become his neighbors.

Next morning Henry said to himself, "Well, that was a funny dream . . . but a nice one . . . and darned interesting . . ." and, as he made this remark, he . . .

. . . glanced out his window—

"Holy smoke," said Henry, "it's really happened," . . . only he didn't say it, because what he saw left him quite speechless . . .

Henry whizzed into his clothes and downstairs and out of his back door. . . . In his own backyard! Curiosity bubbled all over him. But then suddenly he felt . . .

a tug . . . an ugly sort of tug . . . that stopped him. It was his Green Devil, who lived inside him. It had . . . slithered . . . out . . . of him. And it whispered, "Don't speak to these people, Henry! You won't like them. They're DIFFERENT!"

And to make matters worse . . .

. . . every one of Henry's new neighbors had his own private Green Devil, and each Green Devil began to whisper to the person he lived in, "psss, pppsss, sss . . . look! . . . They're DIFFERENT . . . stay away from them . . . pppsss." And when Green Devils get remarks like that listened to . . .

Biff! Ugh!! Bang!*?! Zowie!!! . . . which means fight in any language. But fighting leaves you out of breath . . .

. . . and . . . you begin to wonder why you're fighting. Is it because you're afraid? . . .

. . . afraid of each other? Because you're different?

"But there's no getting around it," thought Henry. "We *are* different! Look at their colors! How do you figure that?"

Well, Henry, it began a long time ago. At first . . .

. . . there were only a few people living in a small part of the world, They were tan-skinned people, not very different from each other.

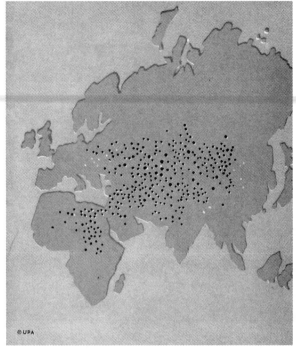

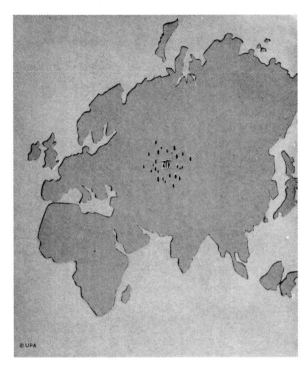

As they spread out over the face of the earth, differences in people's skin color gradually grew more marked.

At the outer edges of the world the extremes of skin color developed—what we call the black, the white, and the yellow skin colors. But scientists know that skin-color doesn't really matter; that you can't classify or judge people by their complexions.

But that sort of talk annoyed Henry's Green Devil.

"You and your science!" he sneered. "Maybe skin-color doesn't matter, but lots of other things do. How about brains. That's what *we've* got. Those others have only brute strength. *There's* a scientific fact for you!"

"I wonder," Henry mused. "I wonder—is it a fact?"

No, Henry, it is *not* a fact. In the first place, strong men come in *all* colors, and secondly . . .

But Henry interrupted, "I can believe what you say about strength, but what about . . . BRAINS?"

All right, Henry, if you really want to know. On the average there *are* small differences in brain sizes. The Eskimos have the largest average brain.

And the *largest* brain on record belonged to an imbecile. So you see, Henry, it isn't the size of a brain that counts, it's what you can *do* with it . . .

The bright ones, as well as the strong ones, . . .
come in all colors.

"Well, yes, but . . ." mumbled Henry, "there's
something about the blood, isn't there?"

There certainly is, Henry. There are four different
blood types, A, B, AB, and O; but the fact is that you can
find all these blood types in people of *every* skin color.

That's interesting," said Henry. "I remember the time
when my neighbor Joe's kid brother Stanley . . .
was an awfully sick boy and needed a blood
transfusion. Joe thought that because he was Stanley's
brother his blood would naturally be best, but . . .

. . . the doctor said that, brother or no brother, their
blood types were different and that if he used Joe's
blood it would be good-bye Stanley! And so . . .

. . . the doctor brought in a man whose blood matched
Stanley's. This fellow was a total stranger but his
blood . . .

. . . did the trick!"

And the wheel, for instance. Imagine trying to
run our civilization without one. But we didn't invent
it. The principle of the wheel was discovered by the
Babylonians, who first used it for their oxcarts.

Later on, the Romans put the wheel on war chariots.

The Chinese used the wheel to bring water to their
rice fields.

And later on we used the wheel to steer our ships.
Wagon wheels took our pioneers to the great West.

And now the wheels of our planes let down on the
flying fields of countries all over the world.

So you see, Henry, all the people of the world have
done their share to build civilization. All human beings
have the same aspirations, the same moving desires
for . . .

. . . love and a home . . .

Henry got the point . . . strength, brains, blood . . .

"But there are some differences, aren't there?" Henry
asked. "What about know-how? We've certainly always
had the edge there!"

Not always, Henry. That's how it is today . . . but
when the caveman lived in Europe about 5,000 years
ago, he was still making crude stone axes . . .

. . . while the Africans were forging them out of iron.

. . . a family growing up . . .

... and the right to worship in their own way ...

... the young ones wanting to work and play as their fathers and mothers do ... according to the ways of their particular street, city, or nation ...

... or climate.

Knowing these things, sensible people learn to live in peace and friendship. They know that the differences in the way people behave are not inherited from their ancestors. They come from something called cultural experience or environment.

Sensible people stop kicking *each other* around and apply their boots to the seats of ...

... the ugly Green Devils of prejudice, stupidity, hate.

But Henry had one more question. "Why don't all people stop hating and fighting each other—right now!"

Well, Henry, science is beginning to understand the real reasons ... to discover why we act as we do. We all know that frightened people are apt to do foolish things, and most people today are frightened of something ...

Some are afraid because they had an unhappy childhood.

Some are afraid they'll lose their jobs or their savings.

Some are afraid they'll be sick and unable to afford a doctor.

Some are afraid of getting old ... of being has-beens ... and losing the respect of their community.

And when people have these fears they are jumpy ... and suspicious ... and too ready to take it out on the other fellow ... especially a *different* kind of fellow.

"Oh," said Henry. "I'm beginning to get it ...

"... we're not born haters. Our Green Devils of prejudice and fear grow inside us ... because we're worried and afraid ..."

You're absolutely right, Henry ...

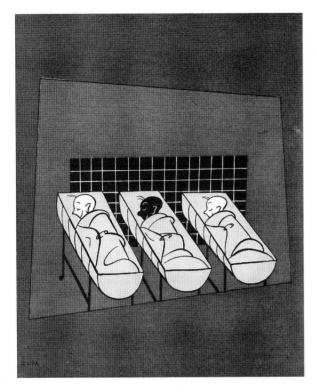

. . . Take children for instance. Nothing worries people more than to have sick children and not be able to get them good medical care. It's only reasonable that every child, no matter where he's born, is entitled to good health . . .

. . . to a good start in life, and to a good school . . .

. . . and those who want higher education should have it . . .

. . . so that no matter where they were born, or what the color of their skin, they'll have the chance to work together at the jobs *that need to be done* . . .

Does that make sense to you, Henry?

Scientists think so. We've just had a look at some of their facts which show that many of our notions about "differences" are—scientifically speaking—just plain ridiculous. Thinking people should get rid of these notions, for . . .

. . . we've only one world and we're all in it. If we can adopt this scientific way of looking at things, we can rid ourselves of useless anxieties and fears, and all get together to contribute to the coming of a better world.

OKAY, HENRY?

43

Three Promises to You (1957)

Munro Leaf (Wilbur Munro Leaf,

1905–1976)

EDITORS' INTRODUCTION

When Munro Leaf was twelve years old, he told his mother, "I'm not going to work for anybody else."[1] The son of Baltimore printer Charles Leaf and the former Emma Gillespie, Leaf decided early on to follow his own muse. The first in his family to attend college, Leaf earned a B.A. in English from the University of Maryland in 1927. Before graduating, he secretly married Margaret Pope, with whom he had two sons: Andrew Munro in 1939 and James Gillespie in 1941. Directly after graduating from Maryland, Leaf borrowed twenty-five dollars from his new bride, caught a bus up to Boston, and talked his way into Harvard's graduate program in English. Leaf received his M.A. in 1931.[2]

While working as an editor, Leaf accidentally became an illustrator. On the subway, he overheard a mother trying to explain to her child why one shouldn't say "ain't." Figuring that he could do a much better job, Leaf wrote his first book, *Grammar Can Be Fun* (1934), sketching some rough drawings to guide whomever would illustrate the book.[3] His editor loved the sketches and said, "We're going to use these." Leaf was amazed, but his editor explained: children would never think that the person who drew these illustrations could *possibly* be talking down to them.[4] Leaf illustrated most of his forty books for children, especially the many didactic ones, such as *Manners Can Be Fun* (1936), *Reading Can Be Fun* (1953), *How to Behave and Why* (1946), and the popular *Watchbirds* series, to name a few.

Leaf's friend Robert Lawson illustrated his most famous work, *The Story of Ferdinand*. When the book was published in the fall of 1936, critics accused *Ferdinand* of being communist, pacifist, and fascist, and of satirizing communism, pacifism, and fascism. Maintaining that the book was written purely to entertain, Leaf said, "if there is a message . . . , it is Ferdinand's message, not mine—get it from him according to your need."[5] Whatever *Ferdinand*'s politics, he became a cultural phenomenon, appearing as a balloon in Macy's Thanksgiving Parade, as the star of an Oscar-winning Disney cartoon short (1938), and as the subject of a popular song. In December of 1938, *Ferdinand* knocked Margaret Mitchell's *Gone with the Wind* (also published in 1936) off the top of the bestseller lists.[6]

Ferdinand was not expressly political, but Leaf did political work. When America entered the Second World War, Leaf wrote *A War-Time Handbook for Young Americans* (1942) and joined the U.S. Army. In 1943, Ted Geisel (aka Dr. Seuss) and Leaf created the pamphlet *This Is Ann* (1943), which told the story of the malaria-bearing mosquito Anopheles Annie, and had a profound effect on reducing malaria losses in the Pacfic.[7] Assigned to solve the problem of poor relations between officers and enlisted men, Leaf spent time with soldiers of lower and higher ranks, including some of the most powerful people in the U.S. Army: Dwight Eisenhower, George S. Patton, and George Marshall. After the war, he kept involved in world politics by illustrating a pamphlet promoting the Marshall Plan. Concerned about the welfare of children around the world, Leaf did several cultural tours for the U.S. State Department, talking with and drawing pictures for children and helping publishers in countries that were just starting to print books for children.[8]

Having made contacts in high places and gained a reputation for compassion towards people of any nationality, Leaf was the natural choice when the United Nations wanted to teach children about its mission. A great admirer of UN secretary-general Dag Hammarskjöld, Leaf gladly accepted the job of writing *Three Promises to You*. The admiration appears to have been mutual. After Hammarskjöld's plane crashed during an attempt to broker peace in the Congo, the Danes asked Leaf to write the memorial book for Hammarskjöld. Undergoing major surgery at the time, Leaf was disappointed to have to decline the honor.[9]

The boy who did not want to work for anyone else grew up working for the children of the world. As Leaf himself writes in *How to Behave and Why* (1946), "Other people have ideas and thoughts, ways to do things, ways to work, ways to play, ways they think of God, and their country, and their race. Their way can be just as right as your way. Remember that, and be glad you have a chance to choose the best of all ways."[10]

NOTES

1. James "Gil" Leaf, telephone interview with Philip Nel, 29 Sept. 2003.

2. Ibid.

3. James "Gil" Leaf, telephone interview with Philip Nel, 1 June 2006.

4. Leaf, telephone interview, 29 Sept. 2003.

5. Margaret Leaf, "Happy Birthday, Ferdinand!" *Publishers Weekly*, 31 Oct. 1986, 33.

6. Ibid.

7. Leaf, telephone interview, 29 Sept. 2003.

8. Leaf, telephone interview, 1 June 2006.

9. Ibid.

10. Munro Leaf, *How to Behave and Why* (Philadelphia: Lippincott, 1946), 52.

In the city of New York,
on the Atlantic coast of America,
is a big and wonderful building.
This building belongs to
YOU
as much as it belongs to anyone else
in the word.

Inside men and women are
working for
YOU.
And day and night thousands more
all over the world
are helping them . . .

to keep
THREE PROMISES
That have been
made to
YOU.

When you know
those
THREE PROMISES
you will understand
why there is a
UNITED NATIONS
and what it means to
YOU.

But first let's talk about
YOU,

You may be tall and thin,

Or
you
may be short
and fat.

You
may be
dark.
You
may be
light.

But whatever you look like, YOU are
an important human being—a person.

YOU
Live somewhere on our earth along with
two and a half billion people.

We know some other things about
YOU, too.

YOU
like to have good food to eat

and
a pleasant place to live.

YOU
want to enjoy a happy healthy life,
don't you?

You hate to be scared!

You don't like to think
that people may come
to hurt you, or your
family, or your friends.

And smash, wreck and destroy things
that make your life good.

That's what happens
in war.

That's why the
UNITED NATIONS
made their first promise.

That they would try to
stop us having any
more wars
EVER!

Probably right now YOU are asking,
"Why were there wars, anyway?
And how can the
UNITED NATIONS
stop them?"

One reason why wars started was
that whole nations were
afraid of each other.

They fought each other
because they were afraid of
what would happen if they didn't
fight.

YOU
are probably wondering
how a nation can be afraid.
Just what is a
nation, anyway?

It's a piece of
land.

And the people who life on
that land.

Some nations are very big.
Some nations are very small.
But they are all made of people
who follow the laws.
made by their governments.

But large or small, most of us
love our country
and obey the rules made by our government.

When members of the
same family quarrel
and each wants
his own way,
that's not a
happy family.

When whole groups of families
quarrel with other groups of
families in the same country
and fight each other,
that's not a happy country.

When whole nations quarrel
with other nations,
that's not a very happy world.

So after a big war the leaders of
many nations got together to
find a way to live without fighting
wars
EVER AGAIN.

This getting together was called the
UNITED NATIONS.

All the leaders of the governments worked together
like a big sensible family.

They decided right away
to make
Promise Number 1:
To try
NOT TO FIGHT EACH OTHER.

When one nation disagreed with another
instead of fighting,
they talked it over
until they found a sensible way to decide
what's right and what's wrong.

To help keep this promise to
YOU

the
UNITED NATIONS
made

Promise Number 2:
that YOU and all
other human beings in
the world, will
be treated fairly
whether they are
weak or strong.

You know yourself if you are
treated as fairly as anyone else

then you usually don't want
to start quarrels and fights.

Promise Number 3:
the UNITED NATIONS
made to
YOU
was
that they would
all work together
to help each
other have
better and happier lives.

So the UNITED NATIONS sends
people out to all parts of
the world to share with other
people what they know
about making life better.

For instance,
isn't it better to teach people how
to raise food more easily
instead of

having them hate you for eating
better?

Of course it is!

So the
UNITED NATIONS
is working day
and night to
keep its
THREE PROMISES.

1
NO WAR
2
Fair treatment for
all human beings.
3
Better living for
everybody by
sharing what we
know.

THREE
PROMISES

to
YOU

44

Excerpt from *Come with Me: Poems, Guessing Poems, and Dance Poems for Young People* (1963)

Written by Edith Segal (1902–1997), Illustrated by Samuel Kamen (1911–1995)

EDITORS' INTRODUCTION

Choreographer, activist, and poet, Edith Segal first expressed herself through dance. Born and raised on New York City's Lower East Side, Segal was the daughter of Russian Jewish immigrants—her mother a hairdresser and wig maker, her father a cigar maker and member of Samuel Gompers's union. He enjoyed dancing, and so did Edith. When she heard the Italian organ-grinder's music, she would run outside to dance in the street.[1] At the Henry Street Settlement, not far from their apartment, the teenaged Edith took dance classes. Her talent enabled her to join the Neighborhood Playhouse and, later, to study with Martha Graham.

Segal became a pioneer in political dance. To quote the slogan for her Workers Dance League, "Dance Is a Weapon in the Revolutionary Class Struggle."[2] In the 1920s, 1930s, and 1940s, Segal staged dances that were, variously, antiracist, antifascist, and pro-labor. Her Lenin Memorial Pageant, staged at Madison Square Garden in 1928, concluded with "some fifty dancers in a hammer-and-sickle formation."[3] In 1934, she performed an interpretation of Langston Hughes's poem, "Tom Mooney," dramatizing the plight of the imprisoned labor leader.

Throughout her career, Segal always felt the need "to have a poem cooking," as she put it.[4] She wrote three books of poetry for children and over a half-dozen other books (many in verse) for adults. One of the works in the latter group, *Give Us Your Hand! Poems and Songs for Ethel and Julius Rosenberg in the Death House at Sing Sing* (1953), attracted scrutiny during the New York State legislature's investigation into alleged communist infiltration of summer camps. In August 1955, the committee summoned Segal, who taught dance at Camp Kinderland from the early 1930s to the early 1970s. Kinderland —Yiddish for "children's country"—was and is a leftist camp, then located in New York's Dutchess County and "operating within the milieu of the Communist-allied Jewish working class movement," according to Paul Mishler.[5] Segal, who employed Kinderland campers in some political dances, invoked the Fifth Amendment in response to most questions but did note that her songs about the Rosenbergs were not taught at the camp.[6]

The children's poems reproduced here reflect the imagination and idealism of Segal's work. "Dreams" speaks to the importance of holding on to one's dreams, and "U.S. Calling UNICEF Friends" invites the world's children to share a common dream of peace and friendship. Established in 1946 as the United Nations International Children's Emergency Fund, UNICEF initially addressed the needs of children in postwar Europe and China but in 1950 extended its efforts to all children in need. Segal signals this global focus, depicting North American, Asian, African, and European children. Expanding on this theme, "The Work of the World" celebrates the variety of jobs that people do. *Come with Me* won praise from Langston Hughes, and Segal's poems gained acclaim from Benjamin Spock and Meridel Le-Sueur, who called her "a singer of the people."[7]

Samuel Kamen, Segal's third (and final) husband, illustrated the book. A Brooklyn-born painter, designer, and lithographer, Kamen studied at the Art Students League and the National Academy of Design. Though less well-known than his wife, Kamen won acclaim for his watercolors, here echoed in the relaxed style of the "UNICEF Friends" sketches. Although he mostly worked as a painter, Kamen illustrated several other books by Segal, including *Poems and Songs for Dreamers Who Dare* (1975) and *A Time to Thunder and Other Poems* (1984).

In the 1960s, 1970s, and 1980s, Segal continued to be both active and activist, marching against the Vietnam War and performing with Pete Seeger. She wrote poems against nuclear proliferation and the U.S.-backed war in El Salvador, and she wrote poems for Paul Robeson and Angela Davis. In 1982, impressed by the 80-year-old Segal's energy, one interviewer observed, "Clearly, solid left-wing causes act on her the way vitamins do on others."[8]

NOTES

1. Albert V. Schwartz, "Edith Segal: Friend and Poet," *Elementary English* 50 (1973): 1224.

2. Ellen Graff, *Stepping Left: Dance and Politics in New York City, 1928–1942* (Durham, NC: Duke UP, 1997), 7.

3. Graff, 26.

4. Schwartz, 1225.

5. Paul Mishler, *Raising Reds: The Young Pioneers, Radical Summer Camps, and Communist Political Culture in the United States* (New York: Columbia UP, 1999), 89.

6. "Forward: Looking Back," *The Forward*, 26 Aug. 2005: <http://www.forward.com/articles/3863>.

7. Deborah Jowitt, *The Dance in Mind* (Boston: Godine, 1985), 272.

8. Jowitt, 267.

DREAMS

Dreams we have when we're asleep
Are dreams we never really keep,
Dreams we keep are dreams we make
When we're very wide awake.

U. S. CALLING UNICEF FRIENDS
FAR, SO FAR AWAY,
SHALL WE PLAN A VISITING KIND
OF SISTER-BROTHERHOOD DAY?

We could come by bicycle,
  By tricycle, by train,
We could come by ocean liner
  Or by aeroplane.

We could bring our bats and hoops,
  Play each other's games :
Baseball, checkers, jai-ali, *
  Learn new words and names :

Mi Amigo, Freint, Dodi,
  Droog, Tomo-dakee,
·Different words that mean *My FRIEND,*
  Naanyo, Mon Ami. **

We could share each other's food,
  Sample different sweets,
Walk together, see the sights,
  Strange and winding streets.

We could sing each other's songs:
  Frère Jacques, I-lu-lu,
Santa Lucia, Saturday Night,
  We know those, do you?

We could dance each other's dances,
  Polkas, reels and squares,
Waltzes, horas, cha-cha-cha,
  In circles and in pairs.

So :

Polish up your bicycle,
  Your tricyle, your train,
Book your biggest ocean liner,
  Test your newest plane.

STATION BREAK, SO LONG FOR NOW!
RADIO U. S. A.
IS SIGNING OFF WITH EXPECTATIONS
FOR THAT HOLIDAY!

UNICEF stands for United Nations Children's Fund

*Jai-ali - Pronounced hī-a-lī. A Latin-American game.

**words that mean FRIEND:

Amigo	*- Spanish*	*Tomodakēe*	*- Japanese*
Freint	*- Yiddish*	*Naanyo*	*- Ga (One of the*
	pronounced Frīnt		*principal Ghanian*
Dodí	*- Hebrew*		*languages.*
Drōōg	*- Russian*		*Pronounced Náhnyo.*
		Amí	*- French*

Note:
U. S. CALLING UNICEF FRIENDS has been set to music and made into
a little ballet. For musical score and directions, contact Edith Segal,
The Citadel Press, 222 Park Avenue South, New York 3, N. Y.

THE WORK OF THE WORLD

Guessing rhymes and questions based on THE WORK OF THE WORLD will be found on pages 45 - 48.

The WORK of the world, the wonderful world,
WHO does the WORK, the WORK of the world?

1.

FACTORY WORKERS surrounded by noise,
Making our clothes, our shoes, our toys,
Autos and furniture, scales and rings,
Washing machines and a million things.

2.

FARMERS growing the corn and the wheat
And all the food we love to eat.

3.

MINERS digging where sun never shines,
Deep in the dark and dangerous mines.

4.

STEELWORKERS pouring the hot molten steel
For girders, tractors, utensils and wheels.

5.

ENGINEERS standing alert at their brakes,
Steering their trains, that go winding like snakes.

6.

TRUCKMEN driving their giant-size trucks,
Making deliveries to depots and docks.

7.

FIREMEN ready with hook, hose and hat
To put out a fire wherever it's at.

8.

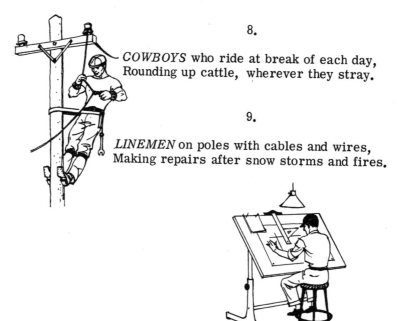

COWBOYS who ride at break of each day,
Rounding up cattle, wherever they stray.

9.

LINEMEN on poles with cables and wires,
Making repairs after snow storms and fires.

10.

ARCHITECTS planning new buildings, new schools,
Cities with trees and parks and pools.

11.

BRICKLAYERS, MASONS, THE WHOLE BUILDING CREW,
Making the architects' plans come true.

12.

CAPTAIN and CREW, up on deck and below,
Braving the windstorms, as seaward they go.

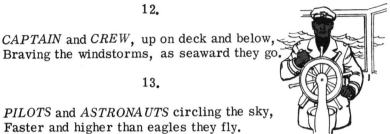

13.

PILOTS and ASTRONAUTS circling the sky,
Faster and higher than eagles they fly.

14.

SCIENTISTS searching, determined to find
Answers to questions that trouble mankind.

15.

PRINTERS at presses that roll at high speed
Turning out books and the papers we read.

16.

TEACHERS who guide us in school every day
Teaching us new things and new ways to play.

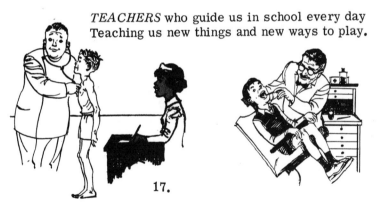

17.

DOCTORS and DENTISTS who care for our health,
Guarding the sources of life's greatest wealth.

18.

SALESPEOPLE showing us things we might buy,
Ready to please us— and oh how they try.

19.

MANAGERS, OFFICE CLERKS sending out mail
All about business, wholesale and retail.

20.

HOUSEKEEPERS cleaning and clearing away,
Washing and ironing day after day.

21.

POETS who write of our joys and our fears,
SINGERS who sing of our laughter and tears,
ALL the world's *ARTISTS* with love in their heart
Weaving our dreams into treasures of art.

22.

PARENTS, whatever the work that they do,
Working all hours for me and for you.
MOTHER and *DAD* are a child's closest friends,
Though *we* grow up, *their* work never ends.

The WORK of the world, the wonderful world,
ALL do the WORK, the WORK of the world!

Sources

Excerpts from Art Young's *The Socialist Primer* (Chicago, IL: Socialist Party of America, 1930) reproduced courtesy of the Socialist Party U.S.A.

A Is for Africa through *F Is for Freedom* copyright © 1992 by Lucille Clifton. First appeared in *The Black BC's*, published by Delacorte. Reprinted by permission of Curtis Brown, Ltd.

Don Miller's illustrations for *A Is for Africa* through *F Is for Freedom* reproduced courtesy of Julia A. Miller.

William Montgomery Brown's "The Brotherhood of Man" from *Science and History for Girls and Boys* (Galion, OH: Bradford-Brown Educational Company, 1932) was apparently not copyrighted.

Charlotte Pomerantz's *The Day They Parachuted Cats on Borneo: A Drama of Ecology* (Reading, MA: Young Scott Books, 1971) reproduced courtesy of Charlotte Pomerantz. Illustrations for *The Day They Parachuted Cats on Borneo* reproduced courtesy of Jose Aruego.

Deb Preusch, Tom Barry, and Beth Wood's *Red Ribbons for Emma* (Stanford, CA: New Seed Press, 1981) reproduced courtesy of Debra Preusch, Tom Barry, and Beth Wood.

Excerpt from *Johnny Get Your Money's Worth (and Jane Too!)*, copyright © 1938 by Ruth Brindze. Used by permission of Vanguard Press, a division of Random House, Inc.

William Gropper's *The Little Tailor* (New York: Dodd, Mead, 1955) reproduced courtesy of Gene Gropper.

Norma Klein's *Girls Can Be Anything* (New York: Penguin, 1973) reproduced courtesy of Erwin Fleissner. Illustrations for *Girls Can Be Anything* reproduced courtesy of Roy Doty.

"Mary Stays after School or—What This Union's About" (Amalgamated Clothing Workers of America, 1939) reproduced courtesy of UNITE HERE! (to the extent that they control the rights).

Text and fourteen illustrations from *Oscar the Ostrich* by Jerome Schwartz, copyright © 1940, renewed 1968 by Random House, Inc. Used by permission of Random House, Inc.

Sandra Weiner's "Doria Ramirez" from *small hands, big hands: Seven Profiles of Chicano Migrant Workers and Their Families* (New York: Pantheon, 1970) reproduced with kind permission of Sandra Weiner (via John Broderick).

Excerpt from Alfred Kreymborg's *Funnybone Alley* (New York: Macauley Company, 1927) reproduced courtesy of Alfred Stephen Kreymborg. Boris Artzybasheff's illustrations for *Funnybone Alley*: these are what the Library of Congress considers "orphan work," as it has not been possible to locate an estate for Boris Artzybasheff.

Lydia Gibson, *The Teacup Whale* (New York: Farrar and Rinehart, 1934): We could locate no estate for Lydia Gibson.

I. Kaminski's *Geyt a hindele ken Bronzvil* [*A Little Hen Goes to Brownsville*], illus. by Nota Koslowsky, lithographic printing by G. Grafstein (New York: Ferlag Kinder Ring of the Workmen's Circle Education Committee, 1937) reproduced courtesy of the Workmen's Circle Arbiter Ring.

Jay Williams's *The Practical Princess* (New York: Parents' Magazine Press, 1969) reproduced courtesy of Victoria Williams. Friso Henstra's illustrations for *The Practical Princess* reproduced courtesy of Friso Henstra.

Selections from Hildegarde Hoyt Swift's *North Star Shining: A Pictorial History of the American Negro* (New York: William Morrow & Co., 1947) reproduced courtesy of Galvin Swift, Barbara S. Brauer, and Deirdre A. Swift. Lynd Ward's illustrations for *North Star Shining* reproduced with kind permission of Robin Ward Savage and Nanda Ward.

Linda Lewis, "Josiah Henson—Kept Right on Traveling to Freedom," from *Freedom* 1:5 (May 1951): 7; Elsie Robins, "How Henry Box Brown Was Expressed from Slavery," from *Freedom* 1:11 (Nov. 1951): 7; "Peter Poyas Said . . . ," from *Freedom* 2:7 (July 1952): 7; "Ida Barnett Fought for Equal Rights," from *Freedom* 3:4 (April 1953): 7; "Heroes in Our History: 'Moses,'" from *Freedom* 3:4 (April 1953): 3; "Heroes in Our History: Ellen Craft," from *Freedom* 3:5 (May 1953): 5. Despite extensive research, we were unable to locate a copyright holder for these stories.

Eve Merriam's "Lucretia Mott" and "Ida B. Wells" from *Independent Voices* (New York: Atheneum, 1968) reproduced with kind permission of Marian Reiner, permissions consultant for the estate of Eve Merriam.

Julius Lester's "High John the Conqueror" from *Black Folktales* (Black Cat/Grove Press, 1969) reproduced courtesy of Julius Lester. Tom Feelings's illustrations for "High John the Conqueror" reproduced with kind permission of Kamili Feelings, for the estate of Tom Feelings.

Langston Hughes's "A Little Boy in a Big City" from *The First Book of Negroes* (New York: Franklin Watts, 1952), copyright Franklin Watts (1952), renewed 1980 by George Houston Bass. Reproduced with kind permission from Harold Ober Associates. Ursula Koering's illustrations for "A Little Boy in a Big City" from *The First Book of Negroes* reproduced courtesy of Lawrence Koering.

"The Sneetches" by Dr. Seuss™ & © Dr. Seuss Enterprises, L.P. 1953. Originally published in *Redbook* (July 1953). All Rights Reserved. Reprinted with kind permission of Dr. Seuss Enterprises.

Excerpts from Walt Kelly's *The Pogo Stepmother Goose* (Simon & Schuster, 1954) copyright © 1954 Okefenokee Glee & Perloo, Inc. Reprinted with kind permission of Okefenokee Glee & Perloo, Inc.

Lois Gould's *X: A Fabulous Child's Story* (New York: Daughters Publishing Co., 1978) copyright © Gould Family Foundation. Reproduced courtesy of Gould Family Foundation. Jacqueline

Chwast's illustrations for X: A Fabulous Child's Story reproduced courtesy of Jacqueline Chwast.

Jeanne Desy's "The Princess Who Stood on Her Own Two Feet" (from Letty Cottin Pogrebin, ed., Stories for Free Children [McGraw-Hill, 1982]) reproduced courtesy of Jeanne Desy. Leslie Udry's illustrations for "The Princess Who Stood on Her Own Two Feet" reproduced with kind permission of Leslie Udry.

Joe Molnar's Elizabeth: A Puerto Rican–American (Franklin Watts, Inc., 1974) reproduced with kind permission of Joe Molnar.

Carl Sandburg's "How Two Sweetheart Dippies Sat in the Moonlight on a Lumber Yard Fence and Heard about the Sooners and the Boomers" from Rootabaga Pigeons, text by Carl Sandburg and illustrations by Maud Petersham and Miska Petersham, copyright 1923 by Harcourt, Inc. and renewed 1951 by Carl Sandburg, reproduced by kind permission of Harcourt, Inc.

Ruth Benedict and Gene Weltfish's In Henry's Backyard: The Races of Mankind (New York: Henry Schuman, 1948) reproduced courtesy of Ann L. Margetson.

Munro Leaf's Three Promises to You (New York: J. B. Lippincott Company, 1957) reproduced with kind permission of James G. Leaf. We have agreed to donate a portion of any profits from our book to UNESCO, in deference to Gil Leaf's wishes.

Edith Segal's "Dreams," "U.S. Calling UNICEF Friends," and "The Work of the World" from Come with Me: Poems, Guessing Poems, and Dance Poems for Young People, illustrated by Samuel Kamen (New York: The Citadel Press, 1963) reproduced courtesy of Shari Segel Goldberg.

The following items are reproduced with kind permission of International Publishers: Ned Donn, "Pioneer Mother Goose," pictures by Bill Gropper (New Pioneer, Dec. 1934); M. Boland, "A B C for Martin" from Martin's Annual, ed. Joan Beauchamp (International Publishers, 1935); Alex Novikoff, "The Races of Mankind" from Climbing Our Family Tree (International Publishers, 1945); Langston Hughes, "Sharecroppers," illus. Fred Ellis (New Pioneer, Feb. 1937); Clara Hollos, The Story of Your Coat, illus. Herbert Kruckman (International Publishers, 1946); Helen Kay, "Battle in the Barnyard" from Battle in the Barnyard: Stories and Pictures for Workers' Children, illus. J. Preval (New York: Workers Library Publishers, 1932); Myra Page, "Pickets and Slippery Slicks," illus. Lydia Gibson, from New Pioneer Story Book, ed. Martha Campion (New Pioneer Publishing Company, 1935); Oscar Saul and Lou Lantz, "The Beavers," illus. Jack Herman (New Pioneer, Dec. 1936); A. Redfield [Syd Hoff], Mr. His (New York: New Masses, 1939); Herminia Zur Mühlen, "Why?" from Fairy Tales for Workers' Children, trans. Ida Dailes, illus. Lydia Gibson (Chicago: Daily Worker Publishing Co., 1925); and Jack Hardy, "American History Retold in Pictures," drawings by Bill Siegel (New Pioneer, June 1931).

The following items are in the Public Domain: Nicholas Klein, The Socialist Primer (Girard, KS: Appeal to Reason, 1908); Caroline Nelson, Nature Talks on Economics (Chicago: Charles H. Kerr & Co., 1912); The Child's Socialist Reader, illus. Walter Crane (London: Twentieth Century Press, 1907); and R. F. Outcault, Buster Brown Goes Shooting and Other Stories (New York: Cupples & Leon Co., 1907).

Credits for Images

Nicholas Klein's *The Socialist Primer: A Book of First Lessons for the Little Ones in Words of One Syllable*, Ned Donn's "Pioneer Mother Goose" (pictures by Bill Gropper), M. Boland's "ABC for Martin," William Montgomery Brown's photo (from *Science and History for Girls and Boys*), Langston Hughes's "Sharecroppers" (illus. by Fred Ellis), "Happy Valley" (illus. by Walter Crane), "Mary Stays after School or—What This Union's About," Jack Hardy's "American History Retold in Pictures" (drawings by Bill Siegel), and "Stories for Children" (from *Freedom*) all courtesy of the Tamiment Library, New York University.

Art Young's *The Socialist Primer*, Myra Page's "Pickets and Slippery Slicks" (illus. by Lydia Gibson), Herminia Zur Mühlen's "Why?" (illus. by Lydia Gibson), and Oscar Saul and Lou Lantz's "The Beavers" (illus. by Jack Herman) all courtesy of Special Collections Research Center, Syracuse University Library.

Charlotte Pomerantz's *The Day They Parachuted Cats on Borneo: A Drama of Ecology* (illus. by Jose Aruego) courtesy of Morse Department of Special Collections, Kansas State University.

Jay Williams's *The Practical Princess* (illus. by Friso Henstra) and Hildegarde Hoyt Swift's *North Star Shining: A Pictorial History of the American Negro* (illus. Lynd Ward) both from the Kerlan Collection, University of Minnesota Libraries.

Joe Molnar's *Elizabeth*, negatives courtesy of Joe Molnar and reproduced by University of Texax Libraries.

Dr. Seuss's "The Sneetches" from the Oolongblue Collection of Charles D. Cohen and The Whole Seuss.

R. F. Outcault's "Buster Brown Plays David and Goliath" from *Buster Brown Goes Shooting and Other Stories* courtesy of the holdings of the Department of Special Collections, University of Florida Libraries.

Other images obtained through Interlibrary Services or the general collections of Kansas State University and the University of Texas Libraries, or from the personal collections of Julia Mickenberg and Philip Nel.

A Working List of Recommended Radical Books for Young Readers

For other ideas, please see the Jane Addams Children's Book Award winners, <http://home.igc.org/%7ejapa/jacba/index_jacba.html>; the Marxist Internet Archive's *Children's Literature Archive*, <http://marxists.org/subject/art/literature/children/>, which includes both online texts and a bibliography; the Minnesota Center Against Violence and Abuse's "Children's Peace Bibliography," <http://www.mincava.umn.edu/documents/pnvcur1-6/pnvcur1-6.html#id2633049>; and the Cooperative Children's Book Center, <http://www.education.wisc.edu/ccbc/>. Also see publications of the Council on Interracial Books for Children, especially their *Interracial Books for Children Bulletin* (no longer published, but available in many libraries). And take a look at the selected scholarship, found at the end of this list.

Part 1: R Is for Rebel

Eve Merriam, *The Inner City Mother Goose*, visuals by Lawrence Ratzkin (1969)

William Steig, *Yellow & Pink* (1984)

Dan Piraro, *The Three Little Pigs Buy the White House* (2004)

Erich Origen and Gan Golan, *Goodnight Bush* (2008)

Part 2: Subversive Science and Dramas of Ecology

Millicent Selsam, *Hidden Animals* (1947)

Herman and Nina Schneider, *You among the Stars*, illus. Symeon Shimin (1951)

Rose Wyler and Gerald Ames, *Life on Earth* (1953)

Benjamin and Sidonie Gruenberg, *The Wonderful Story of You*, illus. Symeon Shimin (1960)

Virginia Lee Burton, *Life Story* (1962)

Bill Peet, *The Wump World* (1970)

Dr. Seuss, *The Lorax* (1971)

Chris Van Allsburg, *Just a Dream* (1990)

Kristine L. Franklin, *When the Monkeys Came Back*, illus. Robert Roth (1994)

Molly Bang, *Common Ground: The Water, Earth, and Air We Share* (1997)

Paul Fleischman, *Weslandia*, illus. Kevin Hawkes (1999)

Molly Bang, *Nobody Particular: One Woman's Fight to Save the Bays* (2000)

Peter Sís, *The Tree of Life* (2003)

Jean-Luc Fromental and Joëlle Jolivet, *365 Penguins* (2006)

Ann Rockwell and Paul Meisel, *Why Are the Ice Caps Melting?* (2006)

Part 3: Work, Workers, and Money

Jack Conroy and Arna Bontemps, *The Fast Sooner Hound*, illus. Virginia Lee Burton (1942)

Eleanor Estes, *The Hundred Dresses*, illus. Louis Slobodkin (1944)

Irwin Shapiro, *Yankee Thunder: The Legendary Life of Davy Crockett*, illus. James Daugherty (1944)

Elie Siegmeister, *Work and Sing: A Collection of the Songs That Built America*, illus. Julian Brazelton (1944)

Irwin Shapiro, *John Henry and His Double-Jointed Steam Drill*, illus. James Daugherty (1945)

Jack Conroy and Arna Bontemps, *Slappy Hooper, the Wonderful Sign Painter*, illus. Ursula Koering (1946)

Mary Elting, *The Lollipop Factory and Lots of Others*, illus. Jeanne Bendick (1946)

Helen Walker Puner, *Daddies, What They Do All Day*, illus. Roger Duvoisin (1946)

Leone Adelson and Benjamin Gruenberg, *Your Breakfast and the People Who Made It*, illus. Kurt Wiese (1959)

Eve Merriam, *Mommies at Work*, illus. Beni Montresor (1961)

Florence Parry Heide, *The Shrinking of Treehorn*, illus. Edward Gorey (1971)

Florence Parry Heide, *Treehorn's Treasure*, illus. Edward Gorey (1981)

Vera B. Williams, *A Chair for My Mother* (1982)

Eve Merriam, *Daddies at Work*, illus. Eugenie Fernandes (1989)

Eve Bunting, *Fly Away Home*, illus. Ronald Himler (1993)

Maurice Sendak, *We Are All in the Dumps with Jack and Guy* (1993)

Julius Lester, *John Henry*, pictures by Jerry Pinkney (1994)

Tim Egan, *Chestnut Cove* (1995)

DyAnne Disalvo-Ryan, *Uncle Willie and the Soup Kitchen* (1997)

Ann McGovern, *The Lady in the Box*, illus. Marni Backer (1999)

Part 4: Organize

Lio Lionni, *Swimmy* (1963)

Jim Aylesworth, *Mr. McGill Goes to Town*, illus. Thomas Graham (1989)

Martin Waddell and Helen Oxenbury, *Farmer Duck* (1991)

Maureen Bayless *Strike!*, illus. Yvonne Cathcart (1994)

Jane Cowen-Fletcher, *It Takes a Village* (1994)

Margie Palatini, *Piggie Pie!*, illus. Howard Fine (1995)

Michael Bedard, *Sitting Ducks* (1998)

Doreen Cronin, *Click, Clack, Moo: Cows That Type*, illus. Betsy Lewin (2000)

DyAnne DiSalvo-Ryan, *Grandpa's Corner Store* (2000)

Toby Speed and Barry Root, *Brave Potatoes* (2000)

Kathleen Krull, *Harvesting Hope: The Story of Cesar Chavez*, illus. Yuyi Morales (2003)

Part 5: Imagine

There are many picturebook versions of Edward Lear's work, such as *The Owl and the Pussy-Cat*, as illustrated by Ian Beck (1995) or as illustrated by James Marshall (1998), and *The Pelican Chorus and Other Nonsense*, illustrated by Fred Marcellino (1995).

Wanda Gag, *Millions of Cats* (1928)

Ruth Krauss, *The Carrot Seed*, illus. Crockett Johnson (1945)

Frank Tashlin, *The Bear That Wasn't* (1946)

Charles G. Shaw, *It Looked Like Spilt Milk* (1947)

Tove Jansson, *The Book about Moomin, Mymble, and Little My* (1953)

Ruth Krauss, *How to Make an Earthquake*, illus. Crockett Johnson (1954)

Crockett Johnson, *Harold and the Purple Crayon* (1955) and its sequels (1956–1963)

Ruth Krauss and Crockett Johnson, *Is This You?* (1955)

Dr. Seuss, *On Beyond Zebra!* (1955)

Remy Charlip, *It Looks Like Snow* (1957)

Ann and Paul Rand, *Sparkle and Spin* (1957)

Don Freeman, *Norman the Doorman* (1959)

Stoo Hample, *The Silly Book* (1961)

Pete Seeger, *Abiyoyo*, illus. Michael Hays (1963)

Maurice Sendak, *Where the Wild Things Are* (1963)

Ruth Krauss, *The Little King The Little Queen The Little Monster and other stories you can make up yourself* (1964)

Donald Crews, *We Read: A to Z* (1967)

Ruth Krauss, *This Thumbprint* (1967)

Leo Lionni, *Frederick* (1967)

Harve Zemach, *The Judge*, illus. Margot Zemach (1969)

Syd Hoff, *The Horse in Harry's Room* (1970)

Shel Silverstein, *Where the Sidewalk Ends* (1974)

Judi Barrett, *Cloudy with a Chance of Meatballs*, illus. Ron Barrett (1978)

Anthony Browne, *Bear Hunt* (1979)

Shel Silverstein, *A Light in the Attic* (1981)

Roald Dahl, *Roald Dahl's Revolting Rhymes* (1982)

Ann Jonas, *Round Trip* (1983)

Chris Van Allsburg, *The Mysteries of Harris Burdick* (1984)

Ann Jonas, *The Trek* (1985)

Jon Agee, *The Incredible Painting of Felix Clousseau* (1988)

Jon Scieszka and Lane Smith, *The True Story of the Three Little Pigs by A. Wolf* (1989)

Faith Ringgold, *Tar Beach* (1991)

Chris Raschka, *Charlie Parker Played Be-bop* (1992)

Jon Scieszka and Lane Smith, *The Stinky Cheese Man and Other Fairly Stupid Tales* (1992)

Istvan Banyai, *Zoom* (1995)

Chris Van Allsburg, *Bad Day at Riverbend* (1995)

Jamey Gambrell, *Telephone*, adapted from Kornei Chukovsky, illus. Vladimir Radunsky (1996)

Shel Silverstein, *Falling Up* (1996)

Calef Brown, *Polka-bats and Octopus Slacks: 14 Stories* (1998)

Mike Lester, *A Is for Salad* (2000)

David Wiesner, *The Three Pigs* (2001)

Michael Chesworth, *Alphaboat* (2002)

Hanna Johansen, *Henrietta and the Golden Eggs*, illus. Käthi Bhend, trans. John S. Barrett (2002)

Stephen T. Johnson, *As the City Sleeps* (2002)

Barbara Lehman, *The Red Book* (2004)

Emily Gravett, *Wolves* (2005)

Antoinette Portis, *Not a Box* (2006)

Deborah Freeman, *Scribble* (2007)

Part 6: History and Heroes

Lin Shi Kahn and Tony Perez, *Scottsboro Alabama: A Story in Linoleum Cuts* (c. 1935), ed. Andrew Lee, with a foreword by Robin D. G. Kelley (2003)

Meridel Le Sueur, *Nancy Hanks of Wilderness Road: A Story of Abe Lincoln's Mother*, illus. Betty Alden (1949)

Muriel Feelings, *Moja Means One: Swahili Counting Book*, illus. Tom Feelings (1971)

Muriel Feelings, *Jambo Means Hello: Swahili Alphabet Book*, illus. Tom Feelings (1974)

Syd Hoff, *Boss Tweed and the Man Who Drew Him* (1978)

Ken Mochizuki, *Baseball Saved Us*, illus. Dom Lee (1993)

Marlene Shigekawa, *Blue Jay in the Desert*, illus. Isao Kikuchi (1993)

William Miller, *Zora Hurston and the Chinaberry Tree*, illus. Cornelius Van Wright and Ying-Hwa Hu (1994)

Robert Coles, *The Story of Ruby Bridges*, illus. George Ford (1995)

William Miller, *Richard Wright and the Library Card*, illus. Gregory Christie (1997)

Ruby Bridges, *Through My Eyes* (1999)

Bryan Collier, *Uptown* (2000)

Doreen Rappaport, *Martin's Big Words: The Life of Dr. Martin Luther King, Jr.*, illus. Bryan Collier (2001)

Tony Kushner, *Brundibar*, illus. Maurice Sendak (2003)

Angela Johnson, *A Sweet Smell of Roses*, illus. Eric Velasquez (2005)

Marilyn Nelson, *A Wreath for Emmett Till*, illus. Philippe Lardy (2005)

Lane Smith, *John, Paul, George, and Ben* (2006)

Part 7: A Person's a Person: Books That Challenge Prejudice

Margret and H. A. Rey, *Spotty* (1945)

Ben Ross Berenberg, *This is the story of the churkendoose: part chicken, turkey, duck, and goose*, illus. Dellwyn Cunningham (1950)

Dr. Seuss, *Horton Hears a Who!* (1954)

Sandra Scoppettone, *Suzuki Beane*, illus. Louise Fitzhugh (1961)

Dr. Seuss, *The Sneetches* (1961)

Ezra Jack Keats, *The Snowy Day* (1962)

Jay Williams, *Philbert the Fearful*, illus. Ib Ohlsson (1966)

Tomi Ungerer, *Moon Man* (1967)

Langston Hughes, *Black Misery*, illus. Arouni (1969)

Charlotte Zolotow, *William's Doll*, illus. William Pene du Bois (1972)

Daniel Pinkwater, *The Big Orange Splot* (1977)

Rachel Isadora, *Ben's Trumpet* (1979)

Robert Munsch, *The Paper Bag Princess*, illus. Michael Martchenko (1980)

Anthony Browne, *Piggybook* (1986)

Eve Bunting, *Terrible Things*, illus. Stephen Gammell (1989)

Sam Swope, *The Araboolies of Liberty Street*, illus. Barry Root (1989)

Vera B. Williams, *More, More, More Said the Baby* (1990)

Chris Van Allsburg, *The Widow's Broom* (1992)

Ellen Jackson, *Cinder Edna*, illus. Kevin O'Malley (1994)

Johnny Valentine, *One Dad Two Dads Brown Dad Blue Dads*, illus. Melody Sarecky (1994)

Tim Egan, *Metropolitan Cow* (1996)

Carolivia Herron, *Nappy Hair*, illus. Joe Cepeda (1997)

Philip M. Hoose and Hannah Hoose, *Hey, Little Ant*, illus. Debbie Tilley (1998)

Subcomandante Marcos, *The Story of Colors/La Historia de los Colores: A Bilingual Folktale from the Jungles of Chiapas*, illus. Domitila Dominguez, trans. Anne Bar Din (1999)

Linda de Haan and Stern Nijland, *King and King* (2002)

Alexis Deacon, *Beegu* (2003)

Cornelia Funke, *The Princess Knight*, illus. Kerstin Meyer (2003)

Chih-Yuan Chen, *Guji Guji* (2004)

Peggy Moss, *Say Something*, illus. Lea Lyon (2004)

Justin Richardson and Peter Parnell, *And Tango Makes Three*, illus. Henry Cole (2005)

Part 8: Peace

Munro Leaf, *The Story of Ferdinand*, illus. Robert Lawson (1936)

Ben Martin, *John Black's Body* (1939)

James Thurber, *The Last Flower* (1939)

Erich Kästner, *The Animals Conference*, illus. Walter Trier, trans. Zita de Schauense (1949)

Ruth Krauss, *The Big World and the Little House*, illus. Marc Simont (1949)

Dr. Seuss, *Yertle the Turtle* (1958)

Jean Merrill, *The Pushcart War*, illus. Ronni Solbert (1964)

Leo Lionni, *The Alphabet Tree* (1968)

John and Faith Hubley, *The Hat* (1974)

Eleanor Coerr, *Sadako and the Thousand Paper Cranes*, illus. Ronald Himler (1977)

Trân-Khánh-Tuyêt, *The Little Weaver of Thái-Yên Village*, illus. Nancy Hom, trans. Christopher N. H. Jenkins and Trân-Khánh-Tuyêt (1977, revised 1986)

Toshi Maruki, *Hiroshima No Pika* (1982)

Dr. Seuss, *The Butter Battle Book* (1984)

David Macaulay, *Baaa* (1985)

Frank Asch and Vladimir Vagin, *Here Comes the Cat* (1989)

Eve Bunting, *The Wall*, illus. Ronald Himler (1992)

Florence Parry Heide and Judith Heide Gilliland, *Sami and the Time of Troubles*, illus. Ted Lewin (1992)

Eugene Trivizas, *Three Little Wolves and the Big Bad Pig*, illus. Helen Oxenbury (1993)

Allan Baillie, *Rebel*, illus. Di Wu (1994)

Patricia Polacco, *Pink and Say* (1994)

David Shannon, *How Georgie Radbourn Saved Baseball* (1994)

David McPhail, *Mole Music* (1999)

Derek Munson, *Enemy Pie*, illus. Tara Calahan King (2000)

Jeanette Winter, *The Librarian of Basra: A True Story from Iraq* (2005)

Anthologies

Marlo Thomas and friends, *Free to Be You and Me* (1974)

Letty Cottin Pogrebin, ed., *Stories for Free Children* (1982)

Jack Zipes, ed., *Don't Bet on the Prince* (1986)

Jack Zipes, ed. and trans., *Fairy Tales and Fables from Weimar Days* (1989)

Ann Durrell and Marilyn Sachs, eds., *The Big Book for Peace* (1990)

Activism "How To" for Children and Teens

Barbara A. Lewis, *The Kid's Guide to Social Action: How to Solve the Social Problems You Choose and Turn Creative Thinking into Positive Action* (1998)

Philip Hoose, *It's Our World, Too!* (2002)

Mikki Halpin, *It's Your World—If You Don't Like It, Change It* (2004)

Barbara A. Lewis, *What Do You Stand For? For Kids* (2005)

Barbara A. Lewis, *What Do You Stand For? For Teens* (2005)

Selected Scholarship on Radical Children's Literature

Jack Zipes, *Fairy Tales and the Art of Subversion: The Classical Genre for Children and the Process of Civilization* (1988)

Herbert Kohl, *Should We Burn Babar? Essays on Children's Literature and the Power of Stories* (1995)

Alison Lurie, *Don't Tell the Grown-Ups: The Subversive Power of Children's Literature* (1998)

Paul C. Mishler, "Primers for Revolution: Communist Books for Children," *Raising Reds: The Young Pioneers, Radical Summer Camps, and Communist Political Culture in the United States* (1999), 109–29

Evgeny Steiner, *Stories for Little Comrades: Revolutionary Artists and the Making of Early Soviet Children's Books*, trans. Jane Ann Miller (1999)

Michelle H. Martin, *Brown Gold: Milestones of African-American Children's Picture Books, 1845–2002* (2004)

Katharine Capshaw Smith, *Children's Literature of the Harlem Renaissance* (2004)

Julia Mickenberg and Philip Nel, eds., *Children's Literature and the Left. Special Issue. Children's Literature Association Quarterly* 30:4 (Winter 2005)

Julia L. Mickenberg, *Learning from the Left: Children's Literature, the Cold War, and Radical Politics in the United States* (2006)

Kimberley Reynolds, *Radical Children's Literature: Future Visions and Aesthetic Transformations in Juvenile Fiction* (2007)

About the Editors

JULIA L. MICKENBERG is Associate Professor of American Studies at the University of Texas at Austin. She is the author of *Learning from the Left: Children's Literature, the Cold War, and Radical Politics in the United States*.

PHILIP NEL, Professor of English and Director of Kansas State University's Program in Children's Literature, is author of *The Annotated Cat: Under the Hats of Seuss and His Cats, Dr. Seuss: American Icon, The Avant-Garde and American Postmodernity*, and *J. K. Rowling's Harry Potter Novels: A Reader's Guide*.

JACK ZIPES is Professor Emeritus of German and comparative literature at the University of Minnesota. Some of his more recent publications include *Sticks and Stones: The Troublesome Success of Children's Literature from Slovenly Peter to Harry Potter, Fairy Tales and the Art of Subversion, Why Fairy Tales Stick: The Evolution and Relevance of a Genre*, and *Relentless Progress: The Reconfiguration of Children's Literature, Fairy Tales and Storytelling*.